# UP AGAINST THE IVY WALL:
*A history of the Columbia crisis*

# UP AGAINST

## A HISTORY OF

ATHENEUM   NEW YORK   1969

# THE IVY WALL

## THE COLUMBIA CRISIS

by Jerry L. Avorn

with Andrew Crane

Mark Jaffe

Oren Root, Jr.

Paul Starr

Michael Stern

Robert Stulberg

of the staff of the *Columbia Daily Spectator*

Edited with an introduction by

Robert Friedman

*Map and drawing on title page by Ava Morgan*

Copyright © 1968 by Members of the Board Associates
All rights reserved
Library of Congress catalog card number 68–57992
Published simultaneously in Canada by McClelland and Stewart Ltd.
Manufactured in the United States of America by H. Wolff, New York
Designed by Harry Ford
First Edition

# Preface

THE EVENTS at Columbia University in April and May of 1968 were among the most significant in the history of higher education in the United States. They occurred rapidly, against a complex background of New Left politics, black power, the role and structure of the university and other broad areas of concern. In addition, they stemmed in large measure from historical sources within the University, sources the authors, as editors and reporters of the *Columbia Daily Spectator*, had lived with and reported on for several years.

This history is to a great extent a record of the first-hand observations of the twenty-five editors, reporters and researchers of the *Spectator* staff who covered the crisis at Columbia. Because of the relationship *Spectator* has developed in its ninety-one year history with various groups on campus, the authors were able to work with the principals in much closer contact than was possible for representatives of the national press. In addition, *Spectator* staff members were often accorded special privileges of access by all parties; for instance, the authors were the only journalists permitted to attend the meetings of the Ad Hoc Faculty Group. Extensive interviews were conducted after the crisis with over fifty faculty members, students, administrators and representatives of the city government and Harlem community. Careful use was made of tape recordings of the events of the crisis, often as a double check against material provided by reporters, sometimes as a unique source of information. A collection of more than three-hundred documents was assembled during the months of turmoil, ranging from strikers' leaflets to confidential memoranda of high administrators. These documents are quoted extensively in the text.

Any opinions expressed in this volume are those of the authors; they do not necessarily conform to those of the *Columbia Daily Spectator*. In addition to the four editors and four members of the news board of *Spectator* who contributed to this account, a number of others have helped significantly. Kenneth Barry and Arthur Kokot of the *Spectator* news board assisted in the organization of material and made valuable suggestions for improving the manuscript. We are indebted to Lida Orzeck and Pat Miklethun who spent long hours transcribing the interviews and typing the manuscript. Neal Hurwitz, a Columbia graduate student, provided the authors with much helpful material assembled immediately after the spring crisis. And finally, our special gratitude goes to Tom Wilson and Michael Bessie at Atheneum, for supplying badly needed encouragement and thoroughly undeserved patience in abundance.

*August 1965* THE AUTHORS

# Contents

| | | |
|---|---|---|
| | Introduction | 3 |
| | Prologue | 23 |
| 1 | The Academic Guerrillas | 28 |
| 2 | Horam Expecta Veniet | 37 |
| 3 | The Second Front | 60 |
| 4 | Enter Alan Westin | 69 |
| 5 | Dick Greeman's Bloody Nose | 96 |
| 6 | The Liberated Life | 117 |
| 7 | Bullshit | 131 |
| 8 | A Bitter Pill | 142 |
| 9 | Amnesty or Bust | 168 |
| 10 | All Necessary Precautions . . . | 181 |
| 11 | Exit Alan Westin | 200 |
| 12 | Amorphatorium | 223 |
| 13 | Déjà Vu | 253 |
| | Epilogue | 277 |
| APPENDIX I | Reflections on Student Radicalism BY Herbert A. Deane | 285 |
| APPENDIX II | Symbols of the Revolution BY Mark Rudd | 291 |
| | Chronology | 299 |
| | Cast of Characters | 302 |
| | Index | 305 |

# *Illustrations*

A GROUP OF ILLUSTRATIONS WILL BE FOUND

FOLLOWING PAGE 150

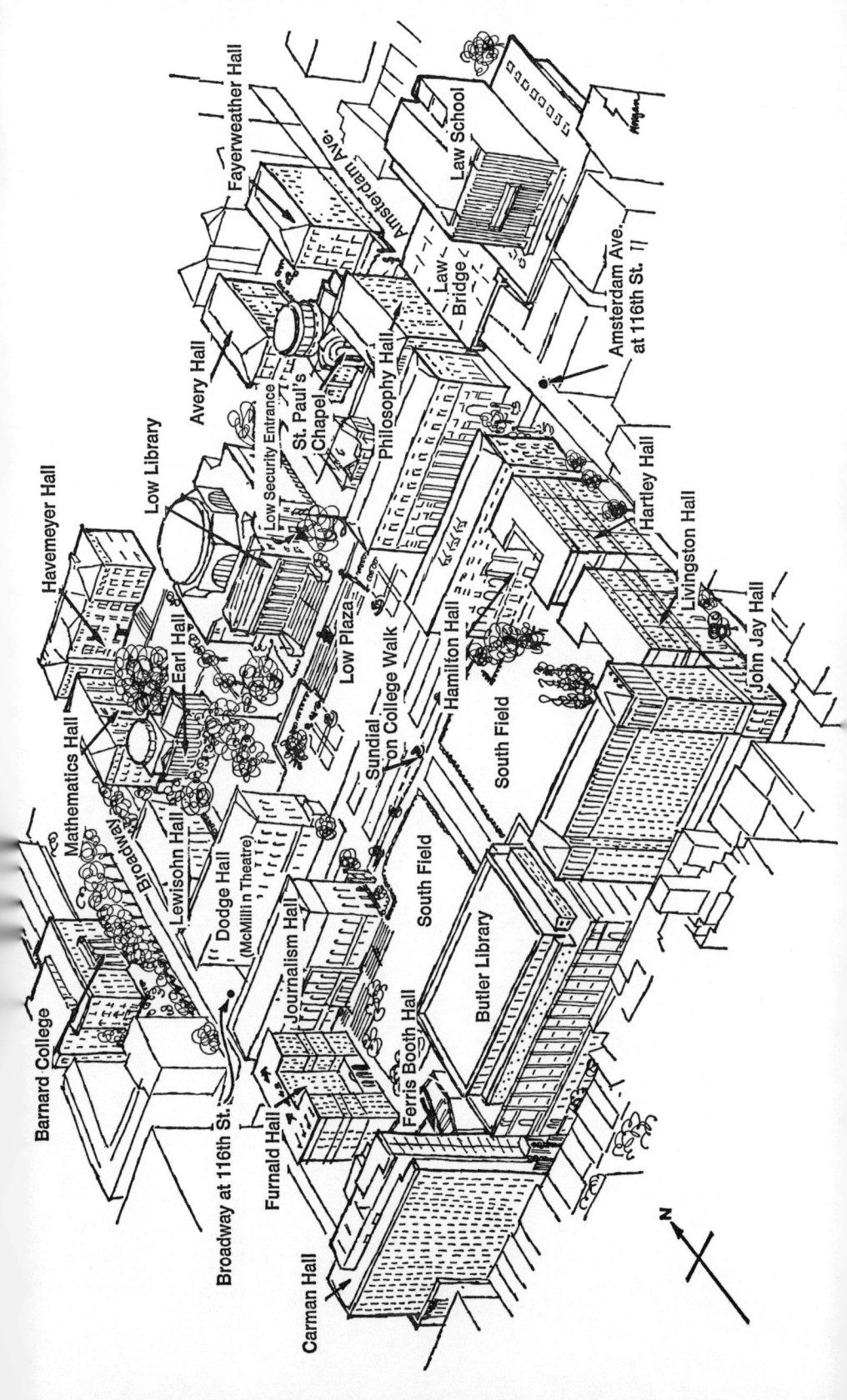

# UP AGAINST THE IVY WALL:
*A history of the Columbia crisis*

# Introduction

## BY ROBERT FRIEDMAN

THE WEEKEND before the revolution at Columbia had its Bastille Day, a group of faculty members who teach the course that is the symbol of the *ancien régime* gathered at the former estate of Averell Harriman to plot quietly the overthrow of a Columbia College tradition. With the help of four students who conveyed the disillusionment of many undergraduates, the thirty professors summarily did away with the survey approach to "Contemporary Civilization" (CC), a course required of all freshmen since 1919. They guillotined the works of Plato, Aristotle and Aquinas which had for so long been required reading and decided that they would begin the study of Western civilization with the Reformation.

What was perhaps most significant about the new CC course developed that weekend at Arden House was that almost an entire semester would be devoted to a topical study of revolutions. As the CC reformers discussed which revolutions should be studied, between meals served on delicate china and walks along wood-lined paths fifty miles north of New York City, the newest revolution, which might be included on next year's reading list, was spreading its vague fingers across a thawing campus.

Educational reform was once again a step behind reality. Studying old revolutions in the classroom while new ones were taking place on the Harlem streets just ten blocks away is typical of the University's relation to society. In recent years students had come to discover that mass urban study programs and courses on revolution were not enough; the University was a social as well as an academic institution and would have to play an active role in the society it once attempted to avoid. Columbia—on the shores of one of the nation's largest black ghettos and adrift in a society sick with war, manipulating the lives of its young people for misguided crusades—was tottering along with the old order it had served so well.

Columbia University in the City of New York is in some respects a strange place for a revolution yet, in others, a likely breeding ground for student unrest. Unlike many large schools such as Berkeley, and many small schools such as Swarthmore, Columbia has little cohesion as a community, for there is little to differentiate it from New York City. There are few trees, and the buildings are cramped onto a six-square-block campus. Columbia is diffused into New York. And in the process something happens that transforms it from the Ivy League school that its alumni and administrators imagine it to be to the urban university that it is in reality. As Columbia flows into the streets of New York, so the society of the streets flows into Columbia. Medieval attempts to keep reflective thought separated from reality only prove futile. New York is life. Its dirt, congestion, motion and art force people to respond; its physical environment has generated a mental climate of liberality and social consciousness, which has permeated the urban campus.

Universities have only recently begun to respond to rapid changes in society and the resulting changes in the psychology and attitudes of their students. One would expect Columbia, because of its location, to be in the vanguard of institutional change. Instead it lags far behind most American universities. Operating under conceptions that were perhaps valid ten years ago, it offers part of its new gymnasium in a gesture of benevolence to a black community that today wants no gifts from white institutions. And with similar lack of understanding, it expects its students to uphold the values of law and order over morality, when those students have seen "law and order" distorted to provide a cloak for white racism and for American involvement in Vietnam.

Today, when students seek to engage themselves actively with society, Columbia is still clinging to the funnel theory of education, trying to protect its students for four years and then channeling them into professional life. This concept of a university as a degree factory with an ovipositor in society is one great source of disillusionment to thousands of students, who on the one hand resist being processed into that society, and on the other refuse to be shunted off from that society during their "incubation" period. So, at Columbia, some students cut classes to get arrested at anti-draft demonstrations, and others devote their hours to community action programs. Their desire to act springs from a deep sense of morality and frustration—frustration that they have no say in shaping the decisions that shape their lives and their world.

The rebellions at campuses across the country this spring had their roots in disillusionment not only with society but with universities as institutions. It was disillusionment with illusion. Columbia has the façade of a great university. It gives the impression of helping society when it is socially bankrupt, and it has the illusion of providing a great education when it is educationally unfulfilling. A survey taken by Columbia's Bureau of Applied Social Research just after the spring demonstrations revealed, not surprisingly, that a large majority of those participating in and supporting the demonstrations were either mildly or very dissatisfied with the University as an educational institution. A slightly greater percentage of students at Columbia were dissatisfied than at Berkeley just prior to the student movement there.

To understand this disillusionment and the activism that it spawned, it is necessary to have a picture of the educational climate of one "great" University, particularly of its undergraduate college, where nearly 15 per cent of the students are now on police blotters. Endowed with some of the best scholars in the world, with hundreds of students whose College Board scores were over 700 and with a wide range of courses and areas of study, Columbia offers an education which lacks what education at most other large universities lacks—spirit. It is an education of mere bones: facts and intellectual theories.

The classroom buildings are across the way from the cinderblock dormitories. Students have classes a few hours a day, and they drift in, listen to their professors and drift back out to their dormitory rooms or apartments. Once in a while they get an exciting professor, but the bulk of their courses are dry and they do not feel guilty about cutting them. Students are forced to seek relationships and involvement in activities outside the classroom. John Locke and the empiricists tell us that we are always learning whether we are in a classroom or not; Buckminster Fuller and the commune-ists tell us that life is to be lived immersed in a group. Students would like to go to such a university where the classroom is not differentiated from the dormitory, where people really live together, where we get into things instead of talk about them. But the Clark Kerrs and the hard-nosed realists tell us that in this mass society we have educational factories.

Columbia is a moderately large university with 17,500 students. Most of these students are engaged in post-graduate work and have little to do with Columbia aside from seminars and the libraries. They do not live on the campus, they do not participate in student activities or in student-sponsored events, they have little contact with the faculty beyond a thesis-oriented relationship with a few professors in their particular department and they have no contact with the administration beyond form letters and registration cards. The 2,700 male liberal-arts students enrolled in the College, however, have a fundamentally different relationship with their University. It is their whole life for four years, a majority live on or near the campus and participate in student activities and all are directly affected by the decisions made by their professors and by the administration.

It is in the College where students are most closely integrated with University life, where disillusionment is keenest, where campus political activity is centered and where the demonstrations began and received their greatest support. Columbia College is, in the traditional sense, perhaps one of the best undergraduate schools in the country for students who seek a sound liberal arts background, preparation for a role in society and a laminated degree. But the traditional student is quickly vanishing. Where students were once swathed in complacency and looked forward to a slice of middle-class life, they now actively avoid it. Their social consciences force them to live in the present and to set aside their plans for the future. Their needs and perspectives have changed radically from the Eisenhower years, reflecting a spiraling hostility toward and loss of faith in society and its institutions.

In 1968 student unrest shifted noticeably from the national scene to the campus, for psychological and tactical reasons. Thrust into a frightening world, the individual tries to make sense of his existence and seeks gratification in having an effect as an individual on his social environment. He is told that he is a citizen of a vast country and slowly learns that his relationship with the government of that country is one-sided. Perhaps this is the failing of mass democracy. Whatever the case, the individual's power extends as far as the ballot box which allows him to vote for officials whose actions and decisions in office can never be known beforehand. His other "legitimate" source of power is dissent. But dissent, students have learned from marching the streets of New York and the steps of the Pentagon, does not change men or their policies; it only incites them to enforce the law. And so students turn back from the Pentagon, where the war machine muffled their protest in tear gas. They are lost in the social context of the nation state. They can protest the war only to find it being escalated before their placards. They can work for McCarthy and pretend to forget that the New Hampshire euphoria will soon be smoke-screened behind the disenchantment of convention politics. And so they return to the framework of their universities, where they can be more effective as individual radicalizers or reformers, and where they hope to find an administration more receptive to their needs and demands.

This is the predicament of an increasing number of college students, which has helped generate a climate for campus activism. Alone, however, it fails to explain: Why Columbia? At many schools, administrations are responsive, either as a result of the personalities of administrators or of the pressures brought to bear upon them through recognized channels of student and faculty participation. Other schools have administrations that can, under tension, adapt quickly to student needs and demands. And a great majority of American universities, particularly those in non-urban environments, are safe for the time being since so many of their students have not reached the level of social consciousness and disillusionment that prevails at Columbia.

In April 1968 social disillusionment and institutional disenchantment finally climaxed at Columbia. The massive demonstrations that resulted, and their widespread support, can only be understood in the context of growing disillusionment with the Columbia administration and with the University as an institution. By following certain trends and issues—none directly leading to the explosion, but each contributing to the atmosphere—the events of spring 1968 no longer appear as an isolated patchwork. Instead they fall into an institutional context, which explains the nature and symbolism of the specific grievances that came to be obscured in the wake of "sensational" tactics.

On any given issue, whether it be the construction of a new gymnasium on public park land or the affiliation of the University with some outside organization, there is something inherently wrong with the method and process by which the action was taken, and most often something intrinsically wrong with the undertaking itself. Bad decisions, however, do not always follow from archaic or faulty decision-making processes. They are frequently the result of the attitudes of men who make decisions while having a limited understanding of the sentiments of those affected by them. At Columbia, however, an archaic system has gone hand in hand with a series of insensitive administrations, and the fruits of this hapless union have been both disastrous and demoralizing to the University community.

The fragmented nature of the University community has allowed Columbia to slip into a disturbing state of affairs. Students who drift in and out of the University as if it were a loading station, and faculty members who closet themselves with their research and latest book, have, by their abdication of any responsibility, left the security of the University precariously in the hands of its administrators. For a large part of the first half of the century Columbia lay under the iron rule of Nicholas Murray Butler, who was both deaf and blind during the latter years of his reign. If a civilian tyrant was not enough, Columbia was saddled in 1948 with a military commander, General Dwight D. Eisenhower, who found little he could do at an academic center and soon realized that it was best to stay away from the campus. His election as President of the United States would have been the best thing for

Columbia had the University's reins not fallen into the hands of Grayson Kirk. Kirk, who had risen from his rural Ohio settings to considerable international reputation as a political scientist, is a highly polished, fundraising, alumni-pleasing, after-dinner speechmaker. He is both distinguished and shy, poised in public and uneasy in private, comfortable in international and corporate circles and rarely accessible to students and faculty. Behind his façade today there is little left.

The twenty-three Trustees to whom President Kirk is directly responsible are securely tied to the corporate structure of American life. Their average age is over sixty and they are far out of the mainstream of University and student affairs. They are invested with ultimate authority over the decisions of the University, and yet not one educator sits on the self-appointed, self-perpetuating board. Most of the men are loyal Columbia alumni who have made it as real-estate magnates, bankers and directors of such corporations as Lockheed Aircraft, Consolidated Edison, IBM and CBS.

The collusion theory that lays the blame for all of Columbia's faults on the corporate interests of the members of the board of Trustees and the President is far too simplistic to explain what happened at Columbia. It is not that the Trustees are out to subvert the University's educational interests. As men who have little contact with University life and who are conditioned to act out of motivations of finance and prestige rather than moral and social concerns, they naturally tend to implicate the University in ventures that go against the consciences of students and faculty members. It is understandable that the Trustees should seek ways to raise money, build the international reputation of the University and fulfill its social and national obligations in manners that are somewhat dubious to members of the academic community. If there were existing channels within the University to check or counterbalance these interests, the incidence of error would be decreased although certainly not eliminated. That there were no such countervailing forces at work at Columbia, however, provided for a faulty system that assured a high occurrence of mistakes. As these mistakes accumulated, questioning turned to skepticism and hostility, and the University administration soon found itself challenged from within and from without. The neighboring community whose existence was threatened by Columbia's future plans began organizing to block University expansion. Internal faculty discontent, generated by inadequate housing facilities, relatively low faculty salaries in a city of high living costs, the decline in the quality of many departments, and the pressures of publishing became more noticeable. Students began attacking what they saw as Columbia's "racist" and "imperialist" policies. The Harlem community was up in arms against "whitey" institutions. The University was on the brink of upheaval.

\* \* \*

It was in this climate that the upheaval spontaneously began on April 23. The eruption would never have taken place, however, if the issues of campus discontent had not been wrapped in a neat package of demands. The student radicals had come to realize that only a multi-issue approach would arouse the generally apathetic campus. Spurts of radicalism at Columbia during the past few years had all centered around one issue at a time—the war in Vietnam, the presence of the Naval Reserve Officers' Training Corps program on campus, recruiting by military and paramilitary organizations on campus—and, while they had served to politicize and awaken the campus, they had not brought about change in the policies of the University. Leftists at Columbia had rarely been able to arouse more than a few hundred sympathetic students to participate in relatively peaceful demonstrations. Their activities were less focused on staging confrontations than they were on educating and building support. Indeed, with the exception of a demonstration in the spring of 1965 at the annual NROTC awards ceremony when the administration called in the police, the New Left at Columbia was never so militant that the administration could not sidestep a potential confrontation by telling military recruiters to stay away from the campus or by agreeing to meet with a few hundred adamant students at a public debate.

It was at one such public debate in the fall of 1966 that the Columbia chapter of Students for a Democratic Society became an active force in campus politics. The chapter had been founded the previous spring by John Fuerst, Harvey Bloom and Michael Neumann, the stepson of Herbert Marcuse. The primary political issue then, as it was in 1968, was the University's involvement with the "military establishment" and with the burgeoning war in Vietnam. On November 15, 1966, two-hundred students marched into a campus building to protest the presence of a recruiter from the Central Intelligence Agency, and on the following day, 150 entered Low Library to present a letter to the administration demanding that the University refuse to allow on-campus recruiting by the CIA. The following week five hundred students, organized and led by the fledgling SDS chapter, marched on Low Library again. This time they confronted President Kirk and forced him into a debate on student rights and Columbia's involvement with the military. In most universities an encounter with the president is a modest achievement, but at Columbia it was a precedent-shattering victory that solidly established SDS. Several dozen students remained in the rotunda of Low that day after Kirk returned to his office and discussed the need for a new radical organization on campus. When they left, the small nucleus of proto-SDS members who had organized the demonstration had grown into a sizable movement. Three months later, in February 1967, eighteen students again protested CIA recruitment on campus, this time by sitting-in in front of an office and blocking a recruiter from interviewing students. Most of the protesters were members of SDS, and the sit-in marked the first noticeable escalation of tactics.

The success of leftist tactics at Columbia tended to vary with the nature of the particular issue. Student radicals were less successful on issues concerning University policies, such as on-campus recruiting by military organizations, than they were on issues which directly affected the well-being of students, such as the draft. Five days after the CIA demonstration a referendum was conducted in the College on whether the University should release information on a student's rank in class to his local draft board. In a major victory for the Left, students voted 1,333 to 563 against releasing class rank. The Columbia College faculty had made a similar recommendation to the University in January, and student sentiment against the draft was almost unanimous. Acting for the first time on a broad base of support, SDS called for a student strike if the administration refused to comply with the results of the referendum. Six other campus groups, mostly non-political, endorsed the threatened boycott and, in March, Grayson Kirk responded to the pressure by calling a special meeting of the University Council—Columbia's normally inactive surrogate for a faculty senate. On March 23, while five hundred students held a silent vigil on Low Plaza, the council voted by a two-to-one margin to withhold class rank information from the Selective Service System. The University had capitulated to the students' and faculty's demand.

SDS returned to the issue of military recruiting, leading, one month later, to the first actual outbreak of violence among students on campus in recent years. In April 1967 the United States Marines made their annual trek to Columbia to recruit potential officers. To bolster their recruiting effort, they received permission to set up their tables in the lobby of one of the busiest College dormitories. Not only did they attract recruits, but they drew a contingent of about three hundred pro-SDS students opposed to the presence of the Marines on campus. The protesters blocked access to the tables, and a wedge of about fifty counter-demonstrators attempted to clear a way through. Fist fights broke out and several students were hurt. The scuffle woke students from their apathy, and when the Marines showed up the next day to finish their recruiting drive, eight hundred turned out to picket them. The administration's decision to have the Marines back that day, when they had the option of cooling things down by asking the Marines to stay away, was the first indication that the administration was more intent on making its stand on principle than on common sense.

They made their point that day, but very tenuously, as over a thousand students lined up on opposite sides of a picket fence and were kept from violence only by a large squadron of faculty members and deans. The campus had become polarized over the recruiting issue; when the fall semester began, recruitment by such organizations as the CIA and Dow Chemical became a focal point for leftists not only at Columbia, but at Harvard, Wisconsin and other universities throughout the country. The Columbia administration wisely avoided confrontation by cancelling all recruiting by controversial organizations during the fall, while a faculty committee worked busily investigating the issue. In November, a College-wide referendum indicated that students supported an open recruiting policy for all organizations by a two-to-one majority, and shortly afterward the faculty committee issued its report also calling for open recruiting. The leftists who had wanted military and paramilitary organizations barred from recruiting on campus had suffered a serious setback. The issue was dropped; SDS remained silent during the next three months and began developing some of the issues that were to become part of the package.

Before examining the package of demands which led to the spring explosion, it will be helpful to evaluate some of the administration's actions during the previous year. Several egregious errors, when they became public, not only impaired the administration's image but served to disenchant various segments of the University community. Eventually, these errors were to become the wrappings of the package of demands put together by the student leftists.

In response to the violent demonstration which marked the annual NROTC awards ceremony in May 1965 the administration established a blue-ribbon Student Life Committee, composed of an equal number of students, administrators and faculty. The committee's mandate was to "re-examine the existing University policies governing student rights and responsibilities as members of an academic community." Following the experience of the Student Life Committee, students at Columbia have justifiably come to distrust the words "recommend" and "committee." After two years of intense work, the committee submitted two reports to President Kirk in August 1967. The majority report, endorsed by the faculty and administration members of the panel, called for a greater advisory role for students in the decision-making processes of the University in addition to recommending that a judicial system guaranteeing due process be established. The minority report, signed by the student members of the committee, stressed in fairly strong language that the majority report offered "too little, too late." They argued that students should be given an actual voice in making many of the decisions and policies of the University. The administration was thus presented with programs for making constructive changes in the structure of the University decision-making processes as early as August 1967. But the reports sat quietly on Kirk's desk. Perhaps he read them and circulated them among some top administrators. Whatever the case, the reports were not made public, and there was no sign of action from the administration. Then, in March, the Columbia University Student Council threatened to release its private copy of the reports if the President did not do so, and finally eight months after they had been submitted, Kirk made them public to the University community. Kirk's covering letter failed to discuss his opinion of the merit of the reports beyond saying that "I am not at the present time prepared to support certain of the committee's proposals." The significance of the Student Life Report quickly became apparent. Students had made a serious effort to bring about change and reform through legitimate channels only to find their recommendations—which were far from radical—suppressed for eight months and ultimately ignored. The administration had bared its unresponsiveness to the University community.

Columbia's affair with the Strickman filter was another exhibition of the University's facility for error. The filter, of unproven value, promised to lower substantially the tar and nicotine intake from cigarettes. Columbia agreed in July 1967 to lend its name to this product and to a business venture of dubious nature, in return for a percentage of the profits. The Trustees' desire to secure a quick but substantial source of income and to ease their social consciences by reducing carcinogenic material in cigarettes led them to the filter. That they had espoused a "remarkable" new product invented by a New Jersey chemist who had spent the last eight years of his life unsuccessfully trying to market that product, before it had been fully tested, raised rasping criticism from Congress, cigarette companies and the public. That they had done so without the slightest consultation with members of the University community served further to irritate students and professors, who are conservative when it comes to lending out the Columbia name. While students began thinking of the day Grayson Kirk would be on national television inhaling a cigarette, urging people to smoke "Columbias," the administration was busy testing the filter and haggling with an impatient Strickman. Finally, after seven months of groping, Columbia turned the filter rights back to the inventor and stated in a public release, "The University feels that it owes it to the public to state candidly that it made a well-intentioned mistake in entering a highly controversial and competitive commercial field." Through their confession they avoided further hostility from the public sector but managed nevertheless to give the University community a clear picture of their ineptness.

While neither of these two issues was mentioned in the course of the spring demonstrations, they and numerous others of lesser importance contributed to the climate. A third issue, however—that of the University's manifest destiny policy and its resulting financial policy—related somewhat more directly to the grievances of the students and of the local residents on Morningside Heights. Aside from the members of the University community who live in the neighborhood, the residents of once-posh Morningside Heights are mostly low-income black, Chinese or Puerto Rican families scattered among a large number of octogenarians and unattached intellectuals, all clinging to their rent-controlled apartments. To them Columbia is the enemy, for it threatens (perhaps not now, but certainly in the near future) to buy their apartment building, if it does not already own it, and to demolish it to make room for new University buildings. Largely to provide for an expanded campus in the future, Columbia has spent the last two decades investing a significant portion of its endowment in the real-estate business, buying property on the Heights. The purchase of this property and the eviction, often preceded by harassment, of more than seven thousand community residents—85 per cent of whom were black or Puerto Rican—over the past ten years have led not only to great fears within the community but also to charges of racial bias. Columbia has been accused of seeking control over property on the Heights in an effort to control the social and cultural tone of the community by forcing out what former Provost Jacques Barzun called the "uninviting, abnormal, sinister and dangerous" elements. The future that is in the minds of Columbia's planners can be found in a special room in Low Library. Set up as a fund-raising gimmick, the room gives a glimpse in white plaster of the future educational park that Columbia envisions for Morningside Heights. In glass cases along the walls of the room are models of all the component buildings for Columbia's expansion, with plaques under each case announcing where the steel and concrete counterparts will be built. That the motives of the University have been racially prejudiced is questionable. That its actions, however, have had racial undertones is apparent, if for no other reason than that so many Negroes and Puerto Ricans have been in the way of Columbia expansion. Few will dispute the need for the University to expand, but an even smaller number can be content with Columbia's disregard for local residents and its "communicidal" policies. The University provides few if any social benefits to the community and has shown little interest in planning for an environment to be shared by local residents and the University. Furthermore, it has engaged in little meaningful dialogue with the community about the future of Morningside Heights, partially because the community is so amorphous and leaderless, and partially because of a lack of University initiative. Residents of the community are treated as "guests" of the

University in much the same manner as the University treats its students. (Tenants of Columbia-owned apartments hold month-by-month leases at the pleasure of the University and students carry identification cards which read "the University is free to cancel his registration at any time, on any grounds which it deems advisable.")

The buying of property in the immediate neighborhood has tied up a large part of the University's endowment in real estate which yields relatively little return. Since the turn of the century, Columbia, like many other universities, has invested heavily in real estate not only on Morningside Heights but throughout New York City and is today one of the largest landholders in the city. After World War II, however, many schools such as Harvard withdrew large parts of their real-estate investments and turned to a rising stock market, thus boosting their endowments significantly. Columbia's conservative Trustees held on to their property and in the process stunted the University's financial growth. The result has been insufficient funds to launch new projects, rapidly rising tuition which has nearly doubled in the past decade and a faculty salary level which has climbed only slowly since the war.

Financial trouble led to plans for fiscal amelioration, and, in October 1966, Columbia launched what was then the largest fund-raising effort in the history of American education. Started on the road to its $200-million goal by a beneficent $35-million gesture of the Ford Foundation, the fund drive lagged during 1967, and as the October 1969 deadline approached, less than half the money had been collected or pledged. While critical to the future of Columbia, the fund drive has had a deadening effect on the present. Administrators, who are soft-talking rich alumni to donate their millions, are reluctant if not unwilling to say or do anything that might appear to be the least bit controversial. They are forced to be unresponsive to student demands for change, because the rich alumni are more interested in preserving the Columbia they once knew than in changing it. The deadening influence of the fund drive has similarly affected many faculty members who are not eager to do anything that might upset chances for major faculty salary increases that the fund drive promises. They are quick to respond to proposals with: "A great idea, but we'll have to wait or else risk upsetting the applecart." These effects of the fund drive came most inappropriately at the time when the University should have been making sweeping changes rather than preserving the *status quo* for the sake of well-to-do alumni and friends.

Student leftists, however, saw that this was just the time to do what the administrators and most faculty feared: rock the boat. It was a time when the administration would be least flexible and responsive and most likely to help set the stage for confrontation and dialectic which the radicals craved. It was further a time when they could enlist the support of more moderate elements, which saw the need for reform or change of policies and had been rebuffed in their efforts to work through legitimate channels. All that needed to be done was to find the issues.

In March 1967 the *Columbia Daily Spectator* ran a story confirming the investigations of an SDS research committee that Columbia was institutionally affiliated with the Institute for Defense Analyses. IDA, as it is known on campus, was founded in 1956 as an independent "not-for-profit" organization to conduct weapons evaluation and other related research for the Department of Defense. It relied for its prestige on the institutional affiliation of major American universities, and in 1959 Columbia was induced to join. According to one of the top IDA officers, Columbia is "one of the three or four primary university sponsors," and Grayson Kirk "has always been an active member of our board." Kirk, as well as Columbia Trustee William A. M. Burden, sits on the IDA board of trustees which determines corporate policy, as well as on the executive committee of IDA which actively administers the work of the trustees. Burden is chairman of both the board of trustees and the executive committee. One officer of IDA described the role played by the member universities earlier this year when he stated, "The involvement of the universities with us is not on a day-to-day basis, but it bloody well does determine the important things, such as the kind of research contracts IDA accepts." The member universities do not lend financial support to IDA, but instead lend some of their top scientists for research, and perhaps most significantly lend their names to these defense-oriented efforts. What has made IDA such an explosive issue on campus is indeed Columbia's agreement to have its name used to enhance the reputation of an organization currently engaged in such work as evaluating counter-insurgency techniques for use in Vietnam and in the streets of American cities. The exact manner in which IDA uses the universities' names is best illustrated in the 1961 annual report where, interspersed between drawings of prominent buildings from the campuses of the twelve member institutions, are such comments as:

> If the Institute for Defense Analyses has produced important studies on problems in national security, much of the credit must go to the university world. Without the efforts of these men and the coöperation of these institutions IDA would not be what it is. We are proud of our twelve member universities as recognition of our debt to the entire university world.

While Columbia does not induce its faculty members to work for IDA, the University's affiliation with the institute makes it particularly easy for Columbia scientists to lend their services either while they are teaching or are on leave. In the past, several Columbia professors have aided in IDA research, and others have been members of the institute's Jason Division. The Jason Division is composed of about forty of the nation's top scientists who devote a significant amount of their time to work on defense problems. According to the 1967 annual report the Jason Division spent much of its time during 1966 "working on technical problems of counter-insurgency warfare and systems studies with relevance to Vietnam."

IDA was an ideal issue for Columbia, for it appealed to people on three levels. First, it is an obvious symbol of the war in Vietnam, and by affiliation the University is accused of aiding the war effort. Thus to protest IDA is, symbolically, to protest an unjust war, and almost everyone at Columbia is opposed to the war. Secondly, IDA raises questions about the moral and social roles of American universities, revealing what many believe to be the universities' inseparable ties with the "military-industrial complex." Students who find the war morally reprehensible find their University's links with that war effort equally reprehensible and maintain that affiliation with such organizations as IDA violates the spirit and purpose of the University as an institution for the continuation of humane ideals. Thirdly, many, including a faculty committee which released its report in June 1968, have criticized the IDA affiliation on the grounds that Columbia became a member as a result of a unilateral action by the administration and the Trustees without consulting students and faculty. Indeed, it was eight years before the ties became known to the University community. These critics contend that the University belongs to the students and faculty as well as to the administrators, and that when it comes to something as controversial as lending the University's name and personnel to defense research, the administration has no right to act unilaterally. What particularly aggravated students were such statements as the ones made by Ralph Halford, former dean of the Graduate Faculties, in reference to Columbia's involvement with IDA. A week before the affiliation was made public, Halford spoke to an inquisitive group of faculty members and students about government-sponsored research at Columbia and explicitly denied rumors that Columbia had any affiliation with IDA. A week later when the ties had become public information, the same administrator commented, "I don't really know what IDA does. These things are not in the purview of faculty or students. . . . This is a matter for the Trustees of the University to decide."

The anti-IDA movement at Columbia began quietly with students questioning the administration on several occasions about IDA and almost always getting the same response: that it is necessary for the government to be able to rely on the resources of its educational institutions. In October 1967 a mild controversy erupted over the disclosure of a non-classified research project that had been secretly funded by the CIA since 1961. The University quickly responded that this was the only CIA-sponsored project at the University and that Columbia would not accept another secretly funded project "unless the purposes were so overwhelmingly important that we could not in good conscience say no." Shortly after the disclosure more than three hundred students, led by SDS leaders, marched into Low to present a letter to Kirk demanding that the University sever all its ties with the defense establishment, including those with IDA. Kirk, following Emily Post, never answered the letter because it had no return address.

In December 1967, at the request of the faculty of Columbia College, the President appointed a faculty committee to study guidelines for the University's relationship with outside agencies including IDA. But the radicals by this time were contemptuous of the slow and frequently ineffective committee process of change, and in response to the administration's lack of direct action on their earlier letter, they again marched into Low Library on March 27. This time things were different. The new SDS chairman, Mark Rudd, presented the administration with a petition demanding an end to all IDA ties signed by more than fifteen hundred students and faculty. Instead of an orderly march into Low, more than one hundred students roamed the corridors of the building for an hour, chanting, using bullhorns and disrupting office activity. Not only were they backing their demand with massive support, but their tactics had shifted to the clearly and intentionally disruptive. Kirk this time responded to the petition in an open letter to Rudd stating that the IDA matter was currently under investigation by a faculty committee. Four days after the demonstration inside Low, the Trustees of Columbia approved a plan worked out by the IDA board of trustees which would end university affiliation to the institute. The disaffiliation plan was a response to growing student protest at the various member institutions and to criticism of IDA ties by the faculties of two of them. The plan's deviousness soon became apparent; the corporate structure of IDA was to be altered so that instead of each university selecting an officer to represent its institution on the IDA trustees, each university would now designate one of its senior officers each year to serve in an individual capacity as an IDA trustee. The new arrangement would cause no significant change in the composition of the IDA board of trustees, and Grayson Kirk would continue to serve as an IDA trustee. That it would be difficult, if not impossible, to differentiate between Grayson Kirk serving in his capacity as President of Columbia and Grayson Kirk serving as an individual seemed obvious to all but IDA and the Columbia Trustees.

From the very beginning of the campus revolt this spring IDA was a prominent issue appealing to a wide spectrum of students because of its multi-level nature. A student referendum taken on the second day of the occupation indicated that of 5,500 polled, over 3,500 favored an end to IDA ties.

As the IDA issue appealed to dissidents on a variety of levels, so too did the planned construction of a Columbia gymnasium in Morningside Park. The gym issue had been developing for several years, and the demand of students and community leaders to stop construction of the gym became a focal point of the spring demonstrations. More so than the IDA issue, the gym was a sticking point for the administration; because of financial involvements, Columbia was not about to compromise. While IDA coalesced anti-war sentiment on the campus, the gym was a catalyst for widespread discontent about black-white relations. The gym not only symbolized racist attitudes of white institutions, but it also pointed to Columbia's shabby relations with the Harlem community, to a conservationist issue and once again to the decision-making process which allowed a gym to be planned without full consultation of students, faculty and most importantly the community.

Columbia had long been in need of a new gymnasium. Its athletic facilities are currently housed in a building constructed at the turn of the century as a temporary structure and long since inadequate. Since the 1920's Columbia planners had been dreaming about a new gym, but for one reason or another the dreams never passed the paper stage. Then, in the late 1950's, Columbia approached the city government with the idea of building a gym in Morningside Park with separate facilities for the community. With the coöperation of Mayor Robert Wagner and his Parks Commissioner Robert Moses, the Trustees worked out a deal whereby Columbia would lease 2.1 acres of park land for ninety-nine years at the bargain rate of $3,000 per annum. It was an unprecedented move—the first time in the history of the City of New York that public park land had been leased to a private institution for the construction of a facility to which the public would have only limited access.

The craggy strip of park had once been an oasis in uptown Manhattan but now served as a narrow no-man's-land buffering Columbia University on the Heights from Harlem which rests at the foot of the park. The paths had become strewn with broken glass, and the crime rate had soared in recent years. Morningside Park was by day a playground and by night a repository for outcasts. It seemed natural that the city and Columbia should team together to make the park safe, while at the same time providing athletic facilities for a deprived neighborhood. That was in 1958, and few raised objections at the time. The civil rights movement had not spread from the South, and Harlem was an inchoate community that was eager to take what it could get regardless of the color of the benefactor. Paternalism was in, and Columbia was out to get its gym, by appeasing the community if necessary. The New York State Legislature approved the lease of park land to Columbia in 1960 with little debate, and the City Board of Estimate a year later held a public session and unanimously agreed to fix the price at $3,000 a year.

While Columbia was raising funds and drawing plans for the gymnasium, however, the black community was fermenting. With the stirrings of the black power movement in Harlem over the past few years, the community had taken on a sense of pride, and the gym had taken on racial undertones. Harlem was no longer to be appeased by a token community gymnasium. Plans had originally allotted 12.5 per cent of the gym's space to the community, and the separate facilities were actually to have a back entrance on the lower Harlem side for the community and a main entrance facing Columbia for the University.

Shortly after becoming Parks Commissioner in 1966, Thomas Hoving spoke out against Columbia's plans to build a gym in the park. Sensing his role as a public official and the shift in the feeling of the black community, Hoving said that if Columbia were to build on public park land it should at least provide for an equal sharing of facilities. As Hoving raised his voice in dissent, he triggered a volley of anti-gym statements from community leaders and local politicians. During the next year and a half they sought to work through legitimate channels to bring about changes in the gym plans. Beginning in February 1967 Columbia officials engaged in a long series of unprofitable talks about the gym with the community which continued through the spring; but it became apparent that Columbia was not willing either to shift the gym site or to make any significant changes in the allocation of space in the gymnasium. Over the summer, however, as Harlem militants scored Columbia's rape of their community and its "racist gym," the University announced that it would add a swimming pool and a locker room to the community part of the gymnasium, thus raising the separate community sector to roughly 15 per cent of the total floor space. As talks with the community resumed in the fall, Columbia kept delaying the groundbreaking date. The University had reached a point where it did not know whom it was talking to, who spoke for the community, or whether it would ever be possible to find out what the community wanted. Many Harlem residents no doubt wanted the gym facilities and the swimming pool for their children, but Columbia got a hint of how some of the more militant community members felt when, in December, H. Rap

Brown turned up at a meeting in Harlem and told his audience: "If they build the first story blow it up. If they sneak back at night and build three stories burn it down. And if they get nine stories built, it's yours. Take it over, and maybe we'll let them in on the weekends." Last-minute attempts to get plans for the gym changed—proposals for alternate sites, redistribution of space or change of control—met with further administration rejections. The gym was for Columbia and, for most observers, a *fait accompli*.

Columbia now plowed blindly ahead toward its groundbreaking date and, perhaps to its surprise, construction began peacefully in the bitter cold morning of February 19, 1968. The next day, however, twenty people staged a sit-in in front of bulldozers and dumptrucks, and six Columbia students and six community residents were arrested. A week later in a larger protest 150 Columbia and community people demonstrated at the gym site, and another twelve students were arrested. It was at this point, when the administration was saying that absolutely nothing could stop the gym and when protests were mounting, that the white radicals and the black students at Columbia took up the gym issue.

To be sure, a few SDS members had participated in the anti-gym demonstrations, but for the most part those arrested were the students who had been exposed to the civil rights movement and who had worked for years in the College Citizenship Council, tutoring and organizing in Harlem. The radicals were latecomers to the gym opposition, but they quickly sensed the importance of taking up a demand of the black militants. At a time when so many people in this country are concerned about race relations, an issue which is at least symbolically racial will attract the attention of everyone, from those who fear the path of black fire to those who would like to throw Molotov cocktails alongside their black brothers.

If it is surprising that SDS waited so long to capitalize on the gym issue, it is astonishing that Columbia's black students were so quiet. The black students' organization—Students' Afro-American Society—which has a membership of about 150, had, until this spring, directed most of its attention toward building a coherent organization for black students on campus. SAS's moderate leaders had steered a course away from the gym issue and the ghetto toward internal problems concerning themselves as black students: working with the admissions office to arrange for more black students to come to Columbia and trying to establish black history courses. Their tactics had been far from militant; instead they worked within the system for a greater tolerance. Founded as a national organization in 1964 by Columbia student Hilton Clark, son of the Negro psychologist Kenneth Clark, SAS attempted to give a sense of identification to a group of black students mislodged in a white institution. The blacks at Columbia had remained somewhat of an enigma, seeking to isolate themselves from white activities and at the same time avoiding extensive involvement with black people outside the University. They had been preoccupied, until this spring, with the trappings of black culture. It was at approximately the same time that a more militant leadership was elected to lead SAS that the blacks took up their role as Harlem's emissaries to Columbia and became involved in the gym issue.

The gym controversy had pointed up, among other things, Columbia's failure to respond to critical changes in the nature of the black community as well as its inability to communicate with that community. In one sense the gym issue was symbolic and in another sense very real. Few people thought on April 23 that the gym could be stopped, yet within a week the administration had called construction to a halt.

The third point in SDS's triangle of demands was discipline. It was the discipline issue that touched off both the April and May occupations of Hamilton Hall and proved to be the stickiest point of all for the Columbia administration. SDS charged, when its leaders were put on probation for the March 27 demonstration against IDA inside Low Library, that the administration was using discipline as a means of political repression to stifle dissent on campus. The administration maintained, on the other hand, that it was merely enforcing the rules that provided for the punishment of students who had disrupted University activities. One such rule was laid down in an edict issued by President Kirk in September banning all demonstrations inside University buildings. SDS took this ruling as another sign of political repression and actively sought to challenge it during the year. But until March 27 the administration, in the interest of avoiding confrontation, had bent over backward not to enforce the rule. Aside from the question of repression, however, the issue of discipline had other implications. Like the gym, the discipline crisis pointed a finger at the University's failure to respond to changes that had been occurring in the nation over the past decade. Increasingly, judicial procedures providing due process had penetrated from the public to the private sector. Private corporations, such as General Motors, had for some time been providing due process for their employees by submitting disputes to an outside court.

Columbia, however, had insisted on family-type justice rather than due process. In a majority of cases family-type justice at an academic institution is workable. A student charged with possession of drugs, with keeping a woman in his room past visiting hours or with plagiarizing a paper is asked in to speak privately with one of the deans, who seeks to "help" him. But family-type justice is not well suited for cases of a political nature. Despite the increasing number of demonstrations and disruptions that have occurred on the campus in the past three years, the administration had failed to institute any sort of legal proceedings which would guarantee students' rights to due process. The symbol of Columbia's obsolete absolutism was a statutory regulation dating back to the founding of Columbia in 1754, which invested ultimate judicial authority in the hands of the President. While in modern times the President had delegated most of this authority to the deans of each of the schools, he retained the right to review sentences and alter punishments at will. Regardless of what ad hoc quasi-legal proceedings might be established to deal with a particular disciplinary case, the President has the power to circumvent due process, since executive, legislative and judicial authority are all in his purview. This indeed became an issue in 1967 when President Kirk altered the punishments meted out by his hand-picked student-faculty-administration panel to a group of students who had participated in a sit-in against a CIA recruiter on campus. The open hearings of this panel marked the first time that the administration had ever set up quasi-legal proceedings to handle political dissent. But the hearings, as they dragged on for two weeks, proved to be disastrous for the administration, and when SDS this year demanded an open hearing the administration bluntly refused. While other schools throughout the country had, or were creating, student-faculty boards to deal with discipline, Columbia insisted that punishment be meted out by deans without any hearings or trial proceedings.

The issue of discipline, which rounded out the SDS list of demands, attracted students and faculty disenchanted with the archaic power structure of the University; the gym had its appeal along racial lines, and IDA picked up the anti-war sentiment. By welding the three together, SDS was able to mobilize a wide range of support, and could capitalize on three separate sources of frustration.

In the chapters that follow we have attempted to show how these frustrations and demands were interwoven with radical tactics to produce the largest and most extended student movement in the history of this country. The spring movement at Columbia, however, provided more than just political action. Living through the crisis was perhaps the best education many Columbia students will ever receive, and reliving it in these pages one discovers a pattern that is not only the basis of most of the world's crises today but promises to duplicate itself two, three, many times tomorrow.

22 August 1968

# Prologue

WHAT IS THE singular of 'swine'?" asked Warren Goodell, vice president for administration of Columbia University, as he walked into the offices of the *Columbia Daily Spectator*.

"It must be 'pig,' " one of the editors suggested. "Why?"

"They called me one yesterday," the vice president said with a nervous smile. "They marched over to my office, and one of them yelled, 'There's another one of these swine around here,' and they came looking for me. But I wasn't in."

The incident had occurred on March 27, 1968, during a demonstration in which over one hundred members of the Columbia chapter of Students for a Democratic Society marched into Low Memorial Library, the domed-and-columned edifice that houses the offices of Columbia's top administrators. Officially the demonstration had been called to protest Columbia's affiliation with the Institute for Defense Analyses, an organization that does military research for the federal government.[1] But beyond this it had another goal: to flout an edict, issued at the start of the academic year by Columbia President Grayson Kirk, banning all protests inside University buildings. SDS claimed that the rule was an attempt at political repression and wanted to draw the administration into a confrontation over the regulation. Inside Low, chanting "IDA Must Go!", the mass of students burst into several offices, including that of one administrator who admitted he was against the war but said he had more pressing problems. The students presented him with a petition calling for Columbia's disaffiliation from IDA, signed by more than 1,500 students and faculty. They then coursed

[1] See Introduction, pp. 15–18.

through the building for the next fifteen minutes, chanting anti-war slogans and distracting secretaries.

Now, as Goodell spoke of the event, he grew agitated. "Take over," he murmured, "the word has gone out from national SDS —take over the universities. . . . Those students have no respect for property," the vice president said. "You should have seen the things they were doing in Low yesterday—writing on the wall, everything. I have a Picasso hanging in my office, you know. Those kids probably won't even know it's a Picasso. If they touch my Picasso they're going to the state penitentiary!

"I guarantee you," Goodell continued, "that we're going to respond to force with force. I've been at Columbia all my life, and I won't stand by and let them destroy the University. Next thing you know they'll be taking over buildings. . . . And let me tell you this—this April, the weeks after this coming spring vacation, will be the most crucial month in Columbia's entire history. This University may well be on the verge of being torn apart."

As spring 1968 came to Columbia University, something unusual began happening to South Field, the large grassy area in the center of the College campus. For as long as anyone could remember, undergraduates on their way from the student activities center in Ferris Booth Hall to their classes in Hamilton Hall had walked by way of the roundabout brick paths set down by Columbia's architects at the turn of the century. But this year an ominous stripe began to appear on South Field along the diagonal which marks the shortest route between the two buildings. Despite fences and signs posted by the administration, students refused to use the meandering routes their predecessors had followed and began to cut a new path straight across the grass. By mid-April the situation had become critical—holes were torn in the fences, hedges were forced apart and the defiant brown stripe worn across South Field seemed destined to remain.

In the midst of a rapidly changing University climate, Grayson Kirk, sixty-four years old, imposing, President of Columbia University, meticulously clad in gray vest and suit, sat in his large Low Library office surrounded by his familiar mementos and objets d'art. He leaned forward in a leather chair and lit his pipe. It was five days before the uprising. His ample jowls swelling red as he puffed, Kirk explained to a small group of student editors why he had refused for eight months to make public the contents of a report he had commissioned on student life at Columbia. The report had been submitted in late August by a committee of students, faculty and administrators who had worked for nearly two years on the project. It contained an extensive set of proposals for student involvement in University decision-making, as well as rules governing student rights and protest. Kirk had finally released the report only after the student council threatened to make its copy public, and now declined to comment on any of the proposals it contained.

"For me to comment on the Student Life Report would foreclose discussion about it on campus," the President remarked with the stammer that mars much of his speech. "I would not want to say at this time in what spheres of University life the students should have a voice, because there hasn't been time to read the report carefully enough."

Discussion turned to the March 27 political demonstration inside Low Library and the disciplining of students that might follow. "The University is free to expel anyone for any reason it deems equitable," Kirk stated, "and that is as it should be. Of course, I have—under the Trustees—the final disciplinary authority." When asked about a particularly controversial incident that had occurred two weeks before, raising questions about the rights of lower-echelon University officials and students, Kirk responded, "There is no part of this University that is immune from the central authority."

April 22, the day before it all began at Columbia, a student sent an open letter to President Kirk. It began with a quotation:

*Our young people, in disturbing numbers, appear to reject all forms of authority, from whatever source derived, and they have taken refuge in a turbulent and inchoate nihilism whose sole objectives are destruction. I know of no time in our history when the gap between the generations has been wider or more potentially dangerous.*
*Grayson Kirk, April 12, 1968*
*Charlottesville, Va.*

*Dear Grayson,*
*Your charge of nihilism is indeed ominous; for if it were true, our nihilism would bring the whole civilized world, from Columbia to Rockefeller Center, crashing down upon all our heads. Though it is not true, your charge does represent something: you call it the generation gap. I see it as a real conflict between those who run things now—you, Grayson Kirk—and those who feel oppressed by, and disgusted with, the society you rule—we, the young people.*
*You might want to know what is wrong with this society, since,*

*after all, you live in a very tight self-created dream world. We can point to the war in Vietnam as an example of the unimaginable wars of aggression you are prepared to fight to maintain your control over your empire (now you've been beaten by the Vietnamese, so you call for a tactical retreat). We can point to your using us as cannon fodder to fight your war. We can point out your mansion window to the ghetto below you've helped to create through your racist University expansion policies, through your unfair labor practices, through your city government and your police. We can point to this University, your University, which trains us to be lawyers and engineers, and managers for your IBM, your Socony Mobil, your IDA, your Con Edison (or else to be scholars and teachers in more universities like this one). We can point, in short, to our own meaningless studies, our identity crises, and our revulsion with being cogs in your corporate machines as a product of and reaction to a basically sick society.*

*Your cry of "nihilism" represents your inability to understand our positive values. If you were ever to go into a freshman CC [Contemporary Civilization] class you would see that we are seeking a rational basis for society. We do have a vision of the way things could be: how the tremendous resources of our economy could be used to eliminate want, how people in other countries could be free from your domination, how a university could produce knowledge for progress, not waste consumption and destruction (IDA), how men could be free to keep what they produce, to enjoy peaceful lives, to create. These are positive values, but since they mean the destruction of your order, you call them "nihilism." In the movement we are beginning to call this vision "socialism." It is a fine and honorable name, one which implies absolute opposition to your corporate capitalism and your government; it will soon be caught up by other young people who want to exert control over their own lives and their society.*

*You are quite right in feeling that the situation is "potentially dangerous." For if we win, we will take control of your world, your corporation, your University and attempt to mold a world in which we and other people can live as human beings. Your power is directly threatened, since we will have to destroy that power before we take over. We begin by fighting you about your support of the war in Vietnam and American imperialism—IDA and the School of International Affairs. We will fight you about your control of black people in Morningside Heights, Harlem, and the campus itself. And we will fight you about the type of mis-education you are trying to channel us through. We will have to destroy at times,* even violently, in order to end your power and your system—but that is a far cry from nihilism.

Grayson, I doubt if you will understand any of this, since your fantasies have shut out the world as it really is from your thinking. Vice President Truman says the society is basically sound; you say the war in Vietnam was a well-intentioned accident. We, the young people, whom you so rightly fear, say that the society is sick and you and your capitalism are the sickness.

You call for order and respect for authority; we call for justice, freedom, and socialism.

There is only one thing left to say. It may sound nihilistic to you, since it is the opening shot in a war of liberation. I'll use the words of LeRoi Jones, whom I'm sure you don't like a whole lot: "Up against the wall, motherfucker, this is a stick-up."

*Yours for freedom,*
*Mark [Rudd]*

# 1

## The Academic Guerrillas

MARK RUDD rose from his aisle seat and walked slowly, deliberately, to the front of St. Paul's Chapel. Several hundred members of the Columbia University community shifted decorously in their seats as Vice President David B. Truman prepared to deliver a five-minute eulogy to Martin Luther King, assassinated in Memphis five days before. Veering to his right, Rudd stepped up into the choir, cut in front of the vice president and placed himself in front of the microphone. Truman stopped; the microphone went dead.

"Dr. Truman and President Kirk are committing a moral outrage against the memory of Dr. King," Rudd said quietly, leaning over the lectern. How, he demanded, can the leaders of the University eulogize a man who died while trying to unionize sanitation workers when they have, for years, fought the unionization of the University's own black and Puerto Rican workers? How can these administrators praise a man who fought for human dignity when they have stolen land from the people of Harlem? And how, Rudd asked, can Columbia laud a man who preached non-violent disobedience when it is disciplining its own students for peaceful protest? "Dr. Truman and President Kirk are committing a moral outrage against the memory of Dr. King," Rudd repeated. "We will therefore protest this obscenity." He stepped down from the stage and walked, shoulders hunched slightly forward, down the center aisle and out the main chapel door into the April sun. Forty others followed him. Truman continued on his way to the microphone and delivered his eulogy as if nothing had happened.

The week preceding the King memorial service had been an extraordinary one. On Sunday March 31 President Lyndon Johnson, in a speech which shocked most and heartened many, announced that he would not seek re-election in November. On Tuesday Senator Eugene McCarthy won an impressive victory in the Wisconsin presidential primary. Thursday, King was shot; in the days that followed, ghetto riots broke out in more than one hundred American cities. In Washington, D.C., federal troops manned machine guns on the steps of the Capitol.

Many feared that King's death had marked the end of non-violent protest in America. As disillusioned citizens—and especially students—looked around them in the spring of 1968, they found that the politics of dignity and order had failed to bring about substantive change: the war in Vietnam continued, the nation had done little to face the crisis of the black ghettos, poverty remained as much a tragically unsolved problem as ever. At Columbia the same frustration grew. Peaceful demonstrations had failed to halt construction of a gymnasium in Morningside Park, lengthy petitions had done little to curtail the University's eight-year affiliation with the Institute for Defense Analyses and committee recommendations had failed to alter the archaic power structure of the University.[1] For several years Columbia students who objected to the *status quo* had confined their dissent to relatively "legitimate" political protest. Their activities had rarely disrupted the normal day-to-day functioning of the University, and they had remained satisfied to carry their demands to the administration and await an answer. But these acceptable forms of protest had proved ineffective in winning any meaningful reforms.

Furthermore, such controlled dissent could not bring about the revolutionary goals which student radicals had come to view as necessary. According to the ideology of Students for a Democratic Society, the radical group that initiated the spring demonstrations at Columbia, it is the whole of American society that must be changed before any meaningful improvement can be made in the policies of America or in the lives of its citizens. The *Port Huron Statement*, drafted by Tom Hayden at the founding convention of SDS in 1962, was the first official enunciation of the organization's position. In its introduction, "Agenda for a Generation," it states:

> Our work is guided by the sense that we may be the last generation in the experiment with living. But we are a minority—the vast majority of our people regard the temporary equilibriums of our society and world as eternally-functional parts. In this is perhaps the outstanding paradox: we ourselves are imbued with urgency, yet the message of our society is that there is no viable alternative to the present.

[1] See Introduction for background on specific issues.

In the years following 1962 SDS moved considerably to the left of the *Port Huron Statement*, but the basic ideas it contained about the vision of SDS remained relevant:

> . . . We are aware of countering perhaps the dominant conceptions of man in the twentieth century: that he is a thing to be manipulated, and that he is inherently incapable of directing his own affairs. We oppose this depersonalization that reduces human beings to the status of things. . . . Men have unrealized potential for self-cultivation, self-direction, self-understanding and creativity. It is this potential that we regard as crucial and to which we appeal, not to the human potentiality for violence, unreason, and submission to authority.

SDS would accomplish these aims through the institution of socialism and, more importantly, through participatory democracy. This process is crucial to SDS theory, which is predicated on the concept that the individual must share in making the decisions which affect his life. In doing so, SDS radicals point out, one can escape the manipulated, powerless role which society would impose on him and, through the same process, one can help realize the goals of social reconstruction which would eliminate this manipulation and domination.

This is, of course, SDS ideology in its purest, most ideal form. Many critics have pointed out, however, that the radicals' practice very often disregarded these noble tenets of individual freedom and social improvement in favor of tactics which made use of manipulation and destruction. Often during the crisis SDS leaders resorted to the very style of coercive measures which they so condemned in the "Establishment." More significant, however, was the preoccupation many in SDS felt with working toward social revolution even when such actions directly contradicted their stated aims of immediate social betterment. As one former member of the SDS Steering Committee noted after the crisis: "If it comes to a choice between acting so as to build a radical movement and acting so as to bring about improvement of conditions, the radical will always give priority to the movement." Thus a major aspect of SDS ideology in practice became the development of political means toward the creation of a radical society. A relatively sedate tactical approach had marked the early days of the Columbia chapter of SDS. It centered on dramatization and politicization; change could be brought about by drawing the attention of members of the community to a given problem, awakening them to the need for change. This emphasis on politicization became known as the "praxis" theory, advocated by those radicals who felt that the best means of converting others to the radical view of the world was through education, propaganda and discussion. Disruptive actions on the part of radicals would, they feared, in many cases only alienate those who might otherwise be persuaded to help work toward the radical reconstruction of society.

A leading proponent of the praxis approach within Columbia SDS was Teddy Kaptchuk, a contemplative senior majoring in the study of Eastern religions. As chairman of SDS from March 1967 to March 1968 Kaptchuk had concentrated on calling the attention of the University community to specific issues such as Columbia's affiliation with IDA, military recruiting on campus or the coöperation of the University with the Central Intelligence Agency. On October 23, 1967, Kaptchuk led over three hundred students into Low Memorial Library to present a letter to President Grayson Kirk demanding an end to the University's sponsorship of IDA. Kirk was not in. An unidentified University official accepted the letter, and the students left quietly. Kirk never answered the letter.

During the next months a number of Columbia radicals became disillusioned with this low-key style of politics and began to advocate more aggressive tactics. At the start of the spring semester the University scheduled a series of recruiting visits for representatives of several controversial agencies, including the Dow Chemical Company, the principal manufacturer of napalm for use in the Vietnam war. The radicals, who had challenged recruiting by the Central Intelligence Agency and the U.S. Marine Corps the year before, were concerned about how to respond to the recruiting issue now. In a referendum held earlier in the academic year students in Columbia College had voted by an overwhelming margin to allow all groups—including military-related organizations—to recruit on campus. Reluctant to alienate the campus and hesitant to focus all their attention on the recruiting issue, SDS planned only a rally and peaceful picket line to protest the presence of the Dow recruiters when they arrived on February 23. But once the demonstration began a group of demonstrators broke away from the picket line and headed to Dodge Hall, where a Dow recruiter was conducting his interviews. Kaptchuk objected, saying, "A picket line has its time and place." One demonstrator retorted, "Who are you going to alienate—some half-assed liberals?" Another yelled, "Leave Ted behind!" The group did and, in a sense, so did the movement. About eighty students went to Dodge and staged a sit-in, preventing the recruiters from keeping appointments.

Mark Rudd was one of the radicals who shared the conviction that the old SDS political style was not leading the movement anywhere. A twenty-year-old sandy-haired junior in Columbia College, Rudd had become involved in politics at Columbia in the end of his freshman year when he joined a campus anti-war group, the Columbia Independent Committee on Vietnam. With the birth of an SDS chapter in the fall of his sophomore year, Rudd was attracted by the radical ideology and multi-issue approach of the new organization and began to attend its meetings. In the spring of his junior year, just before the annual SDS elections, Rudd cut five weeks of classes and went on a three-week tour of Cuba.

Rudd was considered quixotic and undependable by some of the old SDS leaders—he had once advocated stringing barbed wire around Low Library to dramatize the militarization of the University—but other, younger SDS members felt that he might be able to lead the organization to a new level of accomplishment. Soon after he returned from Cuba, Rudd was elected chairman of Columbia SDS.

The change in leadership had immediate effects on SDS activities. Just one week after the elections, on March 20, Colonel Paul Akst, the New York City director of the Selective Service System, appeared on campus to discuss strict new draft regulations with students. The old SDS leadership suggested that the best way to respond to his appearance would be to ask him probing questions to expose the inequity and illegitimacy of the draft. Other members of SDS, however, had a different idea. As Akst began fielding questions from the floor, a group of students created a diversion at the rear of the auditorium, and, as everyone in the audience turned around, an unidentified assailant walked up to the colonel and pushed a lemon meringue pie squarely into his face. Rudd later defended the action enthusiastically, arguing that it was the kind of tactic that served radical goals at least as effectively as leafleting or dormitory canvassing. Few other members of SDS agreed, however, charging that the action had been "terroristic" and silly. But Rudd's style soon won over a large segment of the chapter; the split with the praxis forces was complete.

The new energy and aggressiveness that emerged in SDS under Rudd's leadership were manifested again in the anti-IDA demonstration March 27, when Rudd led more than one hundred students into Low Library in a noisy, intentionally disruptive confrontation with the administration in defiance of President Kirk's ban on indoor demonstrations. By the time of the IDA demonstration a new sub-group had come to dominate SDS. It became known as the "action faction," and advocated a new tactical approach—confrontation politics—to replace the dramatization-politicization style of the "praxis axis." The superficial dynamic of the tactic was simple: a physical confrontation—a sit-in, a blockade, the takeover of a building—is set up to discomfit the adversary who holds the power, in this case the University administration. He can respond by giving in to the substantive demands of the radicals or by crushing them with coercion of his own. If he is unusually perceptive, he may be able to trace a third course, resorting to neither capitulation nor repression, but making small concessions to "co-opt" the dissidents and seduce them to coöperate with the power structure. But, in the coming days, such political sophistication was to prove beyond the resources of the men who ran Columbia.

The tactical elegance of confrontation politics lay in the fact that the radicals had a good chance of winning whether the administration gave in to their substantive demands or overcame them by repression. The use of coercive force on the part of the adversary—whether it came in the form of University discipline or police violence—could be a powerful force to "radicalize" liberal or moderate students. For the crucial part of the SDS view is that while escalated tactics are necessary to bring pressure for change on substantive issues, the "radicalization" of large segments of the population is far more important. As Rudd said later:

Confrontation politics puts the enemy up against the wall and forces him to define himself. In addition, it puts the individual up against the wall. He has to make a choice. Radicalization of the individual means that he must commit himself to the struggle to change society as well as share the radical view of what is wrong with society.

Without a major shift in political orientation within the community, SDS leaders point out that the gains they make on particular demands will remain irrelevant phenomena within the context of a fundamentally unfree society. Through confrontation, the radicals felt, other students can be shown that the ultimate source of the administration's authority is not its moral right but its power to suppress those who disagree with it. Because confrontation is by definition a mass action, it involves many people *through active participation* in political struggle.

Shortly after the March 27 demonstration in Low the administration formulated its response to the confrontation. It had carefully sidestepped a disciplinary encounter with the radicals until now, classifying the earlier SDS indoor protests as "being in the gray area." But the March 27 demonstration had finally forced it to respond. Six students were singled out—Rudd, four other members of the SDS steering committee and the chairman of a campus draft-resistance organization—and summoned to the office of a dean to discuss their participation in the protest. Several dozen other students who had taken part in the demonstration signed a "complicity statement" and demanded that they be given punishment equal to that of Rudd and the others. But the administration refused, arguing that the six students who were called in were the only ones the deans had recognized and so would be the only ones punished.

For nearly two weeks the six refused to see the dean, insisting that they be tried at an open hearing at which they could air the issues involved. Platt informed them that they would all be suspended if they did not come in to see him to resolve the matter. On April 22 the students—who came to be known as the "IDA Six"—finally agreed to meet with the dean but declined to discuss their participation in the IDA demonstration. They were summarily placed on disciplinary probation.

That evening SDS called an emergency general assembly meeting in a classroom in Fayerweather Hall. From forty to seventy students attended the meeting, the size of the group varying as members drifted in and out through the night. Other SDS general assemblies earlier in the year had attracted upwards of two hundred people. Rudd chaired the discussion, which centered on the disciplining of the "IDA Six." "We think this is an out-and-out political repression against us," he began. "Kirk is making a conscious attempt to bust us." Rudd observed that left-wing political groups at Columbia seemed to have two-year life spans; both the Independent Committee on Vietnam and the May Second Movement, SDS's two New Left predecessors, had disintegrated soon after their second birthday. And, as SDS at Columbia neared its two-year mark, there was the fear that it, too, might shrink to the current scale of the ICV: a minuscule core of die-hards with a following composed entirely of themselves.

Rudd emphasized this fear in building strength for the next day's challenge. He suggested that what SDS did the next day would determine whether it would be able to continue at all. "All year we've sort of seen SDS declining, and all year we've been unable to get our politics through to people," Rudd lamented, in a direct stab at the old praxis leadership. Paul Rockwell, a graduate student long active in Columbia radical politics, put the problem more succinctly: "We have a tactical problem in that we are trying to save our ass." Concern was not limited to the speakers. At one point, a praxis-oriented SDS member leaned over to a *Spectator* reporter covering the meeting and said, "Take good notes. This may be the last meeting of Columbia SDS."

The "ideal" course for SDS to take was suggested in a rather remarkable proposal presented by sophomore Steve Komm, who several weeks before had lost to Rudd in the race for the chairmanship. His manifesto was entitled, "PROPOSAL FOR A SPRING OFFENSIVE AGAINST COLUMBIA RACISM," and was marked in heavy letters, "For internal circulation." It stated the problem in the following way:

> [The administration's action] comes at a time when SDS is vociferous but isolated from a mass student and faculty base of

support. . . . Moderation would give credence to and ratify the administration's conduct regulations, which amount to a political castration of SDS. Our reply to the administration's attack must be a political offensive against the University on substantive issues which maximize the opportunities for student and faculty support.

Komm went on to outline immediate and longer-range tactics. The former were fairly conventional for SDS. The demonstrators would first stage a rally at the Sundial. Following the rally the demonstration would flow inside Low Library where Rudd would present President Kirk with a written demand for open hearings for the "IDA Six" on Monday April 29.

The remainder of Komm's proposal—in which concrete plans gave way to less "realistic" but strangely prophetic suggestions—was offered lightly, even whimsically, with the understanding that the actual plans for longer-range tactics would be developed at a steering committee meeting the next night. It read:

> CONTINGENCY A: Fistfights, police violence, similar excitement. Steering Comm. Tues. night plans larger demo. Wed., perhaps with campus anti-racism coalition [black students]. We all pull out quotations from M. L. King. Dorm canvassing late into night. If Wed. all right, see "Escalate," below (d). (Two scenarios: one, ever-bigger demonstrations effectively shutting down afternoon classes until they give in; two, Thurs. 500 or more people sit in [take over] Kirk's/Platt's office until demands granted; Fri. morning they call a sympathy strike.) . . .

As ex-chairman Ted Kaptchuk commented after the disturbances:

> All SDS tactics are based on the assumption that you use the sit-in, takeover and strike when you can. That much is taken for granted. We knew that day that we would try to get into Low to demonstrate, because that was the natural consequence of our politics. When someone gets busted for breaking a rule, like demonstrating inside a building, the thing to do is for everyone to break the rule *en masse;* it flows from our egalitarian ideology. After all, these assumptions are common to all SDS chapters' tactics. They are the unwritten standard radical student tactics.

Komm's scenario continued, "Open struggle, perhaps with city cops, will develop. WE FIGHT! Community support, black students, libs begin to come in," and then for a week later, "Occupation and blockade of Low, continue pressure until University capitulates on demands." The long-range plans in the proposal were presented sketchily, amid considerable laughter; they were accepted only tentatively, after hardly any discussion.[2]

After some minor procedural discussions, the last SDS general assembly meeting of the 1967–68 academic year came to an uninspiring end. The members planned to reconvene the following day at the Sundial, hold a noon rally and protest discipline, IDA and racism. They would then march into Low Library and present a demand to the administration that the IDA Six be given an open hearing. Having made their demand and established their confrontation, the protesters then would leave.

---

[2] Though the Komm proposal has not come to the attention of the national press, other plans—most notably a set of proposals drawn up by Rudd in October, and rejected by the SDS membership, for protest culminating in April with a sit-in inside Low Library—have been seized upon by many as evidence that the events of April and May at Columbia were the product of an elaborate "conspiracy" developed by the radicals. This is true only in the sense that SDS leaders have often advocated student control of the universities, and many have suggested the fairly common tactics of student strikes and sit-ins to achieve that end. From experience, the radicals knew that student activism reaches a sharp peak in the spring months before final examinations and so expected that any mass student action would probably come in April. Both Komm's proposal and Rudd's "October Plan" called for sit-ins, and not the prolonged communal occupation of several buildings. Both were simply articulations of dispositions and ideals radicals had shared since the coming of the New Left onto campus. That they worked this year at Columbia was the result of a complex intertwining of specific administration actions and general student attitudes, especially those related to new draft regulations and the Vietnam war, which served to give force and urgency to the revolutionary visions of the radicals.

# 2

## Horam Expecta Veniet

THE SUN broke through a gray cloud cover shortly before noon Tuesday, April 23, 1968. Nearly one thousand Columbia students and faculty milled on Low Plaza waiting for the featured event of the afternoon—a march into Low Library sponsored by Students for a Democratic Society. At the south end of the plaza more than four hundred students gathered at the Sundial to hear the SDS speakers present their case. At the top levels of the broad-tiered plaza, nearly three hundred counter-demonstrators—including many student athletes—gathered in front of Low, watching the Sundial rally below. Many of the counter-demonstrators seated themselves on the steps, while forty-five others formed a picket line on the plateau above. The picketers marched slowly, carrying signs reading, "Order Is Peace," "Send Rudd Back to Cuba," and "Fire Cannon"—a reference to the University chaplain who had defended Rudd's actions at the King memorial service two weeks before. On the plaza between the demonstrators and their adversaries, the curious and uncommitted stood and waited. At the Sundial, Alexander Platt, the young dean whose disciplinary rulings touched off the Tuesday rally, gazed across Low Plaza, shook his head and muttered, "It doesn't look promising."

Former SDS Vice Chairman Ted Gold stood on the Sundial, shifting his weight from foot to foot, ready to deliver the first speech of the afternoon. Beneath him, imprinted in brass on the top of the Sundial, lay an unnoticed Latin inscription: "HORAM EXPECTA VENIET"—"Await the Hour, It Shall Come." For decades, student activists had stood on this platform, flared against the evils of the world, and waited. Now the hour had come.

Although most SDS actions in the past had been directed against some specific grievance, this rally was called to protest a multiplicity of issues. "We believe that people should be allowed to present petitions indoors, which is what we did on March 27 and is what we're going to do today," Gold shouted. "But that's not what's at issue. What's at issue is not whether *x* hundred people decide to go indoors and break a crummy rule or not. Why did the administration have this rule? What's behind it? It seems clear to me that what's really at issue is what we've been demonstrating about. We don't go indoors to break a rule, to flout the administration, to be defiant youth, to show that we don't respect them. It's got nothing to do with that. What's an issue here is politics— the policy of this University."

Cicero Wilson, newly elected president of the Students' Afro-American Society, stepped onto the Sundial. In a sense, Wilson's presence at the SDS rally was as significant as his speech. SDS had never been able to unite with black militants on campus and, until now, the white radicals had been unable even to get a representative of the blacks to speak at an SDS function. On several occasions before the Tuesday rally, SDS members had unsuccessfully approached the blacks to try to arrange a jointly sponsored demonstration against the proposed gymnasium. For years, most of the black students at Columbia had been reluctant to take political action at all. The blacks had never held a major political rally on campus and had generally left political agitation to the whites. In an internal SAS newsletter circulated in early March, more militant black activists had called for increased political action by black students. After outlining the arguments against the proposed gymnasium, the letter declared:

> Despite the pleas of community leaders for student support, black students have failed to respond. The community needs strong support which thus far has only been supplied by white students. It will be interesting to see if black students will give any aid or assistance to the community in its vital struggle against Columbia.

Until April 23, the failure of Columbia SDS to mobilize an effective black–white coalition was not a new phenomenon for the New Left. When national SDS was first founded in 1962 the organization attempted to organize in the black ghettos and met with little success. Just eight months before this rally the black delegation at the radical National Conference on New Politics broke with the white majority and formed its own caucus. Despite their failures to enlist the blacks, however, the white radicals at Columbia continued to press for unity and on the evening before the Tuesday rally a tenuous alliance between SDS and SAS was confirmed. Cicero Wilson had agreed to speak at the SDS rally and now the black sophomore stood on the Sundial, angrily condemning the Columbia administration and lashing out against all things white, including the audience before him.

"This is Harlem Heights, not Morningside Heights," Wilson told the crowd that had now grown to five hundred. Waving his fists in the air, he attacked the University's plans to build a gymnasium in Morningside Park. "What would you do if somebody came and took your property? Took your property as they're doing over at Morningside with this gym?" Wilson asked. "Would you sit still? No, you'd use every means possible to get your property back—and this is what the black people are engaged in right now." Wilson's discussion of the gym drew extended applause from the crowd, but his comments which followed were not so warmly received.

"You people have criticized Rudd for standing up during the memorial services for Dr. Martin Luther King. Now you should be corrected because you—you white people—will be responsible for a second civil war because of your ignorance and your inactivity." There was scattered applause and one black student yelled, "Tell 'em about it, Cicero." The whites were silent as he continued. "You're going to have to reëvaluate your situation," Wilson instructed the whites. "When they're speaking about racists, if you want to know who they're talking about, you go look in a mirror—because you know nothing about black people. You will be the educators and the administrators, but yet and still you cannot handle yourself in an inter-racial confrontation." Suddenly a short girl standing in the front of the crowd interrupted, "How do you know?" and tried to point out to Wilson that he was talking to sympathetic students and not to white racists.

"I'm talking to students, I'm talking to faculty and I'm talking to the white administration also," Wilson shouted back. He paused and then turned on the crowd, yelling, "How many black faculty do you see at Columbia? What percentage of the school population is black? How much information is being disseminated into the community so that they will understand what's going on in this world of social change? You people had better realize that you condone Grayson Kirk with his roughriding over the black community. But do you realize that when you come back, there may not *be* a Columbia University? Do you think that this white citadel of hypocrisy will be bypassed if an insurrection occurs this summer?" For the students at the Sundial, Wilson's queries were largely rhetorical. But for President Grayson Kirk and the rest of the Columbia administration, the vision of waves of angry blacks scaling the academic acropolis and setting fire to Low Library was a real threat and became a vital consideration in the days ahead.

"Now if you want a free campus," Wilson concluded, "don't stand out here and riot today. That will not complete anything. The University will still be up there. The injustices which they have perpetrated, not only on the student body, but also on the black community, will not be corrected. If you *do* believe in a free campus, if you *do* believe in justice, freedom and equality—if there are such things—then you should support the efforts of SDS to get an open hearing. If Columbia is right, let them prove it." When Wilson completed his remarks he left the Sundial to an extended, enthusiastic ovation.

Meanwhile the course of the rally was being decided privately behind the Sundial. During Wilson's speech Dean Platt had stepped out of the crowd, approached Mark Rudd and presented him with a sealed envelope containing a letter from Vice President David Truman. The letter stated that Low Library had been locked, but that the vice president was prepared to meet with the entire group in the largest auditorium on campus to discuss the issues.

The letter had been drafted just a few hours before the Sundial rally at a meeting Tuesday morning of administrators inside Hamilton Hall, the main office and classroom building of Columbia College. At that meeting Acting Dean Henry Coleman conferred with the proctor of the University, the chief security officer, and several other administrators, including Dean Platt, to decide how to handle the planned demonstration inside Low. Although the administrators could have found out before the weekend that SDS had scheduled a demonstration for Tuesday, they waited until that morning to prepare for the action. At the meeting in Hamilton it was decided to close the main doors of Low and to prepare a letter, signed by the vice president, inviting the protesters to meet with him in McMillin Theatre. About a dozen faculty members would sit behind Truman on the stage "to see that rational discussion took place," as Coleman later phrased it. In addition, the administration asked faculty members—a group so politically diverse or unaligned that they could not be considered partisans of any one side—to disperse themselves throughout the Sundial–Low Library area to protect SDS from counter-demonstrators, counter-demonstrators from SDS, the officers of the administration from both, and the University at large from the excesses of all three.

The administrators' main worry was that a violent clash might occur between conservative and radical students at Tuesday's rally. Concern had been fanned by a mimeographed leaflet distributed on campus Thursday and Friday of the previous week. Copies of the leaflet had been stuffed into every faculty mailbox in Hamilton Hall and gave many professors cause for worry over the weekend. The word "TIRED?" was emblazoned twenty-one times across the top of the flier. The message below read in part:

Tired of a two-standard University that gives virtual immunity to SDS agitators while you are subject to immediate suspension if you toss a paper airplane out of a window? Tired of an environment where you cannot listen to a guest speaker and be sure he won't be physically harassed by SDS? Of an environment where your sacred privacy of worship is allowed to degenerate into political showmanship? Must one group be allowed to dictate this University's future?

On Tuesday, April 23, SDS plans another demonstration against IDA. . . . Be there; lend your presence to a more healthy balance at Columbia University. Don't be there and you might as well hang forever. Can democracy survive at Columbia University? Will Mark Rudd be our next dean? Be there on the 23rd—prepared.

The "prepared" worried a lot of people. Later it was learned that the leaflet had been circulated by a group calling itself Students for a Free Campus, a loosely organized amalgam of students strongly opposed to SDS. Thomas Colahan, vice dean of Columbia College, spent much of Tuesday morning phoning faculty members, asking them to be out on the campus later that day during the demonstration to make sure that no student-student violence occurred.

"This is very big," Colahan told one history professor.

"Big enough for me to cut my class?" he was asked.

"Yes," Colahan answered, "big enough."

When Dean Platt first handed Truman's letter to Rudd at the Sundial the SDS leader was confused about the administration offer. One of the students went up to the Sundial to tell the speakers to stall for time while the SDS leaders caucused. Another student was sent up to Low to confirm Truman's statement that the doors were locked. After a short conference Rudd turned to Dean Platt and told him that the group could not accept Truman's offer unless the vice president would allow the students to set the ground rules for the McMillin meeting. According to those ground rules a student would chair the meeting and the audience would serve as a "popular tribunal" to decide the disciplinary case of the "IDA Six." Dean Platt rejected Rudd's proposals and insisted that discipline could not be decided in such a way, since the group in McMillin would not be "a representative sampling of students."

"We must have these ground rules," Rudd told the dean. "Otherwise, we will not go to McMillin."

"Look—now you have a chance to let your entire SDS group confront the administration," Platt replied.

"That's a mockery. We must have an open hearing."

"That's ridiculous. To take a voice vote on the discipline cases? That's impossible." Platt suggested that Rudd lead the group over to

McMillin and then ask Truman to allow them to determine the format of the proceedings.

Several weeks after the demonstration Platt recounted why he suggested that Rudd first agree to talk with Truman and set ground rules later:

> This was clearly, to some extent, a ploy on my part. I knew that Dr. Truman wasn't going to accept these ground rules, but I hoped for two things: either Dr. Truman would be able to convince them to give up this idea in the hope that they could get down to the business of discussing some issues, which I think was unlikely, but possible. The second aspect of the ploy was to get them into McMillin, get them cooled off, so that, when they came out of McMillin, there would be a lessened possibility that they would go on to do something else. . . . One of the most effective things you can do with a group like this is to, for example, get them into a row of seats. The mere fact that some order is superimposed by a row of seats dissipates the effect of a mob. This is one of the ideas that we had in mind in having the students go into McMillin in the first place.

The dean's strategy did not work. The administration tried to appease SDS and thereby avoid a physical confrontation, but they did not understand that the students would no longer be satisfied with a verbal exchange. In their view, Truman's offer was a device which would produce nothing meaningful and would effectively blunt any power which the student Left could exert on the campus. SDS had passed the stage of "dialogue." After conferring again with his fellows, Rudd mounted the Sundial and—in keeping with the open style of SDS rallies—informed the crowd about what had happened.

"The doors to Low Library have been locked," he announced. "The administration building has been closed down by us. Whether they realize it or not, they are locked in and we, the free men, are outside." Rudd informed the crowd that he had received a letter from Vice President Truman and offered to read it. "Listen and you will understand this man's mind," he said. He read the text of Truman's message, interspersing his own comments:

> Dear Mr. Rudd:
> You are aware of the University rule against demonstrations or picketing within University buildings. Since it is the announced intention of the SDS to conduct a demonstration inside Low Library today and since there would be a hazard both to people [*that's important, we agree*] and to property [*maybe that's not so impor-*

*tant*] if a large number of students were to be in the building for purposes other than a regularly scheduled meeting, Low Library has been closed except to individuals who have scheduled business there [*maybe the head of IDA!*].

If your group wishes to present a petition or to meet with me, however, I shall be glad to meet with you in McMillin Theatre immediately.

Sincerely yours,<br>
David B. Truman,<br>
Vice President and Provost

"He gives us this alternative because he is a very *li-ber-al* man," Rudd shouted, soaking the word "liberal" with all the contempt radicals reserve for those whose politics lie immediately to their right. "After we've gone to the son of a bitch a million times and he hasn't responded to us, now he asks to meet with us in McMillin. Our force has brought him down," Rudd boasted. "But this letter creates a problem."

He outlined the alternative courses of action the demonstrators could now take. "We could have a demonstration inside McMillin, with chanting and picketing. We could have Truman talk to us about IDA and the rest. And we could have the students decide about the discipline stuff against us."

"But if we go to McMillin," Rudd warned, "we will just talk and go through a lot of bullshit." He posed the other alternatives: suggesting that the group could march to Low, "if it's open," or could move to Dean Platt's office in Hamilton Hall. At this point Rudd looked up toward Low and saw his runner signal that the huge front door was indeed locked. "The doors are locked at Low," Rudd yelled. "We won't get in the fucking office. Maybe—"

Suddenly, before Rudd could complete his sentence, Tom Hurwitz, a radical junior sporting a revolutionary red bandana around his forehead, leapt onto the Sundial and shouted, "Did we come here to talk or did we come here to go to Low?"

Raising his right arm to the sky, Hurwitz started toward Low. The six leftist leaders who had been disciplined the day before linked arms and pushed to the front of the crowd that was following Hurwitz across the plaza. As the demonstrators strode swiftly up the steps to Low, chanting "IDA Must Go! IDA Must Go!" several administrators frantically tried to stop the surging crowd. Back-pedalling in front of the marching students, Erwin Glikes, a short, balding assistant dean, pulled at Rudd's sleeve, pleading with him to stop the march. Dean Platt ran alongside the demonstrators urging them to wait. Orest Ranum, Columbia's expert on seventeenth-century French politics, dashed ahead, trying to hold the crowd back, yelling, "Come on now, come *on* now." But the students would not stop. They veered slightly to the east and, as they reached the top plateau of the plaza, stood face to face with 150 counter-demonstrators seated on the steps of Low. A small scuffle broke out when one demonstrator tried to march over the opposition, but the rest of the protesters stood still, not knowing where to go. Someone yelled, "Mark —don't wait," and Rudd turned east with the crowd toward the security entrance of Low, which is always kept open. As the students surged around a narrow path leading to the open door, Professor Ranum and Dean Colahan hurdled a hedge and cut in front of the crowd. Three security guards inside Low slammed the door shut, but about twenty-five students pushed against it, forcing it open nearly a foot. The security guards strained against the door from the inside, and suddenly the students backed off, permitting the guards to lock the entrance.

"Let's go get 'em," a counter-demonstrator yelled from the steps of Low.

"Wait a minute," another shouted. "Just stay here. They've broken the rule and they deserve hell."

"They won't get it, though."

A few black students standing by the counter-demonstrators reacted angrily to the opposition's comments. "Don't you motherfuckers speak to me anymore, because I just may shoot you," one yelled.

Rudd jumped on top of a trash can just outside the security entrance and asked for quiet so he could address the crowd. Jeff Sokolow, a sophomore member of SDS, tugged at Rudd and said, "Tell 'em we could have gotten in, but someone would have gotten hurt." Rudd told the crowd just that and then once again outlined the alternatives open to them. In the middle of Rudd's speech, however, someone in the front of the crowd shouted, "To the gym, to the gym site!" and nearly three hundred of the demonstrators streamed away from Low toward a gate at Amsterdam Avenue and 117th Street. The students moved off the campus led by Cicero Wilson and several other SAS members. As Rudd was left, standing by the security entrance, Orest Ranum paced by, shaking his head and mumbling, "They have absolutely no strategy, absolutely no strategy." Walking with head bent, Rudd moved slowly through a group of counter-demonstrators standing by the plaza. "Let's start chanting," he called to Ted Gold, who trailed behind. The two bewildered leaders started to yell, "IDA Must Go, IDA Must Go," but were hooted down by the delighted opposition. As they walked across the plaza, Ted Kaptchuk ran up to them. "Your demonstration's at the gym," he said, "there are over two hundred at the gym."

Rudd ran off campus and caught up with the marchers at 116th Street and Amsterdam. The crowd proceeded down 116th to Morningside

Drive and slipped into the park by a dirt pathway near 114th Street. They poured into the construction area through an open gate in the twelve-foot-high chain-link fence surrounding the site. As students continued to stream in, three New York City policemen—who patrolled the site as part of a regular twenty-four-hour guard set up after a recent series of anti-gym demonstrations—ran down the hill from the main gate and attempted to close the entrance. But students flung the gate back, pinning the police against the fence. More students rushed into the site, while many others began kicking and pulling the metal fence along the northern boundary. By 12:30 P.M., just one-half hour after the protest had begun at the Sundial, students had pulled down nearly forty feet of fence at the gym site. As protesters continued to rush down the hill toward the open gate fifteen more policemen converged on the demonstrators and started pulling people away from the fallen fence.

Several scuffles broke out between students and police. An officer from the 24th Precinct grabbed Fred Wilson, a white student, and tried to arrest him. A large circle of students gathered around the pair as they struggled. The crowd began shouting, "Let him go, let him go! Take all of us!" and pushed in around the policeman and his prisoner. The officer slipped in the loose dirt and fell to the ground, dragging Wilson down on top of him. The circle of demonstrators piled onto the policeman, kicking at his hands and body, trying to free Wilson. The arrested student broke loose but did not move away. Another policeman seized him; the crowd collapsed on them, throwing both against a large dirt pile. Once more the supporting students joined the scuffle, hitting and kicking the officer. Five additional policemen charged down the hill, swinging their nightsticks. After a brief scuffle the crowd backed off. Wilson was handcuffed and led away, charged with felonious assault, criminal mischief and resisting arrest. The policeman who first grabbed him stood near the demonstrators, with dirt on his face, and mumbled, "They kept hitting me; they kept kicking me. I can't understand it."

In the midst of the confusion which followed Fred Wilson's arrest, a number of students at the gym site asked Rudd to quiet the demonstrators. Surrounded by more than a dozen policemen, Rudd climbed onto a high mound of dirt and began to speak. But the drone of the nearby construction machines drowned out his words. He turned to a police captain and ordered: "Get that stuff turned off so I can talk." The captain pointed to the machinery below and drew his index finger across his throat. The signal was passed along a line of construction workers down the slope to the excavation area. The machines fell silent.

"Is there an administrator around?" Rudd asked. Dean Colahan stood silently near the side gate to the gym site. Several students spotted him and pointed him out to Rudd. "Oh, it's Colahan," Rudd said. "Okay, you have fifteen minutes to get that guy unbusted," referring to Fred Wilson, whom he did not know. "Get up to Low Library and see Truman now," Rudd ordered. "Go now! We'll wait here."

Colahan listened passively and, after a pause, replied calmly, "Get your people out of the park, Mark."

Rudd, pressing his demand, said, "We won't leave until that guy comes back. If not, we'll shut the site down."

While Rudd stood on the dirt pile the crowd debated the next move. "There are three hundred people at the Sundial," one student shouted. "Let's go to Low—that's where the power is," another yelled. Rudd rejected the suggestion and proposed that the radicals make use of one of their most potent tactics by calling a student strike for Thursday. The idea was shouted down by the demonstrators who insisted that it would be impossible to organize a strike on such short notice. Robbie Roth, a thin Columbia sophomore from Queens, suggested that the entire crowd regroup at the Sundial. "We're going to have to go back and get together," he said, "with the crowd building, we can still salvage it." The group filed out of the gym site, walking slowly back through the park toward the campus.

On campus, meanwhile, Ted Gold was trying desperately to reassemble the pieces of what he believed to be a shattered demonstration. The protesters had split their own ranks; most of the students who remained on campus were certain that the SDS rally was over for the day. While the three hundred students had gone to the gym site, Gold led nearly two hundred stragglers to the Sundial to reorganize the protest. "We must honestly sit down and start to think about what happened," Gold said. "We screwed things up because we weren't united enough and we weren't organized enough. We have to have better organization so that this doesn't happen again."

Shortly after 1 P.M. Ted Kaptchuk came back to the Sundial. Speaking over a bullhorn, he told the crowd what had happened at the gym site and suggested that those on campus organize a march to Morningside Park to join the others. Proctor William Kahn, standing by the Sundial, sputtered, "He can't use that megaphone!" trying to invoke a minor University regulation banning the use of amplifiers on campus. The students followed Kaptchuk and marched four-abreast down 116th Street.

As the marchers reached Morningside Drive the students returning from the gym demonstration were emerging from the park. The two groups met at the corner and clogged the intersection. Kaptchuk climbed onto a lamppost and held the speaker section of a bullhorn above his head. Ted Gold, standing on a parked car and leaning against the same post, took the microphone. Not realizing that the amplifier was turned on, Gold remarked to Kaptchuk, "I don't know what's happening."

The former SDS leaders suggested that the entire group return once again to the Sundial "to get our shit together"—an SDS euphemism for organizational discipline. As the group moved back toward the campus Kaptchuk took Rudd aside and advised him to move the demonstration indoors. Kaptchuk was one of many students trying to give Rudd advice. "I told him to go into a building—any building," Kaptchuk later recalled, "because I knew that if you go into a building, you're not running around like infants."

At the Sundial again, Rudd yelled, "We're learning to criticize and learn from our mistakes." He announced that he had sent runners to various points on the campus to scout the alternatives.

"Now the way I see the situation," he continued, "we've got about four hundred, five hundred people who'll do anything now." The crowd cheered. "On the other hand, I don't know if we've got four hundred or five hundred people who'll do anything tomorrow—but I think you will. I don't think four hundred or five hundred people can close down this University. Either we've got to build for a strike on this, which I think is very difficult at this moment . . ." Rudd never completed his thought. Instead, he went on to discuss the arrest at the gym site and then yielded to Cicero Wilson of SAS.

Wilson's speech began calmly and slowly. "I spoke before about white racism," he said, "but I think I was underplaying it a little bit, because I'm finding out very rapidly that it's not covert at Columbia; it's very open. Now what you're going to have to realize is that the black students on this campus are no longer going to sit back and let this shit go on." The crowd warmed to Wilson's rhetoric and cheered his comments. But his tone soon changed. During Rudd's speech one black student, irritated by the whites' apparent lack of organization, had muttered, "Let's take this thing over." Now it seemed that Wilson was trying to do just that.

"SDS can stand on the side and support us," he said, "but the black students and the Harlem community will be the ones in the vanguard."

"What are your proposals?" Rudd broke in.

"We're not proposing anything," Wilson snapped back.

"Look—let me put it this way," Wilson went on. "You people are going over there protesting the gym. Well, I'll tell you something. You're not too much better than Columbia. You're deciding what black people should be doing."

"What are *you* doing?" challanged several white students.

"A referendum hasn't been taken," Wilson said, ignoring his hecklers. "You don't know whether black people want that gym or not." The crowd laughed. Wilson concluded his speech and, when he stepped off the Sundial, there was little applause. The whites in the crowd were upset by Wilson's speech; the cohesion between the black and white students seemed to be weakening. But the next speaker, Bill Sales, a graduate student in International Affairs and an active member of SAS, reëstablished the union.

"Okay," he shouted, "I want you to check something out. I thought up until this stage of the game that white people weren't ready. But I saw something today that suggests that maybe this is not true. Maybe you *are* ready. Because when the deal hit the fan, you were there, you were with me. And this is what we want. If you're talking about revolution, if you're talking about identifying with the Vietnamese struggle, if you're talking about supporting German students, you don't need to go to Rockefeller Center, dig? You don't need to go marching downtown. There's one oppressor—in the White House, in Low Library, in Albany, New York. You strike a blow at the gym, you strike a blow for the Vietnamese people." His audience cheered. "You strike a blow at the gym and you strike a blow against the assassin of Dr. Martin Luther King, Jr. You strike a blow at Low Library and you strike a blow for the freedom fighters in Angola, Mozambique, Portuguese Guinea, Zimbabwe, South Africa." Sales paused.

"You did pretty well today. Hope it's not an isolated incident. It was *beau-ti-ful*. It was almost soulful. All we need is some sophistication—and some organization. The only way you win in a technological society is by your superior organization and superior commitment. And that's what we need. We went down there in a big group once. Next time we go down there, TPF [1] will be waiting for you. An incoherent mob will not be able to deal with them. So we have to be more sophisticated. Now, need I say more? I don't want to get arrested for sedition." Sales received an extended ovation.

Rudd stepped onto the Sundial again. "We don't have an incoherent mob; it just looks that way. I'll tell you what we want to do. We want to win some demands about IDA, we want IDA to go. We want the people under discipline to get off of discipline. We want this guy who got busted today to get the charges dropped against him; to get unbusted—I guess that's how you say it. We want them to *stop* the fucking gym over there. So I think there's really only one thing we have to do and we're all together here; we're all ready to go—now. We'll start by holding a hostage."

"Where are we going to get one?" one student asked.

"We're going to hold whoever we can," Rudd said, "in return for them letting go of the six people under discipline, letting go of IDA and letting go of the fucking gym. We can't get into Low Library. We can't

---

[1] The Tactical Patrol Force (TPF) is an elite division of the New York City Police Department, used for riot control and in high crime areas.

hold the administrators in Low hostage because we can't get in that place and, also, it's too big a place. *But*—there is one part of this administration that's responsible for what's happened today—and that's the administration of Columbia College."

Someone in front of the Sundial boomed, "SEIZE HAMILTON!" and Rudd shouted, "Hamilton Hall is right over there. Let's go!" The crowd surged along the narrow path leading to the classroom building. Within minutes the lobby of the building was overflowing with four hundred students chanting thunderously, "IDA MUST GO! IDA MUST GO!"

Like Proctor Kahn tilting at megaphones earlier, many administrators failed to grasp the significance of events, even as those events grew to clearly historic dimensions. With several hundred angry student invaders ensconced in the nerve center of Columbia College, Assistant Dean Glikes complained that he would be unable to hold a meeting scheduled that afternoon to honor members of Columbia's Phi Beta Kappa chapter. Discussing the work waiting for him in his office, the dean explained that he would have to finish his chores at night, after the disturbance was over.

Inside Hamilton, as the students were chanting "Racist Gym Must Go! Racist Gym Must Go!" Acting Dean Henry Coleman appeared at the entrance to the building. The incantation modulated within seconds to "WE WANT COLEMAN! WE WANT COLEMAN!" As the dean later recalled:

> I came into Hamilton and there was a mob inside. It was a mixed group, not just SDS. When I arrived, Mark arranged for an opening up the middle and invited me in. I had to make a decision on whether or not to go in, and it seemed to me that it was my office, my secretarial staff was in there, and my initial reaction was that I should walk in. I didn't know Rudd at all at that point, really.

The square-faced, crew-cut dean stood silently outside the door to his office, jabbing tobacco into his pipe with his thumb and staring at the students around him. The lobby was hushed.

"Now we've got the Man where we want him," Rudd told the crowd. "He can't leave unless he gives into some of our demands." A roar rose from the demonstrators.

"Now, let me tell Dean Coleman why we're here; We're here because of the University's bullshit with IDA. After we demand an end to affiliation in IDA, they keep doing research to kill people in Vietnam and in Harlem. That's one of the reasons why we're here. We're here because the University steals land from black people, because we want them to stop building that gym. We're here because the University busts people for political stuff, as it tried to bust six of us, including myself and five other leaders of SDS for leading a demonstration against IDA. We're not going to leave until that demand, no discipline for us, is met." After sustained applause, Rudd continued, "Another demand is that our brother who got busted today—he got some sort of assault charge—that brother is released, and all the other people who have been busted for demonstrating over there. So it's clear that we can't leave this place until most of our demands are met."

"Most?" one student said. "We've got to *stay,* man."

Displaying the easygoing style which so appealed to the demonstrators during the initial stages of the protest, Rudd shouted, "I just want to ask people, is this a demonstration, incidentally?" The crowd screamed, "YES!"

"I want to ask people, are we disrupting the University's function?"

"YES!"

"Is the University disrupting people all over the world?"

"YES!"

"Are we going to stay here until all of our demands are met?"

"YES!"

"No deans leave this building?"

"YES!"

The crowd began clapping again and chanting the slogan of the draft resistance movement: "Hell No, We Won't Go."

Rudd pointed to Coleman and Proctor William Kahn, who had been standing beside him: "We know that Coleman and Kahn are only lackeys for the Man. We're going to hold them here but we want Truman and Kirk to come and give in to our demands. We can stay here for a while. If you're hungry, remember that there are a hell of a lot of people suffering because of Columbia University. We've got to put pressure on these guys to change Columbia University."

After waiting nearly five minutes Coleman, very pale and noticeably upset, answered Rudd: "I have no control over the majority of the demands you have made, Mark," he said, "and I have no intention, Mark—I'll make this very clear to you—I have no intention of meeting any demands under a situation such as this." He paused, as students heckled and yelled obscenities. "As far as disciplinary actions taken are concerned, our policy on discipline has not yet been changed. And I certainly am not going to change it under circumstances like these— even if I could. . . . I have no intentions of calling the President or vice president under circumstances like these."

When he completed his statement Coleman turned and opened the door to his office. Rudd asked, "Do you want me to go inside with you?" The dean replied tersely, "When I go into my office, I'll go by myself, thank you, Mark." Coleman went inside with the proctor and an aide, locking the door behind them. Three of the counter-demonstrators who had stayed with the demonstration stood silently, arms behind their backs, in front of the door.

In the lobby of Hamilton the demonstrators cleared two side corridors to allow students to enter the building and attend classes if they wished. The protesters had no intention of obstructing the lobby or blockading the building and hoped to avoid a clash with opposing factions of students. While SDS leaders conferred outside the dean's office, the crowd began to sing "We Shall Not Be Moved," a defiant heirloom of the civil rights and early labor movements. The students composed their own verses as they sang:

*No more suspensions, we shall not be moved,*
*No more suspensions, we shall not be moved,*
*Just like that tree that's standing by the wa-a-ter,*
*We shall not be moved.*

The demonstrators added a new demand with each verse: *"No more defense work, we shall not be moved," "Free Fred Wilson, we shall not be moved," "Gym Crow must go, we shall not be moved," "Open hearings, we shall not be moved,"* and finally:

*No more bullshit, we shall not be moved,*
*No more bullshit, we shall not be moved,*
*Just like the tree that's standing by the wa-a-ter,*
WE SHALL NOT BE MOVED.

On the upper level of the lobby Rudd was busily gathering names of student leaders to form a steering committee that would guide the Hamilton demonstration. He gazed around the lobby, looking for familiar faces and writing down the names of those he wanted on the committee. "All right, look, can I have your attention? I'd like to propose the names of some people for a steering committee for this thing. A lot of decisions have to be made on the spot. I've been making some decisions—before I made some pretty bad ones, but I think it came out okay in the end."

Calling out names like a stadium announcer at a football game, Rudd yelled, "I'd like to propose the following people: From SAS, Ray Brown, Bill Sales; from Citizenship Council, Joel Ziff; unattached liberal, Jon Shils; from SDS, Nick Freudenberg, vice chairman, myself, Mark Rudd, and Ted Gold, ex-vice chairman." Cicero Wilson was later added to the list. While the committee members argued over where to hold their meeting and whether to leave the lobby, several students began to drift out of the building. Bill Sales turned quickly and shouted, "Hey, look, people! Now if you want to get a whole lot of people strung up today, just drift out of here and you'll fuck up good. The brothers at Howard [2] tied that place up and they won. Now I want to see what you grays can do. Can you white people tie up Columbia? Can you beat these administrators like those guys at Howard beat those cats down there? That's what it's all about." The demonstrators responded with a loud "YES!"

"All right," Sales said, "we're going to stay here. We're going to feed you. If it gets cold tonight, we're going to keep you warm. We're going to get this place together, but don't walk out the door."

As the steering committee assembled and started upstairs to hold a meeting Stu Gedal, a sophomore member of SDS, took charge of the demonstration and announced in a paraphrase of Bob Dylan, "We've got something going here and now we've just got to find out what it is." There was confusion in the lobby, as counter-demonstrators mingled with protesters and taunted the speakers. "I'm awfully glad that you hecklers are here," one student yelled, "because we can talk to you and also you're helping us block the building up."

At the steering committee meeting, meanwhile, the eight students sat down in a hallway and began to draft an official statement of the protesters' demands. The meeting began shortly after 2 P.M. during the afternoon class change, and passing students and faculty members stared curiously at the radicals caucusing in the corridor. Six demands that were to lay the groundwork for protest in weeks to come were adopted with little debate:

1. All disciplinary action now pending and probations already imposed upon six students be immediately terminated and a general amnesty be granted to those students participating in this demonstration.
2. President Kirk's ban on demonstrations inside University buildings be dropped.
3. Construction of the Columbia gymnasium in Morningside Park cease at once.
4. All future disciplinary action taken against University students be resolved through an open hearing before students and faculty which adheres to the standards of due process.

---

[2] At Howard University, a predominantly black institution in Washington, D.C., a group of students staged a sit-in in March to protest the disciplining of thirty-nine campus activists. The students took over the central administration building, and university officials ended the demonstration by consenting to most of the students' demands and granting them *de facto* amnesty.

5. Columbia University disaffiliate, in fact and not merely on paper, from the Institute for Defense Analyses; and President Kirk and Trustee William A. M. Burden resign their positions on IDA's Board of Trustees and Executive Board.
6. Columbia University use its good offices to obtain dismissal of charges now pending against those participating in demonstrations at the gym construction site in the park.

One student at the meeting suggested that the steering committee also demand changes in the power structure of the University. The committee rejected the proposal, however, after one member said, "We'll get to that later on."

Rudd suggested to the committee that he should go down to the lobby to determine the opinions of the entire group before making any final decisions. But Sales and the other blacks advised him to stay, discuss with the committee what to do, then go downstairs and tell the crowd what the leaders had decided. Rudd agreed to the tactic even though it violated his political style. SDS had always tried to conduct its business with at least an appearance of participatory democracy. Major decisions were rarely made until they had been thoroughly discussed and voted on by the general membership. Now, however, Rudd was being asked to work within the framework of the black students' political structure—a structure entirely alien to SDS. For the blacks, strong central leadership was the key to any decision-making process. At the steering committee meeting and throughout the weeks of protest the blacks demonstrated a tight, disciplined political structure in which the top leaders made most of the decisions for the group. Although Rudd had now accepted their suggestion to present the six demands as a *fait accompli,* the sharp difference between the political processes of the whites and the blacks would create difficulties by nightfall.

The remainder of the steering committee meeting was spent in discussion of practical problems involved in holding a prolonged demonstration inside Hamilton. Provisions were made for food and water; the problem of ventilating the packed lobby was considered; and a list of newspapers, radio stations and television networks was drawn up for obtaining publicity. In addition, the steering committee made plans to gather support by informing sympathetic groups on and off the campus about the situation in Hamilton.

Just before 3 P.M. the group walked downstairs to the lobby and Rudd read the six demands. "We propose that we stay until these demands are met," he said. The crowd shouted agreement. "Look," Rudd continued, "we really can't tell at this point who's with us by yelling and clapping, although that's fine. People who plan to stay here until we meet these demands, raise your *left* hands." The democratic ritual concluded, Rudd went on. "Okay, now we think the one way we're going to get the University to capitulate is outside pressure. Really, if the people of Harlem and the people from all over, from other SDS chapters, have demonstrations in support of us and get things going, we're going to have a lot better chance." Ray Brown, a spokesman for SAS, announced that the black students were in the process of obtaining support from the Student Non-Violent Coördinating Committee, the Congress of Racial Equality, the students at Howard University, the United Black Front and several other local black organizations.

Rudd then appointed groups of students to "liberate" a huge floor fan from Butler Library, solicit funds and buy food. The lobby was now packed; students began to shuffle about restlessly and talk among themselves. Soon after 3 P.M. the first supplies of food began moving into the hot, stuffy lobby and students passed around bunches of bananas, cans of soda and bags of potato chips. Later, in the evening, the cuisine and atmosphere improved as visitors brought in hot dishes of pork and beans and plates of warmed sauerkraut.

Dean Coleman emerged from his office shortly after 3:30 P.M. Before he could address the crowd standing around him, he was confronted by Stu Gedal who repeated the six demands and asked Coleman for his response. "We have yet to hear any answer on these demands from you," Gedal said. "All that you've said is that you won't consider them. We'd like some answer at this time. Students have the intention of staying here until our demands are met and we hope that there'll be further action from the rest of the student body that isn't here right now."

"May well be," Coleman snapped. "Am I to understand then that I am not to leave this building?"

"Yes, you are," Gedal answered. "Well, wait. Let me ask. Is he to understand that he is not to leave this building?"

"Yes," the crowd yelled. "No," several counter-demonstrators shouted back.

"Are those students who aren't going to let me leave willing to sign a statement to that effect?" Coleman asked.

"NO," the demonstrators answered. "How about the demands?" they shouted. "Tell us about the demands." Coleman, put off by the students' insistence, said firmly, "I have already told you that as far as the demands are concerned, I have no control over any of those demands."

"I would like to know, sir," Gedal challenged, "who *does* have responsibility around here? It seems that nobody has responsibility for anything and that the net effect is that the University is totally irresponsible toward the community and toward its students."

Coleman, now irritated, replied, "I would remind all of you that this afternoon, at approximately 12:30, the vice president was prepared to meet all of you to discuss these demands. You did not choose to meet with him at that time. McMillin Theater was set up. The vice president was prepared to meet with you there, as were members of the faculty."

"Excuse me, sir," Gedal interrupted. "I think you used the correct word when you said that it was 'set up.' . . ."

"Once again I state, as I stated just a few minutes ago, you have asked who is running the University, who is in charge of this—"

"We're telling you, motherfucker," one student cried.

Coleman turned and looked angrily at the demonstrator. "I don't know, maybe you gain a great deal by that kind of language somewhere else. But it doesn't carry a lot of weight in an educational institution and you should *know* it."

While the students shouted insults and demands, Proctor Kahn, standing nearby, pulled gently at the dean's suit coat and whispered, "Reiterate." Coleman repeated his earlier statement that the students had already had an opportunity to meet with the top administrators to discuss their demands. He returned to his office several minutes later, Proctor Kahn and Dan Carlinsky, a public relations officer, trailing close behind.

Outside Coleman's office several students in the crowd argued that holding the dean hostage would tend to obscure their demands and would result in unfavorable publicity. As the debate proceeded, however, a number of left-wing leaders, including several black students, spoke in favor of holding Coleman.

"Look, brothers and sisters," Bill Sales yelled over a bullhorn, "now we're in this place for justice and there's only one way we're going to get it. We're going to have to make the Establishment uncomfortable, dig? If we let the Man go, he'll be going home to eat a nice dinner, go to bed and he'll act like you don't exist. AND YOU WON'T EXIST. . . . We want you to keep Coleman in his office and let him sweat."

Cicero Wilson took the bullhorn and argued that holding Coleman hostage represented the only bargaining point which the students had. "We're making the dean's office and Grayson Kirk make a decision," Wilson said. Several students in the lobby heckled the speakers, and at one point a student took the bullhorn and accused the leadership of manipulating the group with "mob psychology." Ray Brown of SAS addressed the crowd, wielding the black militant's favorite weapon against a hesitant white radical. "There was a lot of talk at that Sundial about revolution," Brown taunted. "Well, it's about time you people made some kind of commitment. It's about time you people stopped talking about revolution and started acting in a manner that is going to bring some meaningful changes." A vote was taken and the students in the lobby reaffirmed by a small margin their decision to hold the dean.

Discussion about Coleman continued among the white leadership.

Cicero Wilson, irritated by the seeming indecision of the white students, paced in front of the dean's office and told a fellow black protester, "If Coleman leaves, all the black students leave." The message was passed along to Rudd and other white leaders.

At 4:30 P.M., shortly after the vote was taken, Coleman and Kahn made their third and last appearance of the day in the Hamilton Hall lobby. Coleman stood silently outside his door, waiting for quiet. When the crowd was still the dean began to speak. "I have by telephone presented your demands to the vice president. In spite of the fact that you were unwilling to meet with him earlier today he is willing to meet with you now in Wollman Auditorium."

The announcement did not cause much of a stir in the lobby. Just four hours before SDS had been made a similar offer and had rejected it. Now the radicals controlled one building and held a dean, and it seemed unlikely that they would accept the offer this time. Rudd told Coleman that the eight-man steering committee would agree to meet with Truman in Wollman if the vice president would first grant amnesty for the demonstrators "as a show of good faith." Two votes were taken, and the protesters decided not to leave Hamilton *en masse* but to allow the steering committee to speak with Truman if amnesty were granted.

Coleman and Kahn walked back into the dean's office where they began to prepare for overtime duty. The dean called his wife to tell her that he would probably not be home for supper and suggested that she call his mother to assure her that her captive son was all right. Throughout the afternoon and early evening Coleman received numerous phone calls from angered alumni, inquisitive faculty members and concerned administrators. David Truman, who remained inside Low Library throughout the day of protests, called the dean at regular intervals to find out what was happening in Hamilton. Late Tuesday afternoon, when it became clear that the students intended to hold Coleman in his office, Truman phoned President Kirk who was attending a meeting downtown. When Truman apprised Kirk of the situation, the President became extremely annoyed and suggested that the police be brought immediately to quell the protest. Truman disagreed. "My feeling was," the vice president later recalled, "that with a mix of both sides in Hamilton, any spark would have blown the thing up, and you'd have had a hell of a battle." Truman was told that the situation was in his hands and that he should do whatever seemed wisest. After speaking with Kirk he called Coleman who agreed that police should not be brought on campus. "I felt," Coleman later explained, "that this would simmer down after they had had a night of it and I was perfectly prepared to sit in here for a night. That wasn't going to bother me."

But there were many others who were bothered. During the afternoon four members of the varsity football squad asked Coleman if he would like a personal escort through the protesters, but the dean declined the offer, hoping to avert violent clashes in the lobby. Later in the day several faculty members, led by Orest Ranum, contacted Coleman and suggested that they lead the dean out of Hamilton, but for the same reason Coleman rejected the plan. Finally, late Tuesday night, while Coleman was trying to get some sleep on an office couch, an irate alumnus called from Westchester and told the dean that he was prepared to pick up a contingent of loyal Columbia graduates and drive down to Manhattan to rescue him. Coleman thanked the alumnus for his sincere concern but asked him to stay in Westchester.

The adversaries camped on both sides of Coleman's large mahogany door settled down for the night. Administrators and sympathetic students brought the dean towels, razors, a toothbrush, a bottle of Canadian whiskey and a fifth of scotch. In the lobby students passed around slices of bologna and bottles of soda, and set about redecorating the austere academic surroundings. One demonstrator hung a large poster of Lenin on a pillar in the lobby, but another, who did not share his ideology, objected. After a brief argument the Leninist won out and the demonstration continued under the watchful eyes of the Russian revolutionary. Soon posters of Stokely Carmichael and Malcolm X sprang up and then one student posted a large picture of Che Guevara above the door to Coleman's office. A counter-demonstrator, standing in front of the door, looked up and muttered, "It makes me sick to my stomach to see a filthy communist's picture hanging over the College dean's office." Red balloons and crepe paper were hung around the entire lobby and several students lounged on the floor, reading comic books, playing guitars and doing homework for the next day's classes.

By 7 P.M. several faculty members had come over to Hamilton to talk with the students. One of the first professors to speak was Arthur Danto, a member of the philosophy department. Earlier in the day Rudd had announced that Danto was among a group of faculty members who supported the demonstration, but now it became apparent that the professor did not sympathize with the students' methods. "Discussion at this point is the fundamental thing that is called for," Danto told them, suggesting that they leave the building. One student demonstrator had informed him that Coleman was free to go if he wished to do so. Danto, accompanied by a colleague from the philosophy department, went into Coleman's office to ask him if he wanted to leave. Coleman said that he would very much like to leave, but when the professors went outside to clear a path for him many of the students refused to move. Having failed to halt the demonstration, Danto left Hamilton.

Later in the evening George Collins, a prominent art history professor, came into Hamilton to discuss the gymnasium issue with the demonstrators. Although most of the controversy had centered around political considerations, Collins objected to the proposed facility mainly because he believed that it would mar the natural beauty and planned aesthetic design of Morningside Park. At a faculty meeting one year before, Collins had presented a motion condemning the proposed gym but could find no one to second it. Now the professor stood inside Hamilton with the original plans for the park tucked beneath his arm and again no one seemed to be interested. Collins, like Danto, went home.

While speakers continued to address the crowd, and a rock band set up for a short concert in the lobby, the steering committee moved into a third-floor classroom to discuss further plans for the demonstration. Midway through the meeting a short black man, surrounded by three large bodyguards, walked in and announced, "I'd like to tell you that the Harlem community is now here and we want to thank you for taking the first steps in this struggle." Community personnel were moving into Hamilton, he said, and were ready to take over when they got the word. He turned and left.

At first the students were confused. They knew that local black organizations had been called but were not certain what they had been called to do. The white committee members sitting in the center of the room looked up at the black students leaning against the walls and offered no objection to the community's involvement. "When that guy walked in," one white student at the meeting later recalled, "something clicked. You could feel the change."

Downstairs, as speakers continued to lecture the crowd, black students, then Harlem leaders, began to appear more frequently at the bullhorn. A SNCC organizer stood directly in front of Coleman's door and told the assembled students that contact had been made with black groups throughout the city and that "the troops are on the move." He said that unless the demonstrators' demands were met "We're going to do whatever is necessary to get them met. The black community is taking over."

Students began drifting upstairs to find a comfortable place to spend the night. Demonstrators sat in the hallways of Hamilton, singing songs or studying. In the lobby, tensions increased. Community people were continuing to arrive and, shortly after nine, a brief scuffle broke out when six massive blacks approached five counter-demonstrators standing in front of Coleman's door and told them to move. The students refused and within a very few moments were not too gently bounced out the front door. About ten blacks formed a tight guard around the entrance to Coleman's office.

In Van Am Quadrangle, just outside Hamilton, Dean Platt talked with groups of angered counter-demonstrators milling around the building. "I think we've drawn the line," he said. "We will not accede to their demands." Platt told the students that the administration would never grant amnesty to the demonstrators and said that "there's going to be a limit" to the time the University would allow the protesting students to occupy Hamilton.

An hour later, Dean Coleman, contacted by telephone, stated that no action would be taken on the demonstrators' demands prior to an emergency faculty meeting that had been called for the next day. Earlier in the afternoon Professor of Psychology Eugene Galanter had gathered the twenty signatures necessary to call a special faculty meeting. Dean Colahan remained in his office until 9 P.M., notifying the entire College faculty of the emergency session.

At 10 P.M. David Truman made his first public appearance of the day, speaking briefly to students outside Hamilton Hall. He then moved into the lobby of Hartley Hall, a dormitory immediately adjacent to Hamilton, where he held a "fireside chat." The meeting had been organized by a student in the School of Business and the audience inside was solidly behind the administration. "We will discuss anything," Truman told the audience, "but we will not act under coercion." He stated that the administration would not grant amnesty for the demonstrators or allow them to appeal their cases at an open hearing.

"There will, and necessarily must be, punishments," Truman asserted, "or we will be torn apart by a willful minority that will have its way no matter what." He rejected the idea of a tripartite committee to judge discipline and dismissed the idea that students should exercise decision-making power within the University. "It is not feasible for the University to be run like a New England town meeting," Truman said. After answering students' questions he left Hartley, but was stopped by Sam Coleman, a member of the philosophy department and a veteran of left-wing movements. The professor asked if it would be possible to make some deal with the students to get the dean out of Hamilton. "Is there something, even a promise of discussions, that could be offered in return for Harry's release?" he asked. "No," Truman replied, "there is nothing."

# 3

## The Second Front

WHEN IT BECAME APPARENT late Tuesday night that there would be no new developments at least until dawn, the Hamilton Hall demonstration turned from a sit-in to a sleep-in. As the tired speakers said their last words, the last of the tired demonstrators left the lobby for the upper floors of the building where they made temporary lodgings on corridor and classroom floors. Scattered on blankets, informal groups on each floor held bedtime parties with peanut butter and jelly sandwiches, beer, and guitars. The main classroom building of the all-male College had been transformed for one night into a coed hostel. But, though sexually integrated, the demonstration was becoming racially strained. The fragile alliance between SAS and SDS, born on the Sundial in the afternoon, was dying with the night. The blacks had segregated themselves on the third floor, leaving the remainder of the building to the whites. But the sleeping arrangements were only a sign. Though the integrated steering committee still hung together, a split over tactics was becoming more pronounced. They had their six demands, a viable sit-in to back those demands and Dean Coleman as a hostage. The question was what to do with all three at dawn: the answers offered by the blacks and whites differed significantly.

The white students on the steering committee had been dealing with the black members in a mood of uneasiness throughout the evening. It was the first time any of them had ever been on a committee with SAS leaders, and many felt that, since this was their first "integrated" demonstration, they had to prove themselves to the blacks. For all their anti-Establishment rhetoric the white radicals now in Hamilton Hall had after all never escalated their tactics much beyond sit-ins. And, before coming to Columbia, almost all of them had been children of the middle-class world they now attacked so bitterly. The black students, on the other hand, though their backgrounds were little more severe and their activities at Columbia had hardly been revolutionary, were seen by the whites as being much closer to the traditions of black oppression and black militancy which SDS had only been able to empathize with in one case and imitate tamely in the other. The blacks were well aware that the whites felt this, and they played upon this advantage. In addition, the presence of numerous Harlem militants in Hamilton Hall instilled an element of fear in the whites: fear that they were losing control.

The steering committee finally broke down along racial lines about 2 A.M. when the SDS and SAS factions left to hold separate meetings. The white caucus took place in a large classroom on the seventh floor; Mark Rudd, exhausted and hoarse, chaired the discussion. Cigarette smoke and crowds of tired, uncomfortable students filled the room. Rudd informed the group that the blacks were thinking of barricading the building and denying access to students and faculty. "This proposal would be bad," he said, explaining that it was important to radicalize students to build a mass movement rather than alienate them from the start by barricading them out of their morning classes. SDS had always been concerned with mass support, and to "turn off" the bulk of students in this way would be a grievous tactical error. "Alienating the faculty would also be dangerous," Rudd warned, "because they could approve some of our demands." The blacks, however, were not at this point concerned with the psychological impact that barricading buildings would have on the rest of the University community. They did not share the ideology of the New Left and were not obsessed with visions of mass support from the white world. While the whites wanted to radicalize the rest of the campus and use the political pressure of popular support to win their demands, the blacks preferred to rely only on the more military advantage of holding buildings, regardless of whether the campus liked it or not. "The blacks want a physical confrontation so that they can hold a club over the University's head," Rudd told the white caucus, "this is dictated by the fact that so many community people are involved, who aren't students and aren't interested in student politics."

Rudd added that a difference in political style was also responsible for the black–white split. The slow, wavering nature of SDS's participatory democracy irritated the blacks who preferred more centralized decision making and felt that SDS would not have the discipline or resolve to "go all the way."

"We're going to try to reach a compromise," Rudd said, shifting from analysis to practicality. He called for suggestions from the floor and one student after another stood to speak against barricading. A vote was called; it was overwhelmingly against a blockade. Discussion soon turned to the abstract political romanticizing characteristic of more routine SDS debates. In the words of one student who was at the meeting:

> It was fascinating—here they were presenting this grandiose vision of revolution and a new world, while the blacks were downstairs scaring the shit out of everyone.

John Jacobs, an ultra-militant SDS member, known as "JJ," finally came up with a compromise. He suggested that the demonstrators close down the administrative wing of the building, continue to hold Coleman captive and at the same time allow students and faculty free access to their classes and offices. In the confusion, however, JJ's proposal never came up for a vote. After another show of hands there was still a majority against barricading. Rudd then posed the next obvious question: What would the group do if the blacks decided independently to barricade? A few students argued that SDS had initiated the takeover of Hamilton, represented most of the protesters, and therefore should not allow the blacks to dictate tactics. But when a vote was taken, a vast majority agreed to stay if the blacks decided to barricade. Minutes later, at 3:25 A.M., a runner came up from the black caucus and informed Rudd that the blacks had indeed decided to close down the building and block the entrance.[1] Rudd, Freudenberg and Shils quickly departed for what was the last integrated meeting of the steering committee.

When the three white delegates to the steering committee reached the first-floor room where the blacks had been meeting, they were told, "We want to make our stand here. It would be better if you left and took your own building." Although the whites had expected all night that the break would eventually come, many were nevertheless shaken by what amounted to an order. They were even more upset when the blacks told them that there were guns in the building. Rumors had been circulating all night, but now it seemed that many blacks were prepared to make a violent stand. The prospect scared the white radicals who were becoming brazen about taking buildings but remained timid about actual violence. The blacks tried to ease the bitterness by telling the white leaders that, by leaving the building, they could act as a diversion when the police came and possibly start a second front.

At 5 A.M. Rudd slowly climbed upstairs to return to the remnants of the white caucus on the seventh floor. He was stopped by many supporters who asked him what would happen, but he barely responded. By the time he reached the meeting room it was again crowded. Now there

---

[1] Some observers claimed later that a black had been standing just outside the white caucus and had heard much of the irresolute debate.

was fatigued silence as Rudd spoke to the group in a low voice, his eyes on the floor: "The blacks have asked us to leave the building—" he paused; "—and I think we should." The students began to debate, not realizing that the issue was, in fact, beyond debate.[2]

In an attempt to keep the demoralized group together, Rudd proposed further action. "The blacks have chosen to make *their* stand," he said; "we should—not in support, but in attack of our common enemy, the administration—go and find our own building to make a stand in." Those in the room followed him slowly out the door and down the stairwell. As they descended they informed the ignorant and awoke the sleeping. At 5:30, as the lobby was filled with distraught whites, Bill Sales of SAS announced through a bullhorn, "We have asked all white students to leave the building." Some started to leave and others, half-awake, dragged their blankets behind them through the crowded lobby. Rudd tried to group the whites together so they could at least exit with a façade of organization. One white student grabbed a bullhorn and pleaded that they stay to protect the safety of Dean Coleman, still in his office. The students looked about in confusion, and Rudd's voice came over the loudspeaker: "We've talked this all over before—we don't have to say why we're leaving. The blacks have asked us to go. It's their stand now." Sales began pushing chairs and tables against the side entrances to the building. As the group prepared to leave one black freshman called out after them, "Good luck to you, brothers! We're still together."

The large center doors to Hamilton Hall were opened and the whites filed out, dazed, into the dawn. Behind them the blacks hurriedly piled desks, chairs, file cabinets and anything else that could be used to block the doors. By 6 A.M. the white exodus was over, the building barricaded and locked. From his office Dean Coleman listened to scraps of bullhorn announcements to find out what was happening. As he said several weeks later:

> From our point of view, our attitude changed a great deal at that point. We were worried; we had no way of knowing who the outsiders were who had come in during the night. . . . As students left the building, we had people coming by our windows who said it was exceedingly dangerous inside and that we had to get out somehow. That's when we took this desk and put it against the one door, and my secretary's desk against the other door. So from about 5:30 on, we were playing a slightly different game. . . .

[2] SDS leader Tony Papert suggested after the crisis that the blacks' demand that the whites leave was not a unilateral move. According to Papert, the decision was arrived at with Rudd's coöperation when the SDS chairman saw that the blacks were prepared to make a militant stand and decided that he did not want SDS involved in such an action. Rudd later substantially confirmed this.

Some of the white students left to go back to their dormitory rooms to sleep, some wandered around in front of Hamilton, others gathered at the Sundial. Out of the confusion, a band of about two hundred students shuffled slowly across a deserted College Walk and, as if drawn by a compulsion to repeat an earlier part of their scenario, they marched to the southeast security entrance of Low Library.

Three or four students at the front of the contingent charged the security door, trying unsuccessfully to force it with their shoulders. One student spotted a board lying on a nearby bench. It was picked up and positioned in front of the large plate glass window of the door. Twice, on the verge of launching the plank through the window, the students hesitated and dropped it. On the third attempt they brought the thick board back slowly and then, in one even motion, smashed the pane. The tinkling of the glass was the only sound to crack the clammy quiet of a gray sunrise. The crowd shuddered—some because of the temperature, others because of the act. The protest had crossed another line.

A security guard who had tried to stop the demonstrators now backed off, his arm cut by the shattered glass. The door was opened, but for most the next move was still uncertain. One student at the rear, who had been committed to revolution just a few hours before, moaned, "Oh, I don't go for *this*." But those up front were more aggressive. They crossed the threshold, and most of the students followed, flowing around the University security office, past incredulous security guards and up the nearest flight of stairs. Once they gained the darkened main floor of Low they headed straight for the offices of the President and vice president. Their destination was marked by a small wooden sign, standing outside Kirk's office, meticulously labeled in gold leaf, "Office of the President of the University." Lifting the signpost, a student, hardened by the earlier breakthrough, shattered a small rectangular pane in the door. This time there was no shuddering as the door was unlocked and the crowd surged into the suite of offices.

The students toyed with office equipment, sipped Kirk's sherry and puffed his White Owl "President" cigars. There was the President's huge mahogany desk, his sofa, his telephones, his private bathroom, his $450,000 Rembrandt "Portrait of a Dutch Admiral," his sculptured ebony lion statuette. Everything was there just as Grayson Kirk had left it.

While the students ferreted through the eight-room administrative complex the SDS leaders arrived. Somewhat more cautious than the rest of the students, they herded the group out of the offices and into the hallway encircling the rotunda to hold a meeting to discuss what to do next. Dawn was filtering through the high windows as the group stood, numbed by the events of the last hour. Mark Rudd, disheveled and discouraged, stood on a bench and leaned against one of the massive black marble pillars. He spoke softly and his familiar voice eased the eeriness as it echoed faintly in the still rotunda.

"No one on the outside must ever know what we say here," he stated solemnly. "The reason we were asked to leave Hamilton was because we weren't solid. I didn't want to tell you this before, but the blacks have guns and are prepared to make a stand; I'm not." He paused and then went on sadly, "I'm not ready to sacrifice my life. There are still things I want to accomplish and I didn't want any of my people to get hurt. That's their fight, we have our own. For some of us our academic careers are already ruined. The only thing we can do is make our stand and try to win our fight." As a footnote to a chapter of history over which he had lost control, he said, "I didn't want to leave Dean Coleman there with guns and all that in the building, but I had no choice." The group swayed noiselessly in the semi-darkness. Stu Gedal leaned against one of the columns for support; Robby Roth's eyes filled with tears.

But the protesters could not dwell on remorse; they had to act. More students from the groups at the Sundial and Hamilton had entered Low, and a plan of action became necessary. The meeting of almost two hundred students was shifted from the hallway to the center of the rotunda, a place normally reserved for formal receptions and lectures by distinguished speakers. Rudd stood before the crowd and in the well-established SDS tradition, outlined the alternative actions available to the demonstrators. Suggestions to leave Low or barricade the entire building were summarily dismissed. A proposed sit-in in the rotunda was rejected for tactical reasons, after Rudd pointed out that the administration could simply lock the huge iron gates that surround the rotunda and leave them sitting there forever. At this point a runner brought news that the New York City police had arrived on campus, were stationed in the basement of Low and would probably be ordered to clear the building. Rudd suggested that the group return to Kirk's office and barricade the doors. The plan was accepted, and the students reëntered the suite, moved into both Kirk's and Truman's private offices and placed desks, chairs and file cabinets against the three doors that lead to the hallway. They filled wastepaper baskets with water from the President's sink to be used as protection against tear gas, and they waited.[3]

Meanwhile, as the demonstrators inside Low were deciding whether to occupy his office, Vice President Truman arrived on campus. Wearing a trench coat, his hat pulled down over his forehead, Truman paced

---

[3] Tear gas dissolves in water. By soaking rags or handkerchiefs in water and putting them to the face one can protect himself from the irritating effects of the gas. The wastepaper baskets were filled because the students feared that the water might be shut off when the police came.

worriedly back and forth on College Walk. The vice president, who normally smokes a pipe, chain-smoked cigarettes as he walked. Several students attempted to speak to him, but he brushed by them. Dave Gilbert, a 1966 graduate of the College and one of the founders of New Left student politics at Columbia, rushed past on his way to the demonstration in Low. Truman called out "Dave, where are you going? Haven't you done enough already?" Gilbert turned his head, made a brief reply and kept running.

The vice president had gone home to bed at three that morning and had been awakened by a phone call from Henry Coleman at six. The dean told him that all whites had been evicted from Hamilton and that the building was being taken over by blacks from Columbia and Harlem. He added that he had been told the whites broke into Truman's own office as well as Kirk's. The administrators agreed that it would be wise to call in a detail of city policemen in case they might be needed, and so Coleman called Columbia Security Officer Adam DeNisco who in turn called the police. Ten minutes after arriving on campus, Truman went to the security office of Low to meet the first squad of city police. His scowl encountered a smile plastered on the face of Captain Richard DiRoma, who was in charge of police operations and had little experience with Columbia or with student protest. The smile left DiRoma's face when he saw Truman, but his bewilderment lingered. (At one point, when calling for reinforcements, DiRoma had shouted over the telephone, "I'm here at Fordham University. . . .") Neither the administration nor the police seemed to know exactly who was in charge, what was happening or what should be done. "Don't ask me what's going on, I just take my orders from the administration," DiRoma told a reporter about 7 A.M. A few minutes later Truman was overheard saying, "Don't bother me, this is now in the hands of the police." DiRoma stationed his men at the entrance to Low with the orders, "If anybody leaves and he is a student, he is a prisoner."

Back in the President's suite there was also confusion, as the students waited for the police. Tony Papert, a first-year student at Teachers College and a long-time member of the Progressive Labor Party faction in SDS, had taken a large group into Kirk's private office and was trying to hold a calm discussion about revolutionary tactics. Another, somewhat more confused meeting was going on in another office under Rudd's leadership. But Papert and Rudd were only partially successful in getting the group organized. Many students roamed through the suite, sitting in the President's chair, lounging on his couches, looking at his art work and peering out his windows for the police. Some students rummaged through files, xeroxing anything of interest.

Downstairs in the security office Truman seemed impatient, talking to lower administrators and to police officials who had arrived on campus. All were ready to carry out orders, but no orders were given. At 6:50 A.M. Truman called Kirk to brief him and to ask him to come to the campus. Though Truman had argued against bringing in the police on Tuesday afternoon, with the breaking and entering into Low he changed his mind. Over the phone Kirk and Truman now agreed that it was time for the police to clear out Low. Kirk also expressed concern about the security of the $450,000 Rembrandt hanging in his office and inquired after the safety of Harry Coleman.

At 7:15 A.M. a delegate from the administration was sent up to the President's office with an offer. He spoke to Rudd through the broken pane in Kirk's door and told him that if the students walked out now and turned in their identification cards they would face only University discipline and no criminal trespass charges. Rudd rejected the proposal, explaining later that it would have been foolish to accept the deal when they knew they had another way out—through the windows. The delegate returned fifteen minutes later with the same offer, which was again rejected, but this time he announced that the police would be sent in to arrest them within fifteen minutes. At the thought of a police "bust," most of the students panicked and made use of their other way out. Hurling blankets and belongings to the grassy plot fifteen feet below, some fled through the large windows and scrambled down the gratings to safety; others jumped from the sill.

Meanwhile, Truman was having trouble with the police officials. Kirk had arrived on campus, and the two were trying to arrange for the arrest of any students who remained in the President's office. As firm as they were in their decision that police should be used to clear out Low, they were also set against using the police in Hamilton, for fear of large-scale violence, possibly involving Dean Coleman. The police, however, balked at this selectivity, Truman reported later, telling him that it would be impossible for them to clear out one building and not the other.[4] It was to be all or nothing, and the dangers that could arise in Hamilton Hall convinced the administrators to do nothing. That the police were not brought in proved critical. Had they been used to clear Low, the demonstration probably would have been contained, and the administration would have had to deal only with the blacks in Hamilton.

Although the administration decided against having the white students arrested, it attempted to end the sit-in by threatening police action. The plan proved only partially successful. At 7:45 the police began dismantling the barricades to Kirk's office, causing several dozen more

---

[4] If a complaint for trespass were filed, police officials explained, they would not discriminate between buildings according to race in responding to such a complaint.

students to leave by the windows. In the midst of the pandemonium Tony Papert continued his meeting, trying to convince the group of the need to stay. But most of them headed for the windows. Papert went into a secretarial office adjacent to the President's where the few remaining students had gathered. As the police broke through the barricades Papert persisted in continuing his meeting, explaining the tactical necessity of holding ground. In affirmation, one student declared, "We ran from the gym site, we ran from Hamilton, let's not run from here." By the time the police entered the office the students had formed a circle on the floor. Only twelve remained; all the rest, including Rudd, had fled. Columbia security guards removed Kirk's Rembrandt to safer quarters, as city police herded all the students into the room in which Papert's group was meeting. The other offices were locked and the police watched over the discussion. Soon they were talking with the demonstrators.

The meeting went on for another hour, then another, and the students began to realize that they were not going to be arrested. Later in the morning Orest Ranum, Columbia's only faculty member who teaches in his academic robes, climbed up on a grating under Kirk's office and vaulted in through the window, his gown billowing. Seating himself on the floor, Ranum tried to negotiate a settlement with the protesters. He spoke to them about their demands and then phoned Truman, suggesting offers to the vice president and conducting straw votes among the students at the same time. The students were not eager to negotiate, however, and Ranum soon left. As it became obvious that no one would be arrested, other students—many of whom had fled Low earlier—returned to Kirk's offices through the windows. As the morning wore on, the police left and the protest, which had nearly ended in defenestration, began to regain stability.

# 4

## Enter Alan Westin

THE COLUMBIA CAMPUS awoke on Wednesday morning to a heavy rain. By 8:30 students and faculty—largely unaware of what had taken place while they slept—had begun to move across the wide central quadrangle between Low and Butler Library. In the buildings which had not been touched by the night's events some classes were held as if nothing out of the ordinary had happened; others were turned into nervous exchanges of information and opinion. Details of police walked about the campus, while just off the central University grounds paddy wagons and police cars lined Amsterdam Avenue. In the steady rain an uneasy crowd assembled in front of Hamilton Hall, some trying to reach their classes, many astounded to find that the building had been barricaded. Groups milling in a sea of umbrellas observed that now only black faces were peering at them from behind the barricaded doors. Professor Lionel Trilling stood outside Hamilton's entrance, talking with a colleague who was furious about what had happened. Trilling, one of America's foremost literary critics, had been at Columbia since he arrived as a freshman in the autumn of 1921. He had taught the literature of discontent to thousands of college students and had lived through the politics of two generations. Now he seemed concerned, but not as outraged as his colleague. "There's a political sense to this," he said.

The night before, Trilling had gathered a group of influential Columbia professors at his apartment to discuss the takeover of Hamilton. Daniel Bell, the sociologist, came to the informal meeting and introduced Trilling to Professor of Psychology Eugene Galanter, a comparative newcomer to the University. They were joined by Herbert Deane, a government professor who was close to the administration (named vice provost soon after the crisis), and by Quentin Anderson, son of the playwright Maxwell Anderson and a good friend of Trilling in the English department. Also present was Professor Danto who had spoken to the demonstrators earlier that evening and a colleague of his from the philosophy department, Richard Kuhns.

For many of them this meeting marked the first time they recognized that the situation was extremely serious. Protests were common occurrences at the University; the issues involved in this one had been in the air for months and had never very greatly exercised any of those present. But now it was clear that the conflict was going past the lines of familiar protest and might possibly end, as one of them speculated, in the suspension of as many as 150 students. Trilling warned that SDS must not be allowed to turn Columbia into "some scruffy Latin–American university." It was generally agreed that amnesty for the demonstrators was out of the question. It was also agreed that the police must not be called in to eject the students from the buildings. Professor Galanter posed the key question: Could the faculty face the fact that this might end in just such an unacceptable solution if a compromise could not be worked out? As Professor Deane later commented, the professors at this meeting—and at the others that would follow—were "anxious to avoid the moment of moral horror." Out of the meeting came the framework for a set of proposals to be presented by Professor Bell at the faculty meeting called for the following day.

Home from the meeting at Trilling's apartment, Professor Danto was awakened Wednesday morning by a call from Dave Gilbert of SDS. Gilbert told him that the situation was out of control and asked him to help gather a group of sympathetic faculty members to meet as soon as possible at the statue of Alma Mater in front of Low Library.

On arriving at Alma Mater Professor Danto found that the demoralization which had affected Dave Gilbert earlier that morning had lifted. It had become clear that those who stayed inside the President's offices would not be arrested and that the demonstrators were being allowed free access by window to the offices. In a heated argument with former SDS chairman Ted Kaptchuk, Danto insisted that the demonstrators' actions were out of all proportion to their stated grievances. The group that gathered around Danto and Kaptchuk as they debated attracted the attention of Vice Dean Thomas Colahan. He suggested that the faculty members move their discussion to Philosophy Hall where he had set up provisional headquarters while his own office in Hamilton was in student hands.

About twenty-five professors began an informal meeting in the Graduate Students' Lounge in Philosophy Hall, a spacious room with a piano and flowered rug, normally used for teas and quiet conversation among students. The group grew during the morning as others learned that Philosophy had become the center of faculty activity. Professors of varying outlooks met to plan strategies for the emergency College faculty meeting.

Faculty members were not the only people students mobilized Wednesday morning. At 4 A.M. the blacks in Hamilton had called Manhattan Borough President Percy Sutton, the city's highest-ranking Negro politician, and informed him that the Hamilton sit-in had taken on a racial dimension. Later in the morning Sutton called City Commissioner of Human Rights William Booth. While driving to a downtown appointment State Senator Basil Paterson, another New York Negro politician, heard of the developments over his car radio and immediately headed for the University. On campus Paterson phoned the office of Mayor John Lindsay to suggest that one of the Mayor's Urban Task Force troubleshooters be sent uptown. Lindsay was reluctant to have city officials intervene in the affairs of a private institution and had Deputy Mayor Robert Sweet call the Columbia administration to ask whether such action would be welcome. The administration replied that city involvement would not be necessary, but several minutes later a high Columbia official called back and asked that one of the Mayor's aides be sent to the campus. Barry Gottehrer, a youthful Lindsay assistant who had spent most of his time trying to cool potentially explosive ghetto situations, was dispatched to the Morningside campus. By midmorning a host of city politicians were at Columbia, shuttling back and forth between Hamilton Hall and Low Library, bearing messages and seeking information.

After calling City Hall Senator Paterson went directly to Hamilton to confer with the students inside. Outside the building he met Assistant Chief Inspector Eldridge Waithe, the top Negro policeman in New York City, who was discussing the situation with Victor Solomon, chairman of the Harlem chapter of the Congress of Racial Equality. Paterson and Waithe spoke through a window with several of the black students and were soon invited inside. The Hamilton Hall Steering Committee stated its demands, which had been communicated by runner to the administration in Low Library. In addition the committee explained that there were two preconditions which would have to be met before negotiations could begin: no criminal prosecution, and no University discipline for any of the students involved in the protests.

After leaving the black students Paterson and Waithe went to speak with Kirk and Truman in the security office of Low Library. Most of the administration's attention and worry were focused in Hamilton Hall where the political difficulties were compounded by racial tension and a threat of bloody violence. For Kirk and Truman at that point the problem of SDS students roaming the President's offices and snooping into his files paled next to the prospect of an all-out shooting war with neighboring Harlem over the occupants of Hamilton and their hostage, Henry Coleman.

Fearing for Dean Coleman's safety, the administration had developed plans for getting him out of the building. It was suggested that the police rip, saw or burn away a section of the thick iron grating barring the window of the dean's office to enable him to exit ingloriously through the rear. The bars' sturdiness was investigated, and it was found that those furthest to the right were weakest and could be pulled out by a truck with a hook if sudden need for escape arose. But the procedure would have taken too long, attracting students who might seek to block the exit.

The administrators told Paterson they would be willing to yield on the blacks' first precondition, amnesty from criminal prosecution; they would not, however, give in on the second, amnesty from University discipline. Kirk told Paterson that Columbia had to stand firm as an example to other schools. A political scientist before becoming President, Kirk took a John Foster Dulles stance: If the administration gave in at Columbia students throughout the country would be encouraged to attempt similar takeovers at their universities and expect to win. This domino theory accounted for a large measure of the intransigence of both the administration and the students. Each side viewed the University as a miniature version of full-scale national revolution. Just as the administrators saw themselves as the representatives of law and order, the student leaders often cast themselves in the role of vanguard of impending global insurrection. There was some truth to both perspectives; the Columbia uprising did occur in the context of a spring of nationwide student unrest.[1] But when this analysis was exaggerated—as it was by both sides—to the point where the Battle of Morningside Heights became *the* decisive engagement in the War Between the Generations, its only result was highly principled stubbornness in each camp.

State Senator Paterson asked Kirk if the University would set an upper limit to discipline—"at least promise no expulsions." The Presi-

---

[1] Occupying campus administration buildings had become a tactic of student protest in the weeks before April 23 (Howard University, Bowie State College, Colgate University, University of Michigan, Trinity College), and the Columbia experience gave the new trend added impetus, with similar tactics appearing after April 23 at larger, generally urban schools such as Northwestern University, Brooklyn College, Boston University, Stanford University, the University of Chicago and San Francisco State College).

dent refused. Before departing, Paterson reminded the administrators that Harlem was near and suggested that they do their best to settle the conflict before nightfall.

Barry Gottehrer, the Mayor's man, also conferred with University officials on Wednesday morning. Like most of those involved in the crisis at that point he was concerned far more about Hamilton than Low. Gottehrer pointed out to the Columbia officials that though he had no first-hand evidence that there had been guns in Hamilton, there had been "some pretty revolutionary people" there who frequently carried guns. Most, however, left by Wednesday morning. The urban troubleshooter reported that although Harlem had vied with the black students for control of the demonstration during the night, most community leaders had left that morning at the request of SAS. For months the Mayor's staff had been working inside Harlem, gauging the pulse of the ghetto, and Gottehrer now suggested that the "community support" threatened by the black students was a myth conjured up to pressure the University and would never materialize. Even so he recommended that the administration accept the two preconditions. Kirk and Truman refused. "The Columbia people didn't really know what they were doing," Gottehrer later said. "They couldn't quite believe it was happening."

The rain continued throughout the morning. Roy Innis, assistant national director of CORE, stood outside Hamilton and told a reporter that he was on campus to "offer support" for the students inside the building. "I'm awfully proud of those kids," he said. "They hold the high ground. They've got the dean in what you might call an extended dialogue." No meaningful communication was taking place, however. Coleman spent the morning resigned to his fate. As the dean described his morning some time afterward:

> Things had gotten completely out of our hands. All we knew about what was happening was what we could find out by way of the window and the few phone calls we were able to get through to the security office. . . . We were told to sit tight. Somebody passed us a hot breakfast through the windows—scrambled eggs and bacon and toast and sweet rolls and orange juice and coffee. I called home but didn't tell my wife about the black students. We took turns trying to get some sleep while someone watched the phone. We always kept wondering when the police were to come around; and we called occasionally to ask where they were.

Outside Low Library the police were making half-hearted attempts to stop students from climbing into the President's office. The administration's desire to avoid violent incidents, coupled with its wish to prevent hundreds of students from streaming into Kirk's office, resulted in a peculiar set of ground rules governing the actions of the police. If a student could climb past the grating enclosing the ground-level windows of the building he was allowed to scramble along a ledge and leap through the window of Kirk's office. If he could not make the grating he was turned back by a policeman and would have to start over. About fifty students—many of whom had fled Low earlier Wednesday morning—climbed back via the approved route. When SDS leaders returned during the late morning they shared in the spirit of the people who had stayed and of those who had rejoined them. As one strike leader later recalled, "On Wednesday Low was the energizer of the strike."

About 11 A.M. the faculty group which was meeting informally in Philosophy Lounge decided to send a delegation into the administration-controlled section of Low Library to speak with the President or vice president. The men met with Truman in the first-floor offices of George Fraenkel, Dean of Graduate Faculties, which had become the temporary headquarters of the central administration. They discussed the problem of the students' access to Kirk's offices, which Truman said would have to be maintained because the police were under orders not to create incidents. It was an unquestioned assumption at that point, according to one professor, that the police would not be used to clear the buildings. A major concern of the faculty delegation was negotiation with the protesting students. Truman informed the professors that he was in touch with the black students through Chief Waithe, but Professor Bell suggested that perhaps it would be better for members of the faculty to serve as the administration's negotiators if talks could be arranged in some "neutral building." Nothing came of the suggestion until later when the faculty delegation decided that one of its members, sociologist Immanuel Wallerstein, should try to talk with the students in Hamilton. Wallerstein had been head of the Faculty Civil Rights Group and, as a specialist in the field of contemporary African politics, had come to know many of the black students who had been in his classes. A meeting was arranged by a black student not participating in the protests, and clearance was obtained from the Hamilton Hall Steering Committee for Wallerstein and Professor Samuel Coleman to enter the building.

At 2 P.M. the two professors climbed over the file cabinets and chairs that formed the Hamilton barricades and were ushered into Dean Platt's office, which the steering committee had established as its headquarters. According to Sam Coleman, Cicero Wilson sat behind the main desk, clearly in charge. Wilson would look at Wallerstein who would ask a question, and then look at one of his colleagues who would answer. When the student—Bill Sales or Ray Brown—finished, Wilson's eyes would return to Wallerstein who would then pose another question.[2] Sales did most of the talking, but "Wilson had an amazing quality of dominance," Coleman recalled. "He reminded me of a strike leader I knew twenty years ago." The professors tried to discover exactly what the blacks' position was, but ran up against a wall of reserve and formality. The dean would not be released. The students would not negotiate in a "neutral location" outside Hamilton. They would not yield on their demands. In Professor Wallerstein's words:

> The four guys on the steering committee [Wilson, Sales, Brown, and Andrew Newton, a Columbia law student] had certain rules about what they would say to me. They would only discuss certain things, such as the demands, which made it very difficult to have a conversation about anything. The point of this tactic was, I think, that wrapped in mystery, they felt they could get more concessions.

Leaving the session Wallerstein stopped in the lobby of Hamilton to talk with an African student about Dar es Salaam, the capital of Tanzania, which Wallerstein knew well. The student was later chastised for having spoken to him.

All afternoon Wednesday the students in Hamilton continued preparations for a lengthy stay. Large cartons of food—much of it supplied by Harlem CORE—were carried inside, as were medical supplies. Leaders of the black community filed in and out, including a Negro State Assemblyman who had been active in trying to block construction of the gymnasium, representatives of CORE, the United Black Front and the Student Non-Violent Coördinating Committee. Human Rights Commissioner Booth, Senator Paterson and Lindsay aide Gottehrer also visited Hamilton again about three. They informed the students that they could be charged with kidnaping as well as criminal trespass if they did not let Dean Coleman out. Reversing the position they had taken before Professor Wallerstein, the steering committee replied that Coleman was not being detained and that his door was locked from the inside. Paterson suggested that the dean be informed that he was free to go, and a vote of the entire assembly of students approved such a decision. Dean Coleman later said what followed:

> Finally at 3:30 in the afternoon, we heard a rap on the door we had locked. We opened it somewhat cautiously, but it was a group of our own students—I recognized Bill [Sales] and Ray [Brown] and one other—and they said they hoped that we would like to

---

[2] Other observers have interpreted Wilson's reticence as an indication that he was *not* the dominant force among the blacks, and so deferred frequently to Sales or Brown.

leave the building. I allowed as how we would, and they said fine, because they wanted us to leave. So I got my briefcase and my raincoat and walked out into the lobby, which was pretty crowded. There were barricades against the [outside] door and somebody said, "Make him crawl out under the table." And I said, "No." I wasn't going to crawl out under the table, if they wanted me to leave the building they'd move the table, and they said, "Move the table, move the table." . . . People have often said that I could have walked out any time I wanted to. Out of curiosity, I checked that out with Barry Gottehrer, and he said, "Don't you believe it."

Coleman, Proctor Kahn and Dan Carlinsky emerged from Hamilton Hall, having spent twenty-six hours inside. Coleman spoke briefly with reporters, noting that he had been treated well and that there had been no conditions for his release. Counter-demonstrators thronged Van Am Quadrangle outside the building. Weaving through them, Coleman passed Dean Platt and said, "Alex, I've just got to get to the faculty meeting."

The official College faculty meeting had begun some twenty minutes before in Havemeyer Hall. The ancient chemistry building had been chosen because it houses one of the largest classrooms on campus, seating more than three hundred people. Almost immediately after the group came to order President Kirk, who was chairing the meeting, recognized Professor Bell. That Bell was called on first was not an accident. Working from ideas generated at the gathering the night before in Trilling's apartment, Bell had spent the morning drafting a set of proposals that would be acceptable to the administration. He had worked in Philosophy Lounge with a close advisor to Truman, Professor Deane, who had conveyed the substance of the resolution to the administration before the meeting. Bell read:

(1.) A university exists as a community dedicated to rational discourse and the use of communication and persuasion as the means of furthering that discourse.

(2.) In this light we deplore the use of coercion, and the seizure of Dean Coleman as hostage. Further we condemn the act of invasion of the President's office and rifling of his files.

These measures were *pro forma*—the sort of statements that had to be made by liberal men about radical tactics before they could get down to the issues. The last two proposals, however, were to prove controversial:

(3.) We believe that any differences have to be settled peacefully, and we trust that police action will not be used to clear Hamilton Hall.
(4.) To the extent that the issues which have arisen in the University community are due to a failure of communication and discussion within the University, we call upon the administration to set up a tri-partite body to discuss any disciplinary matters arising out of the incidents yesterday and today, the issue of the gymnasium and any other matters which are subjects of legitimate concern to the University community.

In an effort to prevent his motion from becoming entangled in political discussion, Bell suggested that the substantive issues—IDA, the gym, amnesty—be left for later consideration.

Before debate began on the Bell package, Vice President Truman presented a summary of the administration's view of the events of the past two days. Professor Wallerstein then described to the group his meeting with the students in Hamilton and their apparent refusal to compromise. As Wallerstein concluded his remarks Dean Coleman walked through the tall, swinging doors at the front of the room, touching off sustained applause from the faculty that had been so concerned about his safety. "It was the only standing ovation I ever received," Coleman remarked wryly a few weeks later. He stepped to the microphone and explained that his release was not, in his estimation, a result of a break in the students' position, but rather a sign that "his incarceration had become an embarrassment to his captors." [3]

The four sections of the Bell resolution were considered separately. The first two parts—defining the function of a university and condemning coercive tactics—were approved substantially as submitted. The third section, which opposed police action as a solution, was a source of conflict between conservative and leftist professors. One conservative suggested that the phrase "we trust police action will not be used" be changed to "we trust police action will not be necessary." Professor Danto moved that the resolution be broadened to condemn "the use of police action in *any* University problem." These modifications were defeated, though another change was made, one which would prove to be important: the third resolution was extended so that it called for the administration to refrain from police action to clear any University building, not just Hamilton Hall.

Bell's fourth proposal, dealing with a tripartite body to deliberate on the issues of the crisis, then came up for discussion. One faculty member

[3] From the minutes of the special meeting of the faculty of Columbia College, April 24, 1968.

asked Kirk what role such a committee would play in resolving the problems at hand. The President answered that its function would be merely advisory, and that he could not guarantee that its decisions or recommendations would be binding in any way. At this point Professor Marvin Harris, a radical professor of anthropology, introduced an amendment to the Bell proposal, which he and three other members of his left-wing-oriented department had prepared earlier in Philosophy Hall:

> (a.) That there be a moratorium on all standing disciplinary decisions which have been made regarding political events on campus until the relevant facts can be made public and until open hearings involving due process can be held.
> (b.) That there be an immediate suspension of construction of the gymnasium until the faculty and students have a voice in deciding whether this project is in the best interests of the University community.
> (c.) That there be an immediate suspension of *all* forms of participation in and affiliation with the Institute of Defense Analyses until the faculty and students have a voice in deciding whether the continuance of these ties is in the best interests of the University community.

The first part of Harris' amendment, which many professors saw as a disguised demand for amnesty for the demonstrators, was defeated 99 to 56. The third part, calling for an end to IDA ties, was also rejected, probably because many professors did not want to undercut a faculty committee which was then in the process of evaluating such ties and preparing its recommendations for the President. One professor later suggested that the defeat of the Harris resolutions was as much the result of the way he presented them as of their content: "He made every proposal sound eighty per cent to the left of where it actually was. When he got through, you felt as if you were voting for the Bolshevik Revolution." Harris' proposal calling for a halt to gym construction was dropped in favor of a substitute motion which, in more equivocal language, asked that the University determine the opinions of community representatives, rather than students and faculty, before going ahead with construction plans:

> This faculty respectfully petitions the University administration
> (a.) to arrange the immediate suspension of on-site excavation of the gymnasium facility in Morningside Park.
> (b.) to be prepared to review the matter of the gymnasium site with a group of community spokesmen; the administration will

immediately invite the Mayor to designate a group who will take counsel with the University with respect to the location and character of the gymnasium.

This substitute motion was passed, as was Bell's original proposal for a tripartite committee of students, faculty and administrators to consider the substantive issues involved in the crisis.

The faculty meeting ended at 6:15 P.M., and Joseph Blau, secretary of the faculty, presented a copy of the approved resolutions to the administration for publication and distribution. When the printed version of the resolutions appeared on campus, a curious note had been appended by Dean Coleman at the bottom beneath the five resolutions and Blau's signature:

> (Note from the Dean: I wish to make absolutely clear that in passing resolution number 4 [Bell's tripartite committee] the faculty reaffirmed that discipline is the responsibility of the President of the University, subject to delegation to the dean of the College.
>
> The Trustees alone can act on resolution number 5 [calling for cessation and reconsideration of gym construction]. President Kirk will ask the chairman of the board of Trustees to call a special meeting of the board to consider this matter.
>
> —Henry S. Coleman)

This parenthetical addition, which was intended as a "clarification," irritated the faculty. They had begun to take a stand on the issues, and many felt that Coleman's addendum was meant to undercut their position. The faculty had never formally "reaffirmed" anything about the powers of the President. The statement that according to the Charter and Statutes of the University all disciplinary power rests with the President had been an *ex cathedra* reminder made by Kirk during the meeting and was hardly a mandate of support. Though Coleman apologized for the addition at another faculty meeting several weeks later, the statement pointed to a turn in faculty-administration relations.

The faculty decisions on the gym and amnesty were the subject of much retrospective analysis. Associate Professor of History David Rothman later observed that his colleagues had acted out of conscience rather than pragmatism, thereby hampering their effectiveness:

> What one might have expected would be for the faculty to give *de facto* amnesty [i.e., pass the first part of Harris' radical proposal] and then clamp down very hard on the issues. This argument has a

logic to it. It says, "Look, children, you don't know what you're doing, and we can't deal with your substantive demands. We'll give you amnesty, get out of the buildings. And then maybe we can sit down and talk substance." In fact, the College faculty did something which I think got us all in a bind. They invoked their consciences: they stood back from granting amnesty for moral reasons and then, also for moral reasons, gave in on a key substantive issue [the gym] by acclamation. What this did from the very beginning was to give a moral force to the sit-in that I think remained with it.

It is unlikely, however, that the granting of amnesty alone would have brought the students out of the buildings.

Several other faculty members voiced an opinion different from Rothman's. They felt that the faculty should have given in completely on the gym, recognizing that pressure from Harlem would make it a dangerous venture anyway. Then, the argument goes, the faculty could have threatened immediate police action if the students did not leave the buildings. This would have allowed the radicals to claim a substantial victory but it would have terminated the crisis quickly. According to this "drastic devaluation" approach, if the faculty had persuaded the administration to make one major concession—on the gym, for instance—and then to stand firm, instead of gradually and grudgingly yielding on several small points, perhaps the students—particularly the black students—would not have speculated on further concessions and would have come out. But again the faculty chose not to follow the course of political expediency.

At the same time that the faculty meeting was going on SDS was holding its own strategy session in the Ferris Booth Hall offices of the campus humor magazine. The two factions which had long divided SDS were having it out in a bitter battle. The "praxis axis," the soft-sell radicals, including former SDS leaders Gold and Kaptchuk as well as Dave Gilbert, feared that many potential supporters might be alienated by further coercive action. They now urged a program of dormitory canvassing, propagandizing, and public discussion of the campus situation. But Rudd and the more militant radicals of the "action faction" felt that open confrontation, such as the takeover of Low, was the most effective form of radical activity since such action itself was a powerful means toward radicalizing others. Rudd proposed that the group in Ferris Booth go to Low to support the approximately seventy-five students who were then in Kirk's offices. The movement needed revitalization, he said, and there was the pressing bio-tactical need to recapture

Kirk's private office, since it contained the suite's only bathroom. His proposal was voted down overwhelmingly, 70 to 3. Rudd then suggested that the group take another building—an idea that was defeated by a comparable margin. After one more such proposal of his was voted down, Rudd, now red in the face, stormed out of the meeting, shouting on his way to the door, "I resign as chairman of this fucking organization!" Excited and exhausted, he went with strike leader Juan Gonzalez to Low where he tried to take charge of the demonstration, irritating those students who had stayed in Kirk's office since the original takeover. On the verge of being told to leave, he went home to sleep for the first time in over thirty hours. In Ferris Booth Hall, Vice Chairman Nick Freudenberg took charge of the meeting, and the group decided, in praxis fashion, to organize a program of speakers for that evening, hold educational discussion in each of the dorms that night and call for a student strike the next day.

Outside Hamilton Hall, meanwhile, counter-demonstrators had massed on the grassy area in front of the building taunting the students inside. The slackening of the rain in the later afternoon had brought students of all political sentiments out to Hamilton's entrance. Now eggs were thrown from a nearby dormitory at a group of black students standing on a balcony of Hamilton. The blacks replied with spurts from fire extinguishers. Having reports that a large number of Harlem residents were planning a march on Columbia under the auspices of Harlem CORE, the administration sent Dean Platt to Hamilton Hall shortly after four to announce that all evening classes had been canceled and that all entrances to the University except those on College Walk would be sealed off for the night. A few minutes later Dean Coleman was called out of the Havemeyer faculty meeting to go over to Hamilton and defuse the situation. A former oarsman on Columbia's crew, Coleman had long been on good terms with the athletes who composed a large and volatile part of the counter-demonstrating faction. Amid periodic exchanges of epithets and eggs, Coleman told the crowd of about five hundred, "We're having a faculty meeting to try and solve this. But we can't meet if we have to continually come out here and police this situation." He and Dean Platt sought to clear space between the opposing factions.

Inside Hamilton the blacks were holding a press conference. Newsmen had made their way through the opposing factions of students and climbed indecorously over the barricades. Ray Brown, a College senior majoring in history and a leader of the demonstration, stood at the top level of the lobby. He would identify himself only as "a spokesman for the steering committee," and announced that he would read a statement. No questions would be answered, and all representatives of the press would then leave. Reciting the release very rapidly, Brown explained that the Students' Afro-American Society wanted to dramatize Columbia's attempt to take over the community. He listed four demands: (1) End gym construction; (2) drop all charges made as a result of gym protests; (3) sever all ties with IDA, including faculty contracts; and (4) grant total amnesty to the students involved in the current demonstration.

Shortly after Coleman was called away from the faculty meeting in Havemeyer, President Kirk was summoned from the chair to Low Library. There, in Dean Fraenkel's office, he met with Borough President Sutton, State Senator Paterson and State Assemblyman Charles Rangel, all of whom had taken public stands against the gym. At 5 P.M. Kirk called Truman and he, too, left the faculty meeting for Low. The black politicians went over the entire stormy history of the gym project, lambasting the Columbia administrators at each turn. The most that Kirk and Truman would concede, however, was a promise to call a meeting of the Trustees as soon as possible to bring the matter to their consideration.

When the gym had first been announced in 1960, the enterprise had seemed in the best tradition of white liberal aid to the disadvantaged. Columbia, the wealthiest and most powerful institution in or near Harlem, would give a small share of its resources to the surrounding community, which would never have been able to build a gym of its own. Out of touch with the changes that had taken place in the ghettos, the Columbia administrators and Trustees could not understand that now paternalistic liberalism was no longer wanted—indeed, was spat upon—by the Harlem community. There has often been speculation that if the gym had been built in the simpler days of the early sixties it would have gone up with no problems. But whether those who ran Columbia University realized it or not, ideas that could have worked in 1960 were to prove disastrous in 1968.

Wednesday evening, Dean Platt proposed to the President that the administration draw up a separate offer to the students in Hamilton Hall. "We were all a lot more sympathetic with the black students than with the white students," Platt later recalled. There were other reasons for settling the Hamilton situation first. There remained the fear that failure to reach a diplomatic solution with the students in Hamilton might bring on an invasion from Harlem. In addition, many expressed the belief that getting the blacks out of Hamilton would "break the back of the situation" and clear the way for an early end to the Low Library sit-in.

Late that evening, having worked out an offer with Kirk, Platt carried the following letter into Hamilton:

To the Columbia University Students in Hamilton Hall:
This is to state that the disciplinary action taken against the students presently occupying Hamilton Hall will be disciplinary probation for the academic year 1968–69 and the remainder of the present academic year, if you leave by 10 P.M. tonight and, when leaving the building, supply your name by signature. Criminal charges will not be pressed if the above conditions are met.

In view of the action taken by the Columbia College faculty, the President plans to ask the chairman of the Trustees, to call a special meeting of the board at the earliest practicable time to consider the faculty recommendations concerning the gymnasium.

(signed)/Alexander Platt/Associate Dean/Columbia College

From the black students' point of view, the administration proposal seemed totally inadequate. Nothing definite was offered about the gym, amnesty from University discipline was not granted. The letter was signed only by an associate dean of the College, whose word would not bind the President to any formal commitment. Furthermore, the students believed that if they accepted disciplinary probation the Students' Afro-American Society would come to an end, since students on probation are not permitted to take part in extra-curricular activities. However, a careful rereading by Platt of the regulations on probation, which had been revised at the start of the academic year, resolved at least the last objection. Students on probation are forbidden participation in *College* extra-curricular activities, and SAS was a *University* activity.[4] This distinction was clarified in a later message to the students.

Some of the community spokesmen who were in Hamilton urged the students to accept the first offer sent them by the administration. Others, however, including Percy Sutton, had told the steering committee that afternoon that they would have Harlem behind them if they stayed and had reminded the students of what their brothers were struggling for in Orangeburg, Selma, Birmingham and throughout the nation.

Their demands had not been met; they had support from Harlem. Still a third factor led the black students to suspect that they had more to win by holding out: the suspicion that the faculty and administration were buckling. This had been suggested earlier by the College faculty resolutions which Professor Wallerstein had shown to the demonstrators

[4] It is not surprising that this distinction was not common knowledge. In addition to the fact that probation regulations were revised in September, neither the 1967–68 official College Bulletin nor the Student Handbook made any mention that disciplinary probation even exists at Columbia.

earlier that evening. The students knew they had faculty support on the gym, and the fact that the administration had promised them that there would be no criminal prosecution led them to believe that their position might improve still more with time.

With the rain continuing into the night, the Harlem rally which CORE had planned to hold on the edge of campus was canceled. The continuing downpour drenched the possibility of violence that had persisted throughout the day, and led one student to comment as he gazed at the deserted, dripping campus, "I knew Grayson Kirk had good connections, but I didn't know he could control the weather." The police, who had moved off the campus early in the afternoon, returned around nine and encircled Low, now crowded with protesters. Students were permitted to leave Kirk's office but could enter only by braving the slippery ledges and gratings at the rear of the building and edging around to the student-controlled windows. Several made it in this way Wednesday night. Outside Hamilton a line of professors stood guard to insure that no violence took place. One professor suggested that they wear white armbands to identify themselves as faculty members. The practice was adopted. Meanwhile, just off campus, units of the Tactical Patrol Force massed on alert.

An SDS rally was held that night in Wollman Auditorium in Ferris Booth Hall. Wollman was kept open throughout the crisis and served as a meeting hall for all sides. A crowd of more than eight hundred radical and moderate students filled the auditorium. The first speaker was Paul Rockwell, editor and sole author of a small radical paper, *Gadfly*, published irregularly at Columbia. Rockwell, who earlier in the academic year had exposed a contract the University held with the Central Intelligence Agency, now tried to justify SDS's actions in terms of what he called "reciprocity." The fiery, blond-haired radical admitted that many students felt a minority of strikers had interfered in their lives by occupying classroom buildings, but he insisted that the real "interference" began with coercive actions by a minority of Trustees who had interfered in the lives of people in Vietnam and Harlem. Since, he argued, the administration had been preventing due process at Columbia by its unwillingness to reply to petitions, by its refusal to seek consent for projects like the gym, by its secrecy on matters like IDA, by the intimidation it exercised through the power of private discipline, the administration had "forced us to act coercively." "Yes, we are being coercive," he declared. "But can we stop horrors by speech alone?"

After Rockwell finished the audience heard reports on the status of the demonstrations. Ted Gold explained that the reason for going into Low was that the whites and blacks in Hamilton had agreed that their position would be stronger if they had two fronts—an explanation that was plausible but at variance with the facts.

The meeting was opened to political discussion. A conservative from the audience approached the microphone, glowered at the radicals, and began an angry attack on left-wing politics. He was interrupted repeatedly by sarcastic applause.

"Back home you're in the minority," the conservative warned. The audience laughed.

A more moderate student followed him and sought to answer Rockwell's reciprocity argument. "I can't see an end to coercion," he said. "I could organize counter-coercion. But I don't want to do that; the only solution is that coercion be limited."

In a room in Ferris Booth above Wollman Auditorium a group of student leaders of varying ideologies was listening to Vice President Warren Goodell. Presenting the administration's views on the situation, he reported that now the students in Hamilton were definitely in control of the building and "behaving responsibly." He contrasted the Hamilton scene with the situation in Low where, he said, the offices had been "messed up," and vandalized by students. "Our job is to get the group [in Hamilton] out by sunrise," Goodell said, explaining that a contingent of Harlem militants was expected before noon. As for Low, "the property damage there we consider to be quite serious. We have no intention of knuckling under. There will be no complete amnesty for the students involved."

Strike leaders were soon informed of Goodell's speech and concluded that the administration was seeking a separate settlement with the blacks. The attempt, of course, had already been made and rejected. Paterson, Sutton and Rangel had been sent to Hamilton by the administration as intermediaries but had left as partisans. Instead of returning to report to Kirk and Truman on prospects for settlement, Sutton had gone to the headquarters of Harlem CORE, where he announced his opposition to the policies of the Columbia administrators. Truman later accused Sutton of "selling out" the administration.

By midnight most of the periphery of the campus was lined by New York City police. Throughout the night faculty members took shifts standing in front of Hamilton, maintaining a token line to discourage outbreaks of violence between students. In Avery Hall architecture students had been working late as they often did. Many were sympathetic with the demonstrations, and when, at 1 A.M., the administration tried to close the building, the students refused to leave. Although the doors remained open and no barricades were constructed, the building became a "Liberated Zone" held by students. Many of the hundred students inside Avery were apolitical compared with the members of SDS and SAS; their antagonism toward the University stemmed in large measure from Columbia's long tradition of mediocre architecture and general insensitivity to its urban environment. The faculty and student body of the School of Architecture had passed a resolution earlier in the year condemning the University's gym plans. The group in Avery accepted the strike's six demands and passed further resolutions of their own, demanding that the University develop policy "that does not overrun adjacent areas," make an effort to recruit more Negro and Puerto Rican students and revise its decision-making structure to allow greater community and student participation. They conducted a "design-in" which produced plans for a new gymnasium to be built on land already owned by Columbia.

In Low students had acted on Rudd's earlier proposal and recaptured Kirk's private office, including the strategic bathroom, by unscrewing the hinges on the thick wooden door. Tony Papert was running a meeting in an adjacent office to discuss whether or not to build barricades. It was conducted in the typical style of SDS participatory democracy: "All right," Papert would say, "now we've heard some people speak in favor of barricading. Would someone like to say something against barricading?" giving priority to those who had not spoken before. The discussion was predicated on the assumption that the administration and police had placed spies in their midst and would thus be aware of all their plenary decisions. One student, who argued in favor of the measure, pointed out that the barricades did not have to be massive affairs, just formidable enough to convince the police and administration that some minimal quantum of violence would have to be employed to eject the demonstrators. This, it was felt, would make a bust less likely than if the administration knew no barricades would be built. Another demonstrator suggested that they take the rare Korean vases on display in the rotunda and place them in front of all doors and windows to discourage intrusion by police. Neither proposal was approved that night.

An ancient radio tuned to WKCR, the campus radio station, provided the group with some of its information about the outside world. Runners periodically entered with news of such events as the mass meeting taking place in Wollman. Rudd arrived with a personal note of support and good wishes from black militant leader H. Rap Brown. It had become clear that Rudd's angry afternoon resignation had been caused by fatigue, and he was now welcomed back warmly by the group in Low. Rumors circulated through the Presidential suite that a "fourth front" was about to be opened now that Hamilton, Low and Avery were secure. Throughout the night discussion continued until only a small core of ideologues remained awake. By 2 A.M. three large offices, including Kirk's private quarters, were fully occupied by sleeping students.

In response to the complaints of the students in Hamilton regarding Platt's first offer—that it was signed only by Platt, left the future of SAS in doubt, was equivocal on the gym—the administration sent a second letter shortly after midnight. This time President Kirk's signature was affixed to the bottom. Kirk spelled out the faculty resolution on the suspension of gym construction and said that he would "recommend [it] favorably" to the Trustees. This was considered a purely sophistical change by the blacks, since the Trustees could easily "consider" the resolution and then reject it. As in the first offer, nothing concrete was offered on the gym. Instead of disciplinary probation, the administration letter now offered "disciplinary warning" which is almost identical to probation.[5] "The second letter was really no different from the first," Platt later said, "but just spelled out the first more carefully, and carried Kirk's signature." Perhaps it was the administration's own press release the next day which best described what the President had offered the blacks on the gym:

> [President Kirk] indicated that, as requested by the Columbia College faculty, he would ask the chairman of the Columbia Trustees to *consider* the College faculty's recommendation that the Trustees *consider* suspending construction of the gymnasium and *consider* inviting the Mayor to designate a group to *meet with* the University on the gymnasium question. [Italics added]

The Hamilton students turned down the second offer as they had the first, though this time they did not bother to send a reply.

The administration also made an attempt to establish contact with the students in Low during the first hours of Thursday. A delegation including Dean Fraenkel, an opponent of the demonstration, and Warner Schilling, a conservative government professor who favored swift action against the students, entered the "occupied" sector of Low to reason with the protesters. After what they considered the fruitless intrusion of Professor Ranum that morning, the Low demonstrators established a policy that outsiders would be permitted to speak only with three student "negotiators," and not with the entire assembly of students. Fraenkel and the others met with Rudd, Papert and Robbie Roth at the top of the stairwell between the administration headquarters and the student-controlled part of the building. Massive double oak doors separated the negotiators from the students inside.

After some preliminary sparring, when it became apparent that neither group had anything significantly new to offer, Dean Fraenkel seized upon an argument which he evidently hoped would make Rudd sacrifice himself for his cause. The dean apparently assumed that Rudd was placing great emphasis on amnesty only because he was concerned

---

[5] The only difference is that students on warning can participate in all extracurricular activities, while students on probation cannot. Each disciplinary status can lead to suspension for future infractions.

with his own future. Fraenkel explained to the SDS leader that he had no right to drag his organization down with him. Rudd had to act as a true leader, the dean declared, not as a student facing dismissal. In what may have been an effort to quash the entire strike by destroying Rudd's last hope of reinstatement, Fraenkel informed him flatly, "You know, Mr. Rudd, that no matter what you do, you're going to be expelled from this University." This dialogue did not result in a *rapprochement.*

At 2 A.M. a group of radical graduate students, led by an instructor in the economics department, let themselves into Fayerweather Hall with their keys and posted guards at the doors. The fourth front was now opened. In Low students affixed a tag marked "OURS" to another building on Kirk's scale model of the University.

Thursday morning a crowd of about 150 students gathered in front of the steps leading to Fayerweather, some of them demanding entry into the building for their regular morning classes. Mixed in the crowd were partisans of both sides of the conflict and spectators; on the steps sat the demonstrators who had taken the building during the night and their sympathizers. Students and faculty members pounded on the doors and tried to force their way in, but could not get through the barricades. The crowd grew to three hundred and, amid loud shouting, several professors made their way to the entrance and spoke to the group through a bullhorn. Amitai Etzioni, an eminent sociologist, expressed his sympathy with the goals of the strike but cautioned, "The disruption of the educational process goes against what you are after." This was challenged by a radical young member of the French department, Richard Greeman, who countered, "There can be no education and no thought divorced from action."

About seventy-five members of the faculty gathered informally in the lounge of Philosophy Hall Thursday morning to discuss the new developments. Vice Dean Thomas Colahan chaired the meeting. Around ten, psychologist Eugene Galanter asked if anyone had heard from Kirk or Truman about the tripartite body which the College faculty had proposed the day before at their meeting in Havemeyer. No one had. Galanter then suggested that a faculty committee of three men be formed immediately to create the commission and that this organizing committee secure approval from the central administration at once. He argued that such a group of faculty would relieve the administration of the effort of finding names for the commission at a time when it was burdened with many other responsibilities. Lionel Trilling supported

Galanter's proposal, and it was suggested that Trilling, Galanter and Carl Hovde,[6] a quiet and well-liked English professor, be chosen as the members of the three-man group to set up the tripartite commission. The delegation was approved by the group in Philosophy, and at noon President Kirk announced that he had named the three professors "to recommend to me the structure, the personnel, and the appropriate procedures for the tripartite commission."

But Thursday afternoon the conservatives on campus had begun to react to the radicals' actions. At 1:30, five hundred counter-demonstrators—many of them athletes—met in University Gymnasium. Jim Quattrocchi, a junior on the wrestling team, suggested that they form a line in front of Hamilton and "not let anyone or anything get in or out." He said he was "sick" of SDS's tactics. "It's just as much our campus as theirs. If this is a barbaric society, it is survival of the fittest, and we are the fittest."

Jack Rohan, who had coached Columbia's basketball team to national prominence that winter, tried to calm the athletes. "I am a little ashamed to see that you are acting like the 'heavies,'" he said. Asking the students to have faith in law and order, Rohan declared, "If you are willing to be a part of mob violence, I take great pity on you and this University. I know you are impatient and so am I . . . but the major issue is whether you want to become part of a situation which would become anarchic." Dean Coleman also spoke to the group in the gym, promising them some definitive action by the evening.

After lunch, Professor of Public Law and Government Alan Westin stopped near St. Paul's Chapel to talk with David Rothman and Robert Fogelson, the two young history professors. Westin, who teaches an undergraduate course on the Supreme Court, was well-liked by the few students who knew him. Distant from college affairs, he had spent most of his time writing and working at the Center for Research in Civil Liberties, which he had helped found. He was respected by his colleagues for his cool, deliberate style and was a close friend of David Truman. Not fully aware of recent developments in the demonstrations, Westin fired questions at Rothman and Fogelson. He began to sense that the faculty should perhaps be taking a more active role in the crisis and asked his colleagues what they had done to organize for such a role. They told him that the President and vice president were conducting a press conference—their first public appearance since the crisis began—

---

[6] Professor Hovde was named dean of Columbia College in mid-July, 1968. He succeeded Henry Coleman, who had served as acting dean since July 1967, and David Truman, who was dean from 1962 to June 1967.

but that no faculty members had been invited to observe. At Westin's suggestion they went to Low and secured permission from Vice President Goodell to attend the conference.

Surrounded by statues of Buddha and bodhisattvas in the Faculty Room of Low Library, Kirk told reporters:

> The University is committed to maintaining order on the campus. We insist that there be respect for the rules and conditions that make University life possible. We have exercised great restraint in the use of police and security forces, because at almost all costs, we wish to avoid physical confrontation. We have constantly tried to communicate with those students who have seized the buildings, and as late as this morning, contact was made with all of the protesting groups, but with no success. We are prepared to talk with the protesting groups, but disciplinary action will have to be taken against those students who flagrantly violated University rules. The students have had ample opportunity to leave the buildings and to engage in *lawful* protest if they so desire.

"We cannot give in on amnesty," Truman said. "This goes far beyond this University." Asked about the gym Kirk replied, "Contract obliges us to continue construction."

Professor Westin was disturbed by the hard-line approach he heard. "It was a disconcerting press conference," he said later, "because the President and vice president took a very strong position—a 'We have no alternative but to turn to law and order' type of presentation." At the close of the conference Westin turned to Vice President Goodell and asked whether it would be possible for Truman to meet with a group of faculty in Philosophy Hall. Westin wanted Truman to discuss the administration's policy with them and, as Westin later phrased it, "to share with us why he felt there was no possibility of give on these issues, and why he seemed to be heading toward such a climax." Goodell said he would try to arrange the meeting, and Westin left Low to gather together as many professors as possible.

After the press conference Truman was told that the demonstrators upstairs in Low wanted to speak to him. He climbed the marble staircase connecting the first floor of Low to the student-controlled sector and knocked briskly on the locked oak doors leading to the hallway of the Presidential suite. "I'm here to speak to Mark Rudd," Truman told a demonstrator who came to the door. Greeted by an inquisitive grin, the vice president explained, "I was told someone here wants to talk with me."

"I don't think so," the student replied, "but I'll go and check." Moments later, he returned with Rudd and several other strikers.

"You have something to say to me?" Truman asked.

"No," Rudd replied. "Did you come here to tell us something?"

"No," said Truman, visibly annoyed. "I was told . . ." The group walked into a corner of the hallway, exchanged brief intransigencies and then the vice president departed.

When Truman arrived in Philosophy ten minutes later more than one hundred faculty members were there to hear him. He recapitulated the development of the crisis, adding at the end in an unsteady voice, "I just don't know how much longer this situation can go on." He maintained that the gym was not a real issue and that the University could not afford to stop construction because it would cost six million dollars to break the contracts. Westin told the vice president that as a lawyer, he could not believe that the contracts could not be severed for less. Truman insisted that this would be impossible.

"Is there anything the faculty can do?" Professor Rothman asked.

"Nothing," Truman answered.

After twenty minutes Truman cut off discussion, saying he was already late for another meeting in Low and that the faculty would have to excuse him. He left the group, probably without realizing that he had greatly alienated many former colleagues, some of whom later said that he had appeared "uncommunicative," "uncompromising," and unable to meet the crisis. Robert Belknap, a professor of Russian who was present during Truman's appearance, later said:

> It was what he didn't say that bothered us. He hadn't said that negotiations were proceeding. He hadn't drawn up a statement saying what could or could not be done. He hadn't appointed a faculty group to advise him. . . . He lost his cool."

Truman had personally raised a substantial part of the five million dollars already collected for the new gym. It had been a College-oriented project, and as dean of the College he had long been one of its key supporters. On the other hand, he had agreed in private that University affiliation with IDA should be terminated but felt unable to say so in public. Known for his willingness to talk to students and faculty members during his years as dean, Truman now was coming to be considered unreachable and unresponsive by both groups. It was common knowledge that Truman was being groomed for the presidency of the University and would probably replace Kirk before the end of 1969. And now all of that seemed endangered.

After Truman's exit, Westin rose and told the group that it was precisely because they had so much admiration for Truman that they were leaving the affair in his hands and were not intervening. There was a tone of subtle defiance in his voice; the remark was plainly a challenge to the group to take the initiative. Professors who were getting up to leave sat down. Westin later described what happened next:

> Professor Metzger said, "That is exactly right. We have business to do here. I am going to ask Professor Westin if he will come forth and take charge. It is not enough to be talked to by the administration. We ought to do something as a faculty." There you have the birth moment of the Ad Hoc Faculty Group.

The group had no formal organization or authority. It emerged Thursday afternoon as an "association of concerned faculty," as Professor Wallerstein described it. Lacking any constitutional means to influence decisions by the administration, its first move was directed to the students. All its power rested on the prestige of its members, among whom would number some of Columbia's most formidable professors. While Trilling, Galanter and Hovde met upstairs seeking names for the tripartite commission, the Ad Hoc Group continued meeting in the lounge, seeking a course of action which could be adopted immediately to ease the increasingly desperate situation on campus. They were quite concerned over a march from Harlem to Columbia planned for that evening by militants of the United Black Front. Professor Fogelson, an authority on urban riots, suggested that it was time for the faculty members to put themselves on the line and take a risk in order to save the University from chaos. He brought forth the notion that professors would have to interpose themselves between their students and the administration and in this way shift the burden of the demonstrators' goals onto their own shoulders. After considerable discussion, a resolution was drafted:

> We, the undersigned members of the Columbia University faculty and teaching staff, make the following proposal to resolve the present crisis:
> (1.) We request the Trustees to implement the immediate cessation of excavation on the gymnasium site, by telephone vote if necessary.
> (2.) We request the administration to delegate all disciplinary power on matters related to the present crisis to the tripartite committee, consisting of students, faculty, and administration.
> (3.) We request the students to evacuate all buildings now, and we pledge our faith and influence towards a solution. Should the students be willing to evacuate the buildings, we will not meet classes until the crisis is resolved along the above lines.
> (4.) Until this crisis is settled, we will stand before the occupied buildings to prevent forcible entry by police or others.

The idea originally proposed by Fogelson—that the faculty strike if necessary—was now extended to what would become known as the "Doctrine of Interposition": the professors would interpose themselves between the police and students. Professor David Rothman, who was active in the drafting of the resolution, later remarked:

> This was a real moment of tension. We understood that when we were signing this document we were really doing something. It was a moment when we saw ourselves taking a truly independent position, and that was not done lightly. Given the nature of the administration and the relation we all had to Truman, this was not easily done. There was an understanding, however, that the time had come for the faculty to act.

After the four resolutions were passed and mimeographed at about 7 P.M., a fifth was put forth by Professor of Philosophy Sidney Morgenbesser. It passed with only one dissenting vote, though it later faded from view. It read:

> (5.) No matter what has happened, we consider these students members of our community. We do not contemplate their being dismissed and we would oppose violently any such action.

The resolutions passed by the Ad Hoc Group were not representative of the sentiments of the faculty as a whole. The professors in Philosophy—including many junior faculty members—were primarily those who were discontented with the way the administration was handling the situation and preferred a more liberal approach. While many conservative professors attended the meetings of the Ad Hoc Group, most of them were content to let Truman and Kirk handle the crisis as they saw fit. Because it was a comparatively liberal coalition, members of the Ad Hoc Group felt that they might stand the best chance of gaining acceptance with the striking students.

Their position determined, delegations of professors fanned out to each of the occupied buildings to convince the students to vacate and let the faculty use its influence to satisfy their demands. By 7:30 one hundred and fifty professors had signed the Ad Hoc Group's statement; eventually three hundred did so. Others, who felt that a faculty strike would not at that point be appropriate, signed a pledge to coöperate with the group.

Professors Westin and Wallerstein took the resolutions to Hamilton. Westin later recounted their experience:

> We sat down and met with four members of the steering committee. They conducted themselves, I would say, with tremendous self-control, and skill and professionalism. I would have a great deal of

confidence if they could represent us in Paris [at Vietnam peace talks] or anywhere else. . . . We showed them the four points and said, "We want you to know that we have come into existence and we want to know whether these can be the basis for a solution." They said, "Well, our procedure is that we will ask you questions, but anything you come in and say to us we will have to clear and take up with our full membership." They asked us a few more questions about how many people were in Philosophy Hall and who the leaders were and then we left.

Three professors sympathetic with the objectives of the demonstration—Peter Haidu, George Collins and Terence Hopkins—went into Low early Thursday evening with the Ad Hoc Group's proposals. Like the administration delegation which had entered Low early that day, they were not allowed to speak with the entire group inside. The student negotiators, now including Juan Gonzalez instead of Rudd, listened to the proposal, brought it in to the strikers, and returned with a rejection after twenty minutes. Ted Gold later explained the attitude of the students toward the Ad Hoc Group:

They were demanding complete abdication of our position, and we were talking in terms of their joining us. We were miles apart. But we didn't want to break off discussion. We were told that they were a more "liberal" faculty group. We said, "All right, if you're on our side, then take a position in favor of amnesty and the other six demands." Those s.o.b.'s said that we should be more reasonable. We would ask them, "What do you think about amnesty?" and they would refuse to give their own positions, and would only say, "It would be absolutely impossible to get the administration to agree to it."

Another crucial encounter between the Ad Hoc Group representatives and the students took place in Fayerweather Hall. Jeffry Kaplow, a left-wing history professor, and Leopold Haimson, an expert on the Russian Revolution, pleaded for acceptance of the proposals before a group of 170 who filled the main lounge on the ground floor. Rudd and other SDS leaders had come in; they moved that the discussion be divided into two parts. During the first, the two professors would plead their case; during the second, there would be a debate from which the faculty members would be excluded. It was a procedural point of little inherent importance. The main objective was to see whether the SDS leaders could command a majority in Fayerweather. After lengthy debate, they did, but only narrowly—the vote was eighty-five in favor of dividing the discussion, eighty-two against. The closeness of the vote foreshadowed difficulties the strike leadership would have with the liberal, pro-faculty graduate student group which held Fayerweather.

Kaplow read the strikers the five resolutions. "This is the maximum you'll get," he said. "It's not enough in the long run, but in the short run it may have to do. There's been a significant change in the attitude of the faculty. Yesterday [at the Havemeyer meeting] I could have retched. It's a damn sight better now. But just remember how far you can push people like David Truman."

SDS Vice Chairman Nick Freudenberg disparaged the slight gains that would come from accepting such a settlement and explained that the strike was being fought over the larger question of "how this community should be run." Paul Rockwell, standing opposite Kaplow on the other side of the room, implored the students to stay in the building. "We're the ones who are giving power to the faculty," he said.

Kaplow took up the argument. "We do not have power. You and us, we are trying to get power in a system where we've never had any." "Why don't you support the six demands?" someone asked. "Look," Kaplow answered, "I and twenty others will support you no matter what decision you make here. We will not stop you from reoccupying the buildings. If you are betrayed, I will join you." The group decided not to accept or reject the proposal, but instead issued a statement to the faculty:

> We appreciate the faculty resolution. However, we will not leave the building under the present conditions. We will leave the building when the University grants our six demands as stated. We thank the faculty for their activities so far, but suggest that the best way they could help arrive at a solution to this crisis would be to support our demands in toto.

# 5

## Dick Greeman's Bloody Nose

WITH THE STUDENTS' REJECTION of the Ad Hoc Faculty proposals, settlement of the crisis by peaceful means receded further into the realm of improbability. The professors met again in Philosophy Hall Thursday evening to survey the situation and decide what action to take next. It was clear to them that the patience of the athletes, administrators and Harlem militants was giving out. Vigilante assaults or police action now seemed certain, and many of the faculty members sitting in Philosophy Lounge feared that if they could not work out a solution on paper, others might work one out by force.

Alan Westin chaired the meeting of about two hundred professors. The group heard reports from people who had been "in the field" working at varying approaches to solution of the crisis. Response to the Ad Hoc Faculty proposals had been negative in all the student-held buildings. Low, Fayerweather and Avery had refused to accept the proposals as a resolution to the conflict. Hamilton had issued a statement reaffirming their demands, but thanking the faculty for its positive efforts.

With the right-wing students who had met that afternoon in the gym now on the verge of becoming as volatile as the leftists, the faculty invited a representative of the conservatives to speak to them. He announced that students opposed to the demonstrations had formed a new group, the Majority Coalition, and had collected the signatures of 1,700 students.[1] He deplored the tactics of the protesters, called for their punishment, and pointed out that while his group would support

---

[1] The group did not, however, comprise a majority of Columbia students any more than did SDS. Their choice of name seems to have been inspired more by political than numerical considerations.

the decision of the faculty, he could not rule out the possibility of violence among students if the current situation were allowed to continue.

SDS spokesman Dave Gilbert then addressed the faculty. In a cogent and passionate speech, Gilbert insisted that the students would not abandon their six demands.[2] No one denies that SDS violated University rules, he said, but it was the fault of the administration and faculty that the students had to resort to such tactics. "We are anxious to avoid violence," Gilbert said. "It's a shame we had to go as far as we did. We distrust the administration; we must hold out for amnesty. If we don't demand amnesty, then we accept the arbitrary power of the University before we begin negotiations." He argued that it was contradictory for the faculty to deplore the students' tactics if those tactics were the only means to secure the very democratic processes that would make such tactics unnecessary. Referring to offers made by negotiators from the Ad Hoc Group, Gilbert pleaded with the faculty to "make no more promises that cannot be kept." Throughout his speech messengers ran into the faculty meeting to bring news of developments outside. The atmosphere was hectic, and more than once Gilbert had to raise his hands to quiet the group, urging, "Cool it, please, people." He spoke to the professors calmly and persuasively, as an equal, and was well received. About 8:30 a runner came into Philosophy Lounge to report on a rally of angry Harlem blacks, taking place on the edge of campus.

Speakers representing most of the ghetto's activist organizations—the Mau Mau Society, CORE, SNCC, the United Black Front, the Peace and Freedom Party—were addressing a crowd of forty Harlem residents and nearly a thousand white Columbia students. The rally was confined to the narrow strip of sidewalk outside Columbia's new wrought-iron gates at the entrance to College Walk, and the participants spoke from the roof of a car parked on Broadway, facing the campus. A row of students opposed to the strike, including a large number of athletes, had lined up inside the gates and now stood guarding the entrance.

Charles 37X Kenyatta, a middle-aged militant wearing a riot helmet with the words "Mau Mau" emblazoned in gold on it, yelled over a

---

[2] As indicated earlier, the six demands, which were formulated Tuesday, and remained fairly constant throughout the occupations, were:
 1. No discipline for the IDA Six or participants in current demonstrations;
 2. An end to gym construction;
 3. No prosecution of students arrested at earlier anti-gym demonstrations;
 4. An end to all University ties with IDA;
 5. Dropping of Kirk's edict banning indoor demonstrations;
 6. A revision of disciplinary procedures to institute open hearings and due process with judgment by a tripartite committee of students, faculty and administration.

bullhorn that the rally had been called "to express support for those students who have guts enough to do something about this University." Omar Ahmed, a tall muscular member of the United Black Front and vice chairman of the National Conference on Black Power, told the crowd that Harlem was waking up and would soon be a force that would have to be contended with. The predominantly white crowd reacted sometimes with light applause, sometimes with roars of approval as the black rhetoric flowed over them. They heard that masses would swarm up the hill from Harlem to burn Columbia to the ground, they heard what would happen to Grayson Kirk and all the other honkies if they did not mend their ways. One speaker, pointing his finger at the cluster of booing athletes at the gates, warned, "If one hair on any black student is hurt, then we'll come in here and wipe out every damn jock."

As the rally ended, someone got up onto the car's roof and announced that the Harlem participants in the rally intended to walk across the campus to the gymnasium construction site. The speakers moved through the audience toward the gates, blocked by the conservative students who had heckled them earlier. A vanguard of blacks formed and launched itself into the line of athletes. The students shoved back. The crowds behind each group began to push, and the entire mass swayed back and forth precariously. A few behind the gates chanted, "Hold that line! Hold that line!" Fifteen policemen, who had been patrolling the rally, made their way along the crowded sidewalk to the gates and formed a wedge, the blacks behind them. The opposing line opened at the sight of uniforms, and both police and blacks were propelled onto the campus. As the police dissolved into the crowd, minor skirmishes broke out between counter-demonstrators and members of the black contingent. Several punches were thrown, but before the situation could get worse, Dean Coleman—a man the athletes respected and regarded as an ally—appeared on College Walk with a bullhorn. "COOL IT!" he yelled to the counter-demonstrators, and through their midst cleared a path for the blacks. Several professors urged the athletes to move back, and they complied. Sociologist Terence Hopkins later noted that this was the last time he felt he could command respect simply because he was a faculty member—"there was still some deference left at that point." With Coleman leading them part of the way, about thirty-five Harlem blacks marched straight across College Walk. A few entered Hamilton Hall, though most continued off campus through the Amsterdam Avenue gate and on to the gym site. There they made a few more speeches and went home.

The march was a victory of sorts for the militants and succeeded in releasing—for them—a great deal of the tension that had built up over Columbia. City officials, who worked closely with Kenyatta, knew that despite the machete he often waved at rallies, he would not begin any dangerously violent demonstration. As one professor observed:

> Both Kenyatta and the police knew nothing would happen as a result of their march across campus. They play a very dangerous game: the tension builds up, then Kenyatta arranges a symbolic victory through his contacts in the police department. This helps his position in the movement and prevents the outbreak of any really serious trouble.

The incident enraged and confused the counter-demonstrators. At a meeting in the gym earlier that day Dean Coleman had promised them that the radical takeover had gone as far as it would go, and that "definitive action" would be taken by the administration that evening. Night had fallen, and now the only definitive action they had seen had been directed by the police and the dean against the athletes themselves. After the disheartening rebuffs and failures at the campus gate the athletes separated. But they were not resigned to defeat. It was clear to them, much as it had been clear to SDS, that the forces of authority—the dean, the police—were unable to run things properly. And, as the radical students had done earlier, the athletes decided to do something about it themselves. About 10:30 knots of athletes began congregating on College Walk. As they talked their determination grew; the situation would have to be resolved tonight. A few tried to organize a Sundial rally but failed. They were joined by other conservative students whose disgust at the demonstrations—and the demonstrators—was great enough to prompt them to violence. Jon Shils, the neatly dressed activist who often served as the demonstrators' liaison with the outside world, went from group to group in the simmering crowd. "What are you going to solve by this?" he begged, as a group of heavyweights surrounded him. Shils urged them not to take matters into their own hands, half yelling at them, half pleading with them. But talk could no longer dissuade them. The crowd streamed up the steps past Low Library and around to the northeast corner of the campus. They stopped at Fayerweather Hall and tried to force their way into the barricaded building, threatening to drag the demonstrators out limb by limb.

The shouting that welled up from Fayerweather penetrated into the Ad Hoc Faculty meeting in nearby Philosophy. A student from inside the occupied building, panting, came running into the lounge to inform the group that Fayerweather was under siege. Several faculty members rushed outside, joining colleagues who had been with the onslaught since its beginnings on College Walk. The faculty members now had yet another peacekeeping function; in addition to interposing themselves between the administration and students, or between police and students, they now had to avert violence between students and students. The professors pushed their way to the center of the action, where athletes were trying to break through Fayerweather's north doors.

One faculty member positioned himself on the top step, facing the attack. "I am Seymour Melman," he shouted in a loud but controlled voice. "Some of you know me. *Do not take the law into your own hands.* Trust the faculty. One act of violence is not an answer to another." The pushing had stopped, and other professors began to speak. "Please, please go back," another yelled. "This kind of action can do nothing but destroy this University." The athletes were now drawn into a dialogue with the faculty members.

"Why don't you tell *them* to stop?" a student yelled from the crowd, pointing to the occupied building. "The dean promised us that we'd have 'definitive action' tonight!" shouted another, almost in tears. "They're destroying my University," one shrieked. Melman tried to answer the conservatives' complaints, assuring them that the faculty and administration were doing everything they could to solve the crisis. The situation somewhat defused, Melman tried a humorous approach. "We ask you to let us handle this," he said. "I know sometimes we seem out of touch—we publish, and you perish."

A student from the crowd took up the repartee. "You've got to get those students out of Hamilton," he shouted. "They've been in there so long they're going to get tenure!"

"No they won't," Professor Westin shot back. "They haven't published yet."

"What do you mean? They're putting out a new leaflet every hour!"

Robert Belknap, the quiet, gaunt professor of Russian, made his way onto a ledge overhanging the stoop where the main assault began. Standing in the light of a lamp near the entrance, he introduced himself, "I'm the head of the Humanities-A program here. All of you have taken or will have to take that course while you are at Columbia." Belknap drew from some of the books read in the Western Literature course, trying to show the angry students outside that the problems they faced were not unique, and that rational discourse is the best way of handling conflict. He did not try to shout down the yelling students, but they soon quieted, straining to hear what he was saying.

Sidney Morgenbesser, an eminent professor whose convoluted patterns of speech had perplexed hundreds of philosophy students, spoke next. As he rambled on about the current problem and tried to convince the crowd of the faculty's good intentions a contingent of unappeased athletes moved around the side of the building to a low, open window. By the time the professors caught up with the crowd one massive sophomore, a second-string tackle on the football team, had wedged himself on the sill, propping the window open with his shoulder. He refused to budge. About eight professors and Dean Colahan ranged themselves on the chest-high ledge surrounding the building and continued to address the crowd, begging them not to surge into the building through the half-open window before them. Philosophy Professor Richard Kuhns was most successful in persuading the counter-demonstrators that violence was not the proper way of resolving problems. "SDS at least has something to propose," he challenged. "What are your ideas?" A student in the crowd protested that he liked things fine the way they were.

One counter-demonstrator now moved through the darkness along the ledge to the east face of the building, out over Amsterdam Avenue, twenty feet below. Students inside Fayerweather were preparing defenses. One spectator later observed:

> That would have done it. With those jocks climbing along the ledge over Amsterdam and trying to force their way into the windows, if one of the people inside the building had resisted and pushed that guy back and he had fallen, you would have seen the bloodiest chapter in Columbia history.

With the action focused on the north face of Fayerweather, desperate faculty members continued their efforts to draw the angry conservatives into dialogue. Finally the athletes were persuaded to send representatives to the Ad Hoc meeting. A small delegation left for Philosophy Lounge to address the professors. The invasion had been turned back.

The Ad Hoc Faculty meeting reconvened in the lounge, now packed with about 250 professors, as students outside peered in through the dirty windows. Professor Morgenbesser introduced Paul Vilardi, a College senior and leader of the Majority Coalition. "We've been asked to cool it," the dark, square-jawed former outfielder on the baseball team told the group. "And we're prepared to cool it. We didn't want them [the Harlem demonstrators] on our campus because they don't belong here. . . . We like the way things are. When we want change, there is an orderly process for getting it. . . . We don't want amnesty for them [the demonstrators]. These people are turning into animals. . . . If you can't stop this, we won't send our children here, there won't be any Senior Fund." By this time many faculty members, unhappy to have to hear out anyone at fist-point, were beginning to take exception to Vilardi's tone. His colleague, Mark Furey, calmed them somewhat. "We're not threatening anybody," he pointed out. "We want to go to classes—occasionally." Some professors laughed. But by the end of his presentation Furey's words, too, seemed menacing. "I'm done talking," he said. "We're going to *do* something about this."

Professor Schilling rose from his seat in the crowded room and told the conservative students, "If they [SDS] break the rules, they will pay the price. The College faculty has not offered amnesty. I commend you for your patience and ask you to maintain it." Vilardi responded that the faculty must act. "You have to stop their food supply. We were told something was going to happen this evening. Something had better." The radicals had forced the faculty into discussion, and now the conservatives were threatening them into action.

Dean Fraenkel attempted to shift the debate toward more promising areas. "Hamilton Hall negotiations have opened up," he announced reassuringly and inaccurately. The dean went on to report that the administration had turned down the pre-conditions to negotiations presented by students in Low. Pressed by a young faculty member to reveal whether he had indeed told Rudd at the outset of talks that he would definitely be expelled, Fraenkel answered, "It's University policy." Having admitted one diplomatic blunder, he went on to make another. "There is no chance that the President will give up to the faculty sole responsibility for discipline. He will listen to advice, but in this crisis he can give the faculty no power in making decisions." Fraenkel's presentation was a major affront to the professors. With internal conflicts intensifying, Vilardi and the other counter-demonstrators were asked to leave. On his way out he warned, "Those people out there aren't going to cool it much longer."

Vilardi's estimation was correct. As the faculty deliberated, a group of counter-demonstrators was meeting in Wollman Auditorium, demanding to know why they should be expected to "cool it" any longer. They had been frustrated in their attempt to invade Fayerweather Hall and were now talking about taking other, similar actions to end the sit-ins.

"I think we're being used by the administration," declared one bitter student. "I think they've put themselves, because of their own stupidity, into a position where they can't back down without a loss of face. They've got to wait until *we* make a move, until there's an actual threat of violence or until some violence has broken out—before they can have a good excuse to use force. As far as I'm concerned, it's just a matter of getting this thing started. I think it's up to us right now to stop this thing from getting any bigger."

The audience agreed, and several conservative members of the faculty and administration reinforced the counter-demonstrators' zeal. Erwin Glikes, the assistant dean whose Hamilton Hall office was being used as a headquarters by the black students, lauded the athletes for the stand they had made earlier that night during the militants' march across campus. "That little group of people was trying to make Columbia the focus of a race riot," he exclaimed. "But you guys were great. You have been everything that Columbia stands for." James Connor, an assistant professor of government, told the group, "I came here as a jock. Columbia was a way out, a big thing in my life. I know how disappointed you are with what you think the faculty is here. But that group [the Ad Hoc Faculty Group] is not the faculty of Columbia College. It is a self-constituted group. Don't let that upset you. Cool people will come out winners."

Roger Hilsman, a popular government professor, carried on this theme. "The guys who are going to win out in this are the ones with the steady nerves," the former assistant secretary of state told them. "Steady nerves are the thing." Students rose to speak, articulating into a microphone what they had felt so strongly on the steps of Fayerweather. The Ad Hoc Faculty Group was condemned as illegitimate, Kirk and Truman excoriated for their inaction. Speaking of the situation in Hamilton Hall, one athlete said, "I'm not blaming those niggers in there. I'm blaming the administration." There was an uproar over his choice of words, and he apologized to the group.

Many of the counter-demonstrators' observations were more reasoned. In an appeal for law and order one student declared, "What's been begun here in the last three days seems like it's a microcosm of what's going on in America." Other comments were on a different level. Another student told the audience, "We want to get these guys from SDS. I'm sure this is what you want. These guys are the troublemakers. I'd like to see them get it right up the ass." As he had done earlier that day in the gym, basketball coach Jack Rohan urged the students not to use violence—"not to slip into a state of nature, so to speak." His approach was typical of the arguments used by faculty and administration that night: first congratulate the athletes and other counter-demonstrators on their spirit and assure them they were right, then ask them not to take independent action because the University was planning action of its own. Many of the professors spoke as if they did not realize that the first half of such a presentation could easily negate the thrust of the last.

The possibility that the angry counter-demonstrators might soon try to end the strike themselves if nothing were done by the administration was one that bothered Kirk and Truman a great deal. As the meeting in Wollman wore on, the two administrators conferred in Low Library over whether the time had come to resort to police force to end the disturbances. The threat of chaos had been raised twice that day even before the volatile counter-demonstrators' meeting in Wollman: the blacks' march across campus and the storming of Fayerweather had each only narrowly missed touching off violence on campus. The administrators feared that the next incident might be the last.

Truman knew, moreover, that if the police were not used now it would be difficult to use them any time again until the end of the weekend. Police officials had informed him that because of the large antiwar demonstrations scheduled for the coming days they would not want to spare their men on Friday, Saturday or early Sunday to end the demonstration at Columbia. Thus the administration felt an added sense of immediacy about calling in the police Thursday night.

During the Fayerweather incident representatives of the Ad Hoc Group had invited a number of strikers as well as conservatives to speak with them. Rudd, Dave Gilbert, Juan Gonzalez, Lew Cole, Morris Grossner and Anne Hoffman now filed into Philosophy Lounge to address the professors. As Rudd spoke, Miss Hoffman, a tall Barnard girl with long brown hair, stood beside him, a small bulge protruding from her trench coat near her stomach. Few of those at the faculty meeting noticed it and none knew that it was a hacksaw.

Earlier that day strike leaders had decided it would be advisable to take over another building. The quarters in Low were becoming increasingly crowded, and radical junior faculty members had suggested that a convincing show of strength at this point would probably be enough to swing the faculty over to supporting amnesty. Consequently, that afternoon Gonzalez had instructed Miss Hoffman to buy a hacksaw and keep it hidden on her. Returning to the strike headquarters in Ferris Booth Hall, she found him in a high-level conference with Rudd, Cole and a pro-strike junior member of the economics department. She produced the hacksaw and asked what it would be used for.

"We're going to take another building."

"The four of you?"

"No, the five of us."

The expeditionary party rounded up some help on the way to its primary target, Lewisohn Hall, home of Columbia's adult-education School of General Studies. But on reaching Lewisohn the group found the building guarded by General Studies students intent on preventing the administration from locking it up and SDS from taking it over. The strikers gave up and went to Fayerweather, where they watched the abortive siege and were invited to discuss their position with the faculty in Philosophy Hall.

Now, in a quite tone, Rudd outlined the political situation as the strike leadership saw it. There were 120 pro-SDS students in Low, he said, two hundred in Avery, 150 in Fayerweather, and over six hundred at a strike meeting that had been held earlier that night in Wollman Auditorium. He reported that discussions were being held continuously among the demonstrators: "We've been talking about what we want—

the six demands—and what the stakes are. These people are putting themselves on the line. From the blacks in Hamilton to the whites in Low, they're going to hold out until they win." The SDS leader charged that the administration had been trying to work out a separate deal with Hamilton but assured the faculty that the blacks had said "No deals" and would continue to do so. "And even if they leave," Rudd added, "we will stay." The only *real* question, he argued, was whether the University policies under fire were, in the final analysis, unjust. If all accepted channels had been exhausted and yet the policies remained, Rudd asked, "Are we to be disciplined for doing the right thing?"

Gonzalez spoke next and explained that the strikers' actions were "liberating" the faculty. (A similar idea had been voiced earlier Thursday by Professor Marvin Harris who told the Ad Hoc Group that the demonstrators should be thanked for saving the University eleven-million dollars in a burnt-down gymnasium.) The students in the buildings do not want to destroy Columbia, Gonzalez said. "They want something better for this University." Michael Goldman, a young professor in the English department, presented the radicals with a crucial question: Would they accept decisions on their demands that were made by due process but did not coincide with their position? Grossner answered that he was sure decisions arrived at justly would agree with their stand. Rudd, however, said that they could not accept injustice no matter how it was arrived at. Several weeks later he elaborated on this concept:

> Look, suppose we do have *n* number of democratically elected committees. They would be pretty much controlled by tweedy types or people of the right wing. Even if the left wing were to participate the others would probably win, because we're still not the majority. And we will be repressed by these groups. The Left often works by a minority taking vanguard action. The reason it does this is that it thinks it understands things better than everyone else. Now this doesn't mean we don't have a faith in democracy. What it means is that in this society the alternatives don't really exist for people to make up their own minds. Here at Columbia the students have for twenty years been fed the line about law and order and, of course, they're reluctant to take direct action. And, of course, therefore, people who do take direct action, for whatever just reason, will be punished because they've broken the law. Even certain democratic societies make unfair laws.[3]

[3] SDS leaders have also pointed out that even if a decision on the gym were arrived at democratically by the students, faculty and administration of Columbia, it could not legitimately be imposed on the people of Harlem, because the community had not been involved in making that decision, and the issue directly affected *their* lives.

The strikers' presentation before the Ad Hoc Group continued to focus on the immorality of the decisions handed down from Low Library and the "arbitrariness" of the men who made those decisions.

"If arbitrariness is to be found anywhere," Professor Danto charged, "it is in SDS, where it is institutionalized."

"Look, we worked out a strategy," Rudd began. "I'm only new at being a revolutionary, but I'm learning fast."

Professor of Sociology Allan Silver, sensing that the radicals' rhetoric was heading nowhere, confronted them with a critical question: "You have set off a chain of events, and you have to bear the consequences. Doesn't the University have any redeeming features that merit your saving it before that chain leads to disaster?" Rudd hesitated, unable to reply, and Silver pressed on. "The fabric of the University must be preserved . . . and SDS must bear the consequences of its actions." He was enthusiastically applauded. Discomfitted, Grossner asked for time to permit the students to prepare an answer to Silver's question. The sociologist had forced Rudd and the others to define their priorities—to make a choice between the welfare of Columbia and the welfare of the radical movement. Ideologically they would have favored the movement, but such a preference would be difficult to justify in the context of a strike supposedly built to remedy problems within the University. Rudd later commented:

> We were really up tight; we had no answer to this huge question. We had to go and form a policy position on the University. And so we asked for some more time. Besides, we wanted to have a strategy talk on what was happening outside.

Professor of English Howard Schless offered the group the use of his office upstairs in Philosophy. Once inside, Rudd phoned Low and spoke to JJ.

"We're gonna move in a few minutes," JJ said.

"Good," Rudd replied. "Need tools?"

"Yeah." Miss Hoffman and her hacksaw were dispatched to Low, where Tony Papert was assembling the rest of a task force. "I want thirty people to do something," Papert announced. A group volunteered, then asked what it was they had volunteered to do. "We are expanding," Papert said. "We need another building."

At the faculty meeting leftist historian Jeffry Kaplow rose to defend the strikers' position. Described as a pedantic lecturer in Columbia's annual student course evaluation booklet, Kaplow now spoke with passion and eloquence. "These people can't be expelled," he pleaded at one point in his speech. "They are trying to save the University from the havoc toward which it has been heading!" His comments were greeted with applause, but, as the response quieted, another professor stood up and said caustically, "We have already heard Mr. Rudd and some of his very sophisticated arguments, but we don't have to hear this from our colleagues!" He was hissed by the group. Another rose and charged that Fraenkel had "undercut" all efforts at negotiation by his "punitive" remarks to Rudd. A third said he was "disgraced" by the actions of Kirk and Truman. Faculty sentiment against the administration was rising. Within minutes word was received that Vice President Truman and Dean Coleman were on their way to the meeting.

As Truman and Coleman left Low by the southeast security entrance and walked toward Philosophy, JJ and his liberation party were silently climbing out of the windows of Kirk's offices on the west face of Low, heading in the opposite direction across a lawn toward Mathematics Hall. The group was soon joined by a supporting force from Fayerweather which, according to one student, "came charging across the campus like a bunch of Vietcong guerrillas." The hacksaw proved unnecessary; the radicals had stationed agents inside the target building Wednesday night before the administration had ordered all halls still under its control to be sealed off. Now, at a predetermined time, these students met JJ's squad and unlocked the door to Mathematics Hall from the inside with little difficulty.

Truman and Coleman arrived at the Ad Hoc Faculty meeting at 1:05 Friday morning. Their faces ashen, their expressions rigid, they moved briskly into the room. Professor Westin, who was chairing the meeting, later described the incident:

> The room was quite crowded, and we were busy at that point trying to decide how we would go forward. Truman walked in, and went to the back of the room. He did not come to the front of the room or ask to have the chair or anything like that. He stood in the back of the room and said, very quickly, "Gentlemen, I'm going to make an announcement I don't think many of you are going to like. . . . We are afraid the situation is one in which we are simply going to call in the police now." And he indicated that in five minutes the President of the University would be on the phone with the Mayor and there would be a decision to call in the police. With that—he didn't ask for any discussion or anything like that—he simply turned around and went out.

The room exploded. There were cries of "Shame! Shame!" as faculty members booed the vice president loudly. The Reverend William Starr, a radical member of the chaplain's staff, shouted, "Liar, liar!" after Truman as he left. Eric Bentley, Columbia's eminent professor of drama, announced, "I resign!" Mathematics Professor Serge Lang called for a vote of censure.

It was 1:10 A.M. On the first floor of Low Library Grayson Kirk spoke to the Office of the Mayor of New York City, arranging for the first massive police action in the history of Columbia University.

On the second floor of Low Library, Tony Papert looked at his watch, interrupted a meeting of strikers and announced, "Mathematics Hall has just been taken."

On the sixth floor of Philosophy Hall a professor ran into the office in which the radicals were caucusing. He told Rudd of Truman's announcement and demanded to know how the demonstrators could have seized another building in the midst of the faculty's efforts at resolving the crisis. Rudd looked up and smiled, "Why, I've been here all night!"

At the rally of counter-demonstrators which had continued in Wollman Auditorium, Dean Coleman walked somberly to the microphone and announced—as Truman had done minutes earlier before the faculty—that the administration had decided to call the New York City police onto campus to clear the buildings. The audience erupted into enthusiastic applause. "Don't cheer," Coleman said grimly. "This is the saddest moment in Columbia's history."

In the lounge of Philosophy Hall Professor Morgenbesser jumped onto a table to seek a clarification despite the clamor that had filled the room since Truman's announcement. As Morgenbesser said later:

> One of Truman's reasons for calling in the police had been the unruly crowd of conservative students meeting in Wollman Auditorium. After he left I asked if the police were going to invade the buildings just to stop the fights between students. The latter would have been okay and consistent with his pretext. "But if the cops are going to clear the buildings," I said, "then we have our commitments."

## 5   Dick Greeman's Bloody Nose

Morgenbesser asked Professor Melman to try to get a telephone message through to Mayor Lindsay. In a slow, deep voice Melman told someone at the night mayor's office to convey a message "with urgent speed" to Lindsay, stating that the faculty of Columbia University wanted him to intervene and call off the police. Melman was informed that members of the Mayor's staff were already on their way to the campus. Most of the faculty members present ran from the lounge to place themselves in front of the occupied buildings to prevent police entry, as they had agreed they would do just six hours before. Melman, Morgenbesser, Sam Coleman and several students rushed to the statue of Alma Mater to await the Mayor's representatives. Two students ran down to College Walk, intercepted Barry Gottehrer and Sid Davidoff of Lindsay's Urban Task Force and brought them up to the faculty delegation waiting on the steps of Low. Melman spoke first.

"These are our children," he implored, his cheeks wet with tears and sweat. "We beg of you, don't let them use the police. If the police go in there and drag the students out it would be a tragedy unprecedented in the history of this University." Melman informed Gottehrer that faculty members had vowed to remain in front of the occupied buildings to prevent violent entry and that the police would have to get past them before they could carry out the administration's orders.

"I speak for over two hundred members of the faculty," Melman continued. "Don't let them destroy this great University. *Please.*" Gottehrer let Melman finish and asked, "If I give you forty-five minutes and stop the gym can you get the kids out?" Without waiting for a reply—none could be offered—the two Mayor's men walked at top speed to the security entrance of Low Library. Melman and the other professors followed.

Alan Westin and Professor Alexander Dallin, a stocky authority on Soviet affairs, had rushed to Low immediately after Truman's announcement before the faculty. Eric Bentley had also gone to Low but was prevented from reaching the top administrators by Dean Fraenkel, who later explained, "He was very emotional and would not have been constructive." The faculty members tried to persuade Truman and Kirk to call off the police, arguing that the use of such force would be a disaster for the University. As the professors spoke in the name of liberalism against the use of police, Sid Davidoff accused Westin and his colleagues of being the kind of intellectuals who would bring fascism to America.[4]

---

[4] Most of the professors present assumed that Davidoff meant that their actions and those of SDS would result in a reactionary backlash. When, however, Davidoff was later asked by one faculty member what he had intended by his comment, the Mayor's aide replied, "What are you going to do when the radical right starts taking buildings?"

In an adjacent office on the first floor of Low, Chief Inspector Sanford Garelik conferred with Kirk over the details of the evacuation. According to one professor, the chief was concerned with the effect the Columbia operation would have on the police force's image, with containing the right-wing officers who would be involved in the action and with the large number of faculty members who were massing outside Low to resist his men. Once the decision to use police had been made and announced to the faculty, specifics not previously considered threatened to cause trouble. Kirk asked whether the police could arrest only the white students. City Human Rights Commissioner Booth objected, however, and said that he could not condone such selective action. Garelik agreed that this could not be done. When Kirk asked what would happen to faculty members who had threatened to obstruct the police non-violently, Garelik told him that they, too, would be arrested. Kirk paled and said that that could not be done.

Mark Rudd and the other radicals left their caucus in Philosophy Hall immediately after they learned of Truman's announcement that the police were coming. The group made its way across campus to the newly "liberated" Mathematics building. Robert Friedman, the editor of *Spectator,* stopped them.

"The cops are coming," he told Rudd.

"I know."

"Do you want to talk to some faculty members?"

Coolly, Rudd replied, "I'll speak to anyone, anytime." As Rudd continued on to Math, Friedman ran toward Low Library where he met Professor Rothman and asked him to find some faculty members or administrators to work out an eleventh-hour negotiated settlement. In the offices of Dean Fraenkel they got through to Truman. The vice president appointed a mission composed of Professors Westin, Silver and Rothman and Dean Platt to meet with Rudd. Unsure of how much time they had to work out a peace before the police arrived, the contingent set out for the student-controlled building.

Access to Mathematics Hall was by window. The delegation climbed onto the stone ledge which surrounds the building at chest height, then—one at a time—squeezed and grunted their way in through the half-open window. More than once they had to be shoved at critical points to clear the sill.

The inelegance of the negotiators' entrance into Math was immediately replaced by the businesslike efficiency with which they got to work. They introduced themselves briskly to Rudd and then proceeded directly into the stacks of the Math Library, passing through a meeting at which the students were making plans for resisting the police. Word of the bust had spread quickly by messenger to all the occupied buildings. As the doors to the stacks clicked shut behind the negotiating party, SDS militant Tom Hurwitz spun on his heel and, with amazed glee in his eyes, pointed toward the stacks. "Do you know what we've got in there?" he asked the others, most of whom were still unaware of the reason for this unexpected visit from the Establishment. Hurwitz, unable to contain himself, jumped into the air, proclaiming, "We got ourselves another dean!" Some in the crowd, remembering the bad press in which their last kidnaping enterprise had resulted, began to protest, as others found rope to tie across the knobs of the stack doors.[5] However, the more pressing problem of preparing for the police quickly overshadowed the attempt at holding a new hostage.

Inside, the negotiating teams made their way to the rear of the stacks, as far as possible from the meeting outside and from the expected point of contact between police and students. They moved aside several small desks and arranged seven chairs into a cramped circle. The group now consisted of Westin, Silver, Rothman, Platt, Rudd, Juan Gonzalez and *Spectator* Editor Friedman. Professor Westin, who was to become the faculty's primary negotiator with the white students, spoke first. Eloquently he appealed to the demonstrators to come out of their buildings as a sign of their faith that the faculty would take up the struggle. Rudd objected that the faculty had given the students no cause for such faith. He said he had been antagonized by Professor Silver several hours before, when the sociologist had questioned him on the effects the rebellion would have on the future of the University. Silver tried to explain that he had not meant his question as an attack, but the opportunity for trust between the two had been lost. Soon a young man with a rugged face entered the stacks and conferred for a moment in whispers with Rudd. After he left, Rudd announced that the man was Tom Hayden, a founder of SDS and a prominent New Left activist.

"Really!" Professor Rothman murmured, "I have one of his books on the reading list for my American Social History course!"

Hayden had assumed leadership of the Math building soon after it was taken. A maestro of participatory democracy, he conducted the mass meetings that night with consummate skill. While such general assemblies often degenerated into chaos and acrimony in other buildings, under Hayden's control discordant bickerings were usually resolved into meaningful debate. As discussions proceeded in ever-narrowing circles

---

[5] The rope was handed to one of the authors (O.R.) who, though he had just entered with the negotiating team, was mistaken for one of those who had taken over the building. He placed the rope under a pile of monographs where it was soon lost.

within the stacks, Hayden quietly prepared the group for the worst. Wearing a karate jacket of thickly matted, coarse cotton ("I found this upstairs—there are a lot up there, so you might want to get yourselves some for protection later"), he quietly explained what measures should be taken for protection against the police. Votes were held on whether to resist actively, passively or not at all. When, after some discussion, it was decided not to resist actively, one stranger, dressed in an unidentifiable dark-green uniform, announced that he was a representative of the National Liberation Front and would fight the police off alone if necessary. Hayden said, "That's fine, man," and continued with the debate on whether to go limp when the police came or to walk out voluntarily. People sneaked nervous glances outside the large windows facing Low, wondering whether that outpost had been taken yet.

Inside the stacks Platt was trying to get the talks down to specifics. "What has to be done to get your people out of the buildings, Mark?" The answer was one that had been heard before and would be heard often again in the next four days: "Meet all our six demands." Its absolute simplicity confronted the negotiators. "All of them?" Platt pleaded. Gonzalez, silent through most of the session, now interrupted. "What Mark means is that first we have to have the demands on the gym and amnesty met." "Right," Rudd agreed. Both were very tired. About midway through the talks, Rudd volunteered a concession which he considered major—so much so that he said he was not even sure he could get it approved by the people in the buildings. A committee of students and faculty—no administrators—would be appointed to try the protesters collectively and judge their guilt, though it would have no power to punish them. The proposal—which amounted to *de facto* amnesty—never got very far.

During these talks, as in much of the later negotiations, Westin and the other faculty representatives found themselves suggesting settlements which they had no power to guarantee. They were emissaries of a bastard body—the Ad Hoc Faculty Group—which had little more power than the authority to disband itself. Even the faculty proper had hardly more to offer on the substantive issues. Because of the institutional structure of Columbia only the President or the Trustees were really in a position to promise the dissident students anything meaningful on discipline, the gym, IDA; and these were the men least likely to initiate compromise. It was true that on occasion the faculty would become exercised enough over a particular issue to make a strong policy recommendation to the President or Trustees, and traditionally the recommendation would be approved. But such instances had been rare in the recent history of the University. Columbia professors generally preferred to let the administration handle major decisions. It was only with the student uprising that faculty members were aroused to differentiate their position from that of the administration and to assume a stand as mediator between the two conflicting sides.

Westin, aware that the police were being mobilized on campus as he spoke, tried to convince Rudd that the strikers had already won a considerable victory. He assured him that no severe disciplinary measures would be taken. He indicated that a faculty committee was on the verge of suggesting an end to all ties with IDA. He predicted that the gym would never be built. But Rudd was aware, as indeed was Westin, that assurances, indications and predictions from the faculty—no matter how well-intentioned—were empty. Furthermore Westin had made it clear that amnesty would never be granted. Dean Platt later noted:

> Westin promised Mark far more at that time than he could deliver, or at least, far more than President Kirk or Dr. Truman would be willing to deliver. . . . He may have been testing. He may have been seeing what Mark's response would be even under these terms, knowing all along that the terms would not be met. And even under these liberal terms Mark met with his group and they turned the proposals of our negotiating team down.

At one point during the talks when Rudd explained again that he could not be sure of any of the promises made to him by the Ad Hoc Group, Professor Rothman remarked that if the students vacated the buildings and put their faith in the faculty, and if the faculty let them down, they could always go back into their buildings. Rudd explained patiently that this would not work; the movement was going on now, the support was there and it had to be kept alive. If the people left the buildings so close to the end of the term, he pointed out, they would return to their dormitory rooms, begin studying for finals, and the movement would collapse. The students were aware how unusual it was for them to possess any measure of power over the administration, and they were not going to give up that rare power until they had won something concrete.

The only substantive agreements reached during the talks in the stacks were that Rudd would carry the faculty offers back to the occupied buildings, and that the administration would restore the telephone service it had cut off in those buildings. Shortly after 3 A.M. the *Spectator* editor was sent to administration headquarters. In an attempt to hold off the long-overdue police invasion, he was told to inform Truman or Kirk that there was some hope of negotiation. As he reached Low the crowd outside was in a frenzy.

\* \* \*

Roughly thirty faculty members had gathered at the entrance to Low Library. Hundreds of students, perched on the high ledge flanking the steps and packed around the southeast corner of the building, strained to find out what was going on at the security entrance. A roaring chant of "KIRK MUST GO!" rose from the crowd into the cold spring air. Clusters of faculty members stood huddled in blankets at each entrance to Low, guarding the building against police attack and sipping coffee. Most of the heat that night came from the klieg lights the television cameramen had ranged around the area.

Roger Berkeley, former general manager of the campus radio station WKCR, announced that the administration had ordered the station off the air, "because Truman feels that WKCR is contributing to an unhealthy atmosphere." As Berkeley spoke, plainclothesmen infiltrated into the edges of the crowd, making their way to the security entrance. When they reached the door they were blocked by three men: Terence Hopkins and Richard Greeman, two leftist members of the faculty, and the Reverend Bill Starr. The three were demanding that every policeman show his identification before entering the building. The plainclothesmen, however, preferred a different tactic: they would back into the crowd at the entrance and, when they were close enough to the doorway, fling back an arm so that it could be seized and they could then be pulled inside by one of their colleagues. During one of these maneuvers Starr found a billy club tucked under the coat of a plainclothesman. He pulled it out and held it up to the crowd, exclaiming, "Say, look what we have here!"

The police, who had been ordered merely to report to the security entrance of Low, now decided that obstruction could no longer be allowed to slow them. Several times an officer asked the students and faculty standing before him to disperse. They did not move. Suddenly the police behind the officer charged. From everywhere in the crowd men pulled clubs out from under trench coats and ski jackets, and a shout went up: "Cops! They're cops! Cops!" Faculty members were thrown to the ground. Greeman, who had been pushed down with the others, struggled to his feet. His hand was on his head, which was wet with blood.

Professor Dallin was at this moment making his way out of Low to inform those outside that the administration had not yet made a final decision on whether police would be used on campus that night. He stepped out of the security office into the pandemonium as Greeman came staggering toward him, his arm extended. Dallin grabbed it. Seeing that his own hand was now covered with blood, he rushed back inside to see Truman and Kirk.

## 5   Dick Greeman's Bloody Nose

A few moments earlier Professor Morgenbesser had made his way into Truman's headquarters. He was furious. "This will be done at the expense of faculty blood," he had warned the vice president. Now Dallin walked into the office, Greeman's blood still wet on his hand.

"Faculty blood has begun to be shed here," he said. Truman blanched.

The vice president strode from the administration headquarters in Low to the security entrance and called, "Dick, Dick Greeman!" He found the instructor and led him into his offices, where others took care of the head wound that Truman later remembered as "Dick Greeman's bloody nose." The original plan to clear the buildings and arrest all student demonstrators which, under faculty pressure, the administration had been reconsidering for the past two hours was now scrapped. Truman suggested that perhaps the police should clear the buildings but not arrest any students. Professor Morgenbesser and the others objected. Truman then proposed that the police spread out over the campus in "sensitive areas" to prevent violence. This solution was opposed by police representatives, however, on the grounds that such new orders would prove confusing in the middle of the night. Truman, Kirk and the police officials finally came to a decision not to use the police at all.

At 3:30 A.M., Friday, Truman walked to the threshold of the security entrance to Low. A crowd of more than a thousand faculty members and students were packed on the brick paths and grassy patches that surround the entrance. Their mood was agitated and hostile as they chanted "KIRK MUST GO!" Word was passed that Truman was about to make an announcement, and the crowd quieted. Speaking through a bullhorn, the vice president read:

> The faculty committee has persuaded the University administration to postpone the request for police action on campus while the faculty and administration continue their efforts to effect a peaceful solution to the situation. Necessary security arrangements will of course be maintained. To encourage these efforts, the University will be closed until Monday. At the request of the Mayor and without prejudice to continuation at a later time, we have suspended construction on the gymnasium pending further discussion.

Applause of relief swelled up from the crowd; the "bust" had been averted, and the students had won their first victory. Despite all the administration's earlier protestations that any action on the gym would have to be taken at the next meeting of the Trustees, construction had now been suspended. Kirk had spent much of the evening on the phone with key Trustees gaining approval for the move, and it soon became a general (though possibly unfounded) understanding that the ill-fated project would never be completed. Although few knew it, the postponement of police action, coupled with the closing of the University through Monday, meant that all parties would have Friday and the weekend to continue working toward a peaceful resolution of the crisis.

# 6

## The Liberated Life

BY FRIDAY some of the strikers' demands seemed well on their way to realization. But victories on matters such as gym construction were not the developments in which the strike leaders took most satisfaction. More significant was the change that had come over the lifestyle of the students who occupied the buildings. This transformation of the quality of life and the existential involvement of the individual were the ends toward which all of SDS ideology pointed. The radicals saw the routinized patterns of society as repressive, manipulative and dehumanizing. The "respectable" lives of businessmen, bureaucrats and professionals to which many of them had once aspired were seen as drab, confining, cardboard existences. Now, insulated from the norms and forms of American culture by several feet of office furniture and barricades, the students inside the "liberated" buildings were able to create social patterns of their own. The takeover of the buildings had begun as a political tactic designed to bring about the goal of social reconstruction. It quickly evolved into the realization, on a small scale, of that very goal. The process of personal liberation was founded in a common existential credential—all the students in the buildings had placed their careers at Columbia in some jeopardy by joining the protest; a common tactic—confrontation; a common enemy—the administration; and a common set of immediate goals—the six demands. In addition, in the day-to-day conduct of the demonstrations each student could feel that he was in direct touch with the sources of power and decision-making within the strike apparatus. This was accomplished through participatory democracy, a central element of SDS ideology as has been noted. Students could, within the strike context, *make the decisions that affected their lives.* All questions, from the most banal administrative trivia to the broadest questions of policy and purpose, were brought up for discussion among all the occupants of every "liberated" building. Eventually the SDS-dominated central steering committee tarnished this phenomenon somewhat, by what some students called "manipulative tactics" of its own; but for the most part decisions were made by a process in which every student was involved. A major segment of each day in the occupied buildings was spent in such discussions, which alleviated the frustration many felt in being so completely removed from the "legitimate" sources of power and decision-making in the larger spheres of the University and the nation. This political participation combined with a similar, social "total immersion" which satisfied the human needs many felt had been bleached out of the sterile routines of normal life.

Once the old social and intellectual patterns were shattered by the demonstrators, students were eager to create their own life-designs. The academic world would be resurrected later in the "liberation classes." But now the first order of business was to restore people's working and living relationships to a condition of humanity.

The communal cohesiveness in the student-controlled buildings began soon after each takeover. The students who occupied Low, for example, had developed considerable *esprit de bâtiment* as early as Wednesday evening. During the following days they formed and joined task forces to serve the needs of the other occupants; some stood guard at points of contact with the outside, some kept up communications via phone and walkie-talkie with friendly buildings, and others—mostly girls—managed food and housekeeping details. The process of working together often became more important than the work itself; at one point a student strode into one of Kirk's outer offices and asked those assembled,

"Anyone want to form an effigy committee?"

"An effigy of what?"

"Anything, man!" he answered. Several volunteered.

Lengthy meetings were held in which the demonstrators engaged in theoretical discussions of radical ideology, the faults of the University and the nature of American life. The students addressed themselves to the latest offers made by the Ad Hoc Faculty Group, and to the more immediate problems of strike tactics and defense. On Thursday night, when word of a possible bust arrived in Low, one demonstrator suggested that, in order to hamper the police, all the occupants remove their clothes when the police came. The proposal passed by a sizable majority, and JJ suggested that with police action so close they begin practice drills immediately. The spirit of the students in Low was partially derived from the distinction that the quarters they occupied were the *sanctum sanctorum* of Columbia University. Kirk's offices had *de facto*

6 *The Liberated Life* 119

been off limits for students of the University, except under extraordinary circumstances. Only a handful of these students had ever, as individuals, even seen the President face to face. It is improbable that any had ever spoken to him. If they had it is highly unlikely that he had answered them. As Eric Bentley once said of Grayson Kirk, "He hasn't spoken to anyone under thirty since he was under thirty." The word that had emanated from Low Library during normal times—sometimes implicitly, sometimes explicitly—was that students, and often faculty members, simply had no business bothering the President of the University. (The only times an undergraduate might with any likelihood come into contact with Kirk during four years at Columbia would be on his first day, at a reception in the rotunda of Low Library, at which the President would shake the hand of every incoming freshman, and on his last day, four years later, when he would sit in cap and gown on Low Plaza to hear the President deliver the commencement address. Because of other commitments, Kirk failed to appear at the freshman reception for the Class of 1969—the class that was now, as juniors, in the vanguard of the uprising. And, because of another set of circumstances, he would not speak at the graduation of the Class of 1968.

The President had consented to hold two or three fireside chats during the past few years at which students could ask him questions about the state and future of the University. But these affairs had been infrequent, stiff and rarely resulted in any meaningful dialogue between students and administration. Many students had attacked Kirk's policies on a wide variety of problems, but the president remained coldly aloof, almost disdainful. When contact was made with some other official of the administration results were generally as frustrating. Students and faculty were told by high University officials that issues such as the gym or IDA were none of their business, that their thoughts on these problems simply did not matter. Discussing the role of students in the University decision-making process, Herbert Deane had phrased the problem this way almost one year to the day before the start of the spring uprising: "Whether students vote 'yes' or 'no' on a given issue means as much to me as if they were to tell me they like strawberries."

For these reasons, the seizure and occupation of Low Memorial Library were especially important to the students involved. They had finally managed to break through the maddening putty-like wall that surrounded the fount of decision-making at Columbia. Accordingly, their first activities centered on research into that power: its sources, its intricacies, its results. Having been told over and over that they had and deserved no power ("You're only transitory birds," Kirk had once told a group of students who confronted him in his Low Library sanctuary, "and therefore should not have a voice"), and having been told equally often that they had no business even knowing about the University's activities beyond the classroom, they seized that power and that knowledge.

Many of the official documents uncovered by the demonstrators in Low revealed only banality in Kirk's activities where evil was expected. There were files of letters to major alumni gift-givers, thanking them for their generous support, inquiring after their wives' health, expressing confidence in the future. There were reams of letters to angry parents, alumni and friends of the University, apologizing for recent political disturbances on campus, assuring them that those students responsible would be punished, explaining, however, that the President was limited by the guarantees of academic freedom. At points the banal yielded to the absurd, as in the following letter found in an old file and posted on Kirk's door by the protesters:

> Dear Sir,
>
> Last night I had a conversation with your late President, Nicholas Murray Butler, and he wishes you to know that he would like to come back among us. He does not plan to work, but to rest here on earth (as we know he had very little rest) and serve you in an advisory capacity. He told me to let you know and I have. It is up to you now to decide such a worthy cause.

The letter, signed in a fine feminine hand, was dated October 18, 1951. Nicholas Murray Butler, former President of Columbia, died on December 7, 1947.

Other documents found by the students were not as occult. One SDS member discovered a rough copy of "A Brief Account of Columbia University in the City of New York," a report prepared by a prominent Trustee and dated January 12, 1967. The copy was a second draft, submitted by the Trustee to Kirk for his comments and suggestions. On page six of the report was the following passage:

> Among the larger grants [to Columbia] is one of $5 million from the U.S. Air Force for studies of the detection and rapid processing of information about ballistic missiles in flight, and another one of the same amount from the Navy for basic research on the underwater transmission of sound.

On the blank facing page, Kirk had made a note with a red felt pen in his distinctively illegible handwriting. It was retyped below by one of his secretaries, so that it could be read:

> I question the tactical wisdom of using this illustration. We have avoided emphasis or publicity about this project because we have

so many students and faculty opposed to all forms of research for the Defense Department. How about using some of the oceanographic or medical projects?

Further on in the report was an account of the neighborhood which surrounds Columbia, and with which the University has long had a troubled relationship:

> By 1959, the local police precinct had the second highest crime rate in the city. (General Dwight D. Eisenhower, who came to Columbia in 1948 as President, obtained a police permit to carry a small pocket derringer on his walks in nearby Morningside Park.)

Kirk had starred the passage and written: "NOTE: I would delete this. It places the problems of regional urban improvement in an unfair perspective."

Other documents found in Low were later released in a pamphlet by the Strike Coördinating Committee. To avoid the reprisals for such publicity threatened by an embarrassed administration, the material was marked as "xerox copies of documents mailed by anonymous sources." For the strikers, the documents represented evidence that the world is to some extent run by a "collusion of elites"; that is, not a conspiracy, but rather a network of "gentlemen's agreements" in which one dirty hand washes another.

One document circulated by the strikers was allegedly a memorandum from Kirk's files regarding a June 1966 telephone conversation he had had with Donald Elliott, a city planning official. The topic was the Morningside Renewal Council, an organization of Heights residents and institutions concerned with the future of the neighborhood, often opposed to Columbia's expansion plans. To the consternation of administration officials, the city felt obliged to hear out the residents' opinions on matters dealing with their neighborhood. According to the replica of the memo, Kirk wrote, in part:

> [Elliott said that] the city was obliged to allow the council to give advice on renewal problems, though, of course, the city was not committed to follow council recommendations. As a solution to the problem, he proposed that, now while many people are away, a small group be set up to consider the renewal problem. To compose such a group he suggested two or three University representatives, to be designated by me—and the officers of the Renewal Council. This group should explore the problem and should see if any agreement could be reached. The University would not commit itself in advance to accept any recommendations by this committee.

[Elliott added that] the city would be prepared to go ahead, regardless of the council's position, if such a form of council consultation could be held. Clearly, he is looking for a way out of a dilemma that is becoming burdensome to him. . . .

To the disappointment of the protesters, no truly damaging material was found when they rifled Kirk's files. But the documents were only one part of the demonstrators' new insight into the personality of Columbia's President. Another aspect of the revelation was the discovery of the Private Life of Grayson Kirk—not his personal correspondence or secret loves but the simple facts of his mortality. When a man has become for so many little more than a collection of half-tone dots on a newspaper page or predictably noncommittal quotations in a news column, the realization that he is to some degree a human being as well can be grotesque as well as amusing. The demonstrators in Low began early to examine the milieu in which the President spent his time. An entire wall of the President's private office was lined with shelves of books, all quite impressive-looking, almost all in mint condition. Many of them were read or leafed through by the students—some quite obviously for the first time. When, for example, one girl wanted to read a French paperback that was part of a collection, she noticed that the pages had never been cut. The same was found to be true of almost every other book in that series. "That's Kirk for you," commented one student, "very impressive on the outside, but inside . . ."

It was the personal detail that caused the cologne-and-cardboard façade to crumble for the students inside Low. They discovered Grayson Kirk the Man: his Ipana toothpaste, his Cornhusker's Lotion, his drops prescribed three times daily to increase dryness of mouth, his Gelusil. The personal side of Kirk was at first pounced on with malice—malice built up from all the distant speeches whose substance no one could recall after they had ended, malice from all the times they had read "President Kirk refused to comment" in *Spectator,* malice from the incident at the Martin Luther King memorial service when he had declined to link arms and sing "We Shall Overcome."

But the students' reaction was not uniformly hostile. The discovery of Grayson Kirk's humanity was quickly greeted with as much delight as anger. There was cooing when an ancient photo of a baby was passed around, supposedly little Grayson. A polite note was left in the President's xerox machine:

Stopped by to visit you, but you weren't in. Sorry to have missed you.

—SDS

A warm, festive summer-camp spirit would spread over the students inside occupied Low with the coming of darkness. On one night, before the entrances to Kirk's office had been sealed, a student sat at a piano within the darkened rotunda and played Chopin. Three girls converted a supply closet into a pantry and set up an assembly line to churn out salami, peanut butter and jelly and American cheese sandwiches. The food had been bought with money solicited on campus and was tossed in the President's windows by sympathizers outside. Another girl was in the office of Helen King, Kirk's special assistant, vacuuming the floor and emptying ashtrays. A cluster of students sat in the carpeted and muraled main reception area sipping milk from champagne glasses and listening to a classical symphony on WBAI. One reporter for the campus radio station crouched in a nearby cubbyhole strewn with cut wires, trying to restore severed telephone connections.

Outside the suite, on the gray periphery of the rotunda, Professor of Music Otto Luening, an early pioneer in the development of electronic music, had come to talk to the students. Sitting in the half-dark in a gray suit and gray sweater, the aging composer observed, "The only difference between being twenty-seven and eighty-seven is this: at eighty-seven, you have all the same drives, the same goals, the same passions. But at eighty-seven you know you don't have the same energy. So you have to be slyyyyy."

He shifted in his chair. "For fifty years I've been teaching young people, and what the hell am I supposed to do tonight? Stay home like my wife told me to do? No; I've got to talk to you people if we're going to get anywhere." Someone brought him an orange from a crate that had been passed inside earlier. In the dark of the rotunda he sat at the piano, demonstrators clustered on the floor around him as he played. Above their heads towered the ebony marble columns of the rotunda and the cold, black dome.

Inside Kirk's suite many of the demonstrators set up for the night. Some offices were used for non-stop meetings, while others—those with the thickest rugs—were designated sleeping areas. The protesters lay in blankets, on coats, faces in the carpet, with signs of the revolution scribbled on pieces of paper and taped to the walls around them:

WE WANT THE WORLD AND WE WANT IT NOW!
Le monde est un fleuve de merde.
¡ARRIBA LA REVOLUCIÓN!

The same sense of community pervaded Fayerweather Hall. But the students of Fayerweather were also considered by many demonstrators to be the most politically deviant. Often, during the week of negotiations with the faculty and administration, leaders of the strike felt obliged to send key speakers to Fayerweather to prevent its more moderate occupants from leaving the fold and settling for less than amnesty. Liberal and moderate graduate students were numerous in Fayerweather and they would often argue bitterly with the radicals over tactics and goals. But what Fayerweather lacked in political coherence it made up for in spirit. Posted on a wall near the barricaded main entrance to the building was a sign probably intended by the radicals for the eyes of the moderates:

> WE SHOULD RID OUR RANKS OF ALL IMPOTENT THINKING. ALL VIEWS THAT OVERESTIMATE THE STRENGTH OF THE ENEMY AND UNDERESTIMATE THE STRENGTH OF THE PEOPLE ARE WRONG.
>
> —CHAIRMAN MAO

An old classroom in the basement had been converted into the offices of the building's steering committee. A typewriter and mimeograph machine had been moved in from other offices in the building to turn out the ubiquitous leaflets and memoranda that served as the central means of communication within and among the occupied buildings. On the blackboard were quotations in Chinese; hanging from a wall over the typewriter, a notice:

> TO ALL WOMEN:
> You are in a liberated area. You are urged to reject the traditional role of housekeeper unless, of course, you feel this is the role that allows for creative expression. Speak up! Use your brains!

In a nearby room physicians and medical students sympathetic to the demonstrations, from hospitals throughout New York, had set up an infirmary; at least one of the medical personnel was on duty twenty-four hours every day. Two wooden tables, used by professors in the *ancien régime* to support notes and lecterns, had been covered with clean white cloth and stocked with an array of medicines and supplies: analgesic jelly, Band-aids, Listerine, tincture zephiran, lollipops, Kaopectate, rubbing alcohol, aspirin. Most complaints were minor and treated on the spot: head colds, stomach pains, muscle strains. But there were provisions for more serious problems as well. On the blackboard at the front of the room were chalked the names and phone numbers of a surgeon and a psychiatrist who had volunteered to help if their services were needed. Beneath these, in the center of the blackboard, was taped a tongue depressor swathed in layers of adhesive tape. It was there in easy reach to be thrust into the mouth of anyone who might suffer an epileptic seizure. Student assistants in white coats marked "Survival Committee" drifted in and out of the room. Similar health precautions were taken in each of the other buildings.

## 6 The Liberated Life

At the height of the demonstrations there were upwards of three hundred people in Fayerweather Hall, each eating three meals more or less per day. Food had been donated by friendly grocery store owners, or had been bought at wholesale cost or in bulk with money raised on campus. A strike food committee was set up in Ferris Booth Hall to coördinate the massive operation of feeding 750 students. Each "liberated" building had its own pantry and food preparation areas. In Fayerweather the classroom used for storing food was excellently equipped, with a complete inventory kept on the blackboard. At one point it read as follows:

Bread: 5 Italian
Towels: 42 rolls
Donuts: 100
Yodels: 50
Toilet paper: 20 rolls
Candles: 72
Paper plates: 300
Plastic forks: 100
Pineapple: 36 cans
Grapefruit juice: 36 cans
Orange juice: 4 large cans
Apple juice: 4 large cans
Applesauce: 24 small, 12 large
7-Up: 36 bottles
Coke: 24 cans

1 Watermelon
Apples: 100
Bananas: 10
Cookies: 48 boxes
Tuna: 192 cans
Canned fruit: 40 cans
Coffee: 24 lb. cans
One 15-lb. Bologna
17 lb. sugar
Peanut Butter: 5 jars
Jelly: 4 cans
Soap: 46 bars
Can openers: 2
Cheese: 144 slices.
**NO EATING IN THIS ROOM**

In Avery Hall, where a group of Architecture students had refused to vacate the building Wednesday night, the doors were not blocked and students and faculty were allowed free access, though few classes were held. Like the students in Fayerweather, the occupants of Avery were primarily graduate students, and a great many of them were moderate. They favored compromise on the amnesty question but were repeatedly convinced by strike leaders to maintain a hard line. Most notable about Avery were its tunnel barricades. The architecture students, helped by their professors, it was said, had constructed them with the skill of professionals. They had built critical stress points that would withstand the onslaught of hordes of police but would yield in seconds if altered in a particular way from the inside. The architects were sure that their barricades were impregnable.

Mathematics Hall had a personality distinct from that of the other occupied buildings. It was the last front opened by the demonstrators; very soon after entering, the students had thrown up a quick barricade and, unsure of what to do next, had resorted to the usual Columbia radical tactic: they held a meeting. Liquid green soap was found in a supply closet, to be applied liberally later to the main stairwell in order to slow the invasion of police, athletes or other unfriendly visitors. It was a very practical meeting; there was no talk of restructuring the University, or the six demands or student power. They discussed fire hoses, barricades, green soap. After the discussions ended the demonstrators scattered throughout the building. The elevator would rise to the top floor, then return to the basement laden with file cabinets, desks and chairs, to be piled at the doors and the entrances to tunnels connecting with other buildings. At the end of the construction frenzy ten solid feet of office furniture had been planted at the exits. (During the same days that the students built barricades in each occupied building the administration was having those parts of Columbia's intricate tunnel system which it controlled barricaded from the other side, to prevent underground expansion of the revolution.)

Over the weekend of the occupation several girls from Sarah Lawrence College came down to visit Mathematics Hall to supplement the activities of their counterparts at Barnard, Columbia's sister institution. A few spent Friday and Saturday nights. For a number, personal mores underwent the same transformation as other aspects of daily life. The concepts of the "liberated male" and the "liberated female" bore ramifications beyond politics, and students in all the occupied buildings joyfully explored this aspect of communal living each night. The residents of Math, like those of several of the other buildings, voted to ban the smoking of marijuana and the use of drugs to avoid the difficulties that a "pot bust" would add to the other police problems they faced.

Math was the most comfortable building the students held. Unlike Hamilton, it contained more than just floor after floor of classrooms; there was the carpeted Mathematics and Science Library which the demonstrators converted into a common room, and the Graduate Students' Lounge complete with kitchen and pantry. Unlike Low and Fayerweather, Math offered plenty of room and sleeping facilities, with couches scattered throughout the building. A xerox and mimeograph machine were available for use. There was a television, in front of which many of the demonstrators would relax and watch the *Late Late Show*. One student brought in a stereo and dozens of records: Dylan, rock, blues. Food was hot and ample; Saturday morning, everyone in one section of the building awakened to find an orange at the edge of his pillow.

Life in Hamilton Hall went on behind a façade that was far different. The easy-going spirit of the buildings held by the white students contrasted sharply with the more austere and closed atmosphere surrounding Hamilton. Only blacks approved by the Hamilton Hall Steering Committee were allowed inside after the first day. Schedules were set up by the SAS leadership to provide eating periods, study periods, relaxation periods and sleeping periods. There was an interval set aside for bathing, beginning at 6 A.M. A hose had been attached to a fixture in one of the bathrooms and stretched over a toilet stall to form a shower. The blacks were not as eager as the whites to rid themselves of "bourgeois fetishes" such as housekeeping. One of their first actions Wednesday morning after evicting the whites was to dispose of three huge bundles of garbage. Even the leaders took brooms in hand to clean up, and the Hamilton group made specific mention in a press release that "we are maintaining the excellent condition of the building." Strict discipline marked their contacts with the outside world as well. As Immanuel Wallerstein, the sociology professor who served as chief negotiator with the blacks, later observed:

> You couldn't get in except by request. I would be out in front of the building and would ask the doorman if I could get in. He would say, "Wait a minute," and send a runner back to the headquarters, who would then come back and say it was okay. Then I would climb over the barricades. It was all a game and I was willing to abide by the rules. . . .
>
> I could never speak to anybody but the four on the steering committee. . . . Often they would tell me that they couldn't talk to me because their four demands had not been met, although they had no objection to my talking to them. This tight organization and discipline is very much a theme of black militancy over the past few years, starting with the Black Muslims and going up to Malcolm X, of impeccable self-discipline and middle-class morality. It's also a standard weapon of any kind of revolutionary movement. They are in that sense Old Leftists. It was something done not to arouse respect from the whites, but to eliminate irrelevant attacks from them. I don't think that they would have tolerated smoking pot or getting drunk, though there certainly was a lot of gaiety in there.

One girl who occupied Hamilton later described the atmosphere inside the building:

> The spirit inside was beautiful; there was singing, talking, dancing to music from small phonographs, watching TV, participating in the interminable meetings. One student, after spending five days

in the building, could not sleep in his bed at home; he had to curl up on the floor.

To coördinate the operations in the four buildings held by white students, a headquarters—Strike Central—was set up on the third floor of Ferris Booth Hall. Strike Central quickly took on a life of its own. Most of the offices of the Citizenship Council were given over to the strikers, as was space donated by the heads of other student activities. In the room that had housed the campus humor magazine a press office was set up, where each day reams of releases were printed for eager reporters. The editors of the yearbook agreed to let their offices serve as a kitchen and food supply station. Hot meals were prepared by Barnard strikers and visiting girls twenty-four hours a day to feed the growing number of students who worked in the central organization or anyone else who was hungry. Cartons of fruit and canned goods lined the walls—at one point there were over two hundred donated grapefruits waiting at Strike Central for distribution. Caucus chambers were set up for top-level meetings of the Strike Steering Committee or negotiating sessions with faculty representatives. The corridor was filled at all hours of the day and night with the clacking sound of mimeograph machines, turning out inter-building memos on the strikers' political position as well as leaflets to persuade the uncommitted. One room was set aside as a "money room"—anyone authorized by the leaders of the strike could come here and get a supply of cash if he needed it. The money, like the food, came from collections conducted on campus and throughout the city.

The influx of female radicals caused a problem on the third floor of Ferris Booth, where there is no ladies' room. The men's room was immediately designated as "liberated," and was used for the rest of the occupation by both sexes simultaneously. And everywhere were signs— "Create two, three, many Columbias," "All power to the communes," and "Up against the wall, motherfucker!" A room with a window overlooking the campus was chosen as a communications center, and students manned walkie-talkies and phones connecting each of the occupied buildings. Another area became temporary sleeping quarters for strike workers who could not make it back to their dorms or apartments, or, in the case of Barnard strikers, did not want to bother with curfews.

Bureaucracies tend to become more powerful than the operations they are meant to facilitate, and Strike Central, too, began heading in this direction. Some students inside the "liberated" buildings soon began to chafe under the administration that sprouted. Many resented the fact that all communication between buildings had to be channeled through

Ferris Booth and felt that the central headquarters was becoming too powerful.

Since the first split with the blacks, the strike had been plagued by problems of divisiveness. The nine-man committee, which was created to organize the original Hamilton sit-in, shrank to six when the blacks left. This soon became the nucleus of a new Strike Steering Committee and was expanded to include representatives from each of the four white buildings. Despite all official statements to the contrary, the students in Low, Math, Fayerweather and Avery never knew whether they could count on the support of those in Hamilton. Within the white camp the problem was no less severe. The Fayerweather and Avery moderates seemed at times close to breaking with the more militant leftists. Even among the radicals the factionalization that SDS had lived with since its birth persisted.

Because the radical strike leadership was having so much trouble with the moderates, it took special pains to preserve the pyramidal structure of the *apparat*. This arrangement frustrated many moderate strikers. One Fayerweather demonstrator who tried unsuccessfully to circumvent the new system and circulate a moderate set of demands, to which SDS was opposed, complained later:

> I went over to see Tom Hayden in Math. He told me I would have to see the people in Ferris Booth. I went to the central steering committee to ask them about the possibility [of accepting a new set of demands]. There they gave me a very paternalistic, patient explanation of why I was wrong. After this experience I came to realize that only an open revolt against the leadership could be effective. They weren't going to give in.

Such a revolution within the revolution never took place, however. Bureaucratic as the Strike Central system was, it was seen as necessary to prevent the faculty and administration from chipping first one building, then another, away from the strike alliance. And it succeeded; the alliance held until the end of the occupation and beyond.

The occupants of the "liberated" buildings were not without their own traditions and sacraments. One night late in the occupation The Pageant Players, a group of street actors, came into Fayerweather Hall to perform "guerrilla theater" for the student strikers. A makeshift stage was put up in a large room, and the actors set their scene with a few painted cardboard props: a castle in a kingdom "very far from here." The story line was simple: the poor people of the kingdom were getting out of control, so the king and queen provided them with welfare, medicare and moldy bread, and sent them off to war. But once they were given guns the people turned full circle and aimed at the king. The king resigned, and the people stormed his castle and knocked it down. The room was packed with almost all the three hundred students who were living in Fayerweather, and with the defeat of the monarchy they all began chanting, cheering and dancing wildly over the castle ruins. An effigy of Grayson Kirk was thrown into the middle of the room, and the strikers tore it to shreds as makeshift drums beat out a thundering rhythm. The students—many of them dizzily waving glowing candles—formed one long chain which snaked around the darkened room as the drums became louder and the tempo faster.

Suddenly, someone at the top of a staircase leading into the room shouted, "Clear the steps!" As the frenzy subsided, a young girl, clad in a white sweater, white jeans and veil, and holding a bouquet of daisies, stood in candlelight at the top of the stairs. To her right stood a boy, wearing a Nehru jacket over an orange turtleneck, beads and a very small black power button. Both were immaculately dressed, freshly scrubbed and blushing. A procession of strikers marched solemnly down the steps, each carrying a candle. Her name was Andrea, his was Richard, and they were about to be married.

The two had known each other for some time before the occupation and had planned to be married later in the spring. But caught up in the spirit of the Fayerweather community, they decided to advance the date and take their vows inside the occupied building, surrounded by the students they had been living with for almost a week. A clergyman had been sent for, and now the Reverend William Starr appeared at the top of the stairs, between Andrea and Richard. The ceremony was short:

"Do you, Andrea, take Richard for your man?"

"Yes."

"Do you, Richard, take Andrea for your girl?"

"Yes."

As the crowd below began noisy cheers of celebration, Starr smiled and said, "I now pronounce you children of the new age."

# 7

## *Bullshit*

**L**IONEL TRILLING was driven in a police car to his apartment two blocks from the campus just before the aborted bust Friday morning. Eugene Galanter, one of the two other members of the prestigious committee appointed Thursday afternoon to form a tripartite commission,[1] was also taken home under police escort. When the police arrived, the administration feared, the campus would not be safe for the three professors, who were scheduled to meet with Truman and Kirk later that morning. Most of the faculty members who had stood guard at the entrances to the occupied buildings, ready to interpose themselves between demonstrators and police, left the campus after the police had been called off. A few stood around talking to students about how close the University had come to violence. In Low Library Vice President Truman picked up a half sandwich from the ever-replenished buffet table in Dean Fraenkel's office and turned to Alan Westin to discuss what had happened at the negotiating session in Mathematics Hall between the three faculty members and Mark Rudd. President Kirk read the announcement of the postponement of police action once more over WKCR and then made ready to leave for the night. The office cleared.

Kirk and Truman were well aware that by not using the police that night they had foreclosed the option of clearing the buildings until at least Sunday night. The long weekend ahead promised possible confron-

---

[1] This was the student-faculty-administration commission recommended by the College faculty Wednesday to investigate the issues involved in the crisis. By Thursday afternoon, however, Trilling, Galanter and Carl Hovde, the third member of the group, had decided that the scope of the commission's activities would be limited to the question of discipline, despite the broad mandate from the College faculty.

tation with peace marchers from the city-wide anti-war rallies, whom leaders of the Columbia demonstration had asked to visit the campus, continuation of the negotiations that had begun Thursday and a prolongation of the student occupations.

Both the negotiations and the confrontation began about the same time, late Friday morning. At 10:30 A.M. Trilling, Galanter and Hovde went to Low Library with a draft of a proposal for the formation of a tripartite disciplinary commission. The Galanter committee had met all day Thursday with students and faculty members in preliminary discussions about the scope and membership of the commission on discipline. The draft they brought to Low on Friday called for the creation of a panel that would have, in effect if not in fact, final judicial authority over discipline. The point was a crucial one, wholly unacceptable to the administration, and was debated for the remainder of the morning. Kirk maintained that since the University Statutes granted him the power "to administer discipline in such cases as he deems proper," it would be impossible for him to give up that authority. The Galanter committee, however, realized that this power would have to be removed from the hands of the President for a disciplinary commission to be recognized by students as legitimate. Due process clearly could not exist when one man had the power to alter sentences arbitrarily. Regardless of what the Charter and Statutes said, they felt, there was no reason why the President could not deal with the immediate problem by delegating his disciplinary powers to the student-faculty-administration commission. The problem has been compared to the issue of tenure: technically, faculty promotions are granted by the Trustees of the University; but in practice tenure decisions are made by senior faculty members and merely rubber-stamped by the Trustees, who in recent years have not dared to use their power to veto faculty recommendations. After several hours of discussion the Galanter committee and the administration worked out a compromise wording on the question of ultimate authority:

> We envisage that the decisions of the commission acting in its appellate capacity will be binding on all parties, but we recognize the statutory responsibilities of the President.

Trilling came away from the negotiations saying that the disciplinary committee would have *de facto* ultimate authority and, though Kirk would have *de jure* authority, he would never use it. The administration, however, did not share that interpretation; Truman said later that Professor Trilling "was running around spouting phrases like *de facto* and *de jure* which he did not understand." The question of Kirk's ultimate judicial authority would prove to be of major consequence in the weeks to come. The power that Kirk clung to for constitutional and personal reasons became for the students the symbol of the patriarchal system they were rebelling against. And the last thing the President wanted to lose was the right to expel those students he thought were destroying the University.

While the negotiations over ultimate authority were proceeding in Low, Columbia was beginning to feel the first ripples of the downtown peace demonstrations taking place that weekend. In the late morning over two hundred black high-school students marched to Columbia and held a rally at 116th Street and Amsterdam Avenue in support of the black students in Hamilton Hall. At 11:15 they streamed onto campus, sprinting toward the Sundial. Echoing the rhetoric of older black militants, the teenagers spoke of an unjust black burden in Vietnam. Shouting "Hell, No, We Won't Go," and "Get Your Gun and Get Whitey," they surged around a narrow brick path to the front of Hamilton. Expecting some trouble, or the occupation of another building by the high-school students, faculty members and Columbia students milled about in front of Hamilton, while several of the visitors scaled the building's walls and climbed through the windows. A few moments later a black Columbia student appeared at the main door, told the kids to "cool it," not to take a building for themselves and to back away from Hamilton. The few who had entered were ejected, and the high-school students retreated docilely to South Field.

The Hamilton leaders had controlled the first of several potentially troublesome situations. An hour later, shortly after one, the two symbols of the black-power movement, SNCC National Chairman H. Rap Brown and his predecessor, Stokely Carmichael, emerged from a car on Amsterdam Avenue. A group of about fifty blacks who were picketing outside the gates at 116th Street surrounded them, as many of the high-school students rushed from South Field to greet the two visitors. A line of police—part of the relatively small detail that was patrolling Columbia Friday—stood shoulder-to-shoulder at the entrance to the campus. The crowd inside and outside pressed tightly against them. Brown extended his arm past the police to shake hands with one of the high-school students inside. The student pulled, the line of police broke and Brown and Carmichael marched triumphantly onto the campus. They went directly to Hamilton Hall, followed by a throng of chanting blacks and surprised reporters. There they met with the student leaders inside for about forty minutes. As they conferred, the crowd outside Hamilton grew. Antagonistic factions began to jeer at each other as many whites became apprehensive about the presence of the two militants on campus. Rows of faculty members, black high-school students, white radicals and counter-demonstrators pressed up tight in front of the building.

Sociologist Immanuel Wallerstein, sensing trouble, moved onto the steps with a bullhorn and made a nervous plea to the students, asking them to refrain from violence: "If one incident of force starts anywhere on this campus I have reason to believe that the police will be here and this University will be destroyed. If you believe that this University is, was or could be an institution for rational discourse, I urge you to keep calm." Shortly after Wallerstein finished, the doors to Hamilton opened and Brown and Carmichael climbed out over the barricades. Carmichael stood quietly at Brown's side as the SNCC chairman spoke. But the white audience, anticipating a verbal whipping, was surprised. Instead of haranguing, Brown calmly read the text of a press statement that had been issued the previous evening by the students in Hamilton. When he finished he added a few words of his own. Shaking his fist, he shouted, "If the University doesn't deal with our brothers in there, they're going to have to deal with the brothers out on the streets." But that was the extent of his vehemence. Brown turned to Carmichael, asking him if he had anything to say. The man who had coined the term "black power" smiled and shook his head. A few moments later the two walked off the campus, followed like celebrities, signing autographs and telling reporters that they would return. The results of the forty-minute conversation between the two leaders and the Hamilton Hall Steering Committee had surprised nearly everyone on the outside. Brown and Carmichael had gone in and offered their rhetoric and whatever support the Hamilton Hall leaders might need. They were told that the rhetoric of Bill Sales, Ray Brown and Cicero Wilson would suffice, that the Columbia brothers had the demonstration fully under control. The most valuable contribution the SNCC leaders could make would be to affirm the stand taken by the Columbia blacks and to draw the attention of the world outside to their demands. This was one of the chief concerns of the blacks in Hamilton, and Brown had devoted part of his short extemporaneous speech to an attack on the press for "blacking out" the actions of the students in Hamilton Hall.

When Brown and Carmichael broke through the police lines at the Amsterdam gate a faculty runner had breathlessly burst into the Ad Hoc Faculty Group meeting in Philosophy Hall, asking for a contingent of twenty professors to go to the gates and help preserve peace. The Ad Hoc Group had reconvened at ten Friday morning after the previous night's near-debacle. They had issued a statement of purpose the evening before and now turned to the task of policing a tense campus to permit negotiations to proceed in peace. This and virtually non-stop discussion occupied them for the next three days. The professors decided to guard the campus gates, assume the responsibility of checking the identification cards of all those who entered and interpose themselves twenty-four hours a day at any point that demonstrators and counter-demonstrators or police seemed likely to collide. A faculty patrol had been set up around Low immediately after the aborted bust Friday morning and by the evening had tightened to a cordon. That the faculty members were negotiating and policing at the same time was seen by the strikers as an indication of bad faith, and by the counter-demonstrators as evidence that the faculty was vacillating and unwilling to end the demonstrations.

While the professors debated in the lounge of Philosophy Hall or manned their posts on campus, the real work of the Ad Hoc Faculty Group was being done in executive sessions of the fifteen-man steering committee, formed Friday afternoon.[2] Most of the group's activities were initiated by the steering committee, which sent out negotiators to meet with students and masterminded strategy. The general meeting in the lounge ratified all steering committee decisions and provided a forum where professors, regardless of rank or political outlook, could come and express their views on the crisis.

The campus remained relatively quiet Friday afternoon after Brown and Carmichael left. Several hundred city policemen patrolled the campus, manning checkpoints at all entrances, stopping all those who wanted to enter the dormitories and demanding to see their keys. Many were rookies, unaware that several University buildings had been occupied for over three days. One said to a student, "We been through this kind of thing before. The best thing that could happen would be if they just sent us home. You don't want us here, they don't want us here and we don't want to be here."

The student demonstrators continued to control five buildings, and campus sentiment shifted toward sympathy with the rebellion. With Vice President Truman's Thursday night announcement that construction of the gymnasium had been halted, that issue moved temporarily away from the center of the crisis. It was becoming apparent that the main points of contention would be the demand for amnesty and the larger question of University discipline. While the students were stating that they would settle for nothing short of complete amnesty, and the administration was making it clear that it would never grant amnesty, the Trilling-Galanter-Hovde committee completed its drafting of a proposal that it hoped would be acceptable to all sides. About four Friday

[2] The steering committee, whose membership underwent several changes and additions, included as of Friday afternoon: Robert Belknap, Daniel Bell, Robert Cumming, Alexander Dallin, Robert Fogelson, Terence Hopkins, Mark Kesselman, Seymour Melman, Walter Metzger, David Rothman, Dankwart Rustow, James Shenton, Allan Silver, Immanuel Wallerstein and Alan Westin (chairman).

afternoon this formulation, tentatively approved by the administration, was read to the Ad Hoc Faculty Group. The Galanter committee was in no way responsible to the Ad Hoc Group but did feel strongly attached to its work. The document that had been drafted called for the formation of a disciplinary commission to be composed of five students, five faculty members and two administrators. The commission was to develop proposals for permanent judicial processes, formulate general guidelines for the discipline of students participating in the current demonstrations and serve as a review board for all disciplinary decisions. The membership of the committee that was proposed Friday proved to be controversial, for it included a faculty member, Leon Lederman, who had formerly worked for IDA, a student who was one of the chief spokesmen for the Majority Coalition, and Dean Fraenkel, who the night before had told Mark Rudd that he would certainly be expelled from the University. In addition, of the five students originally proposed, one favored amnesty, one was a moderate and the remaining three included a student active in the Majority Coalition, a former leader of the Columbia Young Republican Club and a star basketball player who was one of the few black College students who did not occupy Hamilton Hall.

The Ad Hoc Faculty Group recessed shortly after it heard the Galanter committee proposal. As the professors filed out of Philosophy Hall they were met by a crowd of about two hundred members of the Majority Coalition, who had marched with conservative economics professor C. Lowell Harriss across the lawn and now stopped near the statue of "Le Penseur" just outside the doors of Philosophy. Throughout the afternoon members of the Majority Coalition had been huddling first in front of Hamilton, then on South Field and finally in Wollman. A statement outlining their position had been distributed earlier that day:

> We are the Majority Coalition. We represent the two thousand students who signed the petition circulated last Wednesday. Mr. Rudd has made his demands, we demand nothing. We can only request.
>
> We support any reasonable alternative to SDS' ultimatum, including the tripartite commission. It is a positive step, we look for others.
>
> SDS demands amnesty. Amnesty is out of the question. This is the feeling of the majority of students and many of the faculty.
>
> We represent campus moderates, not the right wing as Mr. Rudd would lead you to believe. Internally, we may differ on substantive issues, but we are united in our condemnation of their tactics. We have acted responsibly and rationally in the face of provocation, yet, make no mistake, we are resolute in our purpose.

Often throughout the crisis conservative professors made use of the staunch anti-SDS position of the Majority Coalition to try to persuade their colleagues and the administration that decisive action had to be taken immediately against the demonstrators to prevent widespread student violence. Now Professor Harriss used the conservatives to make a similar point outside Philosophy: these young men have a reasonable point of view; if they are ignored any longer they may resort to unreasonable acts. Unless the insurrection is ended soon, by the police if necessary, there will be widespread student violence, he warned.

Several professors believed that the conservatives constituted the only responsible student voice. But many, hard pressed to handle one dissident faction, were further upset by the growing anti-demonstration force. Their response was to treat the athletes patronizingly, allowing them to speak at faculty meetings, applauding them for "rational conduct" and then dismissing them. Professor Morgenbesser criticized this treatment:

> Everyone was thanking them for not using their muscles. They were virtually being thanked for not machine-gunning the whole place. They were being treated as if calm behavior were a special thing for them. People were saying, "I know you're a nut, but please don't be a violent nut."

Friday evening the spirits of the Strike Coördinating Committee were high, and a press conference was called for 7:30 to convey their elation. Mark Rudd, unshaven and tired, smiled as he read:

> At present the substantive demands of the demonstrators here are well on their way to resolution. The gymnasium will certainly not be built and University and faculty ties with the Institute for Defense Analyses will certainly be broken. The key issue is whether or not the University will grant the demonstrators a general amnesty. . . . First, we cannot enter into negotiations with an administration that holds a sword over our heads. This principle of no reprisals is standard negotiating procedure. The second point is more important. Most of the campus agrees with our demands but some people disagree with our tactics. These people must come to realize that intellectual support without action is worth nothing. During the course of the years we acted through standard channels to get results on IDA and the gym and we were rebuffed at every turn, rudely and irresponsibly. Thus the actions we took were necessary and just and we will not accept judgment or punishment from an illegitimate authority—the administration.

The press statement was perhaps the most confident ever issued by the Strike Coördinating Committee, reflecting growing campus support for the six demands. Rudd went on to urge the faculty, as the demonstrators did throughout the crisis, to cease mediating and to take sides with the students:

> Now the faculty is attempting to devise compromises on account of what they think is a threat of violence either from campus right-wingers or from the blacks. We feel the faculty is unrealistically panicky. The Harlem people on campus have maintained magnificent decorum and control thus far. The right-wingers are disorganized and many of them are leaving campus. The only possibility of violence is from the police at the instigation of the administration. If the faculty wishes to prevent violence and resolve the entire crisis, they should support our demands against a discredited administration which is responsible only to a board of Trustees who want the gym and IDA maintained and not to the students, faculty, and community who want the gym and IDA to go.
>
> The Strike Coördinating Committee reiterates that our six demands, including the demand for amnesty, must be met.

It was the spirit more than the hard line that got through to people and it was the spirit that convinced the doubtful that the demonstration had turned into a full-scale struggle for power between the students and the administration. As the strikers' chance of victory seemed to be increasing, many previously uncommitted students swung over to their side. The radical tactic of politicizing and polarizing the "silent center" was working.

The SCC press conference had followed a long negotiating session Friday afternoon between Rudd, Gonzalez and former SDS vice chairman Ted Gold and the faculty mediating team of Westin, Rothman and Silver. The talks had picked up where they had left off in Mathematics Library the night before but this time were held in a small office in Ferris Booth Hall near Strike Central. Westin again did most of the talking for the faculty and again tried to convince the students to leave the buildings and let the faculty fight for the demands. According to Gonzalez:

> Rudd suggested that the professors join with us. He told Westin, "Students and faculty can take over the University." Westin, shocked out of his mind, said in as intellectual a way as possible that it was impossible and absurd.

Westin later recalled that he sensed a definite hardening of the line among the student negotiators:

> They said that President Kirk and Vice President Truman must resign, that we must change the corporate structure of the Univer-

sity in order to institute the changes they wanted to have achieved, so that faculty and students would have all the decision-making power. . . . They reiterated their six demands.

About two hours after the press conference, talks were resumed in the same small Ferris Booth Hall office. Rudd had taken off the heavy army boots he often wore and propped his feet on a desk, inches away from Westin's face. The student negotiating team began by accusing the faculty members of bargaining in bad faith, of carrying on separate negotiations with the students in the buildings to split the movement's solidarity and of misrepresenting the results of their talks in their reports to the faculty. The professors denied that they had been devious in negotiations and pledged not to carry on separate talks with anyone but the official student negotiators. As in most of the negotiating sessions with the white radicals, the substantive issues of the gym and IDA were avoided by both sides and the discussion centered on the more critical question of discipline. Rudd again brought up the idea, as he had on Thursday night, of a trial by a student-faculty committee that would have power to judge but not to punish the demonstrators. The faculty members then introduced a new idea into the discussions—collective and equal punishment for the students involved in the demonstrations as the only possible way of dealing with mass political activity. The professors' diplomatic rationale was that such a disciplinary approach would virtually guarantee something approaching amnesty—it seemed unlikely that the administration would suspend five hundred students en masse. Their moral rationale was that because of the political and disorganized nature of the protests it would be unfair to single out any individuals for particularly severe discipline. Further, it would be impossible to determine who among the demonstrators had rifled Kirk's files, who had vandalized his office and who had merely sat in. Both Westin and Rothman said later that the idea of collective punishment seemed to interest the students, although it seemed doubtful whether they would have accepted that formula instead of amnesty. Professor Rothman later described the talks:

> We didn't get anywhere but it was very interesting. Rudd was asking very specific questions—nitty-gritty questions such as how are you going to get our ID cards, how do you know who is in the buildings: the sort of questions and discussion one might have expected coming from a party really prepared to begin negotiations.

Shortly before 1 A.M. Saturday, two telephone calls interrupted the negotiating session in Ferris Booth. The first was from Peter Kenen, the young economics professor, who was close to the administration. Kenen asked for Silver and then told him that he had just been at the faculty meeting and that the group was on the verge of voting for amnesty; very excited, and perhaps exaggerating his fears that amnesty would be approved, he suggested that the negotiators return to the meeting to forestall a vote. As soon as he hung up Rudd received a call from a more radical member of the economics department, Robert Zevin, who reported that a vote on amnesty was close, and that if Rudd came over and appealed to the faculty he might be able to swing a victory. Rudd put down the receiver and calmly turned to Westin, "You may want to go back to your meeting; something interesting may be happening." Negotiations were terminated for the night as the group made its way over to Philosophy.

When Westin arrived at the meeting he found that the group had just tabled a proposal to replace the tripartite disciplinary commission with a bipartite committee excluding administrators. The group was now engaged in a brief discussion about amnesty but was nowhere near voting on the question. Westin learned, however, that several leftist professors as well as the president of the Columbia University Student Council had spoken that evening in favor of amnesty and had been loudly applauded. The applause had disturbed Kenen and heartened Zevin to the point where both men were sure—probably incorrectly—that a proposal for amnesty would pass. Westin quickly took the chair and asked for a report from Professor Wallerstein who had been negotiating throughout the day with the black students in Hamilton Hall. Wallerstein painted a fairly optimistic picture of the talks with the blacks, saying, "Dialogue is still open, and the students are taking the night to think about various proposals. I've arranged to see them early tomorrow morning." Westin then rose to give his own encouraging report on the negotiations with the white radicals and told the faculty members assembled that they were making slow but noticeable progress in their talks. At that moment, he said later, he turned to the doorway at his left and saw Mark Rudd standing there, "with a kind of friendly expression on his face; I thought he was going to match what I had just said." On entering Philosophy Hall Rudd had gone to a phone in the building's self-service elevator, dialed the offices of the *Spectator* and said that a major development was about to break. He had then hustled away for a quick meeting with Zevin where he developed a strategy quite different from what Westin was expecting. Westin signaled Rudd, and the SDS leader moved to the front of the room to speak:

> We had exploratory talks . . . very exploratory, more in the line of bullshit. . . . It's going to be impossible to discipline

people at all for these crimes. . . . There is only one solution: recognize that these are political acts and the reasons behind them are political. . . . Amnesty is really the only solution. I ask that this group grant us amnesty with the understanding that what we did was right.

The word "bullshit," though spoken casually by Rudd, negated everything Westin had just said. Rudd's speech was designed to convince the faculty that since negotiations were not getting anywhere they should vote for amnesty. It backfired. Some sympathetic faculty members shouted, "Oh, Mark, what are you doing?" Others demanded, "How can he talk to us like that?" Alan Westin shouted for order and, to prevent a vote, slammed his hand down on the table, stated "This meeting is now adjourned" and walked out of the room.

## 8

## A Bitter Pill

**R**UDD'S "BULLSHIT" SPEECH soon became a landmark of the Columbia uprising, and the already popular phrase joined LeRoi Jones's "Up against the wall, motherfucker" as a byword of the strikers. The incident had caused many faculty members to worry that perhaps their "rational discourse" and negotiations might not be successful. Psychologist Eugene Galanter said later that by Friday night he had concluded that negotiations on rational grounds were impossible:

> The only thing the students would respond to would be actions; no pattern of words, no matter what they meant, would have any effect.

Even the steering committee of the Ad Hoc Faculty Group decided to cut off negotiations, at least temporarily, after Rudd's Friday night speech.

Shortly before noon Saturday hopes for a peaceful mediation of the crisis suffered another setback, more serious than the "bullshit" episode. Members of the board of Trustees, normally distant from campus affairs, were slowly being drawn into the crisis. On Friday morning, William Petersen, president of the Irving Trust Company, who serves as chairman of the Columbia Trustees, made his first major attempt to bring peace to the Morningside campus. He phoned the Mayor of New York City. Lindsay aide Barry Gottehrer later described the conversation:

> Petersen wanted the Mayor to come up to Columbia and settle the situation. Lindsay was willing, but asked what leverage he would be given in mediating. Petersen said they would give him no

leverage. He just asked the Mayor to come onto campus and walk around, talking to people, as he does in Harlem. He expected a miracle.

Lindsay never came, but Petersen continued his search for a solution. Friday evening the Trustees were called together for an informal meeting downtown to discuss what was happening to their University. During times of peace the board normally meets on the first Monday of each month. But since the start of the crisis all sides had been calling for an emergency meeting of the Trustees because these were the only men in a position to make final decisions. Now, however, it seemed that such a convocation would be a very complicated matter. According to the 1810 Charter of the University:

> The said chairman or senior trustee shall not summon a meeting of the corporation unless . . . he cause notice of the time and place of the said meeting to be given in one or more of the public newspapers printed in the City of New York at least three days before such meeting.

No notice had been filed in time for the Friday night meeting, and so, although a quorum was present, the gathering was not official. Nonetheless, Chairman Petersen took it upon himself to issue a public statement Saturday morning stating his interpretation of the opinions expressed by the quorum of Trustees present. The Petersen statement was read to the Ad Hoc Faculty Group late Saturday morning:

> The Trustees of the University met and conferred yesterday (Friday) regarding the situation on the Morningside Heights campus. They expressed approval of the course which has been followed by the University administration and commended the restraint which has been exhibited by the administration and the overwhelming majority of the faculty and students in a most difficult situation. In common with the administration and those great majorities, the Trustees deplore the complete disruption of normal University operations and the illegal seizure and occupation of University buildings, perpetrated by a *small minority of students, aided and abetted by outsiders* who have injected themselves into the situation. . . .
>
> The Trustees have advised the President that they wholeheartedly support the administration position that there shall be no amnesty accorded to those who have engaged in this illegal conduct. Moreover, they not only support the President's stand, but *affirmatively direct, that he shall maintain the ultimate disciplinary*

*power* over the conduct of students of the University as required by the Charter and Statutes of the University.

Insofar as the gymnasium is concerned, the Trustees feel that the attempt to depict the construction of that building as a matter involving a racial issue or discrimination is an attempt to create an *entirely false issue* by individuals who are either not conversant with, or who disregard, the facts. However, the Trustees have approved the action taken by the administration *at the request of the Mayor* of New York City, on Thursday, April 25, to halt construction activities *temporarily*. This action represented an appropriate response, and *a courtesy to the chief executive of the City* at a time of tension. . . .

[The Trustees] have expressly authorized the President to take all further steps which he may deem necessary or advisable to enable the University to resume its normal activities. [Italics added]

In Philosophy Lounge the faculty members listened with amazement to the statement, which seemed to undercut their entire negotiating effort and even to contradict the stance that the administration had taken. Alex Dallin rose as the reading was finished and pronounced in a voice that stilled the murmurings, "This is distressing and extremely deplorable." There was sustained applause, and then his voice flared out once again, "If there had been any doubt of the need for an independent faculty, it is now entirely removed."

The Petersen statement was received with hostility in nearly every quarter of the campus and was seen as written proof that the Trustees were as out of touch with University life as everyone had imagined. Herbert Deane said later that the Petersen statement "almost blew us out of the water." The administration had announced on Thursday night that gym construction had been suspended, a partial concession to one of the Six Demands. Now on Saturday, when the gym had all but dropped out of the picture, the Trustees proclaimed that the gym was "an entirely false issue" and that construction had only been halted temporarily as a courtesy to the Mayor. Before the Petersen statement the administration had seemed ready to modify its stand on discipline by delegating some authority to the tripartite commission proposed by the Galanter committee. Now the Trustees ordered the President to "maintain the ultimate disciplinary power." These men seemed wholly insensitive to the delicate compromises and wordings that had been worked out during the past few days by the administration. The Petersen statement was a trust smasher; now no one knew whom to believe. No one, that is, except the Trustees, who had no qualms about putting their faith in an administration which had been trying to establish its credibility and now found itself further discredited by their resounding support. If Mark Rudd had drafted the statement for the Trustees instead of Petersen it could not have made the situation more critical or the University look worse. At a time when resolution of the crisis hinged on the appropriate use of words, the Trustees picked all the wrong ones. And at a time when all factions on campus—from Kirk's to Rudd's—were at least beginning to share common ideas on decentralization of power and University reform, the one group with the power to institute such changes came out with a hard-line endorsement of the status quo. To the demonstrators a statement like Petersen's was tactically welcome, for in clearly defining the "enemy'" position it further polarized the campus. And when sides were chosen few opted to be on the same team as Petersen.

The paradox of negotiations was now clear: the students had been listening to offers they would never consider; the faculty had been promising them things the administration would refuse to accept; and the administration had been making concessions which the Trustees now rejected out of hand.

The rapport that Professor Wallerstein had built up with the black students in Hamilton Hall during three days of negotiations was virtually shattered. The Petersen statement was not received by the black students until five hours after it was released on campus. When Wallerstein arrived in Hamilton Hall for an early evening negotiating session the blacks were furious. The statement had flatly contradicted many of the offers Wallerstein and Kirk had made. The students had been told that the gym was all but dead and now they felt they had been deceived. Wallerstein had brought Professor Galanter into Hamilton on Friday afternoon to read the blacks his proposal on the discipline commission and to assure them that Kirk would never overrule the recommendations of the commission. Now Petersen was saying that Kirk would—indeed, *must*—retain his ultimate power. The Trustees' statement also ruined hopes for a peace formula that Wallerstein had drafted and the administration had already accepted. The substance of this proposal was no different from what Kirk had promised the black students Wednesday night, but the wording was different enough to make Wallerstein think a breakthrough was possible. As he recalled later,

> I told Truman that the gym was really important to the black students and that coming out of this with a good organizational image was very important. I thought that they had insisted on amnesty only to build their organizational image and thus that it

was secondary. They really weren't afraid like the SDS kids of the consequences because they knew nothing would happen to them other than perhaps disciplinary warning. I said that since they had made amnesty one of their preconditions they weren't going to back down but perhaps we could play a game because they had never actually said amnesty from *what*. So I said let's give them amnesty from civil and criminal prosecution. Truman liked the idea and we suggested to Kirk that he try this formula of amnesty on criminal charges and a statement on the gym and Kirk bought it. It was in the middle of their [the black students'] considering that proposal that the Petersen statement came and then they didn't know which statement to believe.

At the Ad Hoc Faculty meeting, meanwhile, the professors sought a suitable response to the Trustees' action. Marvin Harris indignantly proposed a resolution condemning the Petersen statement and calling it "untimely and ill-considered in substance and spirit." Although most of the members present were disturbed by the Petersen statement they did not at this time want to launch a frontal attack against the Trustees; the Harris motion was tabled. Anger shifted instead to the administration, which Seymour Melman accused of breaking down in a time of crisis. Dean Fraenkel, tired and upset, took the floor and pleaded,

> For God's sake, we're trying to save this University. Now we don't all agree, but please don't attack us for not trying to do our best in what we are trying to do.

With negotiations stalled, the faculty group found that it had little to do but wait and talk. During the morning and afternoon its attention focused on more practical matters such as the faculty cordon of Low Library which had all but disintegrated by Saturday. Edward Leonard, a crew-cut professor of chemical engineering who looked more like a camp counselor than a college professor, stood up on a chair and made a plea for the reëstablishment of the faculty line. Fearful of violent clashes between demonstrators and counter-demonstrators, the faculty group decided to reconstruct their cordon on even stricter terms: absolutely no students would be allowed access to Low except those officially designated as mediators.

That done, the faculty group turned to a matter of more significance but one upon which it had no influence. It had been announced Saturday morning that a meeting would be held in the Law School of all the faculties of the University located on Morningside Heights. The meeting of the Joint Faculties was the first of its kind in the modern history of the University and had been arranged by the administration at the request of a number of more conservative faculty members who felt that their opinions were not being expressed by the professors in Philosophy Hall. The Ad Hoc Group feared that the conservatives would attempt to push a pro-administration proposal through the Joint Faculties. The administration had announced that only voting faculty members—assistant, associate and full professors—would be allowed to attend the meeting. The junior faculty members, who tended to be more left-wing and who had been prominent in the affairs of the Ad Hoc Group, were disturbed by their exclusion. By Saturday the junior faculty—instructors, preceptors and teaching assistants—became a new party in the Columbia struggle, demanding to be recognized and enfranchised. Throughout the day members of the Ad Hoc Group discussed whether they should request the administration to admit younger faculty members to the Joint Faculties meeting in the Law School. Junior faculty members, who had been caucusing in an upstairs classroom in increasing numbers during the day, finally brought the question to a vote at the plenary session of the Ad Hoc Faculty Group that evening. The resolution that passed without substantial opposition requested the administration to allow junior faculty members to participate and vote in the Joint Faculties meeting. The resolution was presented to Kirk and Truman that evening and was rejected on the grounds that the Law School Auditorium was too small to seat all the junior faculty and that they could not be officially notified in time for the meeting. The administration's response annoyed many faculty members who felt that the space problem was only an excuse. One prominent Columbia professor said that if he were President of the University he would have taken his entire faculty to Madison Square Garden if necessary.

While the faculty group debated throughout the weekend in the crowded Philosophy Hall Lounge, the atmosphere on campus was charged with politics and wariness. Hundreds of student demonstrators were in the buildings participating in never-ending discussions of defense tactics, the importance of being radical and the advisability of accepting compromise solutions. Many left their buildings temporarily to go for walks around campus, except for those in Low who knew they would be prevented by the faculty cordon from returning. Out on the campus words were replaced by color symbolism. Red flags waved from the rooftops of Fayerweather and Mathematics. There were armbands for every hue of political affiliation. The strikers wore red ones, sympathetic students who favored amnesty wore green, those who opposed violence (and later on the Majority Coalition) wore light blue, and the faculty tied white handkerchiefs around their arms for peace and neutrality.

Although campus security guards, city policemen and faculty members stood at the two main gates checking identification cards, hundreds of non-Columbia people managed to filter onto the campus. Prominent New York intellectuals—Dwight Macdonald, Conor Cruise O'Brien, Stephen Spender and Allen Ginsberg—wandered about the campus inhaling revolution and climbing through windows to tour the occupied buildings. Downtown, ninety thousand people participated in an antiwar demonstration in Central Park's Sheep Meadow. Similar rallies were held throughout the nation. It was protest weekend in the United States, and Columbia was the place to be.

Inside Low Library the administrators were settling into routinized crisis operations. Kirk and Truman had inched as far as they would go in modifying their position. Faculty members who spoke to the two men over the weekend later said that it was clear then that the administration had no more to offer, especially regarding amnesty. Whatever timid departures they had begun to make from their old stand had been frozen by the Petersen statement, and they now stood rigid and immobile at a point somewhere between partial concession and no concession at all.

In the occupied buildings a similar sort of diplomatic rigor mortis prevailed among the strike leaders and negotiators, if not among their constituents. The strikers had not won their six demands. They had offered and would offer no compromise on any of those demands, especially amnesty. Over the weekend it became clear that the crisis was quickly heading for one of only two possible ends—amnesty or bust.

The Columbia administration relied during the crisis on only two men to make its top decisions: President Kirk and Vice President Truman. Truman had been in the central administration for only ten months yet had been given a relatively free hand in running the internal affairs of the University. As a result of this freedom, however, the position of vice president was somewhat more confining for him during the crisis when Kirk, too, was involved in making on-the-spot decisions. The perspectives and attitudes of the two men were close on most of the issues involved, and in the few instances when Truman disagreed with Kirk it was unlikely that he would take a public stand against the man he hoped to succeed. However Truman, who was normally a smooth administrator whom most people respected, hardened almost to the point of intractability during the crisis. He came close to losing control of himself several times under pressure and he realized that his impeccably drafted future as President of the University might be crumbling with every hour the students remained in the buildings. Kirk was not accustomed to dealing with campus problems, since he devoted most of his time as President to fund-raising and public-relations activities. For a man on the verge of entering dignified retirement this catastrophe seemed a thorough repudiation of all he had done as President of Columbia, of much that he had stood for as a man.

Over the weekend Kirk and Truman surrounded themselves in Dean Fraenkel's suite with lines of communication to various parties in the crisis. One office was turned over to city officials, who divided up their task of keeping an ear to a troublesome campus. William Booth continued to work with the blacks in Hamilton, Sid Davidoff was assigned to talk with the Majority Coalition, Gottehrer kept his eyes on the community and on SDS, and Jay Kriegel, a third Lindsay aide, built up contacts with the Ad Hoc Faculty Group. All were kept informed of the administration's activities.

Another office in the administration headquarters was apportioned to a small group of distinguished and conservative faculty members. The failure of the administration to seek faculty advice until the weekend had been one of the key factors in the emergence of the Ad Hoc Faculty Group and was a continuing source of faculty distrust. On Saturday Polykarp Kusch, a Nobel Prize-winning physicist, historian Richard Hofstadter, Ernest Nagel, a philosopher and one of Columbia's three highly honored University Professors, and several other faculty members moved into Low to offer advice to the administration.

Their first efforts were directed toward drafting an administration-oriented resolution to be introduced at the Sunday meeting of the Joint Faculties. The proposal would assert a broad faculty voice—broader and more conservative than the liberal pronouncements of the Ad Hoc Faculty Group. Late Saturday morning one of the professors in Low phoned economist Peter Kenen, who was asked to come to Low and look at a first draft of the resolution. Kenen had been closely involved in the affairs of the Ad Hoc Group, and while he concurred with the administration he was at the same time well respected by the more liberal faculty members. Kirk's faculty advisors realized that Kenen was the perfect man to introduce the resolution. After making minor changes in the proposal Kenen agreed to sponsor it. He later described the tactic:

> The administration used this device of a pro-administration resolution sponsored by a faculty member on several occasions. They tried to obtain from the faculty a call for action to which they could respond. I did not object to the use of myself as a vehicle in this connection because I liked the proposals and was delighted that the administration was for them.

The economics professor stuffed a copy of the final draft in his coat pocket, where it remained lodged until the next morning, and headed back to the Ad Hoc Faculty meeting.

With no visible steps toward settlement being made in any quarter, a mood of uneasiness began to settle over the leaders of the demonstration.

Saturday afternoon the students in Hamilton Hall sent an open letter to the Harlem community:

> The fight is down to the wire now. The Man is at his wits end in trying to figure out how to deal with us and you. He will have to move soon and if his actions to date are any indication, he will probably move wrong. We need all of your support now. We have been successful in halting the construction [of the gym] but the Man will not meet our second demand which is complete amnesty. This means that he will have to come into Hamilton Hall and take us out by force. Your support and presence might make him think twice about this course of action. Your support is what has kept him from doing it to date. But now, the Man is desperate. Now we ask you to support us with a real show of physical support as well as moral support. We've succeeded in one demand, we can succeed in the other. Our victory is your victory. Your victory is our victory. Every victory for a Black Sister or Brother anywhere is a victory for ALL Black People everywhere. We thank you and ask you to come up and support us tonight. . . . IN FORCE.

The Strike Coördinating Committee also issued a statement Saturday that hinted at uneasiness, but of a different sort. Many students in the buildings seemed to be interested in reaching a compromise settlement, willing to accept something short of amnesty. In an effort to maintain cohesion along the hard line and prevent the movement from splintering, the central leadership issued the following "Internal Memo on Clarifying Our Politics":

> From our present position, we can move in two possible directions:
> To push for the maximum demands that we feel we can realistically attain, even if it means some rhetorical or even substantive concessions;
> Or to maintain political clarity and coherence at the expense of winning certain formal structures. . . . If we make concessions, rhetorical or substantive, on amnesty we may win in return the

A massive rally at the Sundial (above) on Tuesday, April 23, marks the beginning of the month-long Columbia rebellion. Butler Library stands behind the more than 700 demonstrators, counter-demonstrators and observers.   *David Finck*

(Below) Mark Rudd speaks at the Sundial rally, flanked by other members of the "IDA Six." They are, from left, Ted Gold, Rudd, Nate Bossen, Nick Freudenberg (partially hidden) and Ed Hyman.   *David Finck*

(Above) Students tear down part of the fence surrounding the gym site.   *Richard Howard*

Minutes later, police arrest Fred Wilson (below), a sophomore in the College.   *Craig Elle*

By Wednesday morning, black students have sole command of Hamilton Hall (above) while their captive, Acting Dean Henry Coleman (below), peers from his office window.   *Richard Howard*

The Ad Hoc Faculty Group (above) discusses strategy at its first session Thursday in Philosophy Hall.   *Richard Howard*

Its pressure forced Vice President David B. Truman (below) to announce early Friday morning that the administration's request for police action had been rescinded and that construction of the gym had been halted.   *David Clapp*

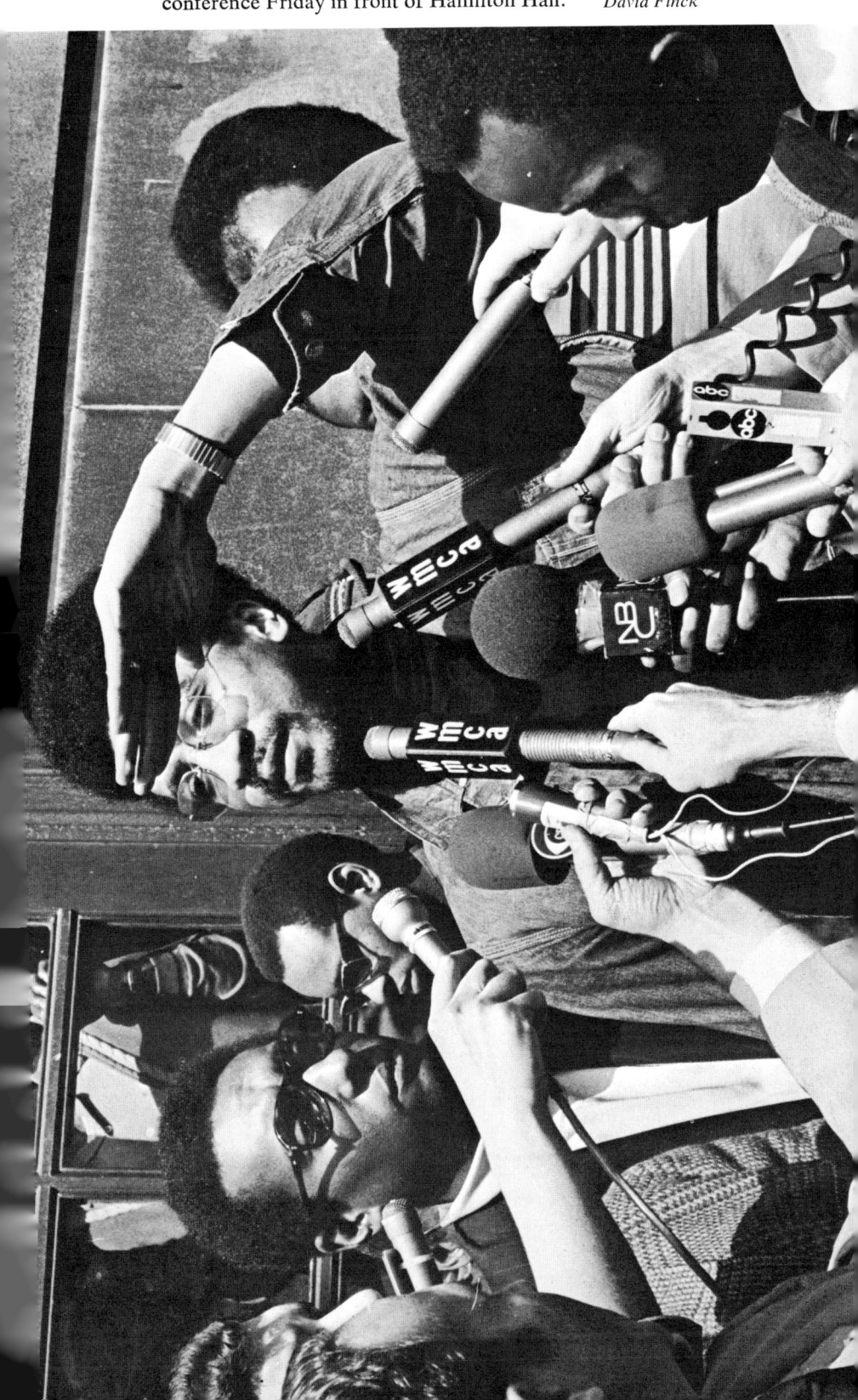

H. Rap Brown (center) and Stokely Carmichael (left) speak at a press conference Friday in front of Hamilton Hall. *David Finck*

Members of the Majority Coalition (top) form a line in front of Low Library on Sunday to keep demonstrators from entering or leaving the building. Meanwhile (above left) Professors James Shenton (right) and Warner Schilling (left) are among faculty who formed their own line outside Low to prevent violence among students. George Fraenkel, Dean of Graduate Faculties (right), also attempts to keep the peace.

*David Finck*

Professors Alan Westin (left) and Immanuel Wallerstein (right) explain the "bitter pill" proposal to the press as members of Ad Hoc Faculty Group Steering Committee stand behind. They are (from left): Dankwart Rustow, Robert Fogelson, Allan Silver, Terrence Hopkins, Robert Cumming, Alexander Dallin and David Rothman. *David Finck*

At Low (left), demonstrators react to the opposition below, and at Mathematics Hall (below), students perch on the ledge overlooking Broadway.

*Richard Howard*

*ard Howard*

The bust begins: outside Hamilton Hall (above), demonstrators block police from the doors as Kenneth Clark (at far right, above) observes. At Avery Hall (right), police charge demonstrators, including an assistant professor of architecture (in jacket).

*Tom Metz*

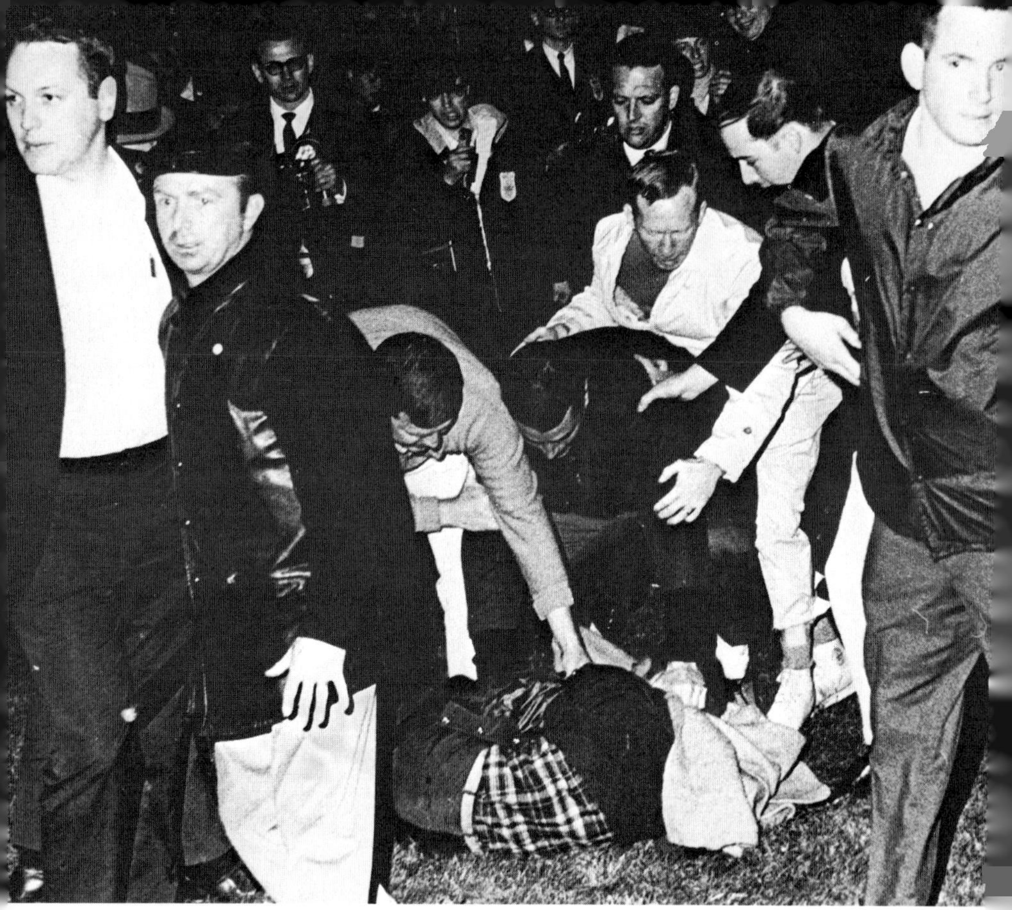

Tom M

At Low (above), a group of plainclothesmen subdues one student while at Avery (below), one of the authors, Oren Root Jr., grimaces after being beaten by police.

Alan Epst

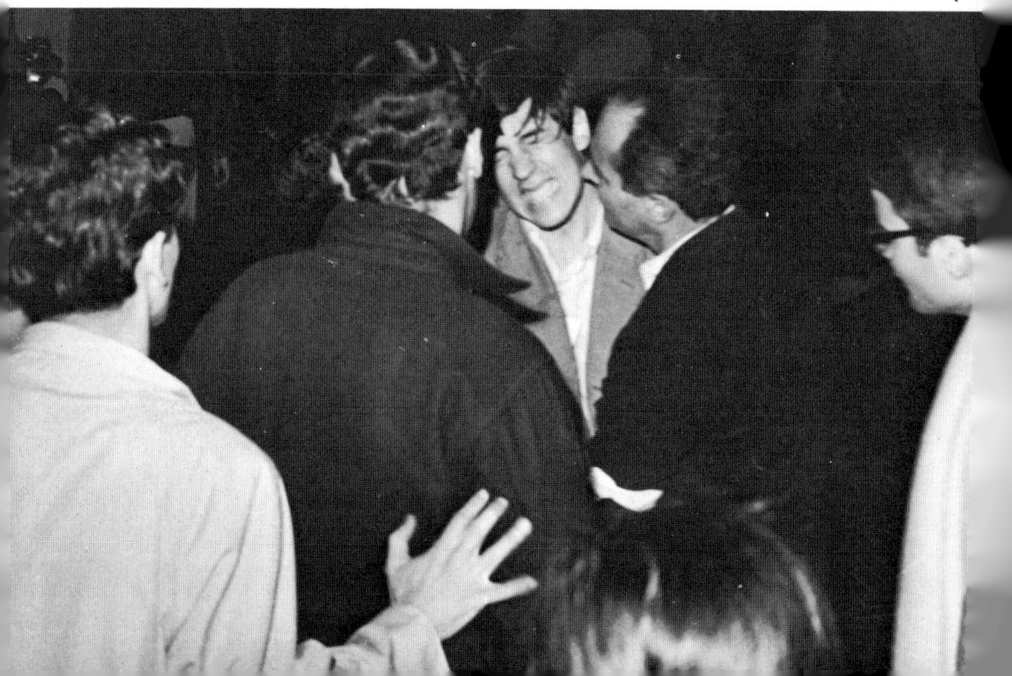

*d Howard*              *David Finck*

Ink drips down a wall in Mathematics (above left). According to several professors, the damage was not done by students.

After surveying his office (below) following the bust, President Grayson Kirk (above right) talks with the press.

An injured cop (above) displays his wound: a girl's teeth marks. *Harvey Fleetwood*

On campus Tuesday evening, Mark Rudd (above right) gives the strikers' victory si
also waved by students (below right) at a mass rally following the bust.

Richard Howard

Allen Wasserman

A few days later, Vice President Truman (left) tours the campus with reporters.

*David Finck*

(Below) The blacks, led by Ray Brown (left), Cicero Wilson (holding sign) and Bill Sales, conduct a victory march.

*Richard Howard*

On May 22, students reoccupy Hamilton Hall (above).

*Richard Howard*

Associate Dean Alex Platt (below left) smiles at the rhetoric of student protester Stu Gedal, but a grim Henry Coleman (below right) tells the students to leave or face arrest and suspension.

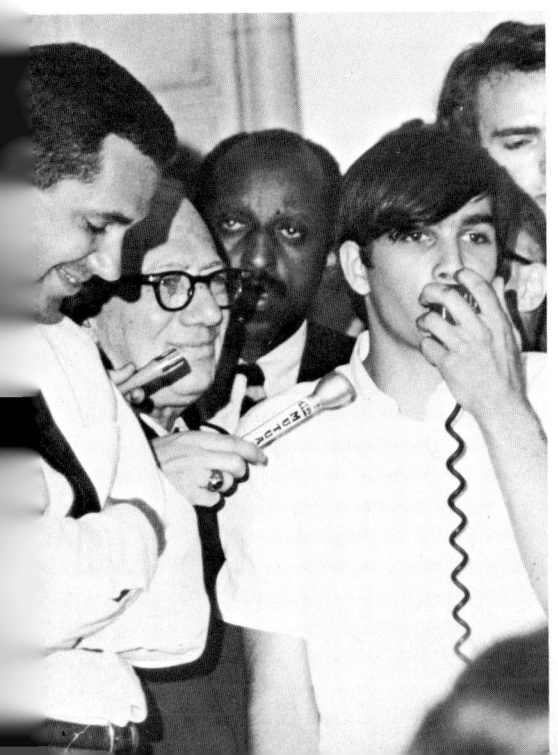

Having cleared the campus a second time, helmeted police guard the steps to Low Library. *Richard Howard*

granting of other of our demands. However, we lose the essential political point that the administration is illegitimate and must be forced to *de facto* declare itself illegitimate by granting amnesty before really substantive structural changes can occur. If we sacrifice political clarity for formal concessions from the faculty and administration, we run the risk that those formal structures will be short-lived, politically empty, and easily co-optable.[1]

The essence of this *clearpolitik* was a demand for unconditional surrender. It was more important to hold to the six demands in order to radicalize the campus than it was to accept partial victory. As Rudd said later:

Formal procedures that we might have won would be empty, because they can be worth nothing without the political consciousness. IDA will be dissociated and there won't be all that much difference in the facility with which the Defense Department gets its research, or in the purity of the University. It won't be *that* much different. But the difference will be in the struggle here. Many students have struggled against IDA, and many have turned left because of this.

Late Saturday afternoon the city-wide peace demonstrations reached Columbia, but not nearly in the proportions anticipated. A Columbia student had invited the crowds in Central Park's Sheep Meadow up to the Morningside campus, and by 6 P.M. over five hundred people had massed at 116th Street between Amsterdam Avenue and Morningside Drive. Columbia strike leaders addressed the crowd with loudspeakers from the Law School Terrace overhead. The speeches—by Ted Kaptchuk, Tom Hayden and Mark Rudd—were somewhat incongruous. The audience was opposed to the war in Vietnam but knew relatively little about Columbia and the issues behind the student movement there. When Kaptchuk denounced "the racism and imperialism" of Columbia and stated that the University "is a good example of what corporate capitalism is all about," his words seemed to go right over the heads of the crowd below. Hayden, too, failed to stir the peace marchers until the end of his speech when he proclaimed: "From the barricades, we'll resist until the end. Our demands are not changed." Rudd took the microphone but hesitated, not knowing what he could say to appeal to

---

[1] On *Spectator*'s copy of this document the last sentence is underlined and at the bottom Mark Rudd has scrawled the following note to the editor: "This is why we're not for 'student power' only, now." The fear that "student power" would lead to co-optation—that partial concessions by the administration would seduce many students to work within the power structure—became a main concern of strike leaders over the weekend.

his audience. The ingrown rhetoric of the Columbia demonstrations had failed to move the crowd, and so Rudd tried to arrange a dialogue.

"You know this is not happening just at Columbia, it's happening all across the country, at Howard, at Northwestern, at Stanford. Where else is it happening?" he cried out.

And in antiphonal response: "At Stonybrook."

"Yeah, at Stonybrook; where else?"

"At Brooklyn College."

"Yeah, at Brooklyn College."

After the interchange, which warmed the crowd, someone yelled, "Hey, get us a black speaker, I thought the black students were involved in this thing, too." Rudd shouted back, "We'll get one," and then mumbled, "Where's Cicero? Get Cicero." Cicero Wilson, however, was with his own demonstration and was no longer available to the whites as a guest speaker. Rudd concluded his speech and thanked the crowd for coming. They clapped politely and dispersed, having paid homage to Columbia as the symbol of student unrest.

As the last peace marchers began trickling back to the suburbs, Rudd, Gold, Gonzalez, Lew Cole and Avery delegate Al Feigenberg settled down to another negotiating session with the faculty at 9 P.M. Although the steering committee of the Ad Hoc Faculty Group had decided to discontinue negotiations after Rudd's "bullshit" speech, they had, according to Westin, received a call Saturday afternoon from the Strike Coördinating Committee apologizing for Rudd's actions before the faculty. Robert Belknap had replaced Westin as one of the three official faculty mediators, because Westin was involved that evening in discussions with the administration. Moreover, the students had repeatedly charged Westin with negotiating in bad faith, and he did not want to place the mediating efforts in further jeopardy.

Again the students asked the faculty members to define themselves politically, and the professors, Ted Gold later recounted, "kept talking about the immense danger of violence; that unless a solution could be worked out the police would come onto the campus." The threats of police action did not seem to disturb the students, and as Gold recalled, "We didn't want a police bust, but we would rather have had that than to give in to the administration." Belknap later said that the student negotiators were willing to make a semantic concession by accepting amnesty under another name. Professor Silver, sensing a possible break, again brought up the idea of group responsibility and collective punishment for the demonstrators. As fair as uniform punishment might have seemed, it was not amnesty, and the radicals indicated that while they would be willing to settle for *de facto* amnesty this did not come close enough. Several other student negotiators seemed interested and asked for certain clarifications about the status of the "IDA Six," who were already on disciplinary probation, before they would give any response. The faculty negotiators could not answer the question and promised to look into it. But by Saturday, they had come to realize the futility of conducting talks with the striking students. Professor Belknap later explained why it seemed unlikely that such discussions would produce a settlement:

> They were organized in such a way that negotiations were impossible. First, proposals would go to the negotiators, then to headquarters, then to the steering committees in the buildings, then to the general membership in the buildings, then back to headquarters, and finally back to the student negotiators. They were not willing to break their solidarity, and they were constitutionally unable to negotiate.

While the negotiations continued Alan Westin reconvened the Ad Hoc Faculty meeting at 10:25 on a portentous note: "It may be that we are reaching a point where some very important action will be taken by this group." Professor Wallerstein, who had been in contact with the black students in Hamilton throughout the day, took the floor and gave a report on his negotiations: "At seven o'clock a problem arose which lowered my high optimism to very low above the zero point." Wallerstein recounted that the black students had been considering his latest peace formula when they found out about the Petersen statement. When they bitterly confronted him with the statement, he went to Low Library to see Truman. "Clarification of the apparent contradictions with the administration leads us into a virtual deadlock on the gym and discipline issues. My estimation of the gym situation turned out to be less accurate than the blacks'." The students in Hamilton and the administration were 180 degrees apart on the gym; the Trustees had agreed to suspend gym construction until they could consider the alternatives, but on re-checking with Kirk and Truman, Wallerstein had learned that the Trustees insisted on the option to go ahead with the original plans if they deemed it advisable. The black students, on the other hand, had made it clear that they would not leave Hamilton Hall as long as the Trustees could return to the *status quo ante*.[2] "This is crystal-clear to me," Wallerstein stated. "In my opinion it is out of the question at the present time that the students will peacefully evacuate Hamilton until that option is

---

[2] As the occupation of the buildings wore on, *status quo* often came to refer to the crisis itself. Thus many began using the term *status quo ante* to refer to "the good old days."

definitively excluded. It is clear and total deadlock, with no give on either side. There is no likelihood—and that is understating it—of bringing students in Hamilton to agreement with the administration on the gym."

On the question of discipline Wallerstein reported that a deadlock with the blacks had also been reached, although it was not quite so total—"they are ninety-eight and not a hundred per cent apart." The students in Hamilton Hall would not accept the President's ultimate disciplinary authority; it would take at least three months to change the Statutes even if the administration wanted to make a change in the distribution of judicial power. Wallerstein had asked Kirk if he could guarantee that, given time, the Statutes would be changed to make this redistribution of power possible. Kirk had said that it was not likely. Would the President guarantee that in this one case he would not use his ultimate power to overrule the decisions of the disciplinary commission? No. "Either the conflict goes on for a very long time during which the students stay in Hamilton Hall," Wallerstein concluded, "or force be used to clear the building."

Westin had a hard act to follow, but managed to give an even more distressing report of his evening discussions with the central administration:

"I have enormous respect for David Truman. He is a tremendously sensitive man. Yet I believe that something has happened, pointing up the dilemma in which this faculty group finds itself. It is my belief that Truman can go no further. *His back is to the wall.*

"Every proposal has been met by the administration with responsiveness. We may be reaching a point where the administration feels that nothing can be done to prevent a showdown. At the moment the administration attitude runs as follows: they've looked at discussions with the students and say that they [the administration] have given many things. Yet there has been no response on the student side—not a single inch of give. There is a sense, having dealt for many months with SDS, that the students do not intend to settle.

"Furthermore, there have been hundreds of calls to the administration from other university presidents that if Columbia does not hold the line there will be sweeps of such student actions across the country. The administration now sees itself as the surrogate for universities throughout the nation. The city administration is no longer eager to hold back the cops. *I believe that we are at a dead end in terms of the administration's belief in negotiations.*"

The suspicions that the faculty members had felt for the past two days were now confirmed. The Ad Hoc Faculty Group would have to move into a new stage of action.

\* \* \*

After a short recess, during which Westin and several other professors conferred with the faculty negotiating team, the meeting was reconvened and Daniel Bell, the group's master tactician, took the floor. He gave just a hint of the strategy that would guide the Ad Hoc Faculty Group for the next two days: it must step from private to public mediation and as an independent body suggest to the University community what it believed to be the fairest solution. The group seemed satisfied, its sense of futility partially dissipated. At midnight Saturday, Professor Shenton called for adjournment: "The steering committee must now get down to the business of considering the last alternatives. I think we still have options and you have to let us use them." The faculty members went home, and the steering committee retired to a deserted office upstairs to spend the time left before dawn planning a last attempt at mediation.

The steering committee, fortified by coffee and compelled by a sense of desperate urgency, worked from midnight to six Sunday morning. Professor Bell stayed at the meeting for less than an hour. He had suggested the strategy of public mediation; it was now up to the other professors to come up with specific proposals. Professors sympathetic to the administration—Fritz Stern and Peter Kenen—sat in on the steering committee deliberations Saturday night. Kenen kept the draft of the resolution he would present at Sunday's Joint Faculties meeting folded in his jacket pocket. Though he conveyed its substance to the steering committee, he was under instructions from Vice President Truman not to let the group see it.

It was evident that the steering committee peace proposal would have to contain a statement about the gym and one about University discipline. Several members of the committee later reported that Westin and Wallerstein were the guiding forces behind the resolution, and that, while the discussion was collective, the drafting was done almost exclusively by Wallerstein. One described him amicably as "the evil genius" of the group. Professor Kenen recalled that about four that morning the group stepped outside for a break while Wallerstein remained inside the office, drafting. Kenen stated:

> We were out in the hall and I said to someone, "This is an exercise in futility. What we are doing is salving our own conscience and drafting what we believe to be a fair solution, knowing full well that it is not acceptable to either side." I thought for a few moments that we were all agreed on that point when Wallerstein

emerged and called us all back in to go over what he had just drafted. And everyone just plunged ahead.

Professor Silver had been working on the idea of collective punishment for the past two days, testing it out with the student negotiators and the administration. (On Thursday afternoon he had drafted a statement on collective punishment that he hoped Kirk would use. Trilling took Silver in to see the President, who read the statement and put it aside, reportedly saying, "It's not my style.") Though the students had shown some interest in collective punishment they had given indications that it would not meet their demand for amnesty. Having found a proposal that satisfied neither side but seemed the most likely synthesis of both, the steering committee made the following proposal on discipline:

1. We recommend that the President establish the tripartite commission in the form defined in the report of the Ad Hoc Committee composed of Professors Galanter, Hovde and Trilling.

We recommend that the University Statutes be revised by the Trustees so that the tripartite commission serve as the body of ultimate judicial review on all matters affecting University discipline.

We believe that the dimensions and complexity of the current crisis demand that a new approach of collective responsibility be adopted, and in this light insist that uniform penalties be applied to all violators of the discipline of the University.

On the gym the faculty members were strongly committed to the idea of community participation in planning the facility. In an effort to resolve the deadlock on whether the University could, once the crisis ended, eventually go ahead as if nothing had happened, the steering committee decided to give the neighboring community veto power over any plans for a gymnasium to be built in Morningside Park. The proposal they finally drafted read:

2. All excavation work at the gymnasium site having been suspended, we now recommend that the Trustees at their next meeting, which we urge occur within three days, request the Mayor of the City of New York urgently to convene a panel composed of:
   a. representatives of the Trustees.
   b. representatives of the community appointed by the Mayor.
   c. representatives of the faculty to be chosen by the faculty themselves.

We recommend that this panel review the gymnasium and adopt an alternative to the present plan. Should the alternative involve remaining on the present site, this plan shall be acceptable to the representatives of the community.

The formulations on discipline and the gym were, in the eyes of the steering committee, the fairest possible on moral grounds and the most practical on political grounds. They realized that they were dealing with two parties entrenched in intransigence and not likely to react to rationality. It was at this point that strategy became crucial. The steering committee was formulating a "bitter pill"—a final set of proposals which would give each side part of what it demanded yet contain certain provisions which each party would find hard to accept. Both sides would have to swallow the pill whole. The mediators would then announce that if the resolution was not accepted by both parties they would terminate their negotiating efforts and leave the disputants, as Alan Westin said, like two scorpions locked in a bottle.[3]

By six that morning a draft of the entire resolution was completed. The last four points outlined the steering committee's strategy:

3. We request that once the President indicates that he accepts these resolutions as his recommendations to the Trustees, we call upon the students now improperly occupying various buildings to vacate these buildings immediately and submit themselves to due process as shall now be established.

4. These proposals being in our judgment a just solution to the crisis our University is presently undergoing, we pledge that,

    a. If the President will not adopt these proposals, we shall take all measures within our several consciences to prevent the use of force to vacate the buildings.

    b. If the President does accept our proposals but the students in the buildings refuse to evacuate these buildings, we shall refuse further to interpose ourselves between the administration and the students.

5. We cannot believe that the Trustees, charged with the welfare of all segments of the University, will not accept a solution regarded as just by students, faculty and the President.

6. As members of the faculty, we are determined to do everything within our power rapidly to resume the full life of this institution in the firm expectation that our proposals will permit a climate to prevail that will once again allow reason, judgment and order to reign.

[3] This tactic is standard labor negotiating practice and is generally successful when both sides are indeed interested in settlement and fear the departure of the mediating body.

The strategy was clear. If one side but not the other would accept the package, the Ad Hoc Faculty Group would swing its support to that party; if both sides accepted, the crisis would be over; and if neither side accepted, police action would be inevitable. At 6 A.M. Alan Westin, convinced that a solution was at hand, told *Spectator*:

> These proposals represent the independent judgment of the faculty as to the most reasonable way of ending this crisis. I believe that the administration, though they may not like the proposals, will be pressed to accept them. If they do not, members of the Ad Hoc Faculty Group will probably take concrete action to persuade them to. A faculty member may not want to teach at a University in which such fair proposals are put to an administration and turned down. If it is the desire of SDS and the blacks to reach a rational fair solution to this, and they do not deliberately seek martyrdom, then I do believe we have found the formula.

Having worked out its solution and its general strategy, the steering committee turned to a plan of attack. The committee had promised the plenary session the night before that the resolutions would be presented to the full Ad Hoc Group at its eight o'clock meeting Sunday. This step posed no problems, for the steering committee knew it could get its proposals accepted by a large majority of the group. But their course of action after that point was somewhat unclear. The Joint Faculties meeting scheduled for ten that morning seemed an ideal place to present the resolution. There would, however, be dangers in such a move. The package of proposals, which to be effective had to remain intact, might be unwrapped and dismantled by the faculty, which could then decide to deal with each of its resolutions separately. Another potential problem was the pro-administration resolution, cached in Kenen's coat pocket, which would probably have no trouble passing and might thus prevent the faculty from adopting the more liberal bitter pill proposals. The conservative professors were likely to be out in force, and since all voting faculty members had been invited there would be a great number of professors who were not familiar with the events and would be likely to defer to the administration. Uncertain of the political climate that would prevail at the Sunday meeting, the steering committee wanted to avoid a possible split within the faculty which would undercut whatever support they could gather for the bitter pill. Finally, the steering committee believed that it would take time for the wisdom of its proposals to "sink in." The decision was therefore made not to bring the resolution to a vote at the Joint Faculties meeting; it would instead be presented for informational purposes only. Shortly before 8 A.M. Professor Kenen called Truman and read him the steering committee's resolution. The vice president was appalled at the faculty statement.

The Ad Hoc Faculty Group reconvened at 8:30 Sunday morning and Alan Westin read the bitter pill resolution. The faculty members responded as the steering committee expected, endorsing the proposals by a vote of two hundred to three. The meeting broke up shortly after the vote, and at ten the professors proceeded to the official meeting of the Joint Faculties at the Law School. Tight security was maintained at the entrance to the building. Students lounged on the grass outside waiting to hear what their faculty would do, as junior faculty members, excluded from the meeting, caucused nearby. Inside Grayson Kirk presided. The first hour of the meeting was spent on a discussion of whether to admit representatives of the junior faculty group and whether these representatives should be allowed to vote. A token agreement was worked out whereby Sam Coleman, the graying philosophy instructor, would be allowed into the meeting as a non-voting spokesman for the junior faculty.

With the argument over seating completed, Alan Westin was recognized and presented a report on the activities of the Ad Hoc Faculty Group up to but not including the drafting of the bitter pill. Truman briefed the professors on administration efforts to resolve the crisis, and then Peter Kenen was called upon to present his resolution. His clothes rumpled from over-wear, his eyes sagging from lack of sleep, Kenen reached into his jacket pocket for the resolution and in a monotone read:

1. We reaffirm the actions taken by the faculty of Columbia College on April 24 and in the committees of instruction of the Graduate Faculties meeting jointly on April 26. With them,
    a. we condemn the violence that has occurred, including the occupation of buildings and the disruption of normal University activities;
    b. we commend the action of the administration in arranging immediate suspension of on-site excavation for the gymnasium in Morningside Park and we urge that it proceed at once to meet with community spokesmen to review the matter of the gymnasium site;
    c. we endorse the establishment of a tripartite commission and express the conviction that its work can result in a fair disposition of the disciplinary problems arising from the current disruption and in progress toward solution of other issues lying within its jurisdiction.

One might have expected a more creative or incisive approach to the crisis from the more than five hundred professors assembled. The only substantive portions of the Kenen resolution condemned, commended and endorsed actions that already had been taken, and offered absolutely no new suggestions on how to deal with the problems confronting Columbia University. But if the first part of the resolution was unimaginative, the rest verged on the insipid. Kenen continued to read:

2. We express our deep appreciation of the patience and restraint shown by the administration and by the great majority of our faculty and students.
3. We recognize that members of the Ad Hoc Faculty Group, meeting in 301 Philosophy, have performed many vital services in the interest of this University. We hope that they will continue their effective efforts at communication and mediation.
4. We are convinced that significant progress has been made toward closer communication among students, faculty and administration in recent days and we pledge our efforts to make this a permanent feature of the University's life.
5. We likewise pledge our efforts to effective, continuing communication with the broader community of which we are a part.
6. We call upon the students who continue to occupy University buildings to recognize that failure to resolve this crisis rapidly and peaceably may result in irreparable damage to all members of this community.

The resolution passed overwhelmingly, 466 to 40. The plea in the sixth point was not backed up by any offers, promises or positive statements, either on the gym or on discipline. Instead, the august body produced a vague affirmation of faith in the administration, the Ad Hoc Faculty Group, non-radical students, communication and the future. The resolution constituted the confession of a faculty that was not able to take a stand.

After the Kenen resolution was passed Westin again rose, this time to present, "for informational purposes only," the Ad Hoc Faculty resolutions. After the reading he yielded to Professor Wallerstein, who analyzed and explained the bitter pill resolution, giving a run-down of who lost what in each of the proposals. The debate that followed focused exclusively on the first of the six proposals—the principle of uniform and collective punishment. William Fox, director of the Institute of War and Peace Studies, attacked the concept, claiming that uniform punishment was counter to Anglo-Saxon law. He was rebutted by historian Walter Metzger, an expert on the American university, who made a passionate appeal to the faculty to realize that Columbia was on the brink of disintegration and that it could be saved only by radically new perceptions. Dankwart Rustow, professor of international social forces, did some quick calculating before the faculty to convince them that collective punishment, while being the fairest solution, was also the only practical one, explaining that to provide individual trial and punishment for five hundred students would be almost impossible. Several other professors who had been close to the Ad Hoc Group also argued for collective punishment and were well received. One member of the Ad Hoc Faculty steering committee said later that by the end of the meeting "we had more support than we expected when we went in," and suggested that they probably could have swung a majority of the faculty behind the resolution. But a vote was never taken. After nearly four hours the meeting was adjourned, and the professors walked out of the Law School, having attended a historic meeting and having done little of historic importance.

While the Joint Faculties were meeting, the Strike Steering Committee was holding a noon press conference in Ferris Booth Hall. Ted Gold read a statement which was directed largely to the faculty and to their bitter pill strategy, although not to the specific proposals:

> We have been very anxious to continue the discussions we had with the Faculty Ad Hoc Committee. . . . But the statement of the Trustees shows us that this Ad Hoc Committee is talking in a vacuum. . . . We thus ask the Faculty Ad Hoc Committee to stop trying to perform a mediating function they cannot carry out. Instead, we think they should constitute themselves as the political body that in fact they are and take a political position in favor of the six demands, including amnesty. . . .

Once again, as in Rudd's disastrous "bullshit" speech, the strike leaders misread the attitudes of the Ad Hoc Faculty Group. The students were receiving most of their information about the group from junior faculty members of the "radical caucus," which over the weekend had taken shape as a semi-independent force within the Ad Hoc Group. Some of them—Mike Ross, Dick Greeman, Bob Zevin—were constantly in touch with the strikers, telling them that the longer they held out the more faculty members would be radicalized and shift left. The members of the Ad Hoc Group had been politicized but they had not been radicalized. They were still unwilling to assume a role other than that of mediator.

Westin gave further evidence of this position at a three o'clock press conference held in Philosophy Hall to announce the bitter pill resolution publicly. Westin sat next to Wallerstein under the glare of television lights and appeared fatigued as he read the proposals. Asked by reporters if he thought the bitter pill would work, Westin replied:

"We believe that SDS will find this acceptable, but it is possible that they would want to be martyrs and go out in a blaze. . . . If they accept they will have gained important democratic procedures in this University. . . . If the demonstrators insist on their demand for amnesty, there will be no chance for faculty support. . . . At the moment of truth they must accept responsibility for their action."

Westin, as he explained later, hoped the bitter pill would appeal to the more moderate students in the buildings. It was the belief of the Ad Hoc Faculty steering committee that there was a small hard core of radicals who would not come out of the buildings under any circumstances, while there were many who could be wooed out by a combination of concession and threat of police.

As the strikers had misunderstood the political mood of the faculty, Westin's analysis appeared to be a misreading of the student situation in all but one of the occupied buildings. In Low, Math and Avery the "hard-core" radicals were many and in control; it was unlikely that the more moderate leftists would desert their leadership. In Fayerweather, however, the militants were having trouble. The constituency, consisting mostly of graduate students, was far more willing to compromise than SDS. Fayerweather's dissidence was confirmed Sunday by a document endorsed five to one among the building's occupants and forwarded to the Strike Steering Committee "for consideration by the rest of the liberated community." Word of the "Fayerweather proposal" leaked to the rest of the campus despite efforts by the Strike Steering Committee to hush up the apparent split. The significant feature of the proposal, which was drafted in response to the Ad Hoc Faculty bitter pill resolution, was that it contained no demand for amnesty:

> In view of the fact that the faculty negotiating proposal originally submitted for our consideration does not accord with our six basic demands, we reaffirm these demands and submit an alternative set of proposals for consideration by the Strike Steering Committee as a possible basis for negotiations with the faculty.
> We propose that a permanent bipartite student-faculty committee be created whose decisions on policy are to be binding and not subject to administrative review. We propose: . . . that disciplinary actions be taken (possibly including amnesty, which we feel we deserve) by the above committee with regard to the present strike and demonstrations leading up to it.

The bipartite committee would be guided by the principle of collective and equal punishment; there would be no suspensions, and all disciplinary sentences would terminate at the end of the academic year. The

## 8  A Bitter Pill   163

Fayerweather proposal seemed to the faculty the sign of a possible breakthrough.

Most demonstrators seriously believed that they were legitimately entitled to amnesty. But for some of the more tactically minded strike leaders, the amnesty question was the point at which their concern with building a radical movement became dominant. They knew that Kirk and Truman were quite unlikely to grant that particular demand. Thus to hold out for amnesty would be tactically fruitful in that if amnesty were not granted, either the occupation would be prolonged, or the administration would be forced to call upon the use of violence to end the strike. The Fayerweather proposal was voted down by the eleven-man Strike Steering Committee.

Thursday and Friday, a referendum had been conducted by three student service societies to gauge student opinion on the demands and tactics of SDS. After a preliminary tabulation Friday, the students conducting the referendum mysteriously decided not to release its results. Sunday, however, they made public the figures representing the sentiments of 5,500 students on the Morningside campus (the Strike Steering Committee officially boycotted the referendum):

(1) I favor amnesty for all students involved in the demonstrations of the last three days: YES: 2,054; NO: 3,466
(2) End gym construction: YES: 4,093; NO: 1,433
(3) End University ties with IDA: YES: 3,572; NO: 1,855
(4) I favor dropping disciplinary probation charges against the six students involved in the prior IDA demonstration: YES: 2,167; NO: 3,263
(5) I favor open hearing by a tripartite committee on all disciplinary action in the future: YES: 4,465; NO: 1,074
(6) The University should use its good offices to have charges dropped against those arrested by the city in gym demonstrations: YES: 2,816; NO: 2,668
(7) I support a student strike in favor of these demands: YES: 2,365; NO: 3,094
(8) I agree with the demonstration tactics used by SDS and SAS thus far: YES: 1,325; NO: 4,124

By Sunday afternoon the Majority Coalition had had enough of faculty mediation, which they felt was only prolonging the occupation. It was time, they thought, to take positive, non-violent action in an effort to win support for their anti-SDS position. On Saturday they had issued a flyer calling for the cordoning off of Low Library to deny the demonstrators free access through Kirk's windows. At 5 P.M. Sunday afternoon a group of more than one-hundred Majority Coalition members assembled on South Field in response to the flyer. To contrast with the image of the protesters each was clean shaven and wore coat and tie. Light-blue armbands were distributed, and then the group made its way in single file to Low Library. There they lined up shoulder to shoulder in front of the low hedge under the windows of the President's offices. Demonstrators balanced on the window ledge, heckling them, while a large crowd of onlookers clogged the paths and lawns nearby. Minutes after the new cordon was formed nearly half the faculty members who had been maintaining their own line inside the hedge left for Philosophy Hall for a meeting to evaluate the new situation; the Majority Coalition moved its cordon inside the hedge.

In a press release distributed shortly after the formation of their blockade the conservative students explained their position, again invoking the tenuous argument that they represented the views of a majority of students:

> During the past evening it has become apparent that the students in the vast majority who have not caused physical violence but acted as responsible members of the University community have been in a sense betrayed by the faculty and administration. . . . After receiving and studying the faculty proposals this afternoon we must state that we find them wholly inadequate and quite inconclusive. . . . We feel, truly, that the student body which has lain dormant since Thursday night is a force to be reckoned with and that many of the faculty have wrongly considered it to be powerless and a force "that can be handled." Since this situation seems to indicate that it is possible for the blockade of the buildings to continue into the coming week, we have decided that we can no longer tolerate the domination of a minority.

The conservatives had attempted to take action before but had been prevented from doing so by the faculty. Their desire to be accepted by authority and to obey authority—the faculty and administration—had forced them to contain their passionate dislike of the demonstrators and their actions. But they had begun to feel frustrated and now attacked "the condescending attitude" of faculty members. Columbia is largely a University dominated by liberal and radical intellectuals, many of whom were now in the buildings. Many of the athletes were at Columbia primarily because of their skill in sports and had come to feel like outsiders, bystanders to the academic currents of the University. The visceral revulsion they felt for the demonstrators led them to join forces with those conservatives who intellectually repudiated the Left and who

## 8 A Bitter Pill 165

formed Columbia's political out-group. They linked forces and chained themselves to the *status quo ante*.

The number of students participating in the counter-demonstrators' cordon increased steadily throughout the evening. At 7 P.M. the Majority Coalition was put to its first test. They had stated that they would not allow either persons or supplies to pass inside. The Strike Committee challenged the counter-demonstrators by attempting to pass food and medical supplies through the cordon. Three demonstrators carrying a box of food approached the athletes' line and were rebuffed. A few minutes later Robbie Roth, a leader of the strikers in Low, sneaked around the end of the Majority Coalition line and started scaling the building's wall. The athletes broke formation, ran to the wall and pulled Roth down by his feet, touching off a brief scuffle between demonstrators, counter-demonstrators and faculty. Roth retreated to Ferris Booth Hall but returned several minutes later with a convoy of ten students bearing cartons of food. Meanwhile, Dean Fraenkel, who had been called to the scene, threw up his arms and asked for a fifteen-minute moratorium on confrontation so that the faculty could clarify its policy on the access of students and food into Low. Roth and his group stood waiting for the faculty response, and at 7:40 Professor Leonard, who had been in charge of the faculty cordon, announced that no food would be allowed up to the protesters. Professor Dallin took a bullhorn and called upon all sides for restraint and de-escalation. Roth returned to Ferris Booth with the food. Several attempts were made later that evening to get food and medical supplies into Low, but on each occasion the carriers were turned back by the Majority Coalition line. At one point a faculty member obtained verbal permission from the Majority Coalition to pass two bags of medical supplies up to the protesters, but as he stepped up onto the grating an athlete left his line and grabbed his arm. Vilardi was called over to check the bags and found only Vaseline and rags. "Hey, they want some Vaseline up there," he yelled over to the cordon; "well, I guess that's all right." Misunderstanding the demonstrators' intentions, Vilardi allowed the bags to pass. The supplies were moved into Low and dispensed as protection against tear gas and Mace.

Frequently throughout that evening the Ad Hoc Faculty meeting was interrupted by emergency crises at the west wall of Low where the faculty and student cordons were standing guard and where hundreds of students milled about, awaiting a conflict. The professors spent most of the evening discussing the faculty cordon, which they had come to refer to familiarly as "ledge in the hedge." It had become apparent, when the demonstrators had attempted to run the blockade that evening, that the faculty policy on its cordon was somewhat confusing, not only to students but to the professors themselves as well. The cordon had served to alienate both the demonstrators and the counter-demonstrators. Furthermore, the flare-ups at Low hinted that the crisis was degenerating from a political conflict into a game of diversions. The students in the buildings interrupted their talk about the University as an institution in society and argued about whether they should attempt to run the blockade. Faculty members were now spending much of their time patrolling and had fewer opportunities to discuss the issues.

Shortly after midnight, while the faculty was debating what to do with its cordon, JJ, the militant who had led the takeover of Math, and a small band of demonstrators tried to break through the Majority Coalition line and enter Low. Faculty members were called to the scene and, in the dim light coming from the President's office, tried to calm the tense crowd. There had been no fighting, but JJ had been turned back repeatedly by both the athletes and the faculty. Professor Kaplow shouted up at the demonstrators, "We are with you, but there is a division of labor, and the faculty must continue what it is doing." Robbie Roth later recounted JJ's attack:

> The student-faculty controversy over access to Low was becoming bitter and divisive. JJ got very perturbed and began to harangue the faculty members. He said, "Listen, I don't really give a shit what you motherfuckers say about ingress and egress. We have a right to come in and out of this place and if you're with us you should join us. If you're not you should leave."

Kaplow told JJ his comments were counter-productive. JJ left in a huff. Once again the ingressors were repelled.

The faculty members returned to Philosophy Hall and decided it was time to draft a formal policy statement on the Low cordon. Professor Wallerstein proposed a four-part doctrine, the last point of which read: "Blockaders at the hedge will not be permitted on the ledge." For a moment the professors laughed at the absurdity. Then they went ahead and drew up a set of rules, incorporating Wallerstein's four points, and retired for the night. The steering committee moved into executive session to plan strategy for winning wide support for the bitter pill on campus Monday.

Throughout the night the Majority Coalition stayed on duty around Low. Their ranks had swelled to nearly 250 students who remained standing and sleeping on the narrow lawn until morning. To counter their show of force a group of more than seven hundred students who supported the six demands held a vigil at the Sundial. Their numbers had dwindled by midnight but several dozen remained until dawn, huddled in blankets and sleeping bags, talking politics and sipping coffee. And inside the President's office the one hundred occupants kept up their watch against the ever-impending police bust.

Sunday night Vice President Truman appeared on a WKCR radio program with five moderate student leaders and again insisted that amnesty was out of the question:

> There can be absolutely no altering on that point [amnesty]. This thing is far bigger than Columbia, and we do not intend to betray our sister institutions. Amnesty would mean forgetting this incident ever happened. Amnesty would mean that any group that wishes to take over this University is free to do so at any time. . . . There are times when order must be maintained because order must be maintained.

# 9

## *Amnesty or Bust*

"THIS IS THE DAY OF DECISION," Alan Westin announced as the Ad Hoc Faculty Group reconvened at 10:30 Monday morning. If the bitter pill were not swallowed that day there would be nothing more that the faculty could do to mediate toward a solution. Early that morning Westin had been informed by one of the Mayor's representatives that the administration would definitely call in the police within twenty-four hours if a settlement were not reached. Now, in Philosophy Hall, Westin's manner was brisk. He asked that no one raise any questions from the floor or bring up new problems. As mimeographed copies of the bitter pill resolution were passed out, Westin reminded the group that they had little time left. He urged those present to spend the next hours circulating on campus to build support among their colleagues and the students for the last-minute proposals. A deadline of 3:30 P.M. had been set for responses from the administration and strikers and, twenty minutes after the meeting began, Westin called for a recess until the afternoon.

One response was shaped at a noon meeting of the Strike Steering Committee in Ferris Booth Hall. The minutes of that meeting read:

> Faculty Ad Hoc Committee gave ultimatum that we meet with them at 3:30 telling them how we feel about their proposal. Westin threatened us by saying that cops will be called tomorrow unless a settlement or decision for a settlement is reached today. The cops are hungry, Westin says.

The strikers discussed the bitter pill, and, though many did not believe that police action was so close, they began to prepare their answer. Another pressing problem confronted them: how to get food past the blockade of counter-demonstrators and faculty and into the students in Low. "The faculty has abrogated its 'moral force' in an attempt to play *realpolitik*," a Low representative charged. The group resolved to break the blockade, hoping to prod the radical faculty members—a group whose size and influence the strikers continually overestimated—to split from the Ad Hoc Group. The delegates from Low put forward a plan in which the pro-amnesty green armbanders would demand free access to Low and if turned back "others will carry the demand out." The proposal was approved overwhelmingly; a moderate Fayerweather counter-proposal to hold a vigil for free access outside Philosophy received only one of the steering committee's eleven votes.

The fidelity of Hamilton Hall was another problem that had caused a great deal of worry among the white strikers. On Sunday the blacks had issued a press release demanding amnesty only "for the persons involved in the present demonstration in Hamilton Hall." Now a black youth came to the Strike Steering Committee meeting and explained that he had word from the renegade hall. As the strikers' minutes recount:

> Hamilton sent a representative. He said they will *not* sell out on the amnesty demand, i.e., they are holding out for amnesty for *all*, not just for the blacks. . . . All buildings have decided that they will resist the police, whether passive or active. Hamilton will resist militantly. Hamilton made a proposal for a new University. Their formulation of it as the Malcolm X University was agreed to by everyone, with the assumption that all buildings will submit ideas and be included. . . . After Hamilton rep. left there was an appeal for unity and for politics that was applauded by everyone.

Strike leaders discovered later that the supposed representative was not an emissary of the students in Hamilton and, according to some reports, was not even a student at Columbia.

The administration spent most of Monday morning and afternoon considering the bitter pill. Westin and Bell tried to persuade Truman and Kirk to accept the entire package, arguing that it was positively the last alternative open to them short of violence. Westin pointed out to Truman that the administrators would be in an excellent position if they accepted the proposals and the students rejected them. This was an argument Westin had used with the strikers as well, one which Truman later characterized as "a little too cute." The administration was willing to accept some of the provisions of the bitter pill but first had to secure the permission of the Trustees. They phoned members of the board to discuss the proposals, and at one point when a Trustee expressed strong reservations about the faculty resolution Truman threatened to resign if the administration were not given the authority to accept those resolutions which it felt it must.

The administration's answer to the bitter pill came exactly at the deadline time of 3:30 when Grayson Kirk issued the following statement:

> I commend and fully share the objectives of the resolution adopted by the Ad Hoc Faculty Group on April 28. I am deeply grateful for the dedicated concern for the integrity of the University that their proposals imply. I am confident that the following decisions carry out the essential spirit of those proposals.
>
> 1. I have already informed the members of the committee I appointed on April 25—Professors Galanter, Hovde and Trilling—that their report recommending a tripartite commission is fully acceptable, and I am prepared to appoint as its members the students, faculty and administrators whose names they have recommended to me.[1]
>
> 2. I will recommend to the Trustees that the Statutes of the University dealing with disciplinary matters be re-examined in the light of the recommendations to be submitted by the tripartite commission.
>
> 3. Matters such as the question of uniform penalties for those involved in this incident will be referred to the tripartite commission, since the Galanter report, which I have already accepted, proposes that such matters be a part of the commission's mandate.
>
> 4. Excavation work at the gymnasium site has been suspended, at the request of the Mayor, as of April 26, pending further discussions, and I shall recommend to the Trustees that they authorize me to proceed with discussions concerning the gymnasium problem, as requested in the resolution adopted at the Joint Faculty meeting on April 28, 1968.

Superficially the Kirk statement seemed to contain many key concessions, and some observers at first believed that the administration had indeed swallowed the bitter pill. But on closer analysis both the strikers and the Ad Hoc Faculty Group concluded that the President had slipped down a placebo instead.

Kirk's first point did satisfy the Ad Hoc recommendation that the disciplinary commission be set up along the lines suggested by the Galanter committee. His second point, however, was less explicit. While

---

[1] After the original names proposed for the disciplinary commission were widely criticized on campus, the Galanter committee proposed a new list. The commission was expanded from twelve members to seventeen: seven students, seven faculty members and three administrators.

## 9   Amnesty or Bust   171

the faculty group had called for a revision in the Statutes to give the tripartite commission ultimate disciplinary authority, Kirk promised only that he would *recommend* that the Trustees *re-examine* University disciplinary regulations *in the light of* recommendations not yet drawn up by the commission. Yet the most recent public statement issued by University officials on disciplinary matters, the Petersen memorandum of Saturday, had stated:

> [The Trustees] not only support the President's stand but affirmatively direct, that he shall maintain the ultimate disciplinary power over the conduct of the students of the University as required by the Charter and Statutes of the University.

In discussions with Westin and Wallerstein on Saturday and Sunday Truman had confirmed that Kirk refused to give up such power.

The Ad Hoc Group had hoped to resolve the amnesty issue by insisting that "uniform penalties be applied to all violators of the discipline of the University." [2] But Kirk demurred at this stipulation, pointing out that he had just set up a commission to make just such judgments. The reservation would have been defensible in times of peace but seemed to many to be more of an evasion during the crisis.

The gymnasium issue posed additional problems. The Ad Hoc Group had asked for adoption of alternative plans by a committee of faculty members, Trustees and representatives of the community, with the latter granted veto power if the new plans were to call for continuation of construction in the park. The President offered instead to *recommend* to the Trustees that he be allowed to begin *discussions* on the gym along lines outlined by the resolution passed by the Joint Faculties in their Law School meeting of Sunday. (This resolution asked only that the administration "review" the matter with community spokesmen.)

Mid-afternoon Monday the Ad Hoc Group reconvened to analyze Kirk's response to the bitter pill and measure the resolution's acceptance on campus. In the hours since the morning meeting 710 faculty and 2,763 students had signed a petition supporting the resolution.[3] The Mayor's aides had suggested to Westin Sunday night that if the group could obtain backing for their package from public dignitaries it might be able to force the administration and strikers to swallow the bitter pill under the pressure of public opinion. Among the supporters announced at the afternoon Ad Hoc Faculty meeting were United States Senator

---

[2] This wording was probably a casualty of the pre-dawn hours Sunday during which the bitter pill was formulated; the proposal was intended to suggest uniform penalties only for the students involved in the current crisis.

[3] There are approximately 2,000 faculty members and 15,000 students on the Morningside Heights campus of Columbia.

Jacob Javits, Columbia Trustee Benjamin Buttenwieser, Borough President Percy Sutton and the Reverend Ralph Abernathy, leader of the Poor People's Campaign. When discussion turned to an analysis of the Kirk reply there was division on how much the administration had actually conceded. Exegeses of the Kirk message were presented, and finally the group decided to recess until it would be able to consider all responses, including that of the strikers, who had not said anything as of the deadline.

While the bitter pill was being regurgitated by the administration, at least one other major plan for settlement was developing. On Thursday eminent Negro educator Kenneth Clark had phoned Truman to offer his help in negotiating with the black students, and on Saturday he had come to campus to confer with the students in Hamilton. Now, Monday, Clark was back, and he brought with him a man who might be qualified to mediate a settlement of the Columbia crisis—Theodore Kheel, one of the country's top labor negotiators. Kheel later observed:

> The faculty was well motivated but totally incapable of dealing with such a dispute. Their minds were too fine, they got lost in the merits of the causes. They could have been good arbitrators but they turned out to be poor mediators. . . . The trouble with the professorial mind in a situation like this is that its passion to rationalize is so compelling that it overlooks and cannot deal with irrational problems—like amnesty. The standard for a proposal must be its acceptability to the people you're trying to persuade, not the overriding commitment of the negotiators.

Kheel spent a large part of Monday afternoon with the Hamilton Hall Steering Committee, "giving them a quick course in dispute settlement."

He came to the conclusion that the amnesty-discipline issue was the key obstacle and drew up a proposal to end the student strike: (1) The students evacuate all their buildings; (2) Everyone returns to class; (3) The administration imposes discipline; (4) The disciplined students can appeal to an outside body composed of, for example, Kheel, Clark and McGeorge Bundy, head of the Ford Foundation. This appeal board would have the right to overrule the administration's decision; (5) Pending completion of the appeal, the *status quo* is maintained, and the students involved remain in school.

"I was trying to appeal to all sides' self-interest," Kheel said. "In cases like this, I never talk to people about what's 'right.' " Clark conferred with the administration about the Kheel plan and was told at first that it would be acceptable. However, when Kirk realized that he would not have final power on discipline, he informed Kheel that he could not go along with the proposal because the Trustees would never approve it.

According to Kheel, a similar yes-then-no response was given late in the day by the blacks. The mediator decided not to approach the students in the other buildings with his proposal unless the administration and the blacks accepted it:

> This was unlike a labor dispute in that it was in the interests of one of the disputants, SDS, *not* to settle. There was no proposal I could name to satisfy them. So I concentrated on working with Hamilton. I knew that if I succeeded with them I would have some leverage with the administration. . . . Kirk has no understanding of group dynamics. When he was appointed President there was nothing in the job qualifications about having the ability to deal with mass movements. This was a mass movement, and he lacked that ability. Kirk was typical of a weak manager afraid to offend his board of directors. If I had been an advisor to the administration, I would have favored amnesty.

His first proposal turned down by Kirk and the blacks, Kheel planned to return Tuesday to try to work out another settlement. He was unaware that, as he negotiated, the administration and the police were completing their own arrangements to end the crisis.

Meanwhile the strikers' plans for running the Low blockade went forward. About fifty students—mostly strikers from Math, with a few green armbanders—began a march around Low led by JJ. They passed parallel to the wall-like line of the Majority Coalition once, twice, three times, chanting, "FOOD! FOOD!" and carrying six large cartons of groceries. As they completed their third circuit, the group veered suddenly toward the cordon and charged. Pro-strike students hurled themselves into the athletes' line. Some of the leftists threw liquid ammonia at the counter-demonstrators. Shoving escalated to punching and kicking; a demonstrator wielding a knife squared off against a counter-demonstrator wielding a soda bottle. The rumble flared, but faculty members quickly intervened and broke it up. The Majority Coalition members re-formed their ranks and linked arms once more, the attack repelled.

Undaunted, supporters of the demonstrators moved back from the cordon, dipped into the cartons of food, and began tossing cans of sardines, loaves of bread, salamis, candy bars, oranges and grapefruits up into the open windows of Kirk's offices. Each successful toss was greeted with applause from most of the spectators, while cheers from the Majority Coalition and their supporters followed every errant throw that bounced off Low and fell to the ground. Unable to halt the airlift into Low the counter-demonstrators began waving blankets and frying pans over their heads to block their opponents' passes. Eggs and intercepted fruit were used as missiles against demonstrators standing on the high ledge near Kirk's windows. Faculty members keeping guard in accordance with their "ledge in the hedge" manifesto rarely intervened on behalf of either side, as fresh groceries splattered around and occasionally on them. The administration responded to the situation by stationing thirty-five police along the disputed border, forming a third cordon.

Late in the afternoon a student from the Graduate School of Business, wearing a dapper three-piece suit, arranged himself on a narrow strip of grass across from the Majority Coalition line. He announced to anyone who would listen that he was about to file a suit against the demonstrators for damages of $500,000 per day. Strikers in Low threw pennies down to him.

When word of Kirk's answer to the bitter pill reached the Majority Coalition line, Vilardi was furious. He saw the President's statement as a sellout to the demands of SDS and declared, "We're not going to get anywhere with those people. Let's leave." The demonstrators had been unable to budge the line, but now it seemed that Grayson Kirk was about to cause it to disintegrate. Frank Dann, former captain of the swimming team, spoke with Vilardi and convinced him that they should continue to maintain their oppositon. The line remained.

The Ad Hoc Group's 3:30 deadline for responses to the bitter pill had long since passed, and the strikers had neither accepted nor rejected the proposals. Finally, around 6 P.M., a statement was released through Strike Central. It was not encouraging:

> . . . We striking students reaffirm our six demands, including amnesty. Amnesty must be a precondition for negotiations. Our demand for amnesty implies a specific political point. Our actions are legitimate; it is the laws and the administration's policies, which the laws have been designed to protect, that are illegitimate. . . .
>
> The resolution of the Ad Hoc Faculty Committee has suggestions in it that could serve as useful approaches to the way the five demands besides amnesty could be met. In addition, the resolution implicitly suggests structures that could be developed within the University after the present crisis is resolved. . . .
>
> The administration, through the threat of police force, has created a sense of urgency and panic which implies that the primary problem on campus is restoration of order and normality, and not the political issues involved. Some members of the faculty have intensified this mood by presenting an "emergency proposal" [the bitter pill] that doesn't get at the root causes of the crisis. The

students who entered the buildings are risking a lot more than the punishments of any of the "compromise" suggestions. We are not afraid of punishment, but the notion of [any] punishment at all undermines the political basis for a solution to the issues we have raised. . . .

Though the strikers' statement also contained a paragraph analyzing Kirk's reply and showing in what areas it was insufficient, the substance of their response to the bitter pill had been formulated at their noon meeting which had ended half an hour before Kirk released his reply. The minutes of that meeting show the protesters' early reactions to the package:

> The building responses went as follows:
> *Avery:* Stick to demands. Reply to faculty that we'd very much like to talk, but that there's no one to talk to who has any power so we cannot accept.
> *Math:* Same.
> *Low:* Unanimously rejects Ad Hoc Committee proposal. . . .
> *Fayerweather:* Would like to talk but agrees with Avery analysis of the situation.

The bitter pill had failed. The strikers had spat it back in the face of the faculty and Grayson Kirk had nibbled off a minuscule portion, politely placing the rest aside like an olive pit. The students in Hamilton had never even responded to it, and the Majority Coalition had called it "wholly inadequate and quite inconclusive." [4] Members of the Ad Hoc Group began to straggle back to Philosophy around 7 P.M., asking each other whether it would now be necessary for them to withdraw as mediators. The popular history professor James Shenton, who like many of his colleagues in the Ad Hoc Group had helped man the twenty-four-hour faculty guard around Low Library, walked to the front of the room and tried to get the attention of the thirty professors who sat listlessly around the lounge. "The SDS response is no response at all," he said. "If you authorize me to do so, I will go out and tell all those guarding Low to leave if they want to." The group discussed such a move but decided not to take any action until the steering committee—which was meeting upstairs—made its official report to the group.

At 8:15 Westin and the other members of the steering committee entered the lounge. Wallerstein, on the verge of complete exhaustion,

---

[4] At 1 A.M. Tuesday morning the Majority Coalition reversed its position and became the only active party to accept the proposals.

announced that in the estimation of the steering committee the bitter pill had failed. Despite their intentions to step aside if their resolution was rejected by all sides, the members of the steering committee had resolved to try one more plan to avert police action. A telegram had been sent to Governor Nelson Rockefeller, containing the draft of a proposal asking him to arbitrate the crisis. If the faculty concurred, Wallerstein explained, Senator Javits would help persuade the Governor to intervene. The idea, as Wallerstein later said, was "an act of desperation; by Monday evening the steering committee was pretty much without hope." They had made this last gesture only because of the sentiment expressed by Professor Bell: "The one thing you do when you're desperate is keep balls in the air."

Debate on the Rockefeller motion ranged beyond the issue of outside arbitration back to the question of whether the administration's response to the bitter pill constituted complete rejection or merely thorough equivocation. Westin reported that Truman had told him that, although the President would not give up his ultimate disciplinary authority, the vice president promised "on his word of honor" that Kirk would never use that power to reverse the decision of the tripartite commission. Kirk would not, however, allow the statutory powers of the President to be diminished under pressure by radical students.

Bell and Westin tried to convince the group that based on their discussions with Truman, they judged that the administration's statement amounted to "a thirty per cent acceptance" of the bitter pill. Others rose to make arguments that suggested five per cent might be a more accurate quantification. Hot debate began over which side had swallowed more of the bitter pill. But the hour was late, and many feared that the police might already be on their way. The lounge had been filling up all evening; now it was packed. Professors stood on tables in the back of the room to be heard, and analysis of statements made earlier in the day soon yielded to discussion of actions that would take place later in the night. The faculty members had pledged that they would "take all measures within our several consciences" to block police action if the President did not accept their proposals. But they had also promised to refuse to interpose themselves further between the administration and the students if Kirk agreed to their resolution and the students did not evacuate the buildings. Caught up in the Götterdämmerung spirit of drafting the bitter pill, the Ad Hoc Faculty Steering Committee had neglected to state what they would do about resisting police action if *both* sides rejected their package. Now that contingency was upon them.

An hour and a half after the steering committee announced it had wired Rockefeller, Professor Galanter rose to object to the move. He warned that the institutional independence of Columbia might be sacrificed "if the faculty gives up its current role to the agencies of the state." Several other professors, including C. Lowell Harriss, also argued against the faculty's abdication of authority. The Rockefeller proposal was called to a vote and defeated. "No one had great hopes for it," Wallerstein said later, "and no one was particularly sorry when the plenary session voted it down."

The food supplies of the students in Low had been cut off by faculty and Majority Coalition lines. Though the strikers claimed that the demonstrators in Low were being starved out, many observers suggested that food stocks in the President's offices were ample and that strike leaders were organizing attempts to run the blockade for political rather than nutritional reasons. As the faculty discussed the Rockefeller motion around ten Monday night, a new confrontation was developing outside Low. The Reverend A. Kendall Smith, a Harlem pastor who had been arrested at a protest against the gym earlier in the year, was attempting to take food past the blockade and through the windows to the demonstrators in Kirk's offices. Smith, accompanied by a young nun and a group of clergy carrying large boxes of canned goods and fresh fruit, clambered up onto a ledge near Kirk's windows. Television cameramen threw spotlights on the contingent, which soon became surrounded by police. The police promised that if Smith came down from the ledge, he could talk with President Kirk or a representative of the administration. The pastor finally agreed and at the security entrance to Low was met by Thomas McGoey, vice president for business. Smith told McGoey that it would be a very Christian act for him to allow the food to be let into Low by the security entrance and left on the doorstep to the President's suite. As McGoey was explaining that he simply could not allow that to happen, a striker from Low emerged and informed Smith that the students inside would not accept food that was passed to them by any route other than the outside windows.

Smith turned to McGoey, took hold of his hands and implored him to arrange for the passage of the food. The vice president, trembling and hesitant, repeated that he had no power, that he could not be held responsible and that for him to allow the food through would be a betrayal of the administration. Above them a choir of strikers began singing, "We Shall Not Be Moved" and "Which Side Are You On?" Smith kept holding onto McGoey's hands, calling on Jesus Christ, as the vice president squirmed nervously and invoked Grayson Kirk. Finally the minister and his flock left for the Sundial where they held a rally and regrouped. About two hundred students were with them when they returned to Low Library, again faced the Majority Coalition line and attempted to push their way through. Between shoves Smith delivered a sermon to the two athletes directly in his path, outlining the need for compassion and brotherly love. Some counter-demonstrators heckled him as David Truman stood silently at a window in a second-floor stairwell and watched. Smith's second crusade ended in failure after only ten minutes.

The strikers did not lose every confrontation over free access, however; the same night one pro-strike graduate student, Mike Golash, edged his way, unnoticed in the darkness, around the end of the Low blockade. Reaching a window grating near Kirk's office he began to climb up. Two faculty members stationed on the ledge above tried to push him down, but he clung to the professors, almost yanking them off the ledge. Pulling himself up and breaking free of the faculty members, Golash made a perilous dash to a window of Grayson Kirk's private office amid a barrage of beer cans and eggs. The window opened and a spray of ammonia showered down on the Majority Coalition. As Golash began to climb in several members of the counter-demonstrators' cordon jumped onto the grating directly beneath him and grabbed his legs. A student leaned out of the window with an umbrella and jabbed it at the opposition on the grating. A second demonstrator used his foot to kick down at the athletes. The contested body was freed as the last of the Majority Coalition members dropped back to the ground and the window closed. Two counter-demonstrators were hurt; one had been kicked in the face.

The members of the Majority Coalition were enraged. Several turned and yelled at the faculty members behind them. One marshal ran up to an already harried professor and screamed, "You said no one would get in; it was your people that let him in." Professor Dankwart Rustow, wearing a bow tie, pullover sweater and a worn tweed jacket, raised his hands for quiet. "Please, please," he called out, "I am sorry to say that your faculty has goofed."

"Not goofed," corrected one angry counter-demonstrator, "fucked up."

Rustow paused, then said, "Correction—your faculty has—fucked up."

At the Ad Hoc Faculty meeting in Philosophy, meanwhile, little progress was being made. "We were at our worst hour," David Rothman later observed. The police seemed only hours away from clearing the buildings, and the professors had come to realize that they were not outside mediators who, when their last proposal was turned down, could make a dramatic "plague on both your houses" exit. "The problem was," one professor said later, "that we all live in the same house." They were members of the Columbia community and if there was one more diplomatic straw at which they could grasp they would try to do so.

With the motion to call in Rockefeller defeated, someone proposed that Mayor Lindsay be asked to mediate instead. Westin suggested to Professor Robert Fogelson that he meet with Barry Gottehrer of Lindsay's office to find out if the Mayor would respond to such a resolution. Lindsay's aides had also begun to oppose the use of police. They were, as Wallerstein later remarked, "hawks at first and then doves five days later." Gottehrer told Fogelson that Lindsay might be persuaded to intervene if he were to receive a strong call from the faculty.

With the Lindsay motion on the floor, Lionel Trilling rose and, in a move that shocked many of his colleagues, called for amnesty for the black students only. He explained that the students in Hamilton had behaved more reasonably than the whites in the past week and urged that the blacks should be treated more leniently because "they are newcomers to our community." After twenty minutes of discussion this motion, too, was buried beneath accumulating strata of last-minute suggestions. Economics Professor Eli Ginzberg, one of the faculty's closest contacts with the Trustees, moved that the steering committee communicate with Chairman Petersen immediately to inform him of the gravity of the situation and to seek the Trustees' mediation. After Petersen's disastrous statement of Saturday few felt that he would be the most sensitive mediator, but all agreed—especially in view of his Saturday statement—that he should be informed of the true nature of the crisis. With little time left to maneuver, the faculty saw that even mediation by the Trustees would be more desirable than police action. The board was the one group that could bring Kirk to change his mind. The proposal carried unanimously.

Shortly after eleven Professor Dallin repeated the motion to call in Lindsay. Fogelson rushed in to tell the group that the Mayor's men said there was "a good chance" that Lindsay would intervene if asked to do so by the faculty. This motion also carried, and Fogelson went off to inform the Mayor's aides. One professor objected, pointing out that the resolution to call Petersen had to be acted upon first. Professor Diamond ran out to catch Fogelson, who later said:

> Diamond came to me and said that the Trustees resolution must come first, so we had a steering committee meeting on the phone for ten minutes and decided we had duly considered the Trustee

motion first. Then I told Gottehrer to go ahead and inform Lindsay.[5]

Trilling's amnesty-for-the-blacks motion was still on the floor. Professor Alexander Erlich now sensed that with a police bust clearly the only alternative to amnesty the faculty might be willing to take a radical position. In a slow, heavy Eastern-European accent, the graying economist declared that if the faculty had to choose between police and infantile behavior, then they must accede to infantile behavior. The crucial issue of amnesty was put on the floor of the Ad Hoc Faculty Meeting for the very first time. The "moment of moral horror" that Professor Deane had first anticipated at the Tuesday meeting in Trilling's apartment had arrived.

All the arguments that had been stridently proclaimed by strike leaflets or quietly suggested in top-level administration conferences were now brought up. As the debate continued, Professor Shenton read the mood of the group differently than Erlich had; he feared that if amnesty came up for a vote at that point it would surely be defeated, with disastrous results for the demonstrators, the faculty and the University. In a short but emphatic speech he urged that the amnesty motion be tabled. A hand vote was taken and counted three times: 118–87, 157–94 and 143–70. The motion was tabled and the meeting adjourned shortly after midnight. The faculty had tried to keep balls in the air, but now the last one had fallen unspectacularly to the ground.

[5] Lindsay aide Davidoff said later that the Mayor was informed of the faculty appeal but did not want to become involved. The hour was late, the administration might oppose and even block his intervention and, with little chance of being able to solve the crisis, the Mayor stood to lose a great deal of political prestige. In addition, Lindsay had checked with his Corporation Counsel earlier Monday and was told that he would have no authority to hold back the police if the Columbia Trustees and administration were intent on filing a formal complaint of trespass. The Mayor told reporters Tuesday that he had never heard about the Ad Hoc Faculty's resolution.

# 10

## All Necessary Precautions...

On April 30, 1968, acting on an official complaint lodged by Columbia University President Grayson Kirk, members of the New York City Police Department effected the arrests of approximately 695 students and other persons who were trespassing in various buildings of the University complex and on the campus and refused to leave upon repeated requests of the University. . . .

Because of the fact that force was used to effect the arrests, a number of injuries were sustained by the demonstrators (92) and by the police (17). Department and hospital records, which are incomplete at this time, indicate the following breakdown:

| LOCATION | NUMBER INJURED |
|---|---|
| Campus | 35 |
| South Lawn | 15 |
| College Walk | 9 |
| Fayerweather Hall | 17 |
| Avery Hall | 5 |
| Low Library | 9 |
| South Hall | 1 |
| Mathematics Building | 1 |
| Furnald Hall | 1 |
| Not Stated | 16 |
| TOTAL INJURED: | 109 [1] |

[1] *Interim report prepared by the First Deputy Commissioner of Police for the Commissioner of Police: Arrests Made on the Complaint of Columbia University Administration of Students Trespassing in School Buildings.* May 4, 1968. More recent figures indicate that 711 were arrested and 148 were injured.

Rumors had been circulating all Monday night that the police would arrive within hours. But the same rumors had circulated Sunday night and throughout the rest of the occupation, and few students paid much attention to them. For hours busloads of police had been unloading at five precinct centers in different parts of Manhattan. Because the Columbia operation would be on such a massive scale the men had been drawn from precincts in all boroughs of the city—Manhattan, Brooklyn, Queens, Staten Island and the Bronx. Shortly after midnight the police began gathering on the periphery of the campus. Word of the mobilization was carried on radio news broadcasts, as breathless students ran among the occupied buildings to report that at the 100th Street precinct house police buses and paddy wagons were lined up for blocks along the street.

At the Majority Coalition line outside Low, Richard Wojculewski, one of the group's marshals, instructed the athletes who stood, arms locked, beneath the windows of the occupied area: "When the word is given, pass over to Alma Mater and then disperse in small groups for protection. Then go back to your rooms or somewhere safe."

In Math the strikers were finishing leftovers of a late dinner of roast chicken, mashed potatoes and green peas. News of the impending bust had arrived, as it had the night before and the night before that. Some ran around nervously, spreading rumors: "They say there are cops in all the underground tunnels"; "They're going to use tear gas on us." Tom Hayden held a meeting of the Math strikers and it was decided that some would block the police by sitting on the steps in their path, others would barricade themselves in upstairs classrooms to continue the resistance.

Detachments of the Tactical Patrol Force began quietly and unceremoniously to enter the campus and head for predetermined positions. A small group of students attached themselves to the end of a band of thirty TPF, playing the theme from *The Bridge Over the River Kwai* on a kazoo as they followed them about.

In front of Hamilton one professor stood just outside the barricaded doors speaking to a black demonstrator who was about to re-enter the building. In a pathetic effort at being witty and constructive, the professor suggested that perhaps a solution to the problem would be for the students inside to invite a Trustee and his wife to spend a night and talk to them. "You know," the professor said, sweating, "get some bongo drums, tell 'em it's a party—they'll come." The demonstrator did not answer.

Since the middle of the occupation the black students in Hamilton had communicated with hardly anyone, except through an occasional press release. Their secrecy had reinforced the growing image of militancy hinted at by their official statements and the conclusions of observers. With the expected police attack, most people on campus expected a small-scale Armageddon. Now, with tension higher than it had been at any other time since the crisis began, the occupants of Hamilton were addressing a rally of Harlem residents from windows overlooking Amsterdam Avenue.

More than 150 demonstrators were marching peacefully on the sidewalk carrying crudely lettered anti-Columbia placards and chanting, "Columbia goes from jerk to jerk—Eisenhower to racist Kirk." As white students joined the demonstration and the rally grew, a window opened on the fourth floor of Hamilton and Cicero Wilson leaned out over the street to deliver his first public address since April 23.

"I'd like to thank you brothers for coming out here tonight," Wilson said. "We're here to stop the gym and to get amnesty for the black students in Hamilton Hall." Teddy Kaptchuk approached a reporter standing near him in the crowd and nervously commented, "You know what he just said really doesn't matter. They're still with us. It's just a tactical thing." But, despite their protestations of unity, the white strike leaders had come to realize that Hamilton was indeed a separate decision-making unit whose actions in the next hours would be completely unpredictable.

"Look," Wilson yelled, "I know they've been trying to whitewash me up here for a while. But they won't succeed. They might try to make me leave this school when it's all over, but I don't care, because if it comes down to a choice for me between being a student at Columbia and being a citizen of Harlem, I'll always be from Harlem first." The crowd cheered and Wilson continued, "We're going to stay here until they meet our demands. We're going to stay and fight until the end." He asked the crowd to remain outside Hamilton for the rest of the night in a peaceful vigil to support the demonstrators inside. "Now you ask yourself what you're living for," the black student shouted, "and whether you're ready to die."

While Wilson spoke more than two hundred students gathered at the Sundial for an impromptu rally. Several professors had decided that if the police were about to begin their action it would be best to draw the hundreds of students milling outside the occupied buildings toward the Sundial. "We must set up a situation where everybody isn't hitting everybody else," one professor explained to another. "Get everyone to sit here quietly." The students sat on the grass and paving stones around the Sundial, holding candles and burning incense. "Police action is imminent," a young man shouted into the thick, fragrant air; "that would mean total destruction of this University. The buildings would remain, but the spiritual and intellectual life of Columbia would not." He called for a vote on whether police action would be a good thing and was answered by loud and completely irrelevant cheers of "NO!" The black rally at the Amsterdam gate was continuing, and now chanting and drumming were supplemented by loud explosions of firecrackers. Melvin Morgulis, an eccentric, occasional part-time student, who had been making a film of the crisis, dashed past winding his movie camera furiously. "We're gonna have a scene here tonight, man," he said, his blond hair trailing behind him, "we're gonna have a real scene." A student stepped onto the Sundial, trying desperately to keep the crowd calm. "Do not go to the Amsterdam gate," he pleaded, "there is nothing there." He sent a runner to find out what was happening—the chanting and pounding had become frantic—and the runner returned with: "What is at the gate is only a man banging a drum."

But it was more than that. As Cicero Wilson continued to speak from the window, someone in the crowd pointed down the street and cried, "Hey, look—the brothers are on the move!" About six blocks south, nearly 250 blacks, lining the avenue from curb to curb, marched slowly toward the campus. Chanting and yelling, the marchers joined the Hamilton protest. "I'd like to welcome you to the *other* part of your community," Wilson called out from inside his building. But the new recruits carried a different mood to the rally—a mood which terrified the whites and upset even Wilson. Small boys waved automobile aerials and older men held long wooden planks in their hands.

While Wilson yelled over his bullhorn for quiet, a tall black man stood up on a parked car and announced, "We're here to support our brothers inside. I think it might be best if whitey just steps out of our way." The whites quickly drifted across the street. Shouting over the clamor, Wilson implored the crowd not to turn on the whites or resort to violence: "We want you to stay here to support us, brothers," he said, "but keep cool."

Now thirty members of the Tactical Patrol Force moved into position around the crowd. Before anyone realized it police barricades had been set up on the outer edges of the rally, and the TPF slowly began to move the crowd toward the sidewalk. In a perfectly coördinated action they pushed the blacks against the wall of Hamilton, swung around and dispersed them down the street.

In the patch of dirt and mud that had once been a flowered quadrangle between Fayerweather and Avery Halls, students and faculty wandered around sullenly while koto music blasted at top volume from a speaker in Fayerweather. As the strident Japanese music bounced between the two occupied buildings the quad took on the appearance of a special corner of hell reserved for left-wing political activists. Knee-level lights at the base of the Business School cast a glare over the north end of the area, throwing distorted shadows high up onto the surrounding buildings. Inside Fayerweather vivid patterns of magenta, turquoise and yellow flashed on and off in coalescing patterns as the Fayerweather strikers—"our low-grade neurotics," Strike Central had begun to call them—put on a light-show to fill the hours or minutes until the police arrival.

Near Low, professors and their teaching assistants pushed their way through the dense crowd that continued to accumulate outside Kirk's offices. "Please don't stand here," they yelled, "it will be very bad if you are standing here when the police come. Go down to the Sundial where there is a rally taking place." Few students moved—most wanted to see the action firsthand. One young girl in tears, a teaching assistant in the English department, began frantically tugging at the sleeves of people she recognized, urging, "Please, please go away from here. You will be badly hurt. Go to the Sundial."

All the occupied buildings were now being sealed off from the inside. Until midnight the students in most occupied buildings, except Low, had continued to allow people to enter and leave relatively freely. Now, however, barricades were strengthened and the word was passed: "The bust is coming; decide whether you're in or out." Some students left, others entered. As the entrances closed for the last time, tables, chairs and desks were piled higher against all doors and windows. Masking tape was striped along the windows to prevent glass from flying in case the police lobbed tear gas into the buildings. Some students smeared Vaseline on every exposed part of their bodies to protect their skin against the incapacitating chemical Mace, and a few broke filters off the ends of cigarettes and shoved them into their nostrils as makeshift gas masks.

Tuesday, 2:10 A.M., April 30: a girl taking a drink of water in Fayerweather noticed that the fountain trickled to a stop. The water supply to the other occupied buildings was also shut off. At Strike Central a student was speaking by phone with occupied Low when the receiver went dead. Two minutes later the phones in the *Spectator* office in Ferris Booth Hall were cut off. The bust was beginning.

Mark Rudd left Strike Central with Lew Cole, Juan Gonzalez and several other strike leaders. Almost running, he crossed the Sundial and headed for Low. As he arrived a student messenger dashed to his side. "They're—leaving—Hamilton—Mark," he panted. Rudd sent another runner to Hamilton to get details.

As knowledge of the bust spread across campus, faculty and students began to assemble at the security entrance to Low, resolved to use all means within their power to prevent a solution of the crisis by force. Rudd walked north around Low, passing a similar group that was forming on the steps of Avery. Behind Avery, at Fayerweather, Professors Shenton and Morgenbesser, as well as Rabbi A. Bruce Goldman, the counselor to Jewish students, were forming the outermost row of a student-faculty cordon to resist the police. Circling the northwest face of Low, Rudd looked toward Math where shouts of "Up against the wall, motherfuckers!" resounded from behind the barricaded doors and windows. As he walked Rudd was followed by a small entourage of Strike Central personnel, manning walkie-talkies to communicate with the students inside each occupied hall. Fayerweather was marshaling its people into predetermined areas—one for those who wanted to resist the police actively, another for those who wanted to resist passively. Math was busy coating its stairs with the green soap found by the first students to enter the hall and saved for just this purpose. Avery was dividing itself between those who would leave when ordered to do so by police and those who wanted to be arrested. (Only one student in Avery had wanted to link arms when the police came and he abandoned this idea when he couldn't find a partner.) Low was furiously strengthening its barricades. What Hamilton was doing was uncertain. The blacks had stopped most radio and phone communication several days before, and now rumors were circulating suggesting everything from total warfare to a complete sellout.

A group of counter-demonstrators spotted Rudd as he completed his circular tour around Low. "There he is," one shouted, "let's get him." But no one responded as Rudd walked purposefully through their midst. As he reached the security entrance once again a messenger from Mathematics ran up to him. The student's face was covered with a puckered film of Vaseline.

"How's it going?" Rudd asked him.

"Fine, man. We're tight."

"Good."

The runner sent to Hamilton now returned. "The blacks are letting themselves be taken out, Mark," the student said incredulously. No shots rang out in the air over Hamilton. No angry masses swarmed across Morningside Park from Harlem. The blacks were allowing themselves to be arrested peacefully.

From the time the final decision to call in the police had been reached early in the evening the administration had been working carefully at arranging for a non-violent end to the Hamilton occupation. Human Rights Commissioner Booth, top police officials and lawyers for the black students had spent much of Monday planning the arrests with the Hamilton Hall Steering Committee. Throughout the occupation, as has been remarked, the blacks had been extremely concerned with their conduct and their image. They had taken care to keep the hall clean, had preserved order and had presented the picture of a "respectable" if militant organization. The coming of the bust had presented them with a choice: they could act in a militant fashion or in a respectable fashion, but not both.

In contrast with SDS the blacks had decided that there was nothing to gain from a bloody arrest episode. Despite Wilson's militant address to the rally just a few hours before, the blacks had already consented to coöperate with the police. Shortly before the police entered the campus some of the occupants of Hamilton had formed a corridor of blankets from the barricaded doors to a neighboring dormitory. Through it passed many of the supplies that had sustained them during their week inside. Large bags of waste paper and garbage were similarly disposed of. Black community residents and high school students, whom the steering committee did not want around when the police came, were told to leave. Now, as the bust was getting underway on other parts of the campus, Assistant Chief Inspector Eldridge Waithe, the black police officer who had been in contact with the Hamilton strikers, approached the front door of Hamilton with a small group of TPF. With two other black officers Waithe slowly made his way through the mass of students and faculty that lined the hall's steps. The crowd was informed that those inside wanted to be arrested peacefully and so offered no resistance. Reaching the main doors, Waithe pulled out a key which the administration had given him and inserted it into the lock. It did not fit and the chief had to settle for a less elegant entrance by crowbar. As the doors were pried apart about two hundred helmeted TPF appeared inside Hamilton lobby, having battered their way through the barricaded tunnels. Gottehrer and Kriegel of Lindsay's office, Kenneth Clark, Booth and representatives of the Columbia administration were on hand inside Hamilton to observe the arrests. One by one the blacks allowed themselves to be arrested, handcuffed and led away without offering any resistance. At Booth's suggestion the handcuffing stopped, and the militant students were led out the same tunnels through which the TPF had entered, into paddy wagons waiting on Amsterdam Avenue. The bust had come to Hamilton and gone. At the other occupied buildings, however, events took a different course.

*At approximately 2:30 A.M., the aforementioned police groups, together with the University representatives, approached the build-*

ings which were under siege, and which had been barricaded and locked from the inside by the demonstrators. In front of each of these buildings a group of students and faculty members stood guard, blocking the entrance to the building. At this point, the University representative, using a bullhorn, read a prepared warning to the group requesting them to stop blocking the entrance and to permit the police to enter. This request was refused. The police superior in charge of the detail then read a police warning requesting the people to leave and this request was refused. At this point, the police forced their way through the crowd to in front of the building and opened the door to each building and entered.[2]

A crowd of about 250 students and faculty was standing in front of the security entrance to Low chanting, "No Violence!" and "Cops Must Go!" They tried to sing Columbia's alma mater, "Sans Souci," but after several false starts gave up because hardly anybody remembered the words. The shouting changed to cries of "STRIKE! STRIKE! STRIKE!" as a column of thirty-five Tactical Patrol Force squared off directly in front of the crowd. The captain in charge of the column struck up conversations with the students standing on the first row of steps. He smiled and joked, occasionally humming along when the crowd sang "The Star Spangled Banner."

While the captain talked Frederick Courtney, an instructor in the Spanish department who was standing at the top of the steps, remarked to students alongside him that he had left his motorcycle helmet and camera under a hedge by St. Paul's Chapel and that he thought the helmet might be a good thing to have. He stepped down and started walking across the grassy plot between Low and the chapel. Suddenly six men leapt out of the hedges and seized him. Courtney was knocked to the ground and, as the demonstrators on the steps watched in amazement, he was punched, kicked and blackjacked. The men were plainclothesmen; some were wearing dark slacks and blue nylon windbreakers, which resembled Columbia jackets, and had looked like students in the dark. Courtney was dragged away, an officer holding each arm and leg.

As administration officials watched from a window above, another column of TPF moved into position behind the first.

The TPF captain in charge announced to the crowd, "You are obstructing police in the performance of their duty. Please move." His order was met with more cries of "No Violence!" and "No Cops!" A few athletes standing on a nearby ledge urged the police to go in and smash the demonstrators, yelling Columbia's football slogan, "Let's go,

[2] *Interim Police Report.*

Lions!" Others yelled, "Beautiful!" and cheered as they spotted more light blue police helmets. Again the captain made his announcement: "You are blocking our progress here." Again no one moved. The captain's jovial face hardened. Suddenly the police pulled out blackjacks and flashlights and charged, ramming them into the nearest faces. Most students were merely grabbed and thrown over the low hedges onto the brick pathways out of the way of police. Some were clubbed as they fell. The front row of resisters was hurled back and to the sides and the police now began plowing through the remaining five rows in a similar manner, throwing people onto the grass or bricks. Dean Platt, standing nearby to observe, was punched in the chest by a badgeless plainclothesman. Screaming, the crowd split; some ran north toward Avery and Fayerweather, others south to College Walk. "Is there a physician in the crowd?" someone yelled, helping a limping girl down the steps of Low Memorial Library, "we need a doctor." "Call Dr. Kirk!" an angry student shouted. The name was greeted with cries of "Butcher, Butcher!" One girl who had been in the security entrance rush now stood crying at the Sundial. "They knock you down but that's not enough, they don't let you up again. They just keep hitting. . . ." "They were pros," another student said, "those TPF guys don't even use clubs." Students returning from the confrontation reported, trembling, that girls were smashed against the stone walks when the police came in. "One guy, in uniform, grabbed me by the hair," said one student bleeding from a gash in his lips, "and said, okay, buddy, you're next. Then wham wham wham wham four times in the face." A Barnard girl who had been in the midst of the attack, nearly hysterical, kept screaming over and over, "Cops suck!" until she broke down into fits of sobbing. "This had to happen," quietly observed one student standing near her in the crowd, "it can't be a thinking process when you come to a stalemate."

The crowd in front of the security entrance taken care of, the police now entered the building. Paul Carter, vice provost of the University, led the police up past the offices where Kirk and Truman were staying to the student-occupied sector of the building. Outside the barricaded doors leading to the President's quarters, Carter read a prepared statement:

> On behalf of the Trustees of Columbia University, the owner of this building, Low Library, I have been authorized to order you not to remain in Low Library and you are hereby ordered to remove yourselves from Low Library forthwith.
>
> All necessary precautions have been taken to assure your safety as you leave the building. The New York City Police Department is here to assure that.

If you do not peaceably remove yourself forthwith from Low Library, the University will make a complaint immediately of trespass to the New York City Police Department in connection with your activities.

We have been informed that the Police Department will take all necessary action in connection with our complaint against you.

This order to remove yourself forthwith is separate and apart from any question of amnesty. You will be subject to proper disciplinary action by the University in any event. Of course, those who leave the building pursuant to this order will have less to answer for than those who do not.

A police officer then made a similar announcement, assuring the students, "Adequate measures have been taken to insure your safety." Still no response came from behind the barricaded oaken doors. The police began methodically to tear them open.

At Avery many of those in the crowd outside sat down as the police approached. Only a few left when ordered to do so. A wedge of Emergency Squad police waded into and over them, armed with crowbars they would use to force the barricaded door. From Math a surging chant crossed the campus—"HOLD ON, AVERY!" A group of helmeted police followed by plainclothesmen continued the rush into the crowd, lifting students and faculty and hurling them out of their way.

> Inside, approximately two hundred demonstrators were located on all five floors of the building. The Columbia statement was again read and most of the demonstrators left the building voluntarily. Fifty-three refused and were placed under arrest; they laid down and had to be carried out bodily by police officers. Mr. Nunne [Edward Numme, the administration observer at Avery] stated that some of the protesters were dragged out instead of being carried out, and that the police could have been more gentle. He described the process as one similar to a hazing line and complained that the police pummelled the students as they passed down the stairwell which was circular. This information has been referred to the Civilian Complaint Review Board for necessary attention and investigation.[3]

Once inside the building the police had made their way up Avery's winding marble staircase to the second floor, where they spotted Robert Thomas, Jr., a reporter for *The New York Times* who was covering the demonstration.

---

[3] *Interim Police Report.*

*Upon being recognized as a member of the press, he was ordered to leave. As he turned to go he was seized and struck about the head and body by plainsclothes and uniformed officers. He then made his way to Dodge Hall where he received twelve stitches on the head and was released.*[4]

No medical facilities were provided by the University. Makeshift medical centers were set up by volunteers in Earl Hall, the building which normally houses the chaplain and his staff, and in the lounge of Philosophy Hall where the Ad Hoc Faculty Group had debated three hours before. Volunteer doctors and medical students organized their own "field units" to care for students who had been hurt. These physicians complained after the bust that the police had hindered their efforts to provide medical care. One volunteer, Dr. June Finer, later stated:

> One of our doctors was beaten [by police] and arrested, a crowd of bystanders was stampeded into a first-aid station with injured, and our white-coated medical personnel were physically prevented by police from reaching injured people, who were taken away without treatment. . . . We saw no evidence that medical and ambulance services were provided by anyone other than ourselves.

Sylvia Steinberg, another member of the emergency first-aid committee, said that she contacted the University Health Service at St. Luke's Hospital across the street from the Columbia campus. According to Miss Steinberg, a nurse told her that no stretcher service was available between the campus and St. Luke's, but that students who came to the Health Service themselves would be treated between the hours of 9 A.M. and 5 P.M.

Twenty minutes after police entered Avery the clearing operation there was complete. Students in Fayerweather looking across the quadrangle toward their sister building saw the lights go on again to reveal police in almost every window. The students at Fayerweather—both inside and on the steps—braced for the attack that they knew would hit them next. Students and faculty stood on the steps at both the north and south entrances to the building. The standard announcement was made by the police at the north steps. Few moved. Faculty and students linked arms and bowed their heads. Helmeted plainclothesmen and booted motorcycle police moved in, some swinging walkie-talkie aerials, and threw the resisters off the steps into the dirt below. Inside Fayerweather five students struggled to keep the barricades intact as the police began breaking through. They could not, however, and the police entered and read their "forthwith" speech, and the University representative read his

[4] *Interim Police Report.*

"forthwith" speech, and minutes later the police began clubbing. Some students resisted and hurled angry taunts at the police, some threw chairs and other objects at them. Several students who were hit and began to bleed from the head were simply ejected from the building and not arrested. Though police had gained access to Fayerweather by the north steps, another contingent now moved to the south steps to disperse the crowd standing there. They ran, shoulders low, into the faculty line. Professors Shenton and Morgenbesser were struck, as was Rabbi Goldman. As he was knocked down Professor Morgenbesser looked up at his assailant and said, "There's no need for all this, you know." All three were later taken to St. Luke's Hospital.

The students from inside Fayerweather and Avery were carried, pushed or dragged face down over the marble steps behind St. Paul's Chapel into waiting police vans on Amsterdam. From Fayerweather alone 258 were arrested, fifty-three from Avery. Some police remained inside the occupied buildings long after all demonstrators had been removed.

*Doctor [Kenneth] Clark stated that at approximately 4:40 A.M., on the morning of April 30, 1968, while he was standing on the southeast corner of 119th Street and Amsterdam Avenue, he observed persons in other than uniform attire, wearing helmets, walking on the third floor of the Fayerweather Building, picking up furniture and dropping the same to the floor. He believes these persons were police officers.*[5]

The violent confrontation between police and students in front of the Low security entrance proved to have been unnecessary. The main force of police assigned to that building had entered through the underground tunnels, never using the entrance the other officers had cleared. Both groups met at Kirk's office and made short work of the desks, chairs and sofas that formed the Low barricades. Inside they met a group of hostile strikers who stood, arms linked, ready to resist arrest passively. The police began to pull the student chain apart, occasionally beating those who did not coöperate. Behind the partially drawn venetian blinds students were seen running from club-swinging police. The students were taken from Kirk's office and run through a gauntlet of officers who kicked and punched them if they did not move fast enough.

*Mr. Carter [the administration observer] stated that approximately one half of the protesters resisted the efforts of the police by*

[5] *Interim Police Report.*

*dragging their feet, and at one point the process became too rapid and caused a pile up.*[6]

With the wounded being carried by faculty members and medical aides into Earl Hall, counter-demonstrators standing on the Earl stoop cheered when students were seen dragged away or hit by policemen, yelling, "Give 'em everything they deserve."

Math was the only occupied building that had not yet fallen. Thought by many to be the most militant next to Hamilton, Math promised to offer the police more resistance than had Low, Avery or Fayerweather. Several hundred TPF lined up in a wide arc in front of the building. From inside came a resounding chant of "Up against the wall, motherfuckers" alternating with responses of "Kirk Must Go!" from the crowd outside. Outnumbered, the few students who stood guard outside the building were soon convinced to leave. The "forthwith" statements were read. In answer, the Math strikers continued, even louder, their chants of "UP AGAINST THE WALL, MOTHERFUCKERS!" Carefully the police dismantled the barricades. The officer in charge told his men to handle the furniture gently, and in less than fifteen minutes the police were inside Math.

*Chief* [Lawrence T.] *Flood* [commander of police operations at Mathematics], *in briefing his men, stressed the necessity of patience and restraint and directed them to leave their nightsticks behind.*[7]

Students seen cursing police in the lower-story windows were suddenly yanked backward and disappeared from view. On the upper floors the police used axes to break into rooms in which militant students held out. The strikers were led or dragged down the steps—soaped to slow the police—and deposited in a pile on the grass just outside the entrance to the building. Policewomen carried out girls who refused to walk.

The police had planned to load the Math students into vans on Broadway at 117th Street, but the large iron gate there was locked; outside a crowd of angry students stood, screaming insults. With them was Mark Rudd. At the suggestion of other strike leaders, who had advised him that it would be unwise for him to be arrested, he had left campus just before the violence of the bust began. Now he was back, hanging from the outside of the gate on the Broadway side of campus, as others bitterly shouted epithets at the police.

Seeing that the Broadway exit was blocked, police took the students

[6] *Interim Police Report.*
[7] *Interim Police Report.* Evidence indicates, however, that some policemen did carry nightsticks or blackjacks into Math.

from Math to paddy wagons parked on College Walk. As each new crowd of prisoners was loaded into a van, the students lining the edge of College Walk cheered in support of the arrested strikers. Television lights blinked on, revealing about two hundred students, most of them from Math, many of them bleeding, holding their fingers aloft in the "V" symbol. The crowd, which included many students who until now had taken no sides in the demonstration, responded by raising its hands in a "V" and chanting, "STRIKE! STRIKE!" and "KIRK MUST GO!" In the crowd of observers someone was listening to a professor on WKCR saying, "We had hoped for a breakthrough. . . ."

Melvin Morgulis, who had been filming the entire bust, went up to one of the police facing the College Walk crowd and earnestly began telling him that what was happening was a tragedy in American history. The policeman turned his back, but Melvin continued talking to him. The long-haired student went on, trying to communicate the misery he felt to another policeman on the line who just kept staring back at him with a blank, bored expression. Melvin began to break down. "Why won't you listen to me?" he cried, "Can't you see what you're doing to my buddies out there?" The rest of his words became unintelligible as he lapsed into tears, winding his movie camera convulsively.

As Melvin screamed at the policemen a tall student staggered toward the College Walk crowd from the area of the police vans. Blood dripped from his left eye and covered most of his face. He was controlled, but on the verge of delirium. "Anyone want to take a picture of me?" he asked calmly, dragging on a cigarette; "Are you going to stay in a University like this? Look what the men who run this University have done to me." Another student approached an officer standing on College Walk. He asked him whether he felt the slightest bit of guilt for what was going on behind him. "I'm a compartmentalized man," the lieutenant answered, smiling. "I do what I'm told, and I do it where I'm told."

As the arrested students were piled into police vans on College Walk, they began chanting and shouting furiously. Choruses of "We Shall Overcome" and "Up against the wall, motherfuckers!" resounded from the metallic innards of the paddy wagons. One group of prisoners began banging rhythmically on the inside of their van, and soon the occupants of each wagon took up the new protest.

The crowd of observers on the south side of College Walk had been chanting anti-cop slogans for some time when they noticed hundreds of police marching in drill formation and regrouping on Low Plaza. Through a series of right- and left-faces and advances the policemen, mostly TPF, maneuvered to within several yards of the crowd and ordered them to move back. The group retreated grudgingly and continued to taunt the police. A group of athletes stood on the Sundial chanting "TPF! TPF!" and shouting insults at the pro-demonstration students around them. A moment later, without warning, the line of uniformed officers and plainclothesmen charged into the crowd. The paddy wagons parked on College Walk swung around, their headlights spotlighting South Field and temporarily blinding the students staring up at the plaza. Flailing their clubs the police chased several hundred students onto the lawn, the glare of the bright lights at their backs as they charged. The athletes on the Sundial were overrun with the rest, their pro-police chants disregarded. The students who ran slowest in the stampede were struck with clubs, tripped or kicked. In the darker recesses of the field plainclothesmen stationed themselves near hedges and pummelled demonstrators who tried to run past them.[8] The students who moved faster found, as they reached the south side of the campus, that all of the gates had been closed and locked. With the police sweeping across South Field, they had no place to go but inside the lobbies of the dormitories which were now filling up with the limping, the bruised and the frightened. One student running for Ferris Booth Hall was clubbed and kicked just outside the building. He lay bleeding near the door, jerking spasmodically, until he was carried away on a stretcher by volunteer medical aides.

For the next hour the police crisscrossed again and again over South Field and its environs, "clearing the campus" by chasing or clubbing the students they found. "It was the only way to disperse the crowd quickly," police spokesman Jacques Nevard explained later, "It is folly for people to stand around and watch when there is trouble. . . . Once you start using force, the chances of excessive force increase greatly."

During the first run across South Field a squad of police had formed a line across College Walk and had marched slowly toward the Broadway gates, forcing over two hundred students off campus. As the first groups emerged onto Broadway four mounted policemen charged into them. The crowd scattered as the horses cantered after them; some students ran down side streets to Riverside Park, others down Broadway. Two students tried to avoid the charge by climbing atop the hood of a car but were knocked down by mounted patrolmen.

When the policemen stopped pursuit the students began slowly making their way back up to Columbia. Many gathered on the corners at 114th and 116th Streets and Broadway. As the police vans rolled off

[8] This tactic was observed by one of the authors (MS) who, when attempting to leave South Field during the police sweep, was struck in the left eye by a plainclothesman. He was taken to St. Luke's Hospital suffering from dizziness and double vision. A nurse who treated him there stated that the wound (a hematoma) was too regular to have been caused by a fist and was probably caused by a blackjack.

College Walk, transporting their cargo to precinct centers for booking, students lining the sidewalks hurled rocks and litter baskets at the vehicles and tried to block the street with benches stripped from the center mall. The police returned to clear Broadway as they had cleared the campus. Plainclothesmen in work clothes (and white riot helmets) charged up and down the street, slamming their clubs menacingly against light poles and parking meters. One of the mounted policemen rode his horse onto a sidewalk and trotted down Broadway toward 115th Street, trapping several students between his horse and storefronts. From windows in Furnald and Ferris Booth Halls soda bottles, water bags and cries of anger poured down on the police.

> *The problem confronting the Police Department on the morning of April 30, 1968, was unique in character. It was greatly complicated by the number of opposing views held by the college administration, members of the faculty and the student body. . . .*
>
> *As the days went by* [before the police action] *the department realized that conditions were worsening, and that each passing day lessened the likelihood of a smooth police operation. This was made known to the University administration.*
>
> *On an overall evaluation, the police used proper restraint in carrying out the request of Columbia University by giving adequate opportunity for the students to leave and vacate the premises, by warning them of the impending arrest action if they did not comply.*
>
> *The University administration, in briefing the department, grossly underestimated the numbers of students inside the buildings and the extent of the involvement of the faculty in sympathy with the students.*
>
> *When, during the course of the operation, the number of students was found to be considerably larger than expected, it necessitated the use of non-uniformed detective personnel* [plainclothesmen] *who originally had been assigned to the operation for investigative rather than operation purposes. They were pressed into service because they were the most immediately readily available force.*[9]

One thousand police were used in the Columbia operation. Conservative estimates of the cost of the action in police salaries alone range from $50,000 to $75,000. As a result of the 148 injuries during the police action, the Civilian Complaint Review Board received 120 charges of police brutality, the largest number of complaints ever received in New York City for a single police action.

[9] *Interim Police Report.*

## 10  All Necessary Precautions . . .

Some of the problems of the bust were the result of poor planning between administration and police officials. As noted in the *Interim Police Report,* the administration notified the police that only two or three hundred students would have to be removed from the buildings—a statement in keeping with Truman's "tiny nihilistic minority" theory but bearing no resemblance to reality. "Our clear understanding," Truman said later, "was that any and all action would be taken by uniformed police." But, as the police moved into the buildings and found twice as many students as the administration had estimated, the most available men, uniformed or not, were called into action. Observing the clearing of one of the buildings, one top police official stared in amazement and said, "My God, where are all these kids coming from?"

Detailed plans for the bust had been worked out Sunday night by Kirk, Truman, McGoey, Goodell, Fraenkel, Business Manager Joseph Nye, Dean Coleman, Chief Inspector Sanford Garelik and other police officials. The police action would have come Sunday night but for the Ad Hoc Faculty's bitter pill which still offered some promise of settlement. The operation was worked out carefully in advance, although once the police entered the campus they seem to have initiated plans of their own. As Truman later said:

> The paddy wagons were supposed to be on Amsterdam and Broadway [only], but somewhere along the line this didn't work out. Our clear understanding was that they would be there so that there would be no need to move the students out onto Low Plaza. . . . On clearing the campus, they specifically asked us what we wanted to do, and we said they should *not* clear the campus. . . . That wasn't the way it was supposed to be.

Kirk, too, was not pleased with the results of the police action, but he seemed to have had at least some idea of what those results might be. In an interview after the crisis, he said:

> No one in his right mind would believe that it is possible to bring a thousand policemen on campus and remove people illegally occupying five buildings and have seven hundred arrests without violence on both sides. This is inevitable. It is regrettable. We did everything we could to minimize or avoid it, but no one believed it could be entirely avoided.

Few in the administration had been aware of the possibility of the sort of spontaneous police takeover that occurred on South Field. In fact, it seems that some of those who made the decision to call in the police had no clear idea of what forceful "evacuation of the buildings" and "restoring of order to the campus" would actually entail. Barry Gottehrer later said:

> On Sunday night, when they were making plans for calling in the police and decided to hold off for a day, one administrator said that he was sorry the police wouldn't be used right then, because if they were the school could go back to normal the next day. Kriegel, Davidoff and I looked at each other and laughed quietly.

In the emergency room of St. Luke's Hospital Robert Zevin, the radical economics instructor who had worked with the strikers, sat dazed, blood crusted on his scalp and staining his face. Shenton and Morgenbesser were there too, the former with an injured shoulder, the latter with a slit scalp. Jack Miller, professor of chemistry, sat in a chair, waiting to help some of his colleagues, and saying, "You must realize we, the faculty, knew what the strike committee wanted, but it was insane. They wanted the University. You think I'm crazy but I'm not." Peter Kenen, the young pro-administration economics professor, also stood in St. Luke's emergency room, telling a student, "It had to come. You think Kirk enjoyed this? I wouldn't have wanted to be in his place in the last forty hours."

Grayson Kirk, neatly attired in a gray suit with vest and gray tie, stood on the right of David Truman in the rotunda of Low Library. Outside the sky was becoming light. Kirk's face was red; both men looked sick with exhaustion. Around them gathered members of the press waiting to hear the official University account of the police action. In an unwavering voice Kirk read a prepared statement:

> With the utmost regret and after nearly a week of efforts at conciliation, I reached the conclusion last evening that I must ask the police to take the steps necessary to permit the University to resume its operations. . . . Despite tireless efforts by hundreds of faculty members and the entire administration, these students have declined to accept any reasonable bases for settlement. They appear to have regarded the University's patience as weakness, although they have been assured repeatedly that we could not indefinitely tolerate a reckless indifference to the integrity of the University and to the standards of conduct on which its life as an academic community depends.
> If Columbia had been prepared to accede to the students' demand for amnesty from all disciplinary action resulting from their

illegal conduct, we would have dealt a near-fatal blow not only to this institution but to the whole of American higher education. Columbia's action tonight thus is not merely in the interest of its own future but that of its sister institutions. . . . It is my earnest hope that the dedicated efforts of faculty, students, and administrators to defend the University in this crisis now will be turned with an equally committed effort toward the renewal of its strength and vitality.

# 11

## Exit Alan Westin

ONE AND A HALF HOURS after the President's suite had been cleared of student demonstrators Grayson Kirk stood in the center of his private office looking at the blankets, cigarette butts and orange peels that covered his rug. Turning to A. M. Rosenthal of *The New York Times* and several other reporters who had come into the office with him he murmured, "My God, how could human beings do a thing like this?" It was the only time, Truman recalled later, that he had ever seen the President break down. Kirk's windows were crisscrossed with tape and on one hung a large sign reading, "Join Us." His lampshades were torn, his carpet was spotted, his furniture was displaced and scratched. But the most evident and disturbing aspect of the scene was not the minor damage inflicted by the students. The everything-in-its-place decor to which Kirk had grown accustomed was now in disarray—disarray that was the result of the transformation of an office into the living quarters of 150 students during the past six days.

In the sullen half-light of an overcast dawn David Truman left Low Library for a walking tour of the campus and the evacuated buildings. As he stepped out onto Low Plaza with Dean Fraenkel and several plainclothes police, Truman was accosted by bands of angry students who spat at him as he passed, shouting, "Fascist Pig!" and "Truman Must Go!" Peter Kenen, leaving the first-aid station in Philosophy Lounge, spotted Truman. Seeing the anger and abuse through which the vice president was passing he ran over to join him. "You ought not to be seen with me," Truman told him, "I don't imagine I'm very popular this morning."

Kenen, however, walked with Truman as the entourage moved about the campus. At each of the occupied buildings, now guarded by police, they encountered professors returning to their offices to see what condition they were in. Math, Avery and Fayerweather were in somewhat worse shape than Low; panes of glass were broken, furniture that had been used for barricades was damaged, the walls were coated with strikers' inscriptions and garbage cluttered the floors. Hamilton Hall, where the black students had made special efforts to maintain the cleanliness of the building, was in fairly good order. Photographers and reporters circulated through the buildings chronicling the damages. The stories they wrote and the photographs they flashed across the country cast the student demonstrators as merciless vandals. But information accumulated soon after the bust indicated that all the damage was not the fault of students. A statement by Samuel Eilenberg, a professor of mathematics who had not been actively involved on any side during the crisis, reflects the level of student-inflicted damage in Mathematics Hall:

> *General Remark:* It appears that the students were extremely careful about personal property of the staff, library property and departmental equipment. As a consequence, damage by students to personal property [in Mathematics Hall] was negligible. A few of the current periodicals of the library will have to be replaced.

But beyond the student damages there was vandalism of a different nature. Immediately after the bust the following report was prepared by members of the social psychology department, which is housed in the uppermost floors of the Mathematics building:

> At approximately 5:15 [A.M., April 30], Professor [Richard] Christie and Warren Goodell, vice president for administration, inspected the 600 floor. *This was half an hour after all student demonstrators had been removed from the building.* Police had forcibly opened doors that had been locked previously. *There was no sign of any damage or looting,* and no evidence of demonstrator presence in the rooms locked prior to police entry.
> Later Tuesday morning, when the police permitted faculty members to go to their offices, Professor Christie noted that the desk drawers in rooms 601, 602, 603 and 604 had been opened and apparently rifled.
> Administrative Assistant Jane Latané came into 601 Math and found that the departmental key box had been broken open and her filing cabinets unlocked. Approximately $30 of petty cash money had been taken, also a radio belonging to Professor Stanley Schachter, and about six bottles of colloquium liquor. The lock was broken on the file cabinet containing student records, but the records did not appear to have been tampered with. The pile of papers on one desk

had been spread all over the desk. The key box had master keys to the department as well as keys to virtually every lock in the department. It is evident that this occurred during the period when the police were responsible for the floor.

In all, three forms of damage occurred:

(1) that caused by demonstrators' moving furniture and other objects for use as barricades.

(2) that caused in the search for and eviction of demonstrators by the police.

(3) *miscellaneous thievery after police occupied the building.*

[Italics added]

A large, dripping ink splatter on the wall of one professor's office became a favorite subject for press photographers covering the aftermath of the occupations. Three members of the mathematics department, however, signed affidavits Wednesday stating that there had been no ink stain in the office when they toured the building as observers at 7 A.M. after all students had been evacuated. Between that time and the appearance of the stain only press photographers and police were allowed in the building. Accounts of similar activities in Math during the post-student hours were filed by other faculty members. One instructor reported:

> I was allowed entry to the Mathematics building at approximately 10 A.M. on Tuesday, April 30, together with Professors Kolchin, Bass, and Verdier. My office, Room 512, was apparently used by the students only for food storage and was in very good condition. Our bookcase and both desks had been cleared for the purpose, and considerable quantities of food were neatly arranged on these. When I returned to my office today [May 1] at approximately 2 P.M., this condition had changed considerably. A large bag (5 lbs.) of sugar and a second larger (10 lbs.) bag of rice had been split open from top to bottom and allowed to spill out over one of the office desks. Further, a large glass jar of tomato paste had been broken on the desk top, its contents spilling over the sugar and rice. Finally, at least half of the food that I had observed yesterday had been removed, including 4 large (2 lbs.) cans of ground coffee and a large box full of oranges.
>
> (signed) James Kelleher
> Instructor

The largest police action in the history of American universities had been completed within three hours. The more than seven hundred students who were carted away by night in the hysterical hours of the bust were transported to seven precinct stations throughout Manhattan for booking. The rides were long, the vans crowded and stuffy. When the vans arrived at the precinct houses, the prisoners were shuttled into large rooms. There police recorded identification and charges of each, as the students sat huddled on the floor, in some cases for as long as five hours. From their respective precinct stations all arrested students were taken in vans to 100 Centre Street for arraignment. They waited in crowded jail cells until their turn came to be called before a municipal judge who informed each of the charges against him. In most cases students were released on recognizance or on small bail. Eighty per cent of the 711 arraigned were Columbia or Barnard students; the rest were students from other colleges, Columbia alumni or faculty and non-students who supported the strike.[1] Most were charged with simple criminal trespass, though many from Low, Fayerweather and Math were also booked for resisting arrest.[2]

While the first students were being arraigned, the others waited through the morning inside their cells. Most slept; the ones who could not tried to break the boredom by distracting guards and chanting strike slogans. At noon, exactly one week after it all began on the Sundial, a guard came to each cell and brought the prisoners their lunch, consisting of weak tea and one slice of bologna between two stale pieces of bread.

As most police left Columbia with the coming of daylight a new armband appeared on campus. Students stood at the gates and on College Walk handing out strips of black crepe paper, signs of mourning for the death of a University. That morning *Spectator* carried a blank editorial surrounded by a black border. A new SDS flyer was hastily produced and distributed:

At 2:30 this morning, Columbia University died. . . . WE WILL AVENGE THE 139 WOUNDED MEMBERS OF THE LIBERATION. . . . DOWN WITH THE UNIVERSITY, UP WITH THE STUDENTS, UP WITH THE COMMUNITY, LONG LIVE THE FORCES OF LIBERATION AT COLUMBIA. . . .

[1] Figures provided by the office of the District Attorney, County of New York. According to the *Interim Police Report,* eighteen of those arrested, or less than 3 per cent, were non-student outsiders. Six faculty members, including Professor Dankwart Rustow, were arrested.
[2] The courts apparently interpret going limp or any other form of passive non-coöperation with police as resisting arrest.

The black armbands were also a sign of outrage. Though the liberals had previously refused to identify themselves completely with the students in the buildings, they were now forced to take sides, and it was unlikely that they would move behind the forces of "legitimate violence." Most Columbia students and faculty had never come closer to mass violence than TV news broadcasts, and the new first-hand experience of police confrontation shook them—at least temporarily—out of middle-of-the-road politics. With many students and faculty members walking around campus wearing head bandages and slings as badges of brutalization, it was hard to remain placidly uncommitted.

The protest that had been born during the occupations grew enormously in scope and support as the newly activated liberals joined its ranks. The crisis developed into its next phase: a full-scale strike against the University. The same phenomenon had occurred at Berkeley in 1964, when a widespread student-faculty strike followed police clearance of a sit-in in Sproul Hall. Now at Columbia the pattern was being repeated. At 7:15 A.M. Mike Nichols, executive vice president of the Columbia University Student Council, stood on Low Plaza amid reporters and shouting students and announced that the student council would support a general strike against the administration. One year ago Nichols had appeared at a campus debate to condemn SDS and the New Left. Now he was joining forces with them against Kirk and Truman. Within hours hundreds of students joined the Strike Coördinating Committee in endorsing the strike.

Late that morning and throughout the rest of Tuesday the first strike activities began. The radicals who were not in jail were holding planning sessions and, outside, hundreds of Columbia students and non-Columbia sympathizers ringed the perimeter of the campus, from 114th Street to 120th Street up and down Broadway and Amsterdam Avenue, carrying picket signs, protesting the police action and supporting the strike. Those who were too tired to walk sat hunched against the walls of buildings. Students straggled back onto campus all morning through the tight identification checkpoints manned by police.

Members of the Ad Hoc Faculty Group filed onto campus for a 10 A.M. meeting in Earl Hall. Frustrated by the fact that their sleepless efforts over the past five days had failed to avert the use of police force, they now began thinking about how they would respond to what the administration had done and to what the students were now demanding. Nearly 750 professors, a large number of whom had not taken part in the pre-bust activities of the Ad Hoc Group, showed up for the meeting, necessitating a move from Earl Hall to the larger auditorium in McMillin Theatre. At noon, after two hours of delay, Alan Westin, trailed by the other members of the steering committee, walked onto the stage of McMillin. A burst of applause accompanied his entrance; the professors rose for the man who had maneuvered the faculty adroitly if not effectively through the first phase of the crisis. As the cheering quieted someone yelled, "Our next President." There was laughter, and then Westin quipped, "That is not the sort of thing one wishes upon a friend."

Outside the doors to McMillin hundreds of students gathered to learn whether the faculty members would, now that the bust had come, take a political stand of their own against the administration. Their shouts of "Strike! Strike!" echoed through the auditorium packed with professors. Westin turned the microphone over to the Reverend John Cannon, the University chaplain, who delivered a long and somber invocation:

"Let not the distress of this present moment dishearten us or incline us to lose faith in this community of learning. Keep us from surrendering truth or giving over freedom to those who in fear or faithlessness prompt us to fight evil with the tools of evil, falsehood with lies, or tyranny with the ways of tyrants. Let this community be a light of truth in a world of darkness. . . . "

Al Moldovan, a doctor who had cared for injured students and faculty the night before, was then asked to give a medical report, which offended many of the professors:

"I was in Meridian, Mississippi, when they had voter registration, and I saw the police and state troopers there; and I was on the Pettus Bridge in Selma, Alabama, when they rode their horses and used the clubs and the tear gas against those defenseless people. Never in my life did I think I would live to see such an occurrence in these halls of ivy. Last night I saw the naked face of fascism at Columbia University. I saw children being beaten, dragged by the hair. . . . "

Westin now returned to the microphone to present a resolution prepared that morning by the steering committee of the Ad Hoc Group. Many members of the committee had been severely shaken by the police action. During the bust one officer had ordered Professor Dallin to get off the campus. When Dallin had angrily replied, "Don't you know who I am?" he was chased along with several hundred others across South Field by club-swinging plainclothesmen and TPF. Shenton had been beaten at Fayerweather, Rustow was in jail. Many of the other members of the steering committee had been asleep during the bust, including Alan Westin. He had gone home Monday night hoping that Mayor Lindsay would intervene. When he had returned at 8 A.M. nearly half the members of the committee were absent, and he had found himself listening to and being led by those who had witnessed the bust. The resolution the group had drafted reflected their fatigue and their outrage.

Now in McMillin members of the steering committee knew the content of the proposal, and most had no idea which way the group would turn. Westin began reading:

> Since Tuesday, April 23, Columbia University has been in the throes of the most fundamental crisis in its history. In the course of this crisis, the Ad Hoc Faculty Group came into existence as a force for peaceful resolution of the conflict, as a force for mediation and equity. Our efforts may have postponed for several days the calling in of the police, but it is obvious that in the end our efforts failed.
>
> On Tuesday, April 30, in the early hours of the morning, the University administration requested the police to clear the buildings of the striking students. These buildings, surrounded by defending members of the faculty and other students, were cleared in a manner which must be said to have involved, stated most conservatively, unnecessary violence.

Westin was reading very slowly, taking his time, letting his words fill the quiet auditorium. The professors listened.

> Was this inevitable? We doubt it. We all share responsibility, albeit far from equally. There are long-standing responsibilities of all those who failed to reserve time and energy for firm reflection upon the nature and policies of this University. We have come to see that its structure is archaic and many of its policies have been insensitive to contemporary political and social realities. More immediately, in the course of this crisis, there has been much intransigence, as we have constantly affirmed. Since those with greater formal power and authority are obliged to manifest greater wisdom, we must first of all condemn the persistent unwillingness of the Trustees and the administration to make a rapid fundamental re-evaluation of the moral ambiguities of their position.

The first applause broke the silence. Westin paused and then went on:

> This is not to say that others are blameless for the precipitation of the violence. Those who thought that refusal to negotiate was a necessary tactic to promote the radicalization of the University contributed to the debacle.
>
> Nonetheless, the fundamental responsibility of a university administration in a time of crisis is neither to support past errors nor to place themselves behind formal impediments to the resolution of the crisis.
>
> Men who understand the nature of a university community must

be able and willing to convince the Trustees, who may or may not be able to understand the nature of a university community, of what is required at the moment of crisis. Since the administration failed thus to persuade the Trustees, it necessarily means that they will receive a vote of no confidence from the faculty and the students. Men who placed the requirements of the continuation of the form and extent of their powers before the preservation of a university community cannot in good faith come to us now and ask us to support their leadership.

Perhaps the striking students would never have been willing to accommodate to the needs of the situation, but the administration failed to test this possibility effectively. They failed to weigh the disproportion of the pettiness of the forms of their resistance and the magnitude of the subsequent calamity.

There was silence. Even the leftist faculty members were surprised at the strength of Westin's words and his call for a vote of no confidence. The Ad Hoc Faculty Group had been critical of the administration throughout the occupation. But for five days they had hesitated to take sides, putting off votes in the interest of unity, struggling to remain neutral mediators. Now came the most critical moment in their short history as a group. Would Westin ask his colleagues to take up arms with the students and strike against the administration? They listened expectantly as he read the crucial part of the steering committee resolution:

> One day soon, we must somehow again bind up the wounds of the University and resume its life in a renewed form. As a first step, however, we must immediately move to do the following:
> A large and representative part of the Columbia University student body has called for a student strike. Normally we would regard the use of a strike by students as academically unwise, and by professors as professionally dubious. In the present situation, however, the student leaders are properly calling for a campus-wide strike. In response to last night's events, we believe we are fully within our professional responsibilities in urging our colleagues to respect this strike.

Thunderous applause filled McMillin. Some faculty members sat shocked; the cheering swelled. One professor ran outside to tell the students of the resolution. Within seconds an approving roar shot back through the auditorium.

There was still more to the proposal—the formation of a faculty fact-finding commission to look into the events, a plea to professors not to resign and a plea to students not to occupy any more buildings—but it was all anticlimax. The significance of the strike endorsement was clear. Until now most faculty members would have viewed themselves as irresponsible if they had come out in support of the demonstrations without having first worked within the system to resolve grievances. Now, after a week in which they had exhausted all legitimate channels for a rational settlement, they were prepared to take radical action and considered themselves somewhat more justified in doing so. Beyond this, as liberals, they were outraged at the police action. The bust became the symbol of their failure and the touchstone of their anger.

Almost immediately after Westin finished reading the resolution George Stade, a tall, youthful assistant professor in the English department, moved that the strike resolution be passed by acclamation. Stade had sensed that the group's fervor would assure passage of the proposal with little opposition. In his enthusiasm, however, he erred. The move for a vote of acclamation was seen by the conservative faculty members as a device to railroad through an extremely questionable resolution and precipitated their dissent. The opposition first attacked the terms of the proposed faculty strike: Was it unconditional support for an unlimited period of time? As Westin recalled later the steering committee itself was not at that time aware of the terms of the student strike. Wolfgang Friedmann, a respected member of the Law School faculty, asked for a clarification of Westin's unconditional support: "I don't think we should take such a drastic action. . . . I urge you, my colleagues, that before we take this drastic action we do fully ascertain the wish of the seventeen thousand or so students, and not act in an emotional response to those who are the most vocal."

One critical speech followed another until leftist historian Jeffry Kaplow stood and addressed the faculty members in an impassioned voice:

"I stand before you wearing a black armband. It is an armband of support and sympathy for the students who have been brutalized by the police. . . . I have personally and with the help of others who share my views prevented the crisis from breaking out many times. It was in the interest of preserving this University community that I did this. . . . The University administration has gone the other way, has precipitated the crisis to a final conclusion. We must stand, we must say that this cannot be allowed to happen, that this is a sign of contempt to the faculty and its efforts to mediate the situation, that we will not go along with it, that we maintain our position, that we pass this resolution in support of the students who have called a sympathy strike. To do anything less would be to open us to the condemnation that is implicit in the words of Jean-Paul Sartre, who said, 'I *detest* people who love their executioners!' "

Kaplow's speech received a long-standing ovation. It failed, however, to stop the barrage. Michael Sovern, a young law professor, rose immediately after the applause subsided. Sovern, who has the distinction of having been appointed a full professor when he was twenty-eight (one of the youngest in the history of the University), had played a negligible role during the crisis. Now his words, spoken with ease and self-assurance, had great effect:

We're here in a mood of outrage this morning because the University administration set in motion forces that led to physical injury to ninety-six of our students. We deplore the effects of the forces they set in motion. I suggest to you that there is a very grave risk that we're about to do the same. The [Ad Hoc Faculty Group's] claim to legitimacy from the beginning has rested on its moral force, its commitment to no coercion, its commitment to reason and avoidance of polarization of this community. We are abandoning those objectives this morning. I do not deny that there has been provocation for that abandonment, but there are hundreds, presumably thousands of our students who will not support the strike, who will want to attend their classes."

"No, No!" several professors shouted from the floor.

"Don't deny the fact, *face* the fact—you're talking about a *strike!*" Sovern responded, raising his voice. There was scattered applause. "You know from the noises you hear that many of the faculty will not support a strike," he continued to increasing applause; "our students are entitled to succumb to the emotions of the moment—we are not. The statement drafted by the committee was necessarily drafted hastily," he went on, his support growing, "under enormous pressure and emotional stress. . . . Let's do this job in an air of reason, peace, and not a divided and potentially violent University campus!" Westin now looked out over the audience and realized that the proposal was running into more opposition than he had expected. Some respected senior members were turning against him, and the points they raised were proving more persuasive than those of the leftists. Only the steering committee, which was doing its best to answer questions from the floor, seemed to be keeping the resolution alive.

"Shall we have an identity if we identify ourselves with the students?" asked Professor Quentin Anderson.

Walter Metzger, a steering committee member sitting near Westin on the stage, took up the challenge. "It seemed to us that we could not say nothing at all. It disturbed me that we might lose our identification as the faculty, but we must for a short time indicate our solidarity with the students. We can't go back to our blackboards as if nothing had happened."

But, despite the efforts of the steering committee, the calm forces of conservatism were gaining ascendency. Fritz Stern, a respected historian, rose from the balcony and delivered what was to be the resolution's *coup de grâce*. Stern had been in Germany when the demonstrations began and had written on April 23 to a colleague at Columbia that, after seeing the German radicals, he far preferred Columbia's SDS. In the few days since returning he had been asked to serve on the Ad Hoc Faculty steering committee and then, when Westin sensed he was too conservative for the group, had been asked to leave. As Stern began to speak the faculty members turned in their seats to look up at him. Seated next to him was Lionel Trilling, nodding approvingly at each point his colleague made. In a level but forceful tone, Stern said: "I am utterly removed from your thoughts and sentiments and I am opposed to both the aims and the contents of your resolution. . . . I remember that it was only twelve hours ago that Professor Bell ended his speech by making it clear that the administration had moved very much closer to the points of our resolution than had SDS. You now come out condemning the administration, but I miss any similar statement condemning the other side."

As respected leaders Westin and the steering committee might still have been able to swing the majority of the Ad Hoc Group behind their resolution. But a very real split had emerged. As chairman of the Ad Hoc Faculty Group Westin had patched one rift after another, forestalling votes and making compromises. While his colleagues spoke he was considering the possible effects of a major faculty split.

Stern was still standing. He offered a compromise: the resolution could be approved, but the strike would not begin for a week, during which time all sides would try again to work out a settlement. Earlier in the meeting the steering committee had accepted an amendment to the strike resolution limiting the initial boycott of classes to two days, after which "we shall re-evaluate our position without prejudice." Now Stern was trying to take the remaining wind out of the luffing resolution. Westin had been chairing the meeting smoothly and at the same time coming to a major decision. He later explained that the situation at that point was analogous to that of a nation state, in which the government no longer had support and in which he was the leader of the opposition. It was the moment, if the analogy were to be maintained, for Westin to become Prime Minister, he said afterward, "But that was not my aim in life." Moreover, Westin realized that he really had little first-hand knowledge of how students felt and what they were demanding. The steering committee had drafted the strike resolution quickly and had not spent much time thinking of the consequences. It was Westin who had guided the faculty from its state of non-involvement Thursday to this crucial moment; a split now might bring about the end of the faculty group as an active force.

Westin called for a two-minute recess and huddled with the rest of the steering committee. He listened to his colleagues and then returned to the microphone. He had made up his mind, but no one, not even the steering committee, knew what course he would take. Wallerstein was sitting at his side reworking the resolution to incorporate the accepted amendments as Westin began speaking again:

"I don't think that this faculty should become split just as the radical element of the student body would like to see. I think it would be very wise to have this resolution withdrawn. I would like to have the opportunity to speak with the student leaders . . . and then I think the steering committee should get together again and discuss the motion. I think you may have a majority to pass this resolution, but if you do so, I will have nothing to do with it."

The room was stunned. Westin lost control of the meeting as professors began jumping up and shouting to be heard. David Rothman, who like Daniel Bell and nearly half of the other members of the steering committee had been asleep when the strike resolution was drafted, now stood up on the stage and said, "Many of us on the steering committee have not had a chance to discuss the motion." He asked for a motion of adjournment, and immediately Eli Ginzberg moved to end the meeting.

"Point of order! Point of order!" professors shouted. One faculty member who got the floor because his voice was louder than the rest pointed out that the meeting could not be adjourned while there was still a motion on the floor. Another argued that Westin could not withdraw his own motion because of the subsequent motion for acclamation made by George Stade. In the confusion—as many as ten people were trying to get the floor at once—Stade withdrew his motion, although hardly anyone heard him.

Morton Fried, a stocky anthropology professor with a full beard, stood up and demanded to know which of the faculty members present had a right to vote on adjournment or on any matter. Fried was challenging the conservative professors who had showed up in force but who had never before been active in the affairs of the Ad Hoc Faculty Group. Hoping to disqualify the conservatives from voting and thereby assure the passage of the strike resolution, Fried gave Westin the out he had been seeking:

"This is an excellent point, sir," Westin said. "There are more than twice the number of people here than have taken part in our deliberations. I am not going to be used by people who have not been part of our meetings. There are students present here, there are others present here whom I do not know. I do not believe we can take ayes and nays in that situation. Therefore I am going to walk off this stage and I call on all the members of the steering committee to do so. We as a steering committee would like time to sit and reconsider, at least I would. . . . I am not going to put this to a vote to the group. That is simply my act. I am going to leave."

Everyone was out of his chair. Some professors were screaming "No!" Some were cheering, and others stood stunned. Alan Westin walked off the stage and out of McMillin Theater, bringing the meeting to a chaotic end. One hundred and twenty-five professors remained behind to sign their names to the strike resolution.

The rest of the steering committee walked out behind Westin. It was a tragic death for the Ad Hoc Faculty Group. Conceived in impotence, the group died just short of seizing power. Although in his final resolution Alan Westin was forced to concede that "in the end our efforts failed," to say that the faculty group accomplished nothing would be misleading. Were it not for their legitimization of the students' demands, their continued efforts to forestall police intervention, and their slow but visible drift to the left, the demonstrations most likely would have been repressed before reaching the proportions and strength they did, and before assuring that fundamental changes would ultimately be made in the University. The Ad Hoc Group had given the faculty a sense of identity and power which it never had before. But in doing so it also gave them a sense of frustration, for its brief life had shown that "faculty power" was still a long way off at Columbia.

A second meeting of the Joint Faculties of Columbia University had been called soon after the bust for 2 P.M. in the Law School Auditorium. The faculty members who had stayed behind in McMillin and signed the strike resolution decided that they would introduce it at the two o'clock meeting. But without Westin's support the vote of no confidence had little chance of passing. In the early afternoon Tuesday, Vice President Truman was discussing another resolution with Professor of History Richard Hofstadter in Low Library. As he had done before the Sunday Joint Faculties meeting, Truman was seeking support from senior faculty members for a pro-administration resolution. Hofstadter, Truman and several other faculty members worked together on the motion, which began:

> While deeply regretting the necessity of police action to restore order on the campus, we believe it essential for all members of the University community to avoid recriminations and devote their efforts to constructive solutions of the problems we confront. . . .

The proposal went on to focus on long-range suggestions for reform within the University but did not concern itself with the immediate problems which Columbia faced in the wake of the bust. It recommended that a seven-man committee be appointed immediately to arrange for the election of a commission which would propose changes in the structure of the University. It called upon the Trustees to issue a statement of willingness to make necessary statutory reforms and urged that Kirk appoint a Trustee-faculty commission to bring about the restructuring.

After helping to defeat the strike resolution Professor Sovern headed back to the Law School. Sovern had been developing his own ideas for a resolution and went directly to the office of William Warren, dean of the Law School, to enlist his support. Warren was in the process of drafting his own resolution at Truman's request but was persuaded by Sovern to work with him instead. Maurice Rosenberg, another law professor, joined them, and together they drew up a resolution to be presented at the Joint Faculties meeting. Sovern had spoken earlier of the need to refrain from emotionalism. The resolution which he helped graft was neutral, apolitical, unemotional and non-committal. There was no condemnation of anyone, no call to arms. Instead, the resolution, drafted in half an hour, dealt with an orderly future:

> In our University's hour of anguish, we members of its faculties must assume responsibility to help return this University to a community of reason. In this spirit we adopt the following resolutions:
> 1. That the University set aside Wednesday for reflection so that without classes, students and faculty may meet and reason together about their University.
> 2. That there be an Executive Committee with power to call the faculty together and to take other needed steps to return the University to its educational task at the earliest possible moment and that the committee be composed of such people as the following: Daniel Bell, Walter Metzger, William Leuchtenberg, Alexander Dallin, Eli Ginzberg, Polykarp Kusch, Ernest Nagel, Michael Sovern, Lionel Trilling, Alan Westin.
> 3. That the recently appointed tripartite committee of representatives of the faculty, student body and administration immediately begin functioning to assure due process and equitable treatment to students facing charges.
> 4. That each member of the Columbia community act in a manner showing respect for his colleagues and assuring the return to life and health of this great University.

The proposed Executive Committee of the Faculty would have the power to bypass the administration by independently calling together a meeting of the faculties. No longer would the President be able to serve as a bottleneck to faculty action. The resolution was significant in terms of faculty power, but at a time when most people were calling for drastic action it appeared a minor step. After drafting the resolution the three law professors left Warren's office to enlist support. Rosenberg sought out members of the Law School faculty, Warren went to speak with the administration and Sovern headed for Philosophy Hall to talk with members of the Ad Hoc Faculty Steering Committee.

When he arrived at Philosophy Sovern showed his motion to Westin, who said that before he could support it two junior faculty members would have to be put on the Executive Committee. After some hesitation Sovern consented, and Westin agreed to support the resolution.

In Low Library Warren was having a harder time. Truman was intent on getting the Hofstadter resolution through the Joint Faculties meeting and told Warren that he could not support the Law School resolution. As they argued Truman became increasingly defensive and, according to one faculty member, said that if the resolution were passed he would resign. Warren left the meeting reluctant to introduce the resolution before the faculty. He was not aware that the threat to resign had become a common pressure tactic for Truman. The vice president had already used it several times with the faculty, and had done so successfully with the Trustees on Monday to convince them to accept his conception of the proper response to the bitter pill. The vice president later commented that while he would not bluff a resignation with the Trustees, "I sure would with the other side [the faculty]."

Because negotiations over the various resolutions were proceeding slowly, the Joint Faculties meeting did not start until shortly after three. When it did, its location had been shifted from the Law School to St. Paul's Chapel so that the overflow crowd of professors could be seated. The acoustics of the chapel, one of the oldest buildings on campus, were not designed for open meetings. From the microphone in the chair where Mark Rudd had denounced the administration, three weeks ago to the hour, a speaker could be heard throughout the hall. But speeches from the floor were lost in the vaults and transepts of the chapel.

As the faculty members began to file into St. Paul's a contingent of about 250 students and junior faculty members gathered at the doors for a silent vigil. A light rain began to fall, and the students covered their heads with newspapers as they heard strike leader Jon Shils explain the purpose of the new campus-wide strike. Most of the arrested students from inside the occupied buildings had returned to campus, and some of them now presented reports of the police action. Outside the Amsterdam

Avenue gate at 116th Street Mark Rudd was speaking to a rally of more than a thousand students from Columbia and other colleges throughout the city. He announced that Columbia was now in a state of revolution and made special mention of the professors who had come out in support of the strike: "For the first time the faculty has seen the light. . . . They have been awakened."

In the darkness of the chapel, however, the Columbia faculty was confused and uncertain. A raucous, bleacheresque tone for the meeting had been set when Grayson Kirk and David Truman walked in. A few conservative faculty members thought it appropriate to applaud the administrators, touching off booing, more applause and cries of "Shame!" The audience quieted, Kirk took the chair, and Truman reported to the faculty on the decision to call in the police and the events which followed. Richard Hofstadter was recognized by Kirk and introduced the administration-approved resolution. But, almost before debate could begin on the Hofstadter proposals, Morton Fried took the floor. The pro-strike professors who had remained in McMillin after Westin's walkout had designated Fried to present the strike resolution to the Joint Faculties. He now read it as a substitute motion to Hofstadter's resolution. Kirk was now in the awkward position of chairing a meeting which was considering a vote of no confidence in him and his administration. Amid the applause for Fried's resolution Kirk renounced the chair and turned it over to Dean Warren, who was sitting in the front row and who, as dean of the Law School, seemed most likely to be able to preside over a disorderly meeting. Once again Kirk's judgment proved faulty; Warren was not an adept chairman. "It wasn't only that Warren didn't know parliamentary procedure; he didn't have the dignity, the presence," one professor remarked. Fried's strike motion was still on the floor; Truman and Kirk were sitting to the side. The vice president recalled later:

> In the mood I was in, I was ready to have the Fried resolution come to a vote . . . maybe it was just my old combative self, but if it had passed, I would have resigned on the spot.

Seconds after taking the chair Warren recognized Sovern, who attempted to cut off debate on the Fried strike resolution. The closure motion was defeated; many professors, in the confusion, thought they were voting on the resolution itself and not on whether to call the question. Faculty members in the back of the chapel rose and demanded clarifications and points of order. Realizing that he was in difficulty, Warren called Sovern to the podium to advise him on parliamentary procedure. The meeting quieted and debate continued from the floor on the strike resolution, although few could hear what was being said. Alex Dallin offered a series of amendments to the resolution which reversed the order of paragraphs and slightly changed its emphasis, serving further to baffle the professors. Sovern again sought to bring the resolution to a vote, but because he was aiding the chair he could not introduce a motion. He signaled to Professor Rosenberg, sitting in the front row, and then whispered to Warren that he should recognize Rosenberg. Rosenberg was called on but apparently misunderstood Sovern's signal and thought that his colleague wanted him to introduce their resolution at this point. He rose and presented the proposal for the Executive Committee as a substitute to the Fried strike resolution which, in turn, had been a substitute to the Hofstadter motion. Most of the professors were just confused, but Warren was infuriated that the resolution was now being read. "You double-crossed me," he muttered to Sovern. Sovern, who later claimed that he was as surprised at Rosenberg's action as Warren was, tried to tell the dean it was all a mistake.[3]

Rosenberg's Executive Committee resolution was now on the floor, along with Fried's strike resolution and Hofstadter's administration-approved resolution. Lionel Trilling sat in his chair musing about what was meant by an Executive Committee composed of "such people as" Lionel Trilling. An amendment was made to delete the phrase "such people as" and the three words were dropped, although again few professors—including William Leuchtenberg, another "such as"—heard the change. After extensive debate on all three proposals it became clear that the Executive Committee resolution was carrying the most support. It was the proposal of moderation. The outraged liberals, thinking it the best they could get, threw their endorsement behind it; the conservatives, fearing that the strike resolution just might pass, also backed it. The question was called, and when a voice vote was taken Rosenberg's resolution passed by a clear majority. A motion was then made to adjourn. The 300–205 vote that followed was seen by many professors as, in effect, a rejection of the strike resolution which might have been reintroduced had the meeting continued.

In the final analysis, enough faculty members were unwilling to depose Kirk, Truman and the rest of the administration because of what had happened. Many of those who were outraged that morning had been appeased by a measure of faculty power, and, although a few faculty members may have been radicalized by the bust, the majority remained

---

[3] After Truman had told Warren of his opposition to the motion, Warren had met with Sovern and Rosenberg and decided that they would await further developments before deciding whether to introduce their motion. With Sovern and Warren on the podium, Rosenberg was the only one of the three left to present the motion. He explained later that he had already independently come to the conclusion that their resolution should be introduced and was about to ask for the floor when he got Sovern's signal.

moderates. With sympathies on the left and commitments on the right the Columbia faculty found itself locked into political neutrality.

Leaving the confused meeting in St. Paul's Chapel the professors were greeted with the plaintive looks of about 250 pro-strike students holding their vigil in the rain on the stone steps of the chapel. Many wore bloodied bandages and held their fingers silently aloft in a "V." Some leftish faculty members returned the sign and went with the students to McMillin Theater for a strike meeting.

The signatures of five hundred students and faculty members had been obtained on the strike resolution, and now the group in McMillin sought to clarify its demands. Marvin Harris led off the meeting by demanding a complete sweep of Low Library: "The faculty has been subjected to every conceivable indignity by an administration that is unable to maintain order. We therefore ask for a change in the administration." Eric Bentley took the microphone and reiterated Harris's demands:

"I said a few days ago that if Kirk brings in the cops, I would not be able to work for an institution like that. We must now change the administration and renounce the President. . . . We cannot hold any truthful discussions before the removal of the President. All depends on one demand: KIRK MUST GO!"

The radical students, however, were still concerned with political clarity. They saw the importance of the six demands as overriding; reaction to the police, demands for resignations were all secondary. The Strike Coördinating Committee issued a statement late Tuesday in which it clearly stated that the strike should not be based entirely on emotional grounds:

> The fact that police were used and the brutality with which they attacked the demonstrators have served to focus attention away from the political issues that caused the sit-in and the strike in the first place. . . . This strike must not only be a response to the police. We must make it absolutely clear what we are striking for. . . . The resignation of President Kirk and Vice President Truman will not alone insure that their unjust policies will not be continued by others, or that the kind of power the administration exercised over the lives of others will not be transferred to a similar elite. To prevent the continuation of those policies we must continue to strike for our demands.

After the Joint Faculties meeting adjourned late Tuesday afternoon, the newly formed Executive Committee of the Faculty held its first meeting and elected Alan Westin and Michael Sovern co-chairmen. It was perhaps the only decision the committee made with ease. Although it did not become apparent for several days, the group was beset by factionalism from the start. On one side were the conservative, administration-oriented professors—William Leuchtenberg, Polykarp Kusch, Ernest Nagel and Eli Ginzberg—who sought to focus the committee's work on its mandate to restore the University to order. On the other side were the former members of the Ad Hoc Faculty Group Steering Committee—Alan Westin, Walter Metzger, Daniel Bell and Alex Dallin—who were now committed to restructuring the University. Sovern and Trilling remained in the neutral middle ground. The results of this factionalism were not at first apparent to the University community, but within the coming weeks the failure of the Executive Committee to take a forceful stand on many substantive issues alienated many students and faculty members, diminishing hopes that the committee would become a powerful new force within the University.

Late Tuesday night the Executive Committee met with a group of about twenty student leaders in a recently evacuated classroom in Fayerweather Hall. The remnants of barricades littered the lower floors; police patrolled the building. After a quick buffet of sandwiches and chocolate cake the professors and students turned to the question of restructuring the University. Schemes were tossed around and optimism was high. Soon Walter Metzger was at a blackboard drawing diagrams of alternative power structures for the University. *Spectator* editors who attended the meeting that night returned to their offices to write a hopeful editorial:

> The opportunity facing Columbia is a unique and challenging one. . . . There are many on the faculty and in the student body who will timidly advocate pretending that nothing really has changed—that if we just go back to our dorms and offices and wait long enough, the scalps will heal, and all will return to the normalcy which precipitated the crisis. First, this will never happen; the trauma has been too great. Second, it should not happen; for we now have the opportunity to do something creative and exciting with this University—our University—that we may never have the chance to do again. Appalled at the past, we are confident for the future.

Wednesday, May 1, Columbia University was officially shut down for the fifth consecutive day. Police continued to guard the campus, and their presence—manning the gates, checking identification cards and patrolling Low Plaza—angered many students who still remembered vividly the events of Tuesday morning. A rally was held at the Amsterdam Avenue gate at 2 P.M. Wednesday to protest the presence of police on campus and to support the strike. Mark Rudd and Charles 37X Kenyatta addressed a crowd of about 750 gathered outside the gates. Students at another rally being conducted by strike supporters at the Sundial drifted over to the gates to hear Rudd's speech. As the rally outside started to break up, a squad of about thirty-five policemen filed onto the campus to join a detachment of twenty-five officers already positioned around the gate. The students on College Walk jeered the police as they entered, shouting, "Cops Must Go!" The police attempted to clear the area, asking the shouting students to move away from the gate. They refused to go and some lining the south edge of College Walk in front of Hamilton Hall linked arms. The police formed a wedge and shoved; several students pushed back, one threw a rolled-up newspaper at an advancing officer and the police charged into the crowd, nightsticks flailing. One student punched a policeman and was grabbed by four uniformed men and one plainclothesman and thrown against the wall of Hamilton Hall, then clubbed and kicked as he fell. Another student standing on a window ledge on the second story of Hamilton jumped feet first onto a policeman in the melee. The officer was knocked down and seriously injured, the student was surrounded and beaten by plainclothesmen.[4] A heavy garbage can was tossed down from Hamilton at the police, and someone in the crowd hurled a broken tree limb at another group of officers. Ten minutes later, when the fighting had subsided, ten students and three policemen were across the street in St. Luke's Hospital. Strike leaders had circulated through the surging crowd, asking people to return to the Sundial. Mark Rudd climbed a window grating of Hamilton and told the students that "the way to win is not to go out and fight cops." Deputy Inspector Joseph Fink, whose white gloves were splattered with blood, ordered his men to pull back. A police official told reporters later that no policemen had received orders from Columbia officials to clear College Walk and that they had not been authorized to use their clubs.

Meetings of various departments, deans, deans' staffs and students continued throughout the afternoon. Eleven divisions of the University decided to cancel classes until Monday in an effort to postpone any confrontation that might be caused by the strike and to provide more time for the multitude of meetings and informal discussions that seemed to be leading the University slowly back to a state of calm.

[4] The policeman spent over a month in St. Luke's Hospital with back injuries.

\* \* \*

A mass meeting had been called for Wednesday evening by the strike leaders to clarify demands and construct a new, broader-based organization for the strike. Proposals for the meeting had been prepared during the day by various groups of students, and the meeting attracted more than thirteen hundred to Wollman Auditorium (seating capacity, 750). The meeting began at eight without a chairman and proceeded in an informal but fiery manner for the next two hours. At ten Dave Gilbert of SDS took the chair and prepared to get down to business. In his soft-spoken manner he told the overflowing audience that democratic procedures would be difficult, but that the group was going to have to "try to participate on a large scale in making fairly complicated decisions."

"The original six demands are no longer sufficient," he told the students; "in addition to winning political demands, we must begin to create a new University." Gilbert then turned the microphone over to Tony Papert, who had led the strikers in Low, and Rudd, who were to introduce a proposal for the formation of a new Strike Coördinating Committee. Rudd began:

"At first we didn't know exactly what to do and I must admit I didn't know whether to go to McMillin and talk to Truman [on the first day], whether to try to get into Low Library, whether to go to the gym site, what to do. But we did them anyway. All along the line people said, 'Hold back, you're really going to turn people off, because your radical politics and especially your radical tactics are just no good.' The fact that there are about a thousand or more people in this room, who are trying to talk and make the strike go, is proof that the sort of politics and tactics we offered were right. . . . This is almost a fact of the strike; I wasn't sure when I went into it but I'm sure now."

He told the audience about a conversation he had had with Professor Westin during the crisis, when he was told that if there were a bust everything would be lost. "Well, we got busted and now look around you," Rudd said, smiling. Cheers of "STRIKE, STRIKE!" rang back. Rudd began to talk about the demands, and warned that it would be foolish to start pressuring for empty trappings of student democracy. As the radicals had done throughout the demonstrations, Rudd argued for political clarity:

"Let's not be timid; let's keep pushing . . . let's be extremely clear on what we're demanding and let's be clear in why we're doing all this. I think it's clear to the seven hundred people who were busted and those who were beat up and those who witnessed it. We're doing this in order to create a human society and to fight exploitation of man by man and we think that this University was an example of this exploitation."

The thrust of Rudd's argument was clear: he was trying to persuade the more moderate students to join the strike on his terms and not seek to change its nature. With the prospect of an influx of liberals onto the new Strike Coördinating Committee, Rudd and the other leaders were faced with the dilemma of rejecting this new support in the interest of preserving the purity of the radical movement or accepting the moderates in the interests of building a mass movement.

Tony Papert spoke of the need to assert the students' power in the University before Grayson Kirk reasserted his. He proposed that the new strike committee take over all University functions as soon as possible: "It's going to mean an orderly process of university life, not the old kind of university life, but as much as possible the kind of life that should go on at a university." Rudd took the microphone again.

"I'd like to comment on what Tony just said," he began.

"Point of order," a student shouted from the audience. "We're here to select a steering committee for the strike." There was applause from the moderates who were becoming annoyed at Rudd.

"But you can't select a steering committee until you've discussed the politics behind the strike," Rudd objected. He was shouted down by the audience. Gilbert tried to quiet the group, and Rudd was given two minutes to comment on the strike before introducing his proposals. After concluding his brief analysis Rudd presented the proposal for a new steering committee—a "provisional government." Membership on the committee would be open to representatives of the entire University community, with the proviso that all delegates must pledge to uphold the original six demands. Representatives would be chosen on a one-man one-vote basis from among students, residents of Morningside Heights and University employees.

When Rudd stepped down from the stage a student representing an ad hoc group of 250 graduate students was given the floor. He proposed an alternative plan under which delegates to the new steering committee would not have to support the six demands. Only support of the strike would be necessary, to insure that the "coördinating committee represents as broad a spectrum of campus opinion as possible." The moderate challenge had been made. Debate ensued for more than two hours, but the lines were clearly drawn. The radicals wanted the six demands and a militant strike; the moderates wanted to focus on resignations, getting the police off the campus and restructuring the University.

Shortly after midnight Gilbert called for a voice vote. It appeared that a majority sided with the radicals, but Rudd and Papert were not quite sure of what to do in the face of a clear split. Papert, who later regretted his words, advised Rudd not to bother with the vote and to accept the graduate students' proposal. Rudd then turned to the audience and, in a wholly unexpected move, yielded to the moderates. The applause for Rudd's conciliation spread rapidly and resoundingly. Delegates would not have to support the six demands, and restructuring would be pressed as a critical issue. The radicals had sacrificed a part of their politics for a massive student strike.

# 12

# *Amorphatorium*

IN THE WEEKS FOLLOWING the bust the Columbia strikers came close to attaining a variant of one goal of classical Marxism: their revolution brought about a classless University. Most undergraduate courses ceased to meet, and it seemed that for much of Columbia the academic year had ended on April 23. The University was officially closed for a week following the bust, and when most of the University's divisions tried to resume their regular academic schedules only part of the Columbia community returned to classes.

With its academic center removed, the conventional life style of most undergraduates disintegrated. In its place arose the post-bust variety of personal "liberation." Students had time to spend long hours engrossed in discussions with the professors they had met in front of buildings during their vigils or with the other students who had been inside the buildings with them. Freed from the fetters of habit and routine, students were able to work on the Strike Committee's many projects, study if they wished, or just lie out on South Field in the sun with one of the girls they had met during the occupation. At the center of the radicals' existence were the communes, the new social units derived from the tribe-like groupings that had formed in each building:

### *On Solidarity—The Communes*

Albert Camus said that the object of rebellion is to make the world safe for Man. America is not safe for Man. Our young men die gratuitously in a war that is without reason or defense. The poor are exploited and made wretched. America is not safe for Man.

A University which orders a thousand club-swinging fascist cops against its students and praises their action, a University which directs plainclothesmen to viciously beat innocent spectators and praises their action, a University that permits mounted police to violate her grounds and to trample students and faculty outside her gates and praises their action, this University is not safe for Man.

We who entered and held the five liberated buildings for seven days know personally the brutality and inhumanity of a system which kills its young men without remorse, and allows the poor to starve without remorse, and wages a dirty war against a free people without remorse. We who were there and busted discovered in that experience a solidarity with each other and with the other students and faculty of this University, all of whom are up against the wall. This solidarity is growing. We will free Columbia of the company men and profiteers and the cake-eaters who control its future and direct its participation in the death industries. Our weapon is our solidarity. Together we support the strike and paralyze this massive institution until Columbia is made safe for Man.

——The Communes.

The Strike Coördinating Committee's immediate constituency grew to approximately four thousand students, and thousands more, with the help of their professors, respected the SCC boycott of classes which were held inside University academic buildings. Some attended the Strike Committee's "free university" liberation classes; more met with their teachers in dormitory lounges, apartments near campus and on South Field to talk about the strike as well as their course material.

On May 2, the Thursday following the bust, two meetings—with two rather different purposes—were held to consider the resumption of regular classes. The College Committee on Instruction, a group of faculty and administrators responsible for all academic affairs in Columbia College, met in Hamilton Hall, and the newly constituted Strike Coördinating Committee convened in a small room on the third floor of Ferris Booth Hall.

Students in the College had missed two full weeks of school, during the crucial period preceding final examinations. It was clear that the two weeks lost could not be made up in the nine days left to the semester. If classes were extended through the end of May no time would be left for the normal ten-day examination period. Stretching the entire academic year into the summer vacation would not be feasible since most faculty members had, like their students, already committed themselves to summer plans.

It would be impossible simply to pick up the term's syllabus where everyone had left off on April 23. And many felt it would be undesirable as well. Flushed with the excitement of revolution, faculty members and students argued that the remainder of the semester should be spent in endeavors more meaningful than cramming for exams. The relevance which so many students had felt their courses lacked was now to be found in discussion of the demonstrations and of the nature of the University.

The usually staid Committee on Instruction proposed, for the consideration of the College faculty, an imaginative solution permitting instructors and students considerable latitude in solving the difficult problem of completing the semester. The two student advisors to the committee were influential in persuading it to accept the proposal which suggested that classes resume May 6, but that "the nature of these classes should be determined by the instructor in consultation with his students." The committee proceeded to overturn—just temporarily—the conventional College grading system. A student would have three options to choose from: in each course he could get a letter grade, a grade of "P" indicating only that he had passed the course, or an "incomplete" which would mean that he would have a year to make up any work necessary to receive a grade.[1] The formal final examination period would be abolished, and the administering of exams left to the discretion of individual professors. The resolution was broad enough to permit students to continue to strike without fear of academic reprisal, yet it enabled professors to meet with any students who wanted to continue course work.

The newly expanded Strike Coördinating Committee held its first meeting Thursday afternoon. Since the mammoth strike meeting in Wollman Auditorium the previous night students of all left-of-center political views had been collecting signatures on petitions to qualify as representative delegates to the Strike Committee. Everyone who could produce the signatures of seventy constituents was given one vote. By the afternoon the credentials of thirty-seven delegates had been approved. Graduate students in several departments, including history, anthropology and English elected delegates.[2] One fraternity gathered enough signatures for representation, as did some members of the local

---

[1] The resolution recommended that no student should receive a failing grade for any course, regardless of what his status was as of April 23, and that even if he attended no further classes he would still be eligible to get a "P." Students in the College are usually permitted to take only one course per semester on the "pass-fail" option. Grades of "incomplete" are normally given only under special circumstances approved by the dean.

[2] The representative of the English department was Edward Tayler, the youngest full professor in the department.

community and some University employees. The bulk of the new committee, however, was formed by the "communes."

At its Thursday meeting, the committee drew up the set of demands it said the University would have to meet before students would return to class. The new demands were practically identical to the pre-bust six demands, as was one of the two preconditions to negotiations: amnesty. But another precondition had now been added: "That the administration recognize our right to participate in the restructuring of the University." The moderates who had joined the Strike Committee had, in the end, agreed to go along with the six demands. They had, however, persuaded their radical colleagues to push for within-the-system changes as well, though the committee did not elaborate on just what such "participation in restructuring" would entail.

Over the weekend the Strike Committee began to outline its tactics for the upcoming boycott. At a mass meeting in Ferris Booth Hall Saturday afternoon over three hundred students passed by acclamation an SCC motion to picket academic buildings on Monday. To prevent the strike from losing the momentum it had acquired from the bust, the group decided to hold a rally every day at noon for the next week.

The committee also created a quasi-formal alternative to University-sponsored classes, the "Liberation School." Saturday the newly formed Strike Education Committee (SEC) prepared an extraordinary memorandum on the "Renaissance of Learning at Columbia":

> To the *entire* Columbia University community, i.e., all students, faculty, administrators and other office workers, clergy, staff, grounds keepers, neighborhood residents, etc.:
> The old administration (represented by President Kirk) has proven itself incapable of meeting the legitimate desire of the University community for a free and democratic, creative and relevant educational institution. . . . Most recently, the old structure has taken a major step toward capitulation by cancelling the old classes for the rest of the term [the College Committee on Instruction proposal].
> The Strike Coördinating Committee can and will meet the legitimate desire for free and democratic learning. . . .
> The SEC *encourages* all participants in counter-classes to exercise their *freedom* to experiment with and create new and different forms and content, according to a continuing *democratic procedure:*
> This means that the *will of the majority* of the participants (students, faculty and others together) in each counter-class should prevail on questions of form and content. . . . Almost anything is

worth a try, and special effort should be made to break the confines of the traditional "lecturer and passive audience" mold.

The radicals issued strong prerequisites for their counter-classes; each would have to be registered with and approved by the SEC, be run democratically and be led by a supporter of the strike. Classes not meeting these requirements, even though they might be conducted informally outside classroom buildings, would be considered counter-revolutionary and liable to be picketed.

The SEC listed three possible types of classes: those considering failures of the "old University structure" and specific ways of remedying them; those dealing with such topics as guerrilla warfare which were "not adequately covered in the old classes"; and those covering the standard subject matter but conducted in the "free and democratic spirit of the new guidelines" and without grades or exams.

A catalogue of liberation classes was mimeographed and posted around the campus. New courses ranged from "The History of the Spanish Student Movement" and "Political Aspects of William Blake" to "Columbia and the Warfare State" and the "History of Buddhism." Most classes were held on South Field or the other plots of grass that dot the campus; some in local apartments or Ferris Booth Hall. Groups of students congregated on the Ferris Booth patio or on the lawn for informal lectures and folk-dancing lessons. The Grateful Dead, an acid-rock band, turned up to put on a free outdoor victory show for over a thousand students, and the communes held solidarity meetings in front of their buildings.

If the strike had disoriented the life patterns of Columbia students, it was also having its effects outside the campus. Both the administration and the Strike Coördinating Committee were deluged with mail hinting at communist conspiracies, praising and attacking actions which the writers knew about only from the superficial, often erroneous reports of the mass media. Some of the hate mail received by *Spectator* was particularly disturbing. A man from Atlanta, Georgia, set down his feelings toward the strikers thus:

> How can you bastards expect to occupy property that *is not your own* and not be thrown out? Tell me!
>
> *Protest, yes!* Picket, yes! Raise all the noise you want to! But to seize property not your own—don't you know this is not FREEDOM! This is ANARCHY! Worse, it's *criminal*. Talk about police brutality. I am against it, of course! But when you INSIST on a *criminal* act, I say, By God, BASH IN YOUR HEADS! Either we have law, or we

don't. What's the matter with you anyway? Have you the mentality of a 4-year old? . . . How do you justify anarchy? Until you learn to respect LAW, I am for BASHING IN your head! How else will you learn?

Parents sent worried letters to their sons and daughters at Columbia, asking if they had taken part in the disruptions, warning them not to be led astray by political opportunists or troublemakers. Some parents, however, were more closely involved. Thursday night the newly formed Concerned Columbia Parents and Alumni Committee, composed primarily of adults who rather hesitatingly supported the spirit if not the substance of what the radical students were doing, held a meeting in Riverside Church to discuss the crisis. As the meeting began around 8 P.M. a graying, husky man in baggy pants and a string tie strode up to the podium in the chapel and, seizing the microphone, declared that he had "liberated" it. Most of the parents smiled, thinking the man was joking. Brandishing the hand mike, the man said he had made himself the "self-appointed chairman" of the meeting and asked if anyone in the audience had "kids who have been arrested." When about twenty of the one hundred present raised their hands, he yelled suddenly in an angry voice that they "were a bunch of suckers," and that their kids had been duped by a band of agitators. Rabbi A. Bruce Goldman, who had been scheduled to address the group, moved toward the platform. As he reached for the microphone, the man resisted, demanding, "Are you trying to take this microphone away from me by force, Rabbi? Don't you want to negotiate first, Rabbi? It only takes one to negotiate." Rabbi Goldman grabbed at the microphone; as several parents rushed up to the stage in an attempt to restrain the speaker, he struck Rabbi Goldman on the head. The man was seized by a number of parents and carried from the stage. Outside the chapel he told reporters who he was—Gandolph Vilardi, the father of Majority Coalition leader Paul Vilardi.

Saturday afternoon Professor of Psychology Eugene Galanter held a private seminar in his elegant Riverside Drive apartment. The subject: the occupations, the strike, the nature of political power and the future of the University. The participants: Mark Rudd, Juan Gonzalez, Ted Kaptchuk, SCC Co-Chairman Ed Robinson and David Bicknell Truman.

The students arrived before Truman did, and Professor Galanter served them coffee from a silver coffee pot, part of a sterling serving set complete with silver creamers and sugar dishes. Rudd later described the encounter:

Galanter kept talking to us about the strike, using images about salivating dogs and rat pellets to illustrate his points. Truman came in, and we shook hands, and we all sat down to talk. I took off my shoes and socks—I have these army boots that really make my feet sweat. We talked about amnesty. Truman went through our six demands, explaining his objections to each. Ed Robinson began to answer him, but I stopped him and said, "Look, we're leftists and we want to fight the policies of this University." Then Truman looked at me as if he knew; there was nothing to talk about. I explained to Truman that we had set up a provisional administration and were prepared to run the University. All he had to do, I said, was to give us the bursar's office so we could pay the people. Then Truman gave me this pained expression—I don't know how to describe it.

The two did not shake hands when they left.

Sunday afternoon the College faculty met for four hours in Havemeyer Hall, to decide what to do about the loose academic threads which the crisis had left hanging about the College. The professors endorsed the work of the Executive Committee and its call for structural reforms to give faculty members a larger share of decision-making power in the College. For the first time in the history of the College, a group of seven students, all members of the Undergraduate Academic Affairs Committee, were permitted to sit in on the meeting. As motions were proposed and amended, speakers would glance inquiringly at the student representatives, seated in the balcony, who indicated by vigorous nods or shakes of their heads whether or not the proposals would meet with student approval. The faculty considered the Committee on Instruction's plan for ending the term and—to the surprise of many—passed it without major alterations.[3]

In the next several days each of the University's other divisions made a separate peace with its students. The School of General Studies adopted a plan similar to that of the College. The School of Architecture, whose students had been involved in the occupation of Avery, made no attempt to return to normality. The Architecture faculty had gone on record opposing the gym several weeks before the occupation began and was in general quite radical. A huge white banner, emblazoned with "AVERY IS ON STRIKE" in large red letters, was hung over the

---

[3] The only significant change made by the faculty was to assure that a student who had done no passing work would not automatically receive a grade of "pass."

building's entrance, and classes were replaced with a series of meetings to reconstitute the administrative and academic structure of the school.

The Law and Business Schools resumed regular classes immediately after the bust. But the spirit of reconstruction penetrated even there. A rump meeting of the Law student body voted Sunday, 103–93, not to strike but passed resolutions calling for the dropping of criminal-trespass charges against the demonstrators and for a total revision of the University's decision-making procedures. At the College of Physicians and Surgeons, far uptown at 168th Street and Broadway and traditionally removed from the political currents on Morningside Heights, the administration of that division announced on May 7 that students would be allowed to sit on the Committee on Instruction to help rule on curriculum. Several student-faculty committees were established to investigate the possibilities of further student participation in decision-making.

In the College Dean Coleman created the Joint College Commission, a committee composed of six students (including two students arrested in Fayerweather) and six faculty members empowered to suggest mechanisms that would give students and faculty control over decisions about curriculum, discipline and dormitory life.

Reaction to the strike in the Graduate Faculties varied from department to department after the faculty members of that division voted to resume regular classes May 6. In the department of Art History and Archaeology students and faculty decided to support the strike and endorsed the six demands. Other departments such as Music and Anthropology attempted to democratize tenure and curriculum-decision procedures by extending representation on faculty committees to junior faculty members and students. Now not only the leftists agreed that the system badly needed change. "Restructuring" was in vogue. Partly out of a new sense of justice, partly out of a sense of fear, those invested with power decided that it should be shared with their disenfranchised subordinates. In the process some of those who had criticized "the system" from outside were now drawn into it—co-opted—and with new vested interests became its defenders.

Surrounded by a multitude of committees with similar names and parallel goals, the Executive Committee of the Faculty began its attempt to establish credibility as a positive force in the drive for reconstruction. One flyer, printed on green paper with the words *"Wrecking or Rebuilding?"* scrawled across the top, bore the appearance and style of an SDS leaflet:

> The Executive Committee of the Faculty is recommending changes in the basic structure of the University. . . . Some strikers are seeking to escalate conflict, which may in fact prevent these

changes. . . . We have been trying to rebuild. Provocation can only jeopardize this. We appeal to all members of the University, including the Strike Coördinating Committee, to join us in our constructive efforts. We have made great gains. We must consolidate rather than risk these gains.
*We are rebuilding now. Join us, everyone.*

If the committee's response to the crisis was different from the strikers', it also contrasted with that of the administration. Whereas Kirk's reaction to a hostile group of students had been the use of violent force, the Executive Committee chose a more constructive approach. In the words of Professor Sovern, one of the committee's co-chairmen: "We want to set in motion procedures and mechanisms to insure that this is the kind of University in which students *wish* to attend classes."

In the days following the bust the Executive Committee met with groups of students, faculty members, administrators and Trustees in an attempt, as one of its members said, to "restore the shattered frame of mutual confidence at Columbia." The committee had another aim as well: to convince all parts of the University community that it was the group to step into the power vacuum which the rebellion and the bust had created. In one "think session" with student leaders, Professor Walter Metzger, an authority on the history and structure of universities, proclaimed:

"The formation of this body [the Executive Committee], and the fact that we're meeting with the Trustees is in the hardest calculation of power extremely significant. Kirk's power derives from the fact that he is the bottleneck through which all power in this University—which comes from the Trustees—must pass."

Trilling, too, emphasized to the students the committee's "pipeline" to the Trustees:

"We are going to have to *explain* students to the Trustees. They are going to ask us, 'What will satisfy them?' I have been dealing with you for some time, and I've learned a great deal. But now you must tell me what you are asking."

The leaders with whom the committee was meeting were generally not proponents of the SCC hard line, but almost all favored some sort of action against the administration. "There are a lot of us who have an amorphous feeling about whether to strike now," one student said. "Then," replied Trilling, "I suppose you could say we're in a period of 'amorphatorium.' "

In another such meeting with students Westin outlined talks which the committee held with the Trustees immediately after its formation. He sounded rather like a missionary who had just returned from a visit to a pre-literate Amazon tribe:

"These men are not normally a group that gets a view of the scene here. Professor Trilling spoke to them eloquently of revolutions and explained that we are in the midst of one. I talked to them about two major trends I have observed: the demand for participation and the demand for due process. They asked us if the gym was *really* an issue. We told them, yes, it was. Isn't that an interesting question! It indicates that they weren't getting the correct answer from their usual sources— the administration. . . . The world they had known and had expected to continue is no longer intact, and we had to provide them with a fantastic amount of information, attitudes, and perspectives that they normally do not get."

For the first time in the modern history of Columbia University the Trustees had come together at the behest of the faculty. The meeting had been held in the Men's Faculty Club and had lasted into the early morning hours of May 2. After listening to the professors the Trustees returned to a private room where they drafted a statement recognizing the efforts of the Executive Committee and establishing their own special committee of the board to consult with students, administrators and alumni and to "study and recommend changes in the basic structure of the University." Boasted Professor Sovern, "The Trustees have transformed us from bastard children into legitimate ones." But in this very act of carving out its own credibility the committee had lost the support of many of the more radical members of the Columbia community. As Sovern observed, "You try to get as close as you can to power, but as soon as you do, you stink. As a result of our working with the Trustees half the campus thinks we've sold out."

In a leaflet released May 3 the Strike Coördinating Committee rejected the efforts of the Executive Committee, comparing it to the disregarded Committee on Student Life and to President Johnson's commissions on civil disorders and the draft. "The committee has neither the proper democratic structure to represent the interests of those studied, nor the power to effect meaningful change," SCC charged. They pointed out that students were not represented on the Executive Committee, and that the two junior faculty members had been appointed by the committee and not elected by their peers. "No real change can take place at Columbia," the leaflet concluded, "until all the faculty and students are guaranteed institutionalized power to make immediate and necessary changes without the veto and modification of the Trustees." Though the Executive Committee was trying to head in just that direction their efforts did not promise immediate or even short-term change. Sunday May 5 the Strike Coördinating Committee sent a letter to the Executive Committee, regretting that the strikers would not be able to meet with them and explaining that "productive discussion is impossible" as long as the students faced civil and disciplinary punishment and the justice of their cause remained unrecognized. Such demands for approval had been a key aspect of the strikers' posture inside the buildings and now seemed to them to make even more sense. They had risked their academic careers because they had been convinced that there was something very wrong with the University. Now, they felt, eminent and formerly complacent faculty members were making precisely the same charges and being lauded as the saviors of Columbia while the students who had initiated the protest were facing jail terms and suspensions.

Over the weekend the Executive Committee suggested a set of restructuring priorities calling for participation in University decision-making processes for professors, students and junior faculty members. The sub-revolutions which the demonstrations set off were thus recognized and legitimated by the Executive Committee, which in turn had been recognized and legitimated by the Trustees, who in the end were, according to the Charters and Statutes of the University, the source of all recognition and all legitimation. Many faculty and students were confident that such respectability would result in meaningful reform while others suspected that once a group—no matter how radical its intentions—began to feel at home in the upper reaches of the power structure it was doomed eventually to become a protector of the *status quo*.

Another issue clouded the actions of the Executive Committee. The group felt that its role was to guide the future restructuring of the University and spent much time trying not to become entangled in the more immediate and less theoretical problems of Columbia University in May 1968. Should criminal charges be pressed? What form should University discipline take? What action should be taken on the rest of the six demands? the strike? The Executive Committee debated these questions and did, in fact, issue a statement asking that criminal charges against the demonstrators be dropped. The committee felt, however, that its main concern should be with larger and more distant questions of power, and in feeling thus lost much of the credibility it wanted so much to attain.

Not all faculty members were content to give their mandate to the Executive Committee. On May 5 a group of professors including Carl Hovde, Seymour Melman, Sidney Morgenbesser, Professor of English F. W. Dupee and Associate Professor of Philosophy Robert Wolff proclaimed the existence of yet another new organization: the Independent Faculty Group. In its first position paper the new organization called for "fundamental change in the entire structure of the University." Moving to the left of the Executive Committee, the Independent Faculty Group also made specific recommendations for clearing up the immediate problems surrounding the crisis. They asked that the University drop all civil and criminal charges against students involved in the recent demonstration; that University discipline taken against the students be administered under new regulations to be established by the tripartite disciplinary commission, "taking into account the *de facto* punishment already inflicted by the police"; "that the University abandon its current plans to build the gym" and give the community veto power over any facility planned for the park; and finally that all ties between officers of Columbia and IDA be severed.

Public and private interchanges between Trustees, administrators, faculty groups and students continued intermittently throughout the rest of May. Slogans of reconstructionism began to flow from the mouths of even Kirk and Truman; the President stated May 8 that "it is agreed on all sides without reservations that the basic structure of the University must be re-examined."

The Trustees, too, had espoused this rhetoric earlier in the week when they announced the formation of the special Trustee committee on restructuring. Having stated that they wished to consult with representative students, the Trustees now faced the problem of finding those students who might best represent the position of the mysterious "majority" that both Kirk and Rudd claimed were behind them. Turning to traditional democratic procedures, they decided to set up elections in each division of the University. But the board of Trustees had become for many students the very symbol of traditionalism and inertia. Few believed that extensive University reform would originate from a Trustee committee, and many suspected that "consultation" with students was merely another meaningless strand of *pro forma* tinsel. The Strike Committee boycotted the elections on the grounds that the Trustees were trying to channel and dissipate student dissent, and the bulk of Columbia undergraduates—who rarely turn out for campus elections in large numbers—ignored the contest. When the ballots were counted only 411 out of 2,700 students in the College had bothered to vote.

The SCC issued a leaflet after the election, stating its willingness to meet "with any or all of the Trustees to discuss the long-standing issues dramatized by recent events." In meeting with the Trustees the Executive Committee had gone over the heads of Kirk and Truman, and now the strikers were trying the same tactic to undercut further an administration whose power seemed to be dwindling. But the Trustees would not coöperate. In a telegram to Mark Rudd the next day Chairman Petersen rebuffed the strikers, declaring that the "Trustees are not the proper body for exchanges regarding settlement of a student strike." The

Trustees did meet with the elected students on May 21 and gave the students two days to prepare a comprehensive program for reorganizing the University. The exchanges were strained, and several of the student representatives later expressed doubt that the Trustees would ever act on any of the ideas they might offer.

Sunday May 5 the Executive Committee of the Faculty announced the appointment of a five-man fact-finding commission "to establish the chronology of events leading up to the recent disturbances on the Columbia campus and inquire into the underlying causes of those disturbances." Chosen to head the panel was Archibald Cox, Williston Professor of Law at Harvard and former Solicitor General of the United States.[4]

The Cox Fact-Finding Commission began open hearings immediately. Within a week representatives from the steering committee of the black students of Hamilton Hall appeared before the commission and read a wordy, legalistic statement:

> The Steering Committee of Hamilton Hall, as representatives of the black students of Hamilton Hall, hereby states:
>
> (1.) That the instant appearance is a special appearance on behalf of the black students of Hamilton Hall.
>
> (2.) That the instant appearance should in no way be construed as, and in fact is not, a recognition of, or in any way, shape, or form an acquiescence to this fact-finding commission.
>
> (3.) That nothing in the instant appearance is, can, or should be construed as testimony before this fact-finding commission.

The blacks went on to observe that no student of community representatives were members of the panel, and that the commission had no mandate to investigate the guilt of the University administration. They then listed their old demands on the gym, amnesty and IDA, and concluded their appearance with:

WE AWAIT WRITTEN RESPONSE FROM THE COMMISSION.

The super-secrecy and refusal to coöperate with any white group which had marked the actions of the blacks during the early days of the Hamil-

---

[4] The other members of the group were Jefferson Fordham, dean of the University of Pennsylvania Law School; Simon Rifkind, a former federal judge and a member of the New York City Board of Education; Dana Farnsworth, director of the Harvard Health Services; and Hyland Lewis, a Negro professor of sociology at Brooklyn College. (Fordham resigned the next day on the ground that he had given a speech specifically condemning the Columbia demonstrators, thus compromising his impartiality. He was replaced the same day by Anthony Amsterdam, a young professor of law at the University of Pennsylvania.)

ton occupation had now intensified still further. In the coming weeks the students who had been arrested in Hamilton consented to speak with hardly anyone, lending an even greater degree of mystery to their activities.

The Strike Coördinating Committee had also been asked to testify before the Cox Commission and their response was no more coöperative, though a good deal more amusing. The same day that the blacks made their "instant appearance," Juan Gonzalez came before the august body and, in the only testimony offered by the strikers, read excerpts from *The Governmental Process* by David Truman:

> The public hearing is usually a haphazard and unsatisfactory device for giving and receiving information. This is one function of such proceedings, but it alone would not account for their continued vitality. A second use is a propaganda channel through which a public may be extended and its segments partially consolidated or reinforced. A third function is to provide a quasi-ritualistic means of adjusting group conflicts and relieving disturbances through a safety valve . . . (p. 372).

The bust had given the strike a tremendous thrust forward, but that thrust had been effectively negated by the official cancellation of classes in most divisions of the University for the four school days that followed. Thus from Tuesday through Sunday the angry students and professors who supported the boycott had been resolutely staying out of classes that were not being held. Monday May 6 was the first day that most divisions of the University officially reopened, giving the dissidents something not to attend. At 9 A.M. groggy placard-carrying student pickets began marching back and forth in front of Hamilton, Mathematics, Fayerweather, Lewisohn, and other principal classroom buildings on the Morningside campus.

That morning Vice President Truman—who since the bust had been getting around campus via tunnel and was accompanied everywhere by plainclothesmen—walked over to Fayerweather to see what effect the strike was having on class attendance. Pickets patrolled both entrances, and a bulletin board outside the building was covered with notices of classes that were being held elsewhere. As Truman, accompanied by Dean Fraenkel, approached, Mark Rudd and Stu Gedal left their picket line at a nearby building to confront them. Standing on the steps of Fayerweather Truman looked at the students and said firmly, "Let me through."

"Let's have a dialogue, Dr. Truman," Gedal replied as the pickets moved to block the doors. A professor tried to enter the building and was repulsed.

"You have no right to do that," Truman said angrily, pushing forward. The adamant strikers pushed him back. Gedal began jumping up and down on the steps, yelling, "Dialogue, dialogue!"

"You shut up," Truman snapped at Gedal, who shot back loudly, "Shut up? Shut up? Do you call that rational discourse?" Truman saw that, in his relationship with those who blocked the doors, they held all the power and were willing to give him none. Realizing that in such a situation rational discourse would accomplish nothing, the vice president turned and walked away.

A pack of reporters had scurried from the University news office to intercept Truman. Asked what would happen if the strike continued, Truman said that the administration might seek a court injunction or call the police back onto campus if necessary. JJ spotted the entourage as it passed behind Low Library. "This University will fall!" the militant SDS member screamed, backpedalling as Truman moved forward. "The kid's crazy, he should be under observation," Fraenkel commented to Truman.

The two administrators moved on to Havemeyer Hall where they were loudly booed. "This campus is being run by hoodlums," Truman said. He walked past Math, then on to Hamilton where he slipped past fifty pickets unrecognized, his hat pulled low over his face. Entering Dean Platt's office he asked a receptionist to announce him. She did not recognize him and asked who she might say was calling. The vice president removed his hat and said, "I am David Truman."

Only ten classes met in Hamilton Hall Monday morning between the hours of nine and eleven, the most heavily scheduled period of the day. Virtually no classes were held in Avery, Fayerweather, Schermerhorn or Kent Halls. For the remainder of the week the strikers' picketing was successful—on Thursday only fifty-five students were attending classes in Hamilton at the peak hour of 11 A.M. By the end of the week the Strike Coördinating Committee had grown to seventy-one delegates, with a constituency somewhat over four thousand students.[5]

Life in the professional schools quickly returned to normal, for these divisions had never been as deeply affected by the strike as had the undergraduate divisions. But life in Columbia College was transformed significantly, with a majority of the students participating in or coöperating with the strike against classes. Yet despite the number of its sup-

---

[5] Of the seventy-one SCC delegates eleven did not represent constituencies. The other sixty each represented about seventy students; the total number of students who respected the boycott is estimated at six thousand.

porters the boycott was paradoxically ineffectual. When the College and General Studies faculties agreed to end formal classes the impact of the strike was dampened. Professors met with their students and worked out arrangements for the remainder of the semester. Only a handful demanded that their students continue to attend class to receive a grade of "pass," and many students took advantage of this opportunity by leaving campus immediately for the summer.

With student interest in a boycott of classes dissipating, SCC decided that new confrontations would have to be set up to keep the strike alive. Since the bust the administration had stationed police and private security guards at every unlocked entrance to the campus. No one was allowed to enter without showing a Columbia University identification card. Students had begun to chafe at this regulation, and the Strike Committee saw a chance for a new confrontation. On May 8 the Reverend William Starr led a group of about thirty students and community residents in an attempt to enter the campus without showing identification to the University guards on duty. They were turned back, and, as the crowd of onlookers grew, nearly two hundred policemen were positioned around the disputed Broadway entrance. Word had been received that a contingent from Harlem was on its way to support the gate-crashers. But the Harlem group, which showed up late, was only twelve strong. Starr and the others stood outside the gate until after midnight and then went home.

The following day SCC organized a brief demonstration inside Hamilton Hall—a deliberate, announced-in-advance violation of the President's ban on indoor demonstrations. The protesters walked into the lobby, read a statement and after chanting "IDA Must Go!" turned and walked out. No action was taken by the administration.

As the days passed and pickets no longer bothered to stand in front of buildings, a more subtle polarization of the campus was taking place. The strike coalition began to experience the open ideological controversy it had tried to repress since the first days after the bust. SCC had to maintain the momentum of the movement and at the same time keep all its factions together. Faced with a concerted liberal effort for reform led by the Executive Committee, many students who still supported the boycott found the framework of reconstruction more congenial than the avowed revolutionary (and extra-University) goals of SCC's radical core. Moreover, the radicals' belligerent political style became increasingly repugnant to their left-liberal allies who supported the six demands.

A considerable number of moderates had been incorporated into the Strike Committee after the organizational meeting May 2 in Wollman Auditorium. But within a week they had formed a distinct sub-group, holding separate informal meetings. As the split between the radicals who led the Strike Committee and the left-liberal minority widened, the "moderate caucus" became increasingly more active.

The moderates lost several crucial votes by narrow margins between May 2 and May 15. The first, just four days after SCC was formed, was the defeat of a proposal which would have replaced the demand for amnesty with one calling for collective judgment before a bipartite committee. On the first vote the proposal passed, 34–31. Ed Robinson, a graduate student in the social sciences who was elected nominal SCC co-chairman with Rudd, called a recess, and the radicals rounded up all their delegates. When the meeting was reconvened the proposal was brought up for reconsideration and lost by a margin of three votes. In the following week the moderates lost several other decisive struggles within SCC.

The final split between the moderates and the radicals on the Strike Committee came on May 15. The previous day, Mike Wallace, a graduate student in charge of the SCC sub-committee on reconstruction, had presented an eighteen-page outline for internal reform at Columbia. The introduction to the document incorporated a well-defined break with previous SCC policy and ideology:

> Beyond question, if fundamental changes are to occur in academia, they cannot be separated from fundamental changes in society. But where are changes to occur first? The committee feels that it is in keeping with general strategies of the Left to radicalize to the degree we can, those institutions in which we have influence. Radicals must carve out a base of operations from which they can act to politicize others, and, as Marcuse suggests, the university, of major American institutions, is most hospitable to the Left, and most likely to afford the needed base of operations. To postpone restructuring of the universities because they are integral parts of a larger system is to deny the Left a fruitful strategy by focusing on the whole and ignoring the part.
>
> But would restructuring along the lines we suggest, supposing for the moment that our proposals were accepted in toto, produce a radicalization of the University? No. Restructuring is not radicalizing. . . . Reconstruction is no substitute for radical political action. . . . On the other hand, the procedural reforms, the accessibility to power levers, the encouragement to organization work in the community—these might aid the Left. The reconstruction committee feels that the reining-in of the administration and the redistribution of power would, if obtained, on balance assist the Left in its work of on-going politicization; at the very least it would provide freedom from current harassment.

The proposals Wallace then presented were admittedly "utopian," but could, he said, "serve as a yardstick" of the ideal university, against which more pragmatic schemes would have to be compared. The focus of power within the University would be shuffled to a new governmental entity, tentatively named the "Joint Thing," which would be elected democratically:

> There shall be a supreme legislative body, composed of the legislative bodies of the faculty and students, and known as the Joint Thing. The Joint Thing shall have full and sufficient power to make policy in all matters whatsoever concerning the central University . . . excepting only that the Joint Thing may make no law which shall abridge freedom of speech, or of the press; or of the right of people peaceably to assemble or to petition the Joint Thing for redress of grievances. . . .
> Legislation may be initiated in either the Faculty Thing or the Student Thing. When passed, a bill goes to the other Thing. If passed by both Things, the bill becomes law. . . .
> The Joint Thing shall have the power to issue Cease and Desist orders restraining the activities of the administration.

The committee went on for sixteen single-spaced pages, outlining the proposed new University government in careful detail, analyzing the roles and relationships of various power factions and interest groups under the old and new systems.

At a meeting of the Strike Coördinating Committee May 14 Mark Rudd and Tony Papert presented a counter-proposal of their own. Their resolution maintained that the Columbia rebellion was only part of a large societal struggle. The SDS motto was "A Free University in a Free Society," but Rudd, like many other radicals, believed that the former could not be obtained without the latter. Because the University is so fundamentally linked to the processes, problems and goals of society, they argued, freedom in a "microcosm" of that society was impossible as long as the whole of that society perpetuated the repressive structures and power relationships that make it unfree. All reforms of the structure of the University would be merely "empty formal gestures," Rudd maintained, of little importance relative to the complete social reconstruction the radicals sought.

Both the Wallace restructuring and the Rudd-Papert proposals were tabled, and the meeting was adjourned. Although Wallace said that he would continue to work within SCC, the moderates caucused and decided that their efforts on the Strike Committee were being stifled by the radicals. Rudd and John Thoms, a graduate English student and leader

## 12  Amorphatorium   241

of the moderates, met privately and agreed that an acrimonious split had to be avoided. At the SCC meeting the next day Rudd read a prearranged conciliatory statement, and then Thoms rose and said that some members of the committee felt it was "necessary to refocus their attention from the mechanics of the boycott to the work of reconstructing the University." He emphasized that his group still supported the strike, made a few jokes to show that there were no hard feelings, observed, "We all have to do our own thing, and I guess it's time to do mine" and walked out. Thoms was followed by twenty-two of the seventy delegates who formed a new organization of their own: Students for a Restructured University (SRU). "We felt it was possible," Thoms said later, "to create a free University as the vanguard of the free society."

After two and a half weeks of steadily diminishing picketing, increasingly ill-attended noon rallies and growing placidity on campus, the Strike Committee temporarily revitalized its moribund confrontation style. During the days before Friday May 17, SCC used leaflets and radio spots to advertise throughout New York City for a "monster rally" to be held on campus Friday evening. The propaganda build-up seemed to augur a major development; many expected the strikers to occupy another building or take some comparably dramatic action.

By 6:15 P.M. Friday almost seven hundred people—many of them non-students attracted by the publicity—had gathered on Low Plaza for the rally. Cicero Wilson of SAS was the first speaker and he gave a meandering, angry speech that drew little response from the crowd. Several other speakers, including Mark Rudd, addressed the crowd which continued to grow during the next hour. At 7:30 two runners pushed their way to the speakers' platform and handed a message to Mike Golash, a radical graduate student involved in community organizing.

Golash read the note and looked up at the crowd. "The community has created a new liberated area in the neighborhood tonight," he announced, explaining that local residents had occupied a building and planned to transform it into a neighborhood action center for Morningside Heights. "I can't tell you exactly where this building is," Golash said, "because that would just be telling the cops, but I can show you." Golash, JJ, Rudd, Lew Cole and other strike leaders started marching down College Walk toward the Broadway gate at 116th Street as the crowd—by now nearly one thousand strong—followed. In the street the group spread out from the sidewalk to the center of Broadway and marched down to 114th Street chanting, "The streets belong to the people." Golash and the others turned right off Broadway and led the crowd to the front of an old tenement at 618 West 114th Street.

About ten days earlier, inspired and supported by student activists on the Columbia campus, several community groups, block associations and tenant organizations had formed the Community Action Committee to fight Columbia's expansion plans in Morningside Heights. The group immediately endorsed the student strike and informed SCC that it would attempt to engineer a community takeover of a University-owned building.

The apartment house at 618 West 114th had been bought by Columbia in 1966. The University planned to tear it down to make way for a new home for its School of Social Work and had already begun to evict tenants. By the time of the takeover only five of the building's twelve units were still occupied. Four of these five tenants (the fifth was in the hospital) agreed to let other community residents seize the building. While the rally on campus was in progress, a sit-in was quietly organized, and word was sent to the SCC leaders that the building had been "liberated." In leaflets prepared on the SCC mimeograph machines in Ferris Booth Hall the demonstrators charged that Columbia was "creating a white ghetto" on Morningside Heights by "deliberately forcing the removal of almost every black, Puerto Rican and Oriental" from the neighborhood. They issued a set of demands calling for Columbia to "renovate and return to the community this building and every other building it has taken from the community," to re-open for occupancy all "apartments and stores now kept vacant," to "irrevocably relinquish all claims to Morningside Park, and to allow the community a role in University expansion planning." In a prepared statement the building's four tenants charged:

> The building on which this demonstration is focused stands as a typical example of Columbia's tenant-removal tactics—buildings are allowed to deteriorate until the occupants find conditions intolerable. Here are some examples in the present case:
> No heat whatsoever in south half of building during winter 1967–68; partial heat, winters 1966–67, 1965–66.
> Sickeningly unsanitary conditions and fire hazards in apartments which have been vacated and sealed.
> Basement grossly neglected, filled with unremoved ashes.
> Front door lock broken (burglaries have occurred recently).
> Halls and stairways in deteriorated condition, with falling plaster.

The tenement had shared the fate of many other buildings in the way of Columbia's expansion. Some of the buildings Columbia takes over are improved and maintained by the University. But in others tenants are often evicted one by one, as was the case with "618." Some are given relocation subsidies. Where this fails less pleasant inducements are employed, such as curtailment of heat and threatening, pseudo-legal letters from Columbia officials.[6] The revenue from rents for the diminishing number of occupied apartments eventually falls below the cost of keeping such buildings in livable condition. Deterioration often becomes advanced before all the tenants have moved out.

This was the case at 618 West 114th Street. Now community activists and Columbia radicals were meeting in a dark, grimy room on the fifth floor of the "liberated" tenement to discuss their tactics. The rhetoric was familiar. "All prescribed channels have been tried," said one resident who had helped plan the occupation. "And what are we left with?" George Hickerson, who had helped organize Kentucky coal-mine workers in the 1930's, went out onto a fire escape facing the street and yelled in a gravelly voice to the crowd below, "This is our building."

The neighborhood residents inside the building urged students not to enter in order to maintain the symbolism of community occupation, and only Rudd and a few other strike leaders were permitted inside. Blankets, cartons of food, mops, brooms, sponges and soap powder were brought into the new "community-owned" building. One vacant room was designated a meeting area, and the old and young activists worked together at sweeping and washing it. A bullhorn was brought over from Strike Central, and for the next several hours various students and community leaders gave speeches to the crowd outside. At one point Rudd spotted a neatly attired man standing at the rear fringe of the crowd. "Hey, everyone!" he shouted from the stoop of the building. "Look who's here—the man who made all this possible—that sonofabitch in the gray hat standing on the other side of the street—William Bloor, treasurer of the University. Good evening, Mr. Bloor!" The treasurer, who manages all of Columbia's real-estate dealings from his offices in the financial district, walked slowly back toward Broadway. By midnight almost half of the one thousand students who had jammed the street at the beginning of the protest had left. The students who remained sat down in the street and lit candles. They sang "We Shall Not Be Moved" and—with Rudd leading—"Oh, When the Revolution Comes" to the tune of "When the Saints Go Marching In."

The administration did not hesitate to call the police. About 11 P.M. Vice President Truman arrived at the scene, and a police command post was set up in a garage at 113th Street and Broadway. Over a hundred policemen were stationed on Broadway and Riverside Drive, and Chief Inspector Sanford Garelik coördinated operations from the garage.

[6] *The Community and the Expansion of Columbia University,* a report of the Faculty Civil Rights Group of Columbia University, December 1967, presents evidence of specific instances of tenant harassment by Columbia.

The next several hours dragged by slowly; by agreement all students stayed out of the community-held tenement. The students in the street knew a bust was coming and wondered why the police, now all around them, did not move in. Dozens of plainclothesmen circulated among the protesters. This time some were in different disguises than those they had used on April 30. In an absurd attempt to look like college students some wore crew cuts, narrow ties, loud sport jackets and pointed black shoes. The long-haired students in the crowd, clad in T-shirts, jeans and sandals, had no trouble picking them out. Food and cider were passed around by candlelight, as familiar protest songs welled up from the adult demonstrators inside the building. A two-hour meeting was held in one of the tenants' apartments and it was decided that those inside would not resist arrest when the police came to evict them.

At 3:45 A.M. six city buses full of Tactical Patrol Force drove by on Riverside Drive. Seconds later three students ran up the street shouting, "They're coming, they're coming!" Eight police vans pulled up on Broadway at 114th Street. About 350 police, all wearing blue riot helmets and plastic face shields, began massing on the north side of the block. Stu Gedal took the bullhorn on the tenement stoop and advised that, to prevent injury from the police, all students in the street take off their glasses and tuck long hair into their collars and that all girls take off their earrings. The memory of April 30 was strong in their minds.

But the memory was also apparently fresh in the minds of Inspector Garelik and Vice President Truman. As the police began moving down 114th Street toward the seated demonstrators, plainclothesmen in the crowd took out their badges and pinned them on. The uniformed men stopped in the street at the edge of the sit-in, and an officer called out over his bullhorn: "Please move down to Riverside Drive. No one will bother you." About three hundred demonstrators let themselves be gently pushed toward the end of the block by the slowly advancing ranks of policemen. "Don't go," the remaining students implored; but in a few minutes less than seventy protesters remained in the street. At this point TPF marched up and down the sidewalks adjacent to the occupied building, instructing neighbors in ground-floor apartments not to lean out and to keep their windows closed under penalty of arrest.

Joseph Nye, Columbia's business manager, stepped forward from the rows of police and stood in front of the remaining demonstrators sitting in the street. "I have been authorized by Columbia University to ask all tenants and their guests to leave the building," he announced over a bullhorn. "All necessary precautions for your safety have been taken. The New York City Police Department is here to see to that." The students laughed, and no one moved. Nye directed the occupants of 618 to leave under penalty of trespass. Policemen then began approaching students, asking them either to leave or be arrested on charges of disorderly conduct. All but one demonstrator quietly submitted to arrest and walked into waiting paddy wagons parked a few steps away. (One Barnard girl crouched on her blanket and refused to get up; she was carried away and charged with resisting arrest.) Rudd, standing on the steps, was arrested by a plainclothesman, handcuffed to the student next to him and placed in the front of one of the vans. At 4:30 Chief Garelik entered the building, and his men peacefully arrested the community protesters. The operation was over by 4:45. Of the 117 people arrested, fifty-six were Columbia students.

The students were taken to the 18th Precinct house to be booked. When Rudd came before the desk sergeant, still handcuffed, the officer looked down at him and smiled. "You must be an Oriental, Mr. Rudd, the way you can relax." The officer who had arrested Rudd was congratulated by his colleagues, and the men in the station house all came out for a look at the arch-revolutionary in chains. The students spent the rest of the night in cells and were taken to 100 Centre Street the next morning for arraignment on charges of disorderly conduct. The house at 618 returned to its old vacated, dilapidated state.

During the first days in May the seventeen-member Joint Committee on Disciplinary Affairs [7] met quietly to decide how best to punish the dissident students for their acts of April 23–30. Thursday May 9, a week and a half after the first police raid, the disciplinary committee released a unanimously approved four-page report on measures and procedures. In a covering letter the committee stated that the entire report "was predicated on the assumption that trespass charges will be dropped." Many groups on campus, including the Executive Committee, had asked the University to drop criminal charges against the demonstrators. Some of them still wanted the students to be granted amnesty; most felt that the April protests were an intra-University affair and should not be dealt with by outside powers such as the courts. Still others objected to penalizing the demonstrators several times for the same acts: many had received corporal punishment from the police, all faced disciplinary punishment from University authorities and now they also faced jail sentences and fines. But the administration maintained that the matter was out of its hands, that once the Trustees had filed a

---

[7] This was the tripartite commission on discipline set up by Professors Trilling, Galanter and Hovde. The membership of the commission was expanded on April 29 to seven students, seven faculty members and three administrators. The commission named itself the Joint Committee on Disciplinary Affairs at its first meeting.

complaint the inexorable wheels of justice must churn, regardless of the mercy of the complainant.[8]

The statement of the disciplinary committee argued that since "voluntary participation in the demonstrations asserted a common responsibility," all known participants in the protest should be given the same sentence: disciplinary probation until the end of the next academic year. The idea of uniform and collective punishment, recommended by the Ad Hoc Faculty Committee, had been adopted as the only suitable disciplinary response to large-scale political actions. The report explained:

> Had any of these acts been committed by a single person or group of persons in an ordinary atmosphere, few would deny that they deserved maximum punishment. But this was not the case in the last days of April. Many of those who participated in the demonstrations acted out of deep commitment, not personal animus, convinced that the University was not responsive to legitimate demands. . . . It is clear, in any case, that no apportionment of responsibility can justify these violations of established rules, whether explicit regulations of the University or the unwritten rules of behavior that govern any community. The actions of the demonstrators were wholly out of proportion to their declared grievances. . . .

Beneath the formal language the committee sought to avoid the mass suspensions which many feared would result from the demonstrations.

The committee was not so lenient with those found guilty of "malicious action" such as theft, deliberate damage to property or "invasion of private papers." The panel recommended that the University carefully investigate these charges and level "appropriate" indictments against the accused offenders.

To insure due process for the demonstrators the tripartite panel recommended a complex amalgam of indictments, tribunals and appellate procedures. The dean of the appropriate division of the University would initiate disciplinary proceedings against a student in his school by summoning that student to discuss the charges made against him. If the

---

[8] A high University official close to the New York County District Attorney's office informed one of the authors soon after the police action that the administration's contention was valid only in the most strained technical sense. While it is theoretically true that, once the complaints were acted on by the police, charges of trespass passed into the hands of the court, the source explained that it is a matter of common practice for the complainant to request extreme leniency and for the court to comply almost automatically and refrain from punishing the offenders. The District Attorney's office itself may also request that charges be dropped. Charges were in fact dropped for several arrested students who were considered innocent by the administration.

student refused to see the dean he would be summarily suspended. If he denied the charges his case would be referred to a five-man tripartite tribunal. The defendant would be entitled to a public trial—an unprecedented modification, satisfying the strikers' demand for open hearings.

The new disciplinary procedure was carefully worked out to clarify all necessary procedural minutiae. But still the central question remained: did the Joint Committee on Disciplinary Affairs have any power to enforce its scheme? On the last page of its report the committee discreetly attempted to clarify the matter:

> The President of the University, on further review of the proceedings, may make such revisions in the decisions of the Joint Committee as he believes to be in the best interests of the University. The President and the Trustees should agree that the President will not increase the penalty which has been sustained or imposed by the Joint Committee.

In the last section of the document the committee warned that the University could not tolerate further demonstrations of a similar nature:

> It is clear that acts which deny the rights of other members of the University threaten its very existence. Future acts which are found, *by due process,* to be in this category must be judged with the utmost severity. [Italics added]

The report of the disciplinary committee was by no means a radical document; it condemned the demonstrators' actions and staunchly declared that they all deserved to be punished. However, the report did try to establish due process where there had been none and, more importantly, attempted to wrest some power from a President not eager to compromise.

Less than thirty minutes after the disciplinary report was released on campus, President Kirk, who had seen it the night before, issued a two-page statement rejecting almost every substantive recommendation of his own committee. His statement read:

> . . . I have studied the document carefully and am prepared to accept the findings and recommendations of the Joint Committee, except for two reservations and two principal comments. I note first the statement in the preamble that the recommendations are predicated on the assumption that trespass charges will be dropped. However, the trespass charges cannot be dropped by the University. A criminal charge, once lodged, is also in the hands of the public prosecutor representing the people of the State of New

York, and of the judge before whom the charges are brought. Furthermore, I am advised that, under the Code of Criminal Procedure, crimes committed riotously may not be compromised.[9]

Second, the recommendation on page five that the President should not increase any penalty sustained or imposed by the Joint Committee is one that I cannot accept. I recognize that decisions arrived at or penalties imposed by the Joint Committee after prior findings by the appropriate dean's office and the disciplinary procedure of the particular school would, in almost all cases, be fair and equitable. In order, however, to safeguard the interests both of the University community and the individual, the present statutory responsibilities of the President of the University must, as recognized by the Galanter Committee, be maintained. In any case, where I believed that it was necessary for me to change a finding or penalty imposed by the Joint Committee, I would, of course, notify the committee in writing of my decision and of my reasons for it before carrying out the action. . . .

Finally, I understand that the procedures outlined in Section II of this report are intended by the Joint Committee to be recommendations that the committee would regard as satisfying the requirements of disciplinary due process, and that they are not intended to be imposed as such on the deans of the various schools, some of whom already have in operation well-defined and equitable procedures. I shall transmit the entire report of the Joint Committee to all deans and directors for their consideration.

Before most people in the University had had a chance to read the carefully constructed report of the disciplinary committee, our President had rejected every significant proposal it made. Within minutes of the release of the presidential edict, Kirk called an impromptu news conference in Low to explain the administration position to the press. He himself did not show up, however, and Dean Fraenkel represented him and parried hostile questions about the Kirk statement.

"Mr. Fraenkel, why does the administration feel it necessary to punish the student demonstrators?" one reporter asked.

"The students occupied buildings in a manner every one of us in the civilized world cannot condone," Fraenkel declared. "We cannot maintain a civilized society if we don't make it clear that we cannot condone

---

[9] "Compromise" in this sense means lessening of charges. According to the source close to the District Attorney's office, however, it is extremely unlikely that a court would consider the acts of April 23–30 "crimes committed riotously" in those cases where the only charges pressed by the University were those of trespass.

this action." Kirk had warned that Columbia must act to protect the security of American universities, and now Fraenkel contended that the very fate of modern man hung in the balance on Morningside Heights.

The newsmen pressed on. "Dean Fraenkel," one asked, "does this statement mean that the University is going to prosecute criminal charges against the students and impose disciplinary measures at the same time?" Fraenkel dodged the question. The reporter tried again: "Sir, do you see some possible difficulty in the spirit, if not the letter, of the law, in bringing disciplinary charges against a student while his criminal case is still pending? Did the University consider this problem?" [10] Fraenkel squirmed in his big leather chair and mumbled, "Let me think about that one for a minute." Then he slouched back, buried his chin in his hand, and finally looked up and said, "You know, that's an interesting question. I really can't answer that right here. I would have to get legal advice from the University counsel on this."

That afternoon the administration found itself under a heavy barrage of criticism. Members of the disciplinary committee and the Executive Committee spoke to both Truman and Kirk, warning them that the rejection of yet another committee report would, at this time, have disastrous results. They further argued that the President's statement appeared autocratic and arbitrary, as if he were wholly unresponsive to widespread demands for due process. By late afternoon Truman had begun looking for ways to mollify Kirk's outright rejection. That evening the Trustees met to discuss the disciplinary report and by the end of the meeting had agreed to adopt a statement, reportedly drafted by the vice president, which backed Kirk nominally and at the same time deviated significantly from the hard line he had espoused that afternoon.

The Trustees agreed that the University could not legally drop criminal charges. The statement added, however, that "the Trustees accepted the view that the University can make recommendations for leniency which the court may or may not accept." In addition the board suggested that the newly formed Trustee committee on restructuring "examine particularly the possibility of revising the University's disciplinary procedures and make recommendations, if they find it advisable, for the review of future disciplinary cases by a University judicial body."

Kirk was now placed in a very difficult position. The Trustees had differed with his stand on the disciplinary report, and many prominent faculty members were incensed that he had undercut the careful work of

---

[10] In addition to the evident fact that demonstrators might be punished twice for the same offense, lawyers for the students argued that testimony and decisions resulting from University disciplinary procedures could be used against the demonstrators in their court trials.

the tripartite panel. The next day Kirk released a letter addressed to the Executive Committee of the Faculty, one of the groups which had expressed disagreement with his action. The letter, said to have been prepared by Michael Sovern, co-chairman of the Executive Committee, contained a stunning retreat from Kirk's May 9 dictum:

> May 10, 1968
>
> The Executive Committee of the Faculty:
>
> As Chairman Petersen's statement of the last evening indicates, Mr. Temple's Special Committee of the Trustees is considering entrusting final review of future disciplinary cases to "a University judicial body." Until the Statutes are revised, responsibility for University discipline necessarily rests with me. However, I wish to assure you, as I did last evening, that *I have every confidence in the Joint Committee on Disciplinary Affairs and would not envisage modifying its decisions.* In the unlikely event that I ever do find myself in disagreement with the Joint Committee, I would be willing to submit the matter to some distinguished alumnus respected by us all.
>
> I note with pleasure the constructive coöperation of students, faculty and administration in the preparation of the Joint Committee report. It seems to me yet another encouraging sign for the future of the University.
>
> I am simultaneously addressing this letter to the Joint Committee.
>
> Grayson Kirk [italics added]

Few thought of Grayson Kirk as a resilient man, and few were able to believe that he did indeed "note with pleasure" anything about the disciplinary incident, which must have been an exceedingly embarrassing and painful experience for him. To issue a statement on Thursday flatly repudiating everything set forth by one of his committees and then to be forced on Friday to mouth, "I have every confidence" in that committee, was clearly a dizzying turnabout. The President had finally been persuaded to delegate most of his disciplinary authority. After reading the letter to the Executive Committee, Kirk's admirers—and there were few—said that he had bent considerably. His critics—and there were many—were sure that he had snapped entirely.

Confident that their mandate had been restored, the committee on discipline went back to work to draft a second memorandum. The new report, issued on May 13, included several significant clarifications which helped to ease many of the administration's apprehensions about the position of the committee. The group reiterated that its recommendations were "predicated on the assumption that trespass charges will be dropped" but suggested that deans begin to implement disciplinary procedures immediately, withholding penalties "pending court action." The administration could accuse a student, indict him and convict him while criminal charges were pending, the committee was saying, but the University should wait on sentencing and punishment until the court cases were resolved. The committee also said in its two-page addendum that any student who fails to appear before the dean when asked "is liable to immediate suspension, even though a trespass charge is still pending against him." For the committee the authority of the deans remained an immutable principle, and anyone who flouted it deserved to be punished swiftly and harshly.

If the disciplinary committee had gained the support of the administration, it had failed to win over the students. The conservatives accused it of appeasing the demonstrators and allowing them to get off with only disciplinary probation. The radicals viewed the rulings of the committee as a clear attempt by the administration to disguise the "political repression" of the University in a "legitimate," powerless body. Many of the strike leaders called the committee "a kangaroo court" appointed by Kirk himself and strictly limited by the mandate which Kirk was willing to give it. The committee had not granted amnesty, and the demonstrators were still not prepared to accept punishments for acts which they believed had created the very groups and processes which were being used against them. And the very act of reporting to the dean's office could be seen by them as nothing short of submission to illegitimate authority.

Meanwhile, the newly patched-up and creaking disciplinary mechanisms began to operate. On May 16 Dean Platt sent letters to SDS leaders Mark Rudd, Morris Grossner, Nick Freudenberg and Ed Hyman, instructing them to come to his office by 5 P.M. May 21 to "discuss" their alleged participation in the demonstrations beginning April 23. None of the other students involved in the demonstrations was summoned. The administration had gathered the names of hundreds of students suspected of participating in the April demonstrations, but chose to call in only four members of the original "IDA Six" for disciplinary action.

Platt explained after the crisis that the central administration had directed him to call in first those students who were already on probation. Platt said he carefully perused the entire list of suspected demonstrators and looked up each individual record to check if the student was on probation. He said that, "coincidentally," the only students who were on probation were the members of the SDS Steering Committee whose disciplining had touched off the demonstrations beginning April 23.[11]

Several weeks after the crisis, Platt was asked by a student if the administration had discussed the chances that this move might bring about another confrontation on the campus. Platt smiled at the question and replied, "Yes—we discussed that possibility."

[11] In testifying before the Cox Commission Platt was asked if he thought the administration's decision to call in four students who surely would not appear could be characterized as "a charade." Platt nodded his head in agreement. Dean Platt resigned from his position as associate dean for student affairs in late July. On several occasions during the crisis Platt had been at odds with the administration. Appearing at the Cox Commission several days after Platt's resignation, Vice President Truman stated that the administration had never given Platt any directives about singling out SDS leaders for swift punishment.

# 13

## *Déjà Vu*

A NEW LEAFLET was tacked to the strike bulletin board in the lobby of Ferris Booth Hall on Tuesday May 21. "SHOWDOWN NO. 2" stood out in big block letters at the top, and "SUNDIAL—3:45 P.M." was written at the bottom. Between, in smaller letters, came a new call to action from the Strike Coördinating Committee:

> Today—Tuesday—Discipline the deans. Four weeks ago today, the insurrection at Columbia began. One of the issues was the discipline of the original IDA demonstrators. Now they have been summoned to report before Dean Platt for the crime of having participated in the demonstrations beginning April 23. Support the strikers' demand for amnesty for all involved. Can an administration which helps make weapons for Vietnam, steals people's land and homes, discipline anyone? SUPPORT DEMONSTRATION AND MASS ACTION FOR MARK RUDD, NICK FREUDENBURG, MORRIS GROSSNER.

Rain threatened throughout the overcast, humid morning and early afternoon, but by 3:30 the sun was out and the first of the curious and expectant began to gather at the Sundial. A magazine writer just back from Paris began a leisurely account of life on the barricades during the student revolt taking place there. A soccer game on South Field continued undisturbed amid scurrying frisbee players and scattered sunbathers, and little children splashed in the fountains on Low Plaza.

Inside Hamilton Hall secretaries hurriedly moved Dean Platt's files from his inner office to an adjacent closet equipped with a heavy padlock. Nothing was left behind. Correspondence, in and out baskets, desk supplies were all carted into the storage area. Platt, in shirt sleeves, locked his office and stepped outside, leaving only one secretary inside, in case the students he had summoned for a hearing actually did decide to show up.

By four, when strike press secretary Ron Carver walked over from Ferris Booth to begin the rally officially, nearly three hundred students had gathered at the Sundial, along with Dean Platt who stood in the front row smoking a pipe and squinting into the sunlight. "I'm proud to announce the fourth weekly anniversary of the Hamilton occupation," Carver said, and the crowd cheered the invocation. He apologized for Mark Rudd's absence, explaining that he was tied up at Strike Central and would be over in a few minutes. "Don't leave," Carver advised the crowd, "because there will be a new action, one which every one of you will be able to participate in."

While Carver was speaking, Rudd, Grossner, Hyman and Freudenburg strolled out of Ferris Booth and across South Field to the Sundial, accompanied by their lawyers and a group of fifteen parents. As students crowded around the four leaders behind the Sundial, asking them what they were going to do, Rudd said: "We're not going in. The lawyers will go in and talk." Morris Grossner said, with a smile, "We're not going in, but everybody else is."

As Ray Brown of SAS stepped up onto the Sundial to speak, Jon Shils walked over to Juan Gonzalez and motioned him aside. "Let's go over now and see how things are set up," Shils said, and they headed over to Hamilton together. After reiterating the demands of the students who had occupied Hamilton Hall, Brown affirmed that none of the black students who had participated in the demonstrations would go in to be disciplined. He declared that the dean's authority was illegitimate and pledged that if any black student were suspended or expelled, every black student who had been in Hamilton would leave Columbia. "This University didn't have the right to take the actions it did," Brown concluded. "Our position hasn't changed one damn bit."

After a professor read a statement in support of amnesty, drafted by several faculty members, Carver announced the surprise guest speaker of the afternoon, Mrs. Isabel Grossner, Morris' mother. She embraced her son and stepped up onto the Sundial. Carver called out, "Let's have a cheer for this poor woman who has endured all this." Clad in an ankle-length raincoat and three-foot-wide black flop hat, Mrs. Grossner announced, "We have several demands of our own." Reading a statement drafted by the Concerned Parents Committee, she called on the administration to drop all civil and criminal charges against the demonstrators. She charged that there was a "dangerous absence of community control" in Columbia's expansion procedures and chided the administration for "closing the way to the democratization of the University." While Mrs. Grossner spoke, reporters asked Dean Platt, who was still standing in front of the Sundial, what he was planning to do. Platt replied that he would speak with the four students he had summoned and then with their parents. If the students refused to see him, he said, "they will be immediately suspended, according to the recommendations of the Joint Discipline Committee."

At 4:40 Mark Rudd began the rally's final speech. The audience had grown to almost five hundred students, and CBS had set up a TV camera on the periphery of the crowd. "I've got that *déjà vu* feeling," Rudd began, and the crowd laughed. Speaking quietly, in his usual informal, bantering style, Rudd asked the students surrounding him, "Why is there any question that the students should go in or not today? I know the administration wants to kick us out; it seems to me as if they've decided already." He cited Dean Fraenkel's statement during the occupation—"No matter what, Rudd will be expelled"—and gaily repeated Vice President Truman's confession that he could not stand to be in the same room with Rudd. "Too much water has gone under the bridge for us to go in now to see the dean," Rudd continued. He looked pointedly at Platt. "I think we can counter-attack."

Rudd then read a complicity statement drawn up by the Strike Committee, pledging its signers to disrupt commencement exercises if any demonstrator were disciplined, to refuse their diploma if any striker were denied his and not to register in the fall if any protester were suspended or expelled. The last declaration brought a cheer from a knot of counter-demonstrators in the rear of the crowd who had been glowering at the speakers. "Dean Platt told us to come to his office," Rudd went on, glancing down again at the unperturbed administrator, "but I see that he's not in his office to listen to us. I'll give him about thirty seconds to start on over there now and if he doesn't go, then we should go over there to see if he shows." Dean Platt smiled benignly and did not move. "The four of us won't see him, but our parents and lawyers want to go over there," Rudd said. "If they want to do their thing, that's all right."

At the end of his speech, Rudd shrugged his shoulders and said, "Let's go," and the crowd started moving slowly toward Hamilton. A cadre of members of the now-defunct Majority Coalition sprinted ahead of the mass, but when they arrived at Hamilton they found that ten strikers had beaten them to the spot and stood with linked arms in front of the central door to the building. This "defense squad" funneled the crowd into Hamilton slowly, asking groups that coalesced outside the entrance to move inside or step back. As the lobby filled, the parents and lawyers, led by Ron Carver, filed into the administrative wing and positioned themselves in front of the door to Platt's office. Carver knocked, and there was no response.

By five the lobby was crammed with nearly five hundred students. Counter-demonstrators had occupied the raised bench to the right of Dean Coleman's office, where they shouted insults at the strike leaders congregated below them on the steps. Students sat down in the lobby. A CBS camera poked in through the center door, and reporters pushed their way toward the positions they had held a month before.

Ted Gold, raising his voice over the taunts of the hecklers, announced to the crowd, "We have not occupied Platt's office. There's no reason why he can't sit down in his office like a reasonable man and discuss his irrational policies." The students began chanting, "Amnesty! Amnesty!" and then switched to "Strike! Strike!" The mood of the crowd was startlingly similar to that of the first occupation—carefree and boisterous. Singing in Hamilton lobby brought back nostalgic memories of the beginning of the strike, and the excitement of direct confrontation was welcome after weeks of shadowboxing with disciplinary committees and fact-finding commissions. And there was the same confusion and uncertainty as on April 23; no one was sure what would come next or what strategy to follow. As Juan Gonzalez stated a few days later, the Strike Committee had not planned to re-occupy Hamilton and had discussed only a vague outline for a brief indoor vigil to dramatize their familiar stand on amnesty.

As the chants continued Rudd moved up to the front of the lobby's steps and began to outline the significance of what had become a sit-in. "We have to make a choice now," he said, straining to project his voice over the hubbub of private conversations and the continual heckling from the hostile enclave on his right. "We could go outside and see Platt, but that wouldn't accomplish much. Four weeks ago there were three hundred of us here. Since then our power has grown. I want to find out if we want to keep it growing—do we want to make a stand here? Make a stand until we win what we want—amnesty." The crowd cheered loudly. Rudd warned, "If you stay, you will probably be busted tonight." He said that people who had been arrested before should not take the risk of being busted again and then asked all those in favor of staying in Hamilton to raise their left hand. About two hundred people indicated that they wanted to stay, although no one bothered to count the arms that shot up. Rudd then asked how many of those who wanted to stay had not been busted before. A few hands were raised. Paul Vilardi, perched on the railing of the Majority Coalition bench, made a quick count and called, "Only thirty-five, Mark. That's not good, Mark, not good."

Juan Gonzalez shouted up from the main doorway that Dean Platt had refused to enter his office. Platt had walked over to the lawn near Hamilton, watching the crowd growing in front of the building. A runner returned to Hamilton from Strike Central with a bullhorn, and Rudd called out for the members of the defense squad to come to the top of the stairs. As they surrounded Rudd in front of Dean Coleman's office, the SDS chairman announced that the lawyers, who were still waiting in front of Platt's door, had made their last offer to meet with the dean. "We should stay here until the administration responds to our lawyers' request, or until it shows that the only force it has is the police," he shouted. A second vote was taken on how many students who had not been arrested previously would be willing to stay and be busted this time. The number of hands was too small to merit counting. About fifteen minutes later Dean Platt appeared at the doorway of Hamilton. A path was cleared, and he walked to the door of his office where the group of parents and lawyers had assembled. Amid a vigorous chant of "Amnesty! Amnesty!" Platt unlocked the door and disappeared inside with the group.

A new outburst of insults and counter-chants erupted from the Majority Coalition bench. One student, tall and blond, stood in the center of the lobby screaming, "Go back to New Jersey, Rudd." Rudd stared down at his antagonist contemptuously, pointing his finger and saying, "I bet you feel lonely down there." The student glared back defiantly but did not reply as the crowd laughed at him. Vilardi suddenly decided that he had had enough and called for his group to pull out. They left quietly, and the demonstrators surged into the vacuum, easing the crush in the lobby.

The crowd thinned somewhat during the next hour, while various strike leaders carried on their well-practiced take-up-a-few-hours rhetoric. By 6:30, when the lawyers and parents emerged from Dean Platt's office, there were about two hundred people in the lobby, most of them active protesters. Platt walked to the center of the lobby and made a brief statement, announcing that he had had "a very useful talk" with the lawyers and parents, and that they would resume their discussions at nine the next morning when Dean Coleman would be present.

As Platt began to leave, stepping over students seated on the floor, someone shouted, "What about the demands? What about IDA?" He turned, stood silent for a few seconds and then said, "Yes, I think we should disaffiliate from IDA." Stu Gedal seized the bullhorn and asked Platt why he was so determined to discipline the protesters if he thought their demands were just. Platt grinned sheepishly, balanced on the steps, and shook his head when Gedal asked him to join the demonstration. "I'll be glad to discuss the issues, however," he said calmly. "On IDA, I think Columbia should disaffiliate immediately." "How about the gym? How about the gym?" a black student yelled out. Having made one confession, Platt replied, "This is an issue over which reasonable men will disagree." Challenging the crowd, he added, "I don't believe there is anyone in this room today who knows a fraction of the factors involved in the issue. If you make an honest attempt to explore the controversy, you might change your opinion." The dean said that since he did not know all the facts he could not make a judgment. He then walked through the crowd and outside.

Rudd took the bullhorn and introduced David Lubell, one of the group's lawyers, who told the demonstrators that Platt had not considered the lawyers' presence in his office an appearance on behalf of the summoned students. Platt, Lubell said, indicated that the four would consequently be suspended for refusing to appear before the dean. Brandishing the bullhorn, Rudd shouted: "We have only one reply to that—Strike! Strike! Strike!" The crowd picked up the chant. At that moment a student climbed up on another's shoulders and taped a three-foot-high poster of Mao Tse-tung over the door to Dean Coleman's office. The chant turned into a prolonged cheer; another familiar face from the first round of protests had returned. Mrs. Grossner then took the amplifier and related her version of the meeting with Platt, stating that she thought the administration was ready to discuss amnesty seriously and that "a new dialogue" had been opened up. She also said, somewhat surprisingly, that Platt "told us he didn't want to suspend anyone." The crowd applauded faintly, and Stu Gedal called out, "Look, either there will be reprisals, or not."

It was not an either/or proposition. After emerging from Hamilton Dean Platt had gone straight to the President's suite in Low Library, where he conferred briefly with Truman and Coleman. Dean Coleman officially approved the suspension of Rudd, Grossner, Hyman and Freudenberg, and it was decided an ultimatum would be delivered to the protesters in the building. At this point Truman notified Police Commissioner Howard Leary that the police might be needed that night.

At 7:20 Coleman—carrying a bullhorn—Platt and a convoy of administrative assistants left Low Library and headed toward Hamilton. As Coleman approached the doors a student inside shouted, "Make way for the honored dean." The demonstrators cleared a path in the lobby leading to the door of his office, but Coleman made no move to enter the building. Raising the bullhorn he called out firmly, "This is Dean Coleman." A burst of laughter greeted this superfluous pronouncement as people yelled, "Up against the wall!" They were shouted down in turn by cries of "Let him talk." Coleman continued: "You are hereby directed to clear out of this building. I will give you further instructions if the building is not cleared in ten minutes."

Coleman walked away from the door and out onto South Field where Platt was waiting. Proctor Kahn made a futile attempt to disperse the crowd of onlookers at the steps of Hamilton. Inside, Rudd began to discuss what would happen if people were arrested again. Bail would be fairly high, he said, and the judges would probably be stiff. He didn't mention the possibility of leaving the building, and no one brought it up from the floor. At 7:30 Dean Coleman returned to the front of Hamilton. "You have ignored my directive," he announced and stated that he would deliver a specific ultimatum shortly. As he waited on the steps, Ron Carver, speaking to the crowd outside, cried, "We're on the offensive now. The University is up against the wall." Dean Coleman stood silently, looking at his watch. "We're here for amnesty," Carver shouted; "regardless of what action we take now, amnesty is what we're fighting for."

Dean Coleman returned to the doorway, shakily raised his bullhorn again, and read his final pronouncement: "As an officer of this University, I have to inform you that we have no alternative now but to call in the police. Any student arrested will be immediately suspended for an indefinite period." There was dead silence inside Hamilton; outside, counter-demonstrators began a brief chant of "TPF, TPF" that was drowned in a sudden crescendo of "Up against the wall, motherfucker" emanating from Hamilton. Coleman started back to Low, surrounded by students and reporters. On College Walk he halted for an impromptu press conference. Asked when the police would come, he said it would be "a while, because it takes time for them to get up here." The police had already been notified, he said, adding that the students in Hamilton would be charged with criminal trespass and "disrupting the proper functioning of the University." Coleman explained that Rudd, Grossner, Freudenburg and Hyman "were suspended today and will receive official letters tomorrow." He then continued on to Low Library where the administration was holding a press conference to announce the suspensions. Grayson Kirk, surrounded by a covey of plainclothesmen, walked into the rotunda, read a brief statement and told reporters he had asked the police to be "gentle." "Our desire is to get the building cleared without violence," he said.

On April 23 and 24 the administration had not been able to employ the police effectively to dislodge the protesters, and the original occupation had built up considerable momentum. The administration felt that hesitation this time, in the face of what was considered an open declaration of war by the "forces of destruction and anarchy" (as Vice President Truman later characterized the students who re-occupied Hamilton), was out of the question. Moreover, a highly successful precedent for this type of ultimatum had been set two weeks earlier at the University of Chicago. After student demonstrators seized the administration building there, they were presented with the threat of arrest and suspension if they did not come out before a specified time. The students left the building well before the deadline.

As news of Dean Coleman's ultimatum spread across the campus, the crowd outside Hamilton grew to nearly one thousand students, some of them hostile to the demonstration. A "Stop SDS" sign was unfurled from a window in Hartley dormitory, and the first of many volleys of eggs hurtled up toward protesters standing on a third-floor balcony of Hamilton. As daylight waned the scene became increasingly bizarre, the TV spotlights and strobes creating pools of glare amid the dark, seething mass of students waiting for the impending bust.

Inside Hamilton a more serious mood now gripped the protesters. They had entered the building without the express intention of occupying it and had been directly challenged by the administration before they had resolved to do so. The threat of suspension was the administration's ultimate weapon, far more frightening than the police, and it raised the protest to a new level. The demonstrators, who had successfully confronted the administration for a month, felt they could not afford to capitulate now to what they themselves had termed an illegitimate authority. As Juan Gonzalez explained a few weeks later:

> It was a confrontation which showed how much we believed in what we were fighting for. If our goals went beyond the University, then we should have been willing to leave it if necessary. Were we students who were politically active, or activists who happened to be students?

The demonstrators had shown that they were willing to confront the police on April 30. It was not clear, however, that provoking another mass arrest—one that would be considerably smaller than the first—would provide any leverage for making the administration act on the six demands. In the eyes of the demonstrators the moral integrity of the movement and its tactic had to be defended. The fear of being forced to leave school was offset by the passion of commitment. The protesters had been inadvertently trapped by the internal dynamic of their struggle and found that they had impelled themselves into another confrontation. Doubt began to increase: Would staying in Hamilton revitalize the floundering strike or would it merely be an unnecessary and unproductive sacrifice?

Although Rudd's earlier statement of intent had been enthusiastically accepted by the group, when the time came for individual decisions few were willing to risk arrest and suspension. But the students were also reluctant to leave. The first demonstrator to speak after Coleman's ultimatum was delivered was Steve Halliwell, who reminded the crowd that even if the police had been called it would take them hours to arrive on campus and that there was no sense in leaving until they had actually appeared. Mark Rudd, surrounded by some students urging him to ask everyone to leave now and others suggesting that they make a stand, said hurriedly that a decision would have to be reached and that open debate on what to do would begin shortly. He called for volunteers to barricade the tunnel entrances, and ten students raced downstairs. By 8 P.M. a pile of planks, furniture and office equipment, reaching halfway to the ceiling and solidly braced against the opposite stairwell, had been constructed in the basement corridor in front of the tunnel doors. The demonstration fragmented into discussion groups as Rudd huddled with several other members of the Strike Committee in a corner of the lobby.

A few minutes after eight Professors Rothman and Fogelson entered Hamilton lobby. "The faculty won't move on this—it's happening too fast," Rothman told a reporter. Fogelson suggested to his colleague that they circulate through the lobby and try to persuade students they knew to leave the building. The two professors met with little success and, after a few inconclusive arguments, they left. During the next half hour members of the Joint College Commission—the student-faculty board created the previous week to study restructuring proposals in the College—arrived for an emergency meeting in the admissions office.

The water supply inside Hamilton was cut off around 8:30; toilets downstairs would not flush and the drinking fountains ran dry. The same action had been taken against each of the occupied buildings three weeks before, presumably to prevent the demonstrators from resisting a police rush with the high-pressure fire hoses mounted in the hallways of each building. Now it seemed clear that a bust was near. Students milled around, asking one another if they would stay and be arrested this time. The situation was not new and almost everyone appeared calm. A few minutes later the lights blinked out, plunging the entire building into an eerie semi-darkness. The klieg lights outside cast wavering patterns on the walls and ceiling of the lobby, while students felt their way around, trying to locate fuse boxes by the flickering glare of matches and lighters. An administrator calling from Low Library asserted to members of the Joint College Commission that the administration had not cut off electric power. Students quickly sent out for candles. The protesters sang the "Internationale" and "Solidarity Forever" in the darkness. A French student reminded the crowd that Charles De Gaulle had offered amnesty to the French students in Paris. "As far as I know," he said, "President Kirk is not as powerful as General De Gaulle." As if on cue, someone in the dorms began playing the "Marseillaise."

The lights in the lobby came back on at nine, and with them returned renewed debate. A spokesman for the Joint Committee on Disciplinary Affairs entered the building and announced to the crowd that the committee had decided it had no jurisdiction over the threatened suspensions, and that the fate of the demonstrators now rested entirely in the administration's hands.

Meanwhile, at the 24th Precinct house on West 100th Street the police had started to plan their operation. Chief Inspector Garelik arrived there about 8:30 and was briefed again over the telephone by the administration. Tow trucks removed the cars along 100th Street to make room for the buses that would be used to carry the police task force up to Columbia. By ten the tow trucks had moved up to the campus and begun removing parked cars. Patrolmen massed at the 24th Precinct house and further uptown at the 26th Precinct house.

At 10:15 a spokesman for the Joint College Commission emerged from the admissions office with a "compromise" solution that the administration had accepted. The University, he said, would call off the police if the protesters would surrender their identification cards and leave the building. Tony Papert conveyed the proposal disdainfully to the crowd. "I'll give the offer, and then we can have the speakers against it," he said, adding with a sour grin that anyone who wanted to could speak in favor of the proposal. No one bothered to debate, and the offer was derisively hooted down. Lindsay aides Barry Gottehrer and Jay Kriegel arrived in Hamilton at 10:20. They huddled with Rudd, Gonzalez and Jon Shils in a second-floor stairwell, informing them that the police were already moving and would probably be ready earlier than on April 30, possibly by 12:30 A.M.

Rudd went back out to the lobby. "This is very important," he called out, his face set. "All people not getting busted please leave immediately. This is very important." A few shouted back that they would not leave until the police showed up. Gonzalez repeated Kriegel's and Gottehrer's warning that the police were already moving, adding, "The bust will come sooner than we think." Still no one moved. After a few minutes of confusion, Rudd called for a vote at 11 P.M. "How many people want to stay?" he asked. The lobby quieted. Thirty people raised their hands as the other 250 demonstrators looked around at each other. "You're succumbing to panic," Gonzalez admonished the crowd as he counted the hands. Tony Papert picked up the bullhorn and called for further debate. No one disputed his action, although many later said it was a blatant manipulation. Many of the demonstrators, reluctant to consider their vote conclusive, were waiting to be convinced to stay. As Rudd explained later:

Yeah, there was a lot of that [manipulation]. I don't want to apologize for Tony because he has a fixed idea and does everything he can to get there. On the other hand, you can say that it is even more democratic to have more discussion.

The resolve of some of the strike leaders to remain in Hamilton had hardened, but the question of unity appeared to be equally important. It would be difficult to maintain a united front if a large number of demonstrators walked out, since the administration could suspend thirty students with little trouble. It would have considerably more trouble, however dealing with several hundred non-coöperative protesters.

During the next hour a battery of speakers exhorted the increasingly apprehensive crowd not to leave. Ted Gold, one of SDS's more persuasive orators, argued that "by leaving and giving in to the administration we will be giving them the credibility we have denied them so far. We must show that we still believe what we are doing is right." He said that either everyone had to stay or everyone had to leave, since a split was the worst possible alternative. Most of the other speakers echoed these arguments. One girl speaking from the floor gave a tearful, angry appeal for staying. Only one leader, Mike Golash, urged everyone to leave: "This time we've taken a vote and have to abide by it. The only way to win is to disrupt the University and to continue to do it. It's a waste to stay." Another speaker from the floor suggested that if only a few people wanted to stay they could; and every successive night another small group would occupy a building and force the University to call the police each night.

Ted Gold went upstairs to the third-floor balcony at 11:45 and made a desperate appeal to the crowd of fifteen hundred standing below. "We need more people inside," he called out over a bullhorn. His voice was barely audible above the rumbling of the crowd below. "I'm asking for people to come inside," he yelled again. On Van Am Quadrangle the rows of athletes and other counter-demonstrators began to chant, "Stop SDS." But the students on the Hamilton steps countered with a roar of "Strike! Strike!" drowning them out. Gold tried again: "We don't have enough people inside. We have to show the administration that they can't punish us. It's not a question of personal commitment now, but political. . . . " A shower of eggs and rocks from the rear of the crowd forced Gold to jump back inside Hamilton. No one joined the protesters.

Shortly after midnight Rudd make a final speech to the demonstrators in the lobby. In a disjointed, sometimes unintelligible presentation, he said, "I think that the illusion of unity should be maintained no matter what. We're basically all in this to win. And if we decide to leave, no one should stay, so there will be no pieces to mend together. Maybe we can come back together tomorrow. The question isn't really what we do tonight, but what we do from now on." Rudd seemed to be saying that the group should leave, although he explained later that he had only been trying to present alternatives.

He walked away from the bullhorn and was immediately surrounded by his confidants—Papert, Gold, Cole, Gonzalez—who began arguing with him. His speech had confused the protesters. Had he said that everyone should leave or not? Rudd returned to the bullhorn. "I'm for staying," he said firmly. "If we all leave, we'll walk our separate ways." He called for another vote.

The lobby fell quiet. "How many will stay now?" Rudd asked. One hundred people raised their hands. "How many want to leave?" Seventy-five hands went up slowly in the stillness. Rudd called for abstentions; there were thirty-five.[1] Mike Golash picked up the bullhorn. "I think you've made the wrong decision," he said and asked for time to continue the discussion, as Papert had done earlier. Rudd grabbed the microphone from his hand. "I'm sorry, but the decision has been made. It's all over," he said. "I've gotten a reliable report that the cops will be here at 12:30. The people who are leaving have to leave now so we can get ready."

Rudd's words were met with cries of dismay from the floor. Most of the students who had voted to leave wanted to remain inside Hamilton as long as possible. But Rudd and the others kept urging them to leave immediately, so the remaining protesters could discuss defense tactics without having their plans disrupted by a hurried last-minute exodus. The departing demonstrators reluctantly started to form a line in front of the center door, many carrying blankets and books in a scene similar to the Wednesday morning a month earlier when the whites had been evicted from Hamilton. A sense of urgency overcame the lobby as the minutes dragged by, and the line of students did not move. Someone suggested that those who were leaving should hold a rally at the Sundial to protest the administration's decision to call the police, and should then march on the School of International Affairs and demonstrate in front of the building. Finally Steve Halliwell opened the doors and the students who were leaving began to move forward.[2]

A volley of eggs greeted the subdued, disheartened demonstrators

---

[1] This vote count is approximate. The totals given are those announced by the strikers, who counted from the top of the stairs; the vote was very close, and there is the possibility that the number who favored staying would have been counted as larger in any case.

[2] Jay Kriegel of the Mayor's office left too. As he walked out, Ted Gold asked him to stay and join the protest. According to Gold, Kriegel demurred, stating, "The cops would rather get me than any four of you."

who filed slowly out of Hamilton into the glare of the TV lights; stray eggs splattered against the building's walls, spraying shell and yolk over the mass of students below. A few protesters began to walk toward the Sundial, but most formed a new line at the base of the steps. Steve Halliwell, leaning against the center door with his bullhorn, explained to the throng that "the people who are leaving fully support the people who are going to be suspended," and that the split was over tactics, not goals. "For four weeks now," he continued, "we've been facing the threat of police action. The cops have been up here more than Lindsay, Kirk or Truman ever expected. The University will cease to exist if every political question raised is answered by police. And suspensions are just a piece of paper."

A WKCR reporter strung a microphone cable over from the Hartley Hall station to pick up Halliwell's speech; a line of students stretching across Van Am Quad and the steps of Hamilton held the wire in the crook of the "V" sign they formed with their fingers. "Strike!" Halliwell called out over the bullhorn, and hundreds of arms flashed the "V" for victory as the chant echoed out over the quadrangle.

On Amsterdam Avenue the first city buses marked "Special," carrying riot-helmeted members of the Tactical Patrol Force, had pulled up at the corner of 116th Street. It was 12:30. The police piled out and began lining up across the street near the Law School. A dump truck piled high with gray police barricades pulled up, and the policemen set up a blockade along Amsterdam down to 114th Street. Other buses parked on Riverside Drive spewed out more TPF who lined up along Broadway between 114th and 116th Streets.

In front of Hamilton Stu Gedal was leading the crowd in interminable verses of "We Shall Not Be Moved," including "Cops don't scare us, we shall not be moved." When the students' enthusiasm for singing gave out, Marty Kenner, a balding student activist from the New School for Social Research, began an impassioned speech about the quality of a Columbia education. In a conventional Marxist critique he accused the economics department of reinforcing capitalist myths, the history department of ignoring or distorting relevant social forces, the physics department of prostituting itself for the government. He attacked professors by name—sociologist Daniel Bell for writing a book with a title as presumptuous as *The End of Ideology,* Soviet expert Zbigniew Brzezinski for working for the State Department, historian Richard Hofstadter for his condemnation of "student nihilists" after the Berkeley crisis. Lionel Trilling, Eric Bentley, Jacques Barzun—Kenner invoked the entire Columbia pantheon, and even his friends became embarrassed as the list expanded. Finally, he was silenced by an emergency announcement from inside Hamilton—a call for water, soft drinks and other liquids.

In the lull a tired student shouted plaintively from a window in a nearby dormitory, "Left, right, center—why don't you all go home and go to sleep?" The crowd laughed, but the moment of lightness faded as word of police lines being set up on Amsterdam reached the quadrangle. The mass of people outside Hamilton thinned somewhat as students raced to the gates on College Walk at Broadway and Amsterdam to intercept the police. Inside Hamilton protesters watched from upper-story windows as the police maneuvered below. Rudd assigned Lew Cole and Juan Gonzalez to organize "defense squads" outside. The two strikers left Hamilton at 1 A.M. and walked over to 116th Street and Amsterdam where a crowd of two hundred students had gathered to confront a line of police on the sidewalk.

One student seized a wooden police barricade and set it down in front of the policemen, who merely stared. "Lew and I looked at each other and said, 'Shit, man, let's do it,'" Gonzalez recalled, and with the help of about ten other demonstrators they began erecting a barricade—a small-scale application of the tactic being employed that week by rioting Parisian students. Trash cans, wooden fences surrounding the shrubbery on South Field, police barriers were piled ten-feet high in a few minutes. Cole and Gonzalez raced over to 116th and Broadway where a smaller crowd of about seventy-five students had gathered. They began hauling pieces of lumber and metal braces from a subway construction site outside the gates, and within minutes another barricade—this one including a metal ramp removed from Low Plaza and two burning trash cans—had been erected.

More and more police accumulated at 116th Street and Amsterdam, lining up three-deep on the other side of the barricaded gate. Ed Hyman, standing atop the barrier, asked the officers why they were willing to work for such low wages and told them that they were dupes, since Mayor Lindsay had sent them up to Columbia and then accused them of being brutal. Watching from inside Hamilton, the demonstrators were amazed. "It's beautiful," one girl sighed as she watched students perched high on the barricade screaming obscenities at the cops. No one had expected that kind of support and resistance. It was getting more like Paris every minute.

At 2 A.M. the detachment of TPF massed outside the Amsterdam gate began crossing the street, moving directly toward the barricade. But the police made no attempt to breach it. About half the detachment marched up Amsterdam Avenue to 118th Street where it was met by Chief Garelik. Ten minutes later the police entered the campus at 118th

Street and disappeared into the underground tunnels leading to Hamilton Hall.

Inside the occupied building the demonstrators had gathered on the lobby steps where they sang softly, continuously, Ted Gold leading them. "Oh, there's no *New York Times* where I'm bound," they sang; Gold kept providing new verses, like "No more war where I'm bound"; "The people decide . . ."; "No Trustees . . ."; finally, "Che is waiting where I'm bound." Then the camp songs began, but with a twist: "You can't get to heaven on the bourgeoisie, 'cause the bourgeoisie won't set you free." Two big jugs of cider, donated by someone in the dorms, were passed around. The singing stopped about 2:30 when the sound of police chopping at the barricades downstairs became audible. "What rhymes with fire hose?" Ted Gold asked, trying to begin again, but no one answered. At 2:40 A.M. a fat TPF in a riot helmet bounded up the east stairwell and entered the lobby. He strode past Gold and Mark Rudd, who was leaning against a railing near Dean Coleman's office, and ripped the poster of Mao off the wall. More police led by Chief Garelik poured up the stairs and into the lobby. At that point a scruffy, booted, long-haired "demonstrator" walked over to Rudd and placed him under arrest, handcuffing him in the process.[3]

The protesters were arrested, without resistance, in groups of four, then lined up in front of the west stairwell. After a pause of ten minutes while Garelik, a shock of black hair hanging limply over his glasses, directed the operation from the top of the steps, the students were marched into the tunnels. No attempt was made to move them out above ground; hundreds of students pressed against the front entrances screaming insults and attempting to force the doors open. One student called for a rush on the lobby, but no one supported him; the struggling at the doors was only token resistance.

Rudd was taken to an unmarked police car and driven downtown alone to be booked; the others were led into paddy wagons at 115th and 118th Streets and Amsterdam. Rudd was later charged with riot, inciting to riot, criminal trespass and criminal solicitation (exhorting others to act illegally)—offenses with a total maximum penalty of over six years in prison.[4]

[3] Police officials later said that the plainclothesman was Detective Frank Ferrara who had been sent up to Columbia two months earlier to investigate drug usage and to engage in political undercover work.
[4] Rudd's bail was set at $2,500. Four other strikers were later charged with felonies. Marty Kenner and Tony Sager were both charged with riot and inciting to riot; they were also charged with conspiracy to commit murder for allegedly

Outside on the campus, just as the heads of policemen became visible inside the occupied building, smoke started pouring out of two windows, one on the seventh floor at the far east end and one on the sixth floor in the middle of the building. Firemen, unable to enter the campus because of the barricades on 116th Street, clambered up ladders extended from trucks parked on Amsterdam Avenue. One fire had been started by igniting the contents of a wastepaper basket overturned in the middle of the room. The other blaze was set among the papers of Orest Ranum, the young professor of history who had taken a public stance against the demonstrators. Ranum's office was broken into, his files were ransacked, and the notes and manuscripts for projected books on the history of Paris and the reign of Louis XIV were burned.[5]

By 3 A.M. the students who had congregated in front of Hamilton had already begun to move toward the north area of the campus in an attempt to find the paddy wagons being used to remove the protesters. Several hundred students swarmed over the raised portion of the Engineering Terrace and the connecting areas in front of Fayerweather and Schermerhorn Halls. Some gouged paving stones out of College Walk on their way over,[6] and they hurled them down at policemen lined up below on Amsterdam Avenue. At 119th Street the police had parked several squad cars, buses and a communications van in a wide driveway leading onto the campus. Students bombarded the vehicles with bricks, shattering three cars' windshields. Another group dragged a small tree, potted in a three-hundred-pound container, from the Engineering Terrace, lifted it over the retaining wall and dropped it onto the van, crushing the roof. A band of almost two hundred students marched on Schermerhorn Hall. Some wanted to start a new wave of liberations, but after several demonstrators broke into the building the crowd decided not to enter. Returning to College Walk, several students hurled bricks through windows in nearby Fayerweather. Another fire erupted shortly after 3 A.M.—this time on the fifth floor of Fayerweather. Twenty minutes later, firemen rushed into the building and joined students who were already inside fighting the flames. A burning wastebasket had ignited curtains and other inflammable furnishings, including a couch, in an office. A group of graduate biology students, afraid that the fires on

---

leading a group of students in a charge at two plainclothesmen, yelling, "Let's get them," over a bullhorn, and their bails were set at $5,000. Ed Hyman was charged with riot and inciting to riot, and, after he allegedly lied to the judge at his arraignment (he said he was a nephew of a State Supreme Court justice), his bail was set at $7,500. Ray Brown was arrested later that night on the campus and charged with assaulting an officer and resisting arrest.

[5] The Strike Committee later repudiated any responsibility for the destruction of Ranum's notes, which he said were "irreplaceable."

[6] Over 130 such stones were missing before the end of the night.

campus might spread and ignite highly inflammable material in the Schermerhorn Hall laboratories, called campus guards and barricaded the entrance to prevent anyone from entering the building. The smouldering furniture in Fayerweather produced considerable smoke but no real danger. The fire was soon brought under control and was out by 3:40.[7]

By this time, the north campus was largely deserted except for several small bands of students still roving around Low Library, tossing bricks at second-floor windows. The crowds in front of Schermerhorn and Fayerweather had returned to College Walk and the barricades. At 116th Street and Broadway demonstrators piled the barriers still higher, as Barnard girls standing on the roof of a dormitory across the street screamed chorus after chorus of "Up against the wall, motherfuckers!" at the police lined up outside the gates. (Some of the policemen yelled back at the students; in one exchange after being asked to "articulate" by one girl, an officer shouted back, "Go articulate behind the barn yourself!") A student on the roof of the Barnard dormitory hurled a soda bottle at a group of police standing near the subway construction site on Broadway. One officer was struck on the head, collapsed and was rushed into a taxi and then to St. Luke's Hospital, where he was later released with no serious injury.

But the excitement seemed somewhat anti-climactic. The barricades erected on College Walk were symbolic acts of resistance; everyone had known that the police would enter Hamilton through the tunnels and that a flimsy pile of saw horses and garbage cans could not hold back a determined charge for more than a few minutes. Moreover, the police had made no move to enter the campus, and the bricks and taunts flung from the Engineering Terrace and from behind the barricades did not impede the arrests taking place inside Hamilton. At most they caused the administration to see that recourse to police force was becoming increasingly more dangerous.

By 3:45 WKCR broadcasted that it was about to wrap up its account of the night's action, and that the campus was quieting down. But inside Low Library administrators had made a far different appraisal of the situation. Dean Coleman, Dean Colahan and Joseph Nye, the University business manager, had been out on the campus phoning in reports to the headquarters in Vice President Truman's office. These reports, which told of large bands of angry students roaming the north campus committing violent and destructive acts, the accounts of arson in Hamilton and Fayerweather, and the tinkling of shattered glass in Low Library

---

[7] The fire department has not made public the results of any investigation of arson in the Fayerweather or Hamilton fires which would indicate whether they were set by Columbia radicals or others.

itself, all gave the impression of an impending riot. As Thomas McGoey, vice president for business, later described the atmosphere in Low:

> Within a period of one half to three quarters of an hour, we received the following reports: (1.) There was a fire in Hamilton; (2.) There was a fire in Fayerweather; (3.) We had a number of false alarms—Furnald, Carman, Ferris Booth Halls. The headquarters during this time was Truman's office. I was returning from the security office after checking one of the false alarms when a brick came through the window. I dropped to the ground, but the venetian blinds stopped the brick as the glass shattered all over. Then, in a matter of seconds, a brick came through the window in Truman's office. The President and Dr. Truman were there. Somebody yelled, "Let's go into the corridor," and we went into the reception area. Then a billiard ball came through the window in the President's office. In this period, six windows were broken.
>
> We also had reports that windows and doors were being broken at Schermerhorn, Fayerweather, Philosophy, and Kent, and that these buildings were being occupied by various groups. I don't say students, because non-students were being observed and reported around the campus. The word was that they were occupying these buildings. Two men were grabbed and pulled in. All right, some of our students are hippie-looking, but these were really bad. They looked like they were straight out of the East Village. They had fire in their eyes. One had a brick in his hand—a non-student, wild-eyed; he was arrested in the security office. Another was running, yelling, "Riot, Riot!" He was pulled in right in front of Low, and was also a non-student, or at least he didn't have an ID.
>
> Then the report came that they were dumping shrubbery containers over the Engineering Terrace. A report came over WKCR that barricades had been set up on 116th at Amsterdam and Broadway, and that fires had been set at these barricades. There were reports that wild-eyed hoodlum types were running around with rocks, yelling. This was a whole emotional riot atmosphere building up. It was clear to us that we couldn't control it. This was the background and atmosphere to the decision we made to clear the campus. It's like a general and an army in a war—we had to make a decision. We had no choice.[8]

---

[8] During this period a representative of the Strike Committee attempted to negotiate with the administration. A few minutes before the police had entered Hamilton, Josh DeWind went over to Low and asked to see President Kirk. McGoey met with him instead, and DeWind proposed that, since it seemed evident the students outside were ready to fight the police, the administration should

On April 30 the clearing of the campus had resulted in considerable violence. The administration's decision to clear the campus once again was based on both misinformation and misinterpretation. Unqualified reports from observers on campus and exaggeration of incidents that seemed to be major but turned out to be relatively minor led to a panicked response by the administration.

McGoey was delegated to inform Commissioner Leary and Chief Garelik, who were in the security office below, that the administration wanted the campus cleared. According to one of Mayor Lindsay's aides on the scene, Leary was furious when he was told of the decision—his men had already begun to pull back from the campus after Hamilton was evacuated. The police began to mass detachments on Amsterdam and Broadway at either end of College Walk.

Inside Low, Dean Coleman and Frank Safran, the manager of Ferris Booth Hall, hammered out details of the operation with the police, Truman and Kirk. Ferris Booth was to remain open to students, and the police were under no circumstances to enter it or the dormitories. The clearing action was to proceed north to south, with the south gates left open until the area was cleared. At 4:10 A.M., Grayson Kirk announced over WKCR:

> The police have been requested by the University to clear all campus academic buildings. The police have also been requested to clear the campus of all persons, under penalty of arrest. Dormitory residents are to remain in their rooms. All other persons, including dormitory residents not in their rooms, must leave the campus immediately via the nearest gate.

But in the area to be cleared hardly anyone was listening to the radio. A group of counter-demonstrators, led by Paul Vilardi and other ex-Majority Coalition personnel, rushed the Broadway barricade around 4:05 and began dismantling it. As they wrenched a metal ramp from its position, another band of students began to struggle with them in an attempt to replace it on the barrier. The latter group won and began to re-pile the debris dislodged by the counter-demonstrators. By the light of a fire flickering in one of the trash cans in the barricade, a brief, vicious fight broke out between the contending students. One of those trying to rebuild the barricade was SAS leader Ray Brown; he was scuffling with an athlete near the trees inside the gate when, simultaneously, the TV

---

suspend all disciplinary proceedings. According to DeWind, he told McGoey that if anyone could control the crowd by holding a rally and announcing a concession the strikers could. The administration refused to negotiate under such conditions. According to McGoey, "he was sitting here with a gun at my head." DeWind was unequivocally rebuffed.

lights outside the gates went on, and the police charged inside, swinging their clubs. As the police penetrated about fifty feet inside the gate, driving the students before them, Brown and his assailant were seized. The counter-demonstrator managed to slip away, but Brown was thrown to the ground, then dragged back behind a line of police in front of the partially rebuilt barricade. "They got Ray, they got Ray," murmured a group of blacks nearby, as students bunched up near the knot of police surrounding Brown, still on the ground. The police formed a circle three-men-deep around their captive, clubs ready, and the group of black students stood by helplessly. The TV lights snapped out, and in the darkness, the blurred shapes of policemen moved up and down like pistons over Brown's prostrate form, kicking and punching him. He was hauled away and charged with assault and resisting arrest.

At the same time a detachment of twenty policemen marched out of John Jay Hall after entering through the gate on Amsterdam at 115th Street. Students grouped around the Sundial spotted them as they entered the campus. A mass of seventy-five, screaming "Cops must go!", descended on them. The detachment stopped and then turned around as the students bore down upon it across South Field. The group of students pushed into the police, who clubbed a few in the front row. The men demanded that their sergeant allow them to "get these fucking kids," but he ordered them to pull back. The students, chanting, pursued the police into Livingston Hall and ripped the iron gate at the 115th Street entrance partially out of the wall in their attempt to force the police off campus.

On College Walk a student who had been listening to his radio stood on the steps of Low Plaza shouting out that the campus was going to be cleared. The few faculty members and hundreds of other students milling around did not listen; several passersby scoffed. The police had withdrawn after capturing Brown and the barricade at Broadway was completely rebuilt.

Dean Platt returned to Low after touring the campus. He recalled later:

> I came in from outside and asked Kirk what he was doing. Kirk said that he had ordered the police to clear the campus. I told him that it wasn't necessary since I had just been at the Sundial and the impression I got was that the action was dissipating. A group of students had agreed to go home. I was told that the decision had already been made.

Platt, extremely upset, grabbed a bullhorn and rushed back outside to College Walk.

Professor David Rothman met him on the way down from Low, and the two men headed for the Sundial together. A crowd of nearly one thousand students gathered around them. Platt stepped onto the Sundial and raised the bullhorn to his mouth. "I have a regretful and unhappy announcement to make," he began, his voice breaking. The roar of the students, chanting, "Cops Must Go!" and "It's Our Campus!", momentarily drowned his voice. "Please let me speak," he began again. "The police will be coming on campus shortly, and I ask all students to leave. The police will occupy all academic buildings." A student shot up out of the crowd and rammed Platt from the side, wrested the bullhorn from him and ran into the crowd with it. Platt, with tears running down his cheeks, stood on the Sundial amidst the students who were screaming—in even greater rage—"It's Our Campus!" "Let's get out of here, Alex," Rothman said and pulled Platt away into the crowd.

It was 4:30. Seconds after Platt left the Sundial the police began to move onto the campus in force. Over five hundred helmeted TPF—backed up by several hundred plainclothesmen—had been massing at 116th Street and Amsterdam while other officers walked among them distributing billy clubs. Within minutes the first ranks had smashed through the barricade at the gate and lined up along College Walk.

Although the administration had requested students to leave the campus "via the nearest gate," it was impossible to get out of the southern half of the campus without climbing a fence. All gates were locked, and the police had surrounded the barricade at Broadway. The students on College Walk were trapped.

About four hundred of the students at the Sundial linked arms and moved slowly toward the line of TPF at the Amsterdam gate. No one chanted, although a few students shouted obscenities as the line of demonstrators approached the police. Plainclothesmen on the edge of the formation, carrying long wooden clubs, started moving along the sides of Hamilton and Kent. A captain stepped out of the ranks with a bullhorn, but before he could speak a student lunged and seized him around the neck, forcing him to drop the bullhorn. The plainclothesmen charged, without orders, toward the Sundial. The line of demonstrators faltered and then broke, and the students turned and fled. TPF ran after them, swiping at their legs and heads with billy clubs. Deputy Police Commissioner Jacques Nevard later described the scene:

> It was one of the most extraordinary things that has ever happened. It was unbelievable. It's a moment that's going to stay in my mind forever. Those *fantastic* kids linked arms and marched on the police and then the look that went over their faces when the front row realized what they had done, where they were, and how des-

perately they wished they were someplace else. But then the melee was on.

TPF chased the students onto South Field. Most who tripped in the stampede on College Walk were kicked and beaten; a few were pulled to their feet and thrown onto the lawn. As the charge swept across the Sundial, police breached the Broadway barricade and began closing in from the paths on the west side of campus. Students dived over the shrubbery surrounding South Field to escape. Those who were caught before they could reach the sanctuary of the dormitories were pummelled by plainclothesmen.[9]

By 4:45 almost all of South Field had been occupied by police. Chief Garelik called WKCR and announced a ten-minute grace period for students to leave the campus unmolested. Most of the students who had made it across South Field had been forced into Ferris Booth and Furnald; uniformed police lined up outside the entrances and shoved stragglers inside. The gates on 114th Street were finally opened, and some students left the campus. Plainclothesmen were still chasing small groups of demonstrators on South Field in front of John Jay Hall. Most of the students hurdled the hedges in front of Hartley and Livingston Halls and scattered on Van Am Quad. The plainclothesmen regrouped, then lined up across the quadrangle and swept down toward John Jay, driving the students who had remained outside into the dormitories. The first assault wave ebbed.

The second massive charge of the night, which produced the most injuries and the most conspicuous brutality on the part of the police, was carried out almost entirely by plainclothesmen, while hundreds of uniformed men stood idly on College Walk. Many of these plainclothesmen wore no visible shields, and others wore their badges upside-down or with tape covering their numbers. In a situation exacerbated by continued verbal and physical provocation from students inside and outside the dorms, under conditions demanding rigid discipline and self-control, individual plainclothesmen were given a free hand. The result was predictably bloody.[10]

---

[9] Many of the students arrested or injured on campus Tuesday night and Wednesday morning had not been participants in or even partisans of the demonstrations. For example, one of those injured was David Malament, a senior who had been named one of the student members of the Joint Committee on Disciplinary Affairs. He had been walking off campus as directed when he was pounced upon and struck by police. Kirk and Truman later offered Malament personal apologies. Bill Ames, a starting guard on the basketball team, was arrested outside Furnald Hall when he asked for the badge number of a plainclothesman he had seen beating a student in the lobby. The charges against Ames were later dropped.

[10] In the interim report issued after the April 30 operation, the police department had stated:

It is department procedure to delegate to members of the uniformed force, the policing of demonstrations such as the ones that occurred on the Colum-

As the police moved away from the entrances to Furnald and Ferris Booth, small groups of students began to scatter back onto South Field. By 5 A.M., when the grace period was over, about two hundred demonstrators had regrouped in the center of the lawn, where they began screaming insults at the police. The assistant chief inspector directing the clearing operation told his lieutenants: "Don't wait any longer. Let the men do what they are here to do." About fifty TPF moved across South Field toward a group of students on Van Am Quad. Plainclothesmen with billy clubs and blackjacks moved after them in pursuit of another band of demonstrators nearby. The students were caught in a pincers in front of John Jay Hall, where several were seized and beaten. The group of TPF wheeled past the dormitories and toward Butler Library, toward another group of students standing near the center of the lawn. As these protesters dashed toward Hartley, about fifty plainclothesmen moved down from College Walk in pursuit. The students ran inside Hartley Hall; several dived through the open bay windows as the police closed in on the building. Students in the lobby jeered at the plainclothesmen, and one officer, standing on a ledge outside the lobby, picked up a beer can and hurled it through a window at an abusive student. Other plainclothesmen, some carrying fenceposts and sticks instead of clubs, entered the lobby and forced the students inside away from the windows.

On the other side of the campus, near Furnald, six plainclothesmen— one wielding a fencepost—cornered one student and beat him. As the students who had returned to the lawn raced back to Ferris Booth pursued by plainclothesmen, a phalanx of TPF charged through the 115th Street gate, cutting many of them off. Several protesters were trapped and clubbed. As the rest struggled to get back inside Ferris Booth, the police lined up on the patio and clubbed and shoved students forward. In the crush a girl was propelled into one of the large glass doors of Ferris Booth, shattering it as she went through. A boy was then shoved into the jagged opening after her. Many students who had made it safely inside the buildings went up to the small lounge on the second floor. Through the large picture windows they could see swarms of police sweeping across South Field, clubbing students who could not keep up with the surge. The police continued their rush onto the patio just beneath the lounge. One student running for the door was caught and thrown head first against the building's stone wall.

---

bia University campus. IT IS RECOMMENDED THAT ALL MEMBERS OF THE FORCE ASSIGNED TO THIS DUTY BE REQUIRED TO WEAR THE REGULATION UNIFORM OF THE DAY [their emphasis].

However, a sudden emergency may occur which requires both uniform and non-uniform personnel to be pressed into immediate service in a crowd-control situation. It is recommended that all such non-uniformed members of the forces affix their shields to their outermost garment while so engaged.

About ten plainclothesmen chased a few demonstrators up to the steps of Furnald. Students were screaming epithets and hurling bottles at them from the windows above. The police charged into the lobby, even though the administration had expressly ordered that no police enter the dormitories. At least three carried guns in their hands. Ron Carver, who was standing just inside the doors, was surrounded and beaten by six of the plainclothesmen (his head required forty-two stitches). The police then charged through the lobby, swinging clubs. A few uniformed policemen also came inside and ran upstairs, breaking into at least one dormitory room and beating several students in the fourth-floor corridor. Six students were dragged out of the lobby and arrested. Policemen also entered the lobby of Carman Hall, another dormitory, forcing the students there into a bathroom, and ranged throughout the first six floors, beating at least two students in the halls.[11]

By 5:30 no students were left outside. Policemen stood guard in most buildings on campus and hundreds more relaxed on College Walk, waiting to be recalled. The night's action had resulted in 130 arrests in Hamilton, forty-seven arrests on campus and sixty-eight reported injuries (seventeen to police). At 5:45 Grayson Kirk announced:

> The University will continue operations as it has in recent days except that only the College Walk gates, at Broadway and Amsterdam, will be open. ID cards will be checked at the gates.

Commissioner Leary, asked by reporters as he was leaving the campus if he was satisfied with the behavior of his men, replied: "No comment. No word at all."

---

[11] Alexander Platt said after this police action that he had seen "gratuitous violence inside the dormitories." After making his announcement on the Sundial, Platt returned to Low Library, then came back out to observe the police action. After seeing beatings inside Furnald lobby he approached two high-ranking police officers and said that the police had not been authorized to enter the dormitories. The officers, standing less than a hundred yards from Furnald, said they "didn't see anything."

# Epilogue

THE DAY after the May 21 reoccupation of Hamilton Hall, Grayson Kirk issued the following statement:

> There may have been some disbelief on the part of some of the rebellious students that the University would ever discipline large numbers of students. I think it important for me to state that if disciplinary probation, suspension, or even permanent expulsion must be dealt to any number of students, this action will be taken. Columbia University must and will honor its commitment to educate those students who genuinely want what a great University can provide them.

Within two weeks the administration lived up to Kirk's tough statement and announced the suspensions of seventy-three students.[1] Thus, despite the steps that had been taken during the crisis toward the institution of disciplinary reform, the sixty-eight students arrested for the reoccupation of Hamilton were suspended before being proved guilty. And despite an earlier recommendation of the Joint Committee on Disciplinary Affairs that all future cases be judged in accordance with due process, the committee sanctioned the suspensions.[2] Other measures

---

[1] Of the seventy-three suspended, seven were disciplined for refusing to appear before their deans and the rest for their participation in the reoccupation of Hamilton Hall. Although 131 were arrested inside Hamilton on May 21–22, only sixty-eight were Columbia students.

[2] The Joint Committee on Disciplinary Affairs later backed down somewhat from this hard-line position. In mid-summer, it informed the disciplinary tribunals that had been established in each division of the University that "the tribunals are free to change the announced decision in particular cases if the circumstances warrant the change." Most appeals on the suspensions, as well as most disciplinary action against students who participated in the April 23–30 demontrations, were postponed until the early fall.

were taken as well to purge the campus of the radicals who had thrown it into upheaval. On May 23, two days after Hamilton II, the University news office issued a short statement:

> Columbia University has consulted its attorneys on the matter of Mark Rudd appearing on campus and expects to have an announcement on this matter in the near future.

The administration acted swiftly against the radicals on other fronts as well. Two days after the suspensions, the University registrar's office mailed a notice to the local draft boards of four students (Freudenberg, Grossner, Hyman and Rudd) stating that they were no longer enrolled at Columbia and were consequently eligible for the draft. Within four days after the suspensions, the University informed the Regents Scholarship Center of the State of New York that three of the four students (Rudd is a resident of New Jersey), because they were suspended, would no longer qualify for state scholarship assistance. And on May 26, a week before the end of the academic year, the following letter was delivered by hand to Morris Grossner in his dormitory room:

> We have been advised by the office of the dean that you have been suspended from Columbia College. You must, therefore, vacate your room no later than 12 noon on Tuesday, May 28, 1968.
>
> Very truly yours,<br>James G. Nugent, Director<br>University Residence Halls

In at least one instance, however, the administration proved that it was as interested in academic affairs as it was in discipline. On the same day that Mark Rudd received notification that he had been suspended, his parents received a copy of the following form letter sent each term to students with superior academic standing:

Dear Mark:
Although the events of the past few weeks make last semester seem a particularly long distance away, I still wish to congratulate you on your fine scholastic record for the fall term. It is particularly important at this time for us all to take cognizance of the primary function of this College. I hope you take appropriate pride in your academic accomplishment.

Very truly yours,<br>Henry S. Coleman<br>Acting Dean

* * *

## Epilogue

On another Tuesday, exactly eight weeks after Mark Rudd seized the microphone in St. Paul's Chapel, six weeks after the first occupation of Hamilton Hall, five weeks after the first bust, and two weeks after the second occupation of Hamilton, Columbia University tried to return to its 214-year-old traditions. A year of disorder was to come to a close June 4 with the measured pomp and ceremony of commencement exercises. For Grayson Kirk and his colleagues, it was a chance to plant a flag of law and order on a mountain of chaos; for the leftists, the opportunity to unfurl their red banners and depart triumphant.

Several weeks earlier, the administration had announced that commencement exercises would be held in the nearby Cathedral Church of St. John the Divine rather than at their customary outdoor location on Low Plaza and South Field. In a further effort to minimize the likelihood of disruption, Kirk announced a few days later that for the first time in his fifteen years as President he would not deliver the commencement address. Professor of History Richard Hofstadter agreed to deliver the address in Kirk's place. But, to replace commencement itself, students were planning their own ceremonies.

The campus was hot and brilliant as graduating students donned their slate-blue robes and strolled on College Walk with parents and friends. For the first time in weeks the campus was open to outsiders, and the atmosphere was relaxed. Melvin Morgulis stood by the Sundial hawking copies of a radical pamphlet, "Who Owns Columbia?" and Ted Kaptchuk, his mortarboard rimmed with "Columbia SDS" buttons, smiled at photographers. But, despite the carnival spirit, everyone knew that commencement was going to be the scene of yet another political protest. Students for a Restructured University had made arrangements for a "counter-commencement"; the Strike Coördinating Committee had scheduled a series of marches and a rally; and both groups planned a walkout from the official ceremonies.

Commencement began at 3 P.M. The entire area around the massive cathedral had been cordoned off by police barricades; onlookers were kept at a block's distance from the church doors. The rally which SCC had planned to hold immediately in front of St. John's was moved by police up to the Amsterdam Avenue gate of the campus at 116th Street, where several hundred people awaited the walkout. Inside the cathedral, rows of seats were slowly filling with the caps and gowns of three thousand graduates and, in the semi-dark, plainclothesmen stationed themselves at exits and in front of valuable reliquaries. As solemn organ music filled the cathedral—the third largest in the world—the long academic procession entered. At the end of the line of professors, Trustees and alumni, all in flowing robes, walked Grayson Kirk. He slowly seated himself near the altar and the ceremony began. Seen from the back of the church, Professor Richard Hofstadter was a point of blue as he stepped to the podium to speak:

> For a long time, Columbia University has been part of my life. . . .

Precisely at this moment, Ted Kaptchuk rose from his seat in the Columbia College section near the rear of the cathedral and asked students to walk out. One by one the mortarboards and tassels turned from Hofstadter to Kaptchuk and the students who rose to follow him. A few faculty members seated in the front rows also joined the walkout. Nearly three hundred students—mostly from the College and Barnard—filed out through the doors into the sunlight, pulled red armbands out from under their robes to tie around their billowy sleeves and shot their arms up to flash the "V" sign at cheering crowds lining the police barriers on Amsterdam Avenue. The students marched to the campus, while inside the dark cathedral Hofstadter continued as if uninterrupted:

> . . . A university is firmly committed to certain basic values of freedom, rationality, inquiry, discussion, and to its own internal order . . . the university is singular in being a collectivity that serves as a citadel of intellectual individualism. . . . It does in fact constitute a kind of free forum—and there are those who want to convert it primarily into a center of political action. . . . To start by assaulting its most accessible centers of thought and study and criticism is not only to show a complete disregard for the intrinsic character of the university but also to develop a curiously self-destructive strategy for social change. Columbia has been a distinguished university these many decades because it has been doing *some* things right. . . . What kind of a people would we be if we allowed this center of our culture and our hope to languish and fail?

As Hofstadter's words echoed through the somber interior, amplified a hundredfold by a coarse public address system, they were simultaneously broadcast in five smaller auditoriums scattered around the campus where parents and friends who could not fit into St. John's listened to the piped-in graduation ceremonies. Meanwhile, counter-commencement exercises were beginning in the open air.

The three hundred graduates who had walked out of the cathedral marched onto the campus, where they were met by hundreds of cheering parents and students and by the Strike Committee rally. A small loudspeaker played spirited march music as the graduates lined up around Alma Mater, behind an informal speakers' platform. The ceremony was opened by Rabbi Goldman and Professor Alexander Erlich, who had introduced an amnesty motion before the Ad Hoc Faculty Group in the tense hours before the first bust. Erlich said he was disturbed that Columbia was having two commencements but added, "It would have been a greater heartbreak if we had not had this particular commencement. This is the beginning of a new struggle for a more excellent Columbia."

Literary critic Dwight Macdonald addressed the group of graduates, now seated on the steps of Low Library, and the crowd of over one thousand standing on the plaza. He applauded the actions of the Columbia radicals but warned, to scattered boos, "You're not going to get any revolution." He said that such disturbances must not be allowed to get out of hand, for that could cause those in power to retaliate with repression. The second featured speaker, noted psychoanalyst and author Erich Fromm, told the group that what had happened at Columbia had been "a revolution in the name of life" in the midst of a culture that was becoming "a society of zombies." He observed that contemporary education and society tended to reduce the freedom men could find in their lives. Sometimes becoming intensely involved in a dramatic action may be the only valid way of behaving, Fromm declared, quoting Nietzsche: "There are times when anyone who does not lose his mind has no mind to lose."

Harold Taylor, former president of Sarah Lawrence College, conferred degrees on the dissident graduates:

> By virtue of the authority vested in me by the trustees of the human imagination, derived from the just powers of human nature and the constitution of mankind, I hereby confer upon all of you here present, in addition to all those absent, a degree of beatification through the arts, in order that the arts may flourish everywhere, and the delights of poetry, political action, dance, theater, and the insight of science and the fruits of technology may descend upon you, everywhere on earth and in the great space surrounding this small planet, for the best use to which it can all be put in the interest of human beings everywhere and to the ultimate benefit of all living things, with the rights and privileges pertaining to our union with nature and our peculiar human condition. . . .
>
> To others who wish to go through life without diplomas or certificates of any kind, I confer upon you a degree of happiness and freedom, and send the best wishes of this outdoor congregation of celebrants of freedom that you will never become addicted to or corrupted by the idea that in order to learn what you need to know, you have to commit yourself to an institution.
>
> May you all learn forever.

\* \* \*

So ended the 1967–68 academic year at Columbia. But despite its peaceful conclusion, there was something disturbing about the end. Perhaps it was simply that it was not an end at all. There was no evidence that with the coming of the summer vacation either the administration or the radicals had moved to abandon their confrontation style of operation. The second occupation of Hamilton Hall had provided proof that the administration, too, was locked in what the Independent Faculty Group called the "confrontation syndrome." Time and again Kirk had stepped into the trap set by the waiting radicals, responding in textbook fashion to the confrontation they had set up. One hundred students had purposely violated Kirk's rule on indoor demonstrations, and the administration singled out six political leaders to punish. Eight hundred students had seized control of University buildings, and the administration responded with a police action that brought it more damage, embarrassment and loss of support than SDS had been able to cause all year. Just as the campus was quieting, beginning to put tentative faith in new structural reforms, Kirk overturned the recommendations of his own disciplinary committee, shattering the very faith which might have replaced violent discontent. Finally, as the academic year neared its close, the administration had again played into the radicals' hands. It summoned four SDS leaders to appear for discipline just before the close of the academic year, when it was common knowledge that the radicals would use the issue for political ends. The result was the second occupation of Hamilton. Clearly, all these confrontations were welcomed by the radicals. But it was the administration's unsophisticated response that in each case made the difference between a difficult political incident and a major disaster.

After Hamilton II, most moderate students were not as willing to move behind the Strike Coördinating Committee as they had been after the first bust. Police violence had lost some of its radicalizing effect on students who had already witnessed brutality. Further, many felt that the protests were getting out of hand; they were queasy about taking to barricades and throwing bricks and were deterred by the prospects of suspension and arrest. The administration had its first real opportunity to isolate the radicals and win the support of moderates. In a press statement released shortly after the reoccupation, Vice President Truman tried his hand:

> The choice is fundamentally a simple one: Do you support the small group of persons who go to any lengths to destroy this University, or do you support those who are dedicated to the use of orderly processes to accomplish the aim of building a stronger and better Columbia, one that will continue to be a great university?

Will you put your trust in those who clearly have no respect for the values that the University represents, who have consistently employed misinformation and half-truths to inflame the situation, and who are willing to resort to coercion and destruction in order to impose their will on the great majority?

It was the same rhetoric, the same sort of black-and-white analysis that many radicals had made. Truman was still talking about the nihilistic minority versus the forces of law and order. His failure to offer any major concessions or to acknowledge that there might be something between nihilism and preservation of the *status quo* made it impossible for many students to move behind the administration. Ensnared in its old patterns of thought, the administration missed its opportunity to coopt the moderates.


The summer, many Columbia professors are fond of saying, is a time when nothing gets done. New York City is muggy and hot; the Columbia campus, empty and uninspiring. Despite pronouncements of dedication to the reconstruction of Columbia, most professors and students fled Morningside Heights as the temperature rose. The summer was to be the time for piecing together the shards of the academic urn. It was feared that unless proposals for widespread reform could be devised before September, the fall would bring a renewal of the struggle—more confrontation, more militancy and more repression. Some feared, however, that regardless of what schemes were invented, the spring had been just prologue to the fall.

Toward the end of the academic year, one group after another announced its intention to spend the summer "restructuring" the University. The Executive Committee of the Faculty became the first, when it announced in mid-May that it would create four task forces to work over the summer developing new mechanisms for University decision-making. Students for a Restructured University also set up a project funded by a $10,000 grant from the Ford Foundation and $30,000 from other sources. The administration then announced the formation of its own two-man task force, headed by Herbert Deane. With the Joint Committee on Disciplinary Affairs trying to formulate guidelines for campus protest and punishment, and committees within each division of the University searching for structural inadequacies to remedy, here was ample employment for anyone who wished to try his hand at renovating an institution whose structure almost everyone suddenly agreed was in need of improvement.

On August 5 representatives from each of the groups engaged in active research on the University held an open forum to outline their progress and their prospects. Each talked about the difficulties of reconstruction. Each spoke of new student-faculty committees, faculty senates, student governments and due process. Each announced confidently that at least some of his committee's proposals would be ready by the fall, and then each observed that he had absolutely no idea about what would be done with them, how they would be implemented, and whether they would be acceptable to anyone.

During the spring demonstrations a certain permanence became attached to the new diagonal path students had worn across South Field to bypass the University's roundabout brick walks. By summer the few tufts of grass which remained in its way had been dried up by heat and footsteps. With the coming of autumn, somewhere in the Columbia bureaucracy a decision would be made: stronger and higher fences would be built to force students to use the old paths, or the new stripe across South Field would be accepted as a legitimate and necessary thoroughfare. Given the attitudes and perspectives of the men in Low Library, it seems likely that they will choose the former course. [3] The life and vigor of the University strongly militate in favor of the latter.

[3] On 23 August 1968 Grayson Kirk announced his early retirement from the presidency of Columbia University. On that same date Andrew Cordier, the sixty-seven-year-old Dean of the School of International Affairs and former Under Secretary-General of the United Nations, was appointed Acting President. Since taking office, Dr. Cordier has made several conciliatory gestures, such as his request that criminal-trespass charges against 391 of the arrested students be dropped and his reinstatement by an act of "executive clemency" of forty-two of the seventy-three students who had been suspended following the riots.

# APPENDIX I

# Reflections on Student Radicalism

## by HERBERT A. DEANE

THE OCCUPATION of University buildings, the holding hostage of the Acting Dean of Columbia College, and the looting of the files of the President which took place at Columbia during April and May of this year are the most recent and most widely publicized in a series of protest activities that have moved far beyond the bounds of peaceful assembly, picketing, and expression of opinion. The first major action of this kind occurred three years ago when a mass demonstration in front of Low Library forced the cancellation of the NROTC awards ceremony. In the same period similar demonstrations and "sit-ins," involving the use of coercion to prevent University activities to which the protesters object or to accomplish aims to which they are committed, have taken place at many other universities and in the larger society, both in this country and abroad. While the events at Columbia are thus part of a much more general pattern, the circumstances and the actions have their own special character to which attention must also be given.

No one can doubt that the continuation and escalation of the war in Vietnam during the past three years have been the major factors responsible for the mood of bitter dissent and frustration of many students and teachers in American universities. Students in constantly increasing numbers have become convinced that the course pursued by the United States government in Vietnam is morally and politically indefensible. More significantly, many of these students and their teachers have come to believe that our political leaders have been a good deal less than candid in their statements about the war, and, at least until Senator

At the time of the crisis, Herbert A. Deane was a professor of government at Columbia University. He has since been made vice provost for academic affairs.

McCarthy's decision to launch his campaign for the Presidential nomination and President Johnson's decision not to seek re-election, many students were seriously questioning whether the ordinary democratic political process and the normal avenues of criticism and protest had any real capacity to influence the course of events and the directions of governmental policy. This growing sense of frustration and disillusion with normal political activities has been reflected in a sharp rise in the level and intensity of campus protests.

A second major factor in generating protest and disillusion on the campuses has been the urban and racial crisis in our country, culminating in the widespread riots of last summer and in the wave of destruction that followed the assassination of Dr. Martin Luther King, Jr., this April. Here again, many students and teachers, especially at urban universities located near ghetto areas, have become increasingly outraged by the miseries and injustices that mark the lives of slum-dwellers. Moreover, they have watched, with deepening frustration, the inability or unwillingness of government at every level to deal effectively with the problems. Despite the clear warnings and prescriptions in the Report of the Kerner Commission, most Congressmen and state and local legislators have been unwilling even to begin the massive and costly efforts required to deal with the economic ills of the slum areas that make up a large part of the central city. The principal lesson the legislative majorities seem to have learned from the riots is the need for more men and more sophisticated weapons to deal with the rioters.

One serious consequence of this highly charged campus mood and this deepening frustration with the ordinary processes of criticism and dissent has been that the more radical students have turned their energies to attacks on their universities and to efforts to interfere with university activities which have (or are alleged to have) some connection with the military establishment and the prosecution of the war in Vietnam or with the racial crisis in our cities. It is no accident that two of the major issues in the Columbia demonstrations this spring involved the University's ties to the Institute for Defense Analyses and the building of the gymnasium in Morningside Park. These issues were selected and emphasized because they could, when presented in highly simplified and stark terms, attract support from a much larger group of students who were opposed to the war in Vietnam and to racism. In the past year, the attacks of student radicals have been extended to the university itself and to its basic functions of teaching and research, even when these functions have little or no connection with the war or the urban crisis, on the ground that the university is deeply enmeshed in the ills of a corrupt social system since it is both an element in the "power-structure" of the society and the training-ground for the employees who man the middle and upper levels of the business, government, and military bureaucracies. To such attacks, when they pass from words to coercive and violent actions, the university is peculiarly vulnerable. It conducts its normal activities by peaceful means and rational discussion, and it has neither the ethos nor the instruments to deal effectively with violence or threats of violence. In our classrooms, libraries, and laboratories disciplinary problems have been virtually non-existent, and our lives together as teachers and students have been governed much more by unspoken conventions than by written rules.

It may be useful to explore some of the common assumptions and value-commitments that underlie the protest activities of radical students at Columbia and its sister institutions during the past three years. Again and again one is struck by the posture of complete self-righteousness and of unyielding moral absolutism in the attitudes and actions of the radical leaders. "I am totally right and completely moral, and you—if you disagree with me—are absolutely wrong and wicked. Therefore, there is no basis for any real discussion with you. You have no rights that I must respect, and you must agree to accept everything that I demand. If you fail to do so, I am justified in using any and all means to insure the triumph of right and justice, of which I am the embodiment and exponent." Faced with this complete moral certainty, one is tempted to cry out, in Cromwell's great phrase, "I beseech you, in the bowels of Christ, think it possible you may be mistaken." For, to the moral absolutist, force directed against the wicked and the unbelievers becomes, as Ortega warned us, the *prima* or *unica ratio* rather than the *ultima ratio*. Discussion, tolerance of difference, compromise, negotiation—all the methods by which civilized men seek to resolve or to sustain their differences so that they can go on living together and learning from one another despite their differences on many matters—have no part in the attitudes of the true believer. He is entranced by the Sorelian notion that politics—the civil and civilizing activity, *par excellence*—is inherently and irreparably a corrupt and corrupting business since it necessarily involves discussion and compromise with other individuals and groups. For him, as for Sorel, only "pure violence," commitment to myth and non-rational appeals, and "black ingratitude" towards all reformers and mediators are strong enough medicine to polarize society into the two hostile groups of savage repressors and advocates of heroic violence and so to save us all from the decadence that he sees as the inevitable end of compromise and rationality.

Closely associated with this moral absolutism is the assumption—as pernicious as it is ancient (and dear to the hearts of anti-radical crusaders like the first Senator McCarthy)—that the pursuit of ends that one regards as supremely good and desirable legitimates the use of all means, including coercion and violation of the rights and freedoms of others, which one believes to be necessary to accomplish his goals. Radical students, who, not so long ago, were among the strongest supporters of civil liberties and freedom of expression for all, and particularly for unpopular minorities, have on some recent occasions abandoned these libertarian principles and resorted to the use of force to prevent those with whom they disagree from exercising their freedom to act and to speak. Because they feel strongly that NROTC has no right to exist on the Columbia campus, they have a "right" to disrupt its awards ceremony even though the NROTC students, their parents, and their friends wish this ceremony to take place. Because of their deep hostility to the war in Vietnam and, in some cases, to all wars except those of "national liberation," they have a "right" to prevent other students from being interviewed on the campus by representatives of the armed forces or of certain corporations and government agencies. They are unmoved by the fact that both the faculty and their fellow-students have overwhelmingly endorsed the principle of "open recruitment" on the campus.

Behind this assumption of a "right" to interfere forcibly with the exercise of the rights of others, even of the large majority, stands the more general postulate that freedom of expression for all members of the community is a "bourgeois" notion and that freedom belongs properly only to those whose views are "right" and "progressive." The ill-concealed elitism of this view is a clear echo of the Leninist doctrine that only the enlightened vanguard understands the historical situation and the mission of the proletariat, while the masses, corrupt and ignorant, must be led, manipulated, and coerced for their own eventual good. And, curiously enough, the elitism of some of our contemporary radical students also echoes the claim that only the elite have a right to freedom found in the pseudo-doctrines of Fascism, supposedly the antithesis of Leninism. (Do we have here an example of the dialectical principle of the interpenetration of opposites?) This view that freedom rightly belongs only to the enlightened minority is clearly manifested when some of the leaders of SDS, for example, talk about the stupidity and political backwardness of their "unradicalized" fellow students and when they admit that they would not be influenced by a student referendum in which their views were decisively rejected.

These attitudes of moral rigidity and self-righteousness, unwillingness to engage in meaningful discussion, and contempt for the rights and liberties of others, including the large majority of faculty and students, were all obvious during the period from April 23 to April 30 when the Columbia buildings were being occupied. The student leaders of the demonstrations were never willing to engage in genuine discussion of their original "demands" and were even less willing to modify those demands or to seek for a compromise solution. The leader of SDS publicly dismissed, with contempt, the last in a series of mediation proposals set forth by the *ad hoc* Faculty Group. The record clearly indicates, on the other hand, that the administrative officers and the Trustees of the University made significant changes in their original positions and genuine efforts to accept in large measure the proposals set forth by the *ad hoc* group. The leaders of the demonstrations presented to the University—that is, to the large majority of the faculty and the students as well as to the administration and the Trustees—only a choice between two almost impossible alternatives: complete capitulation not only to their specific demands, including amnesty, but also to their continuing claims to "power," or calling in the police in order to respond with force to force. Every member of this University was unhappy with the latter alternative, but hardly a single voice was raised in the long hours of faculty discussion in favor of the first course, even by those who were to some degree sympathetic with one or another of the protesters' specific demands.

No one with any sense would argue that Columbia University on April 22, 1968, was a perfect institution which had no need of changes in its organizational patterns, in its means of communication among administrators, faculty, and students, in its relations with the surrounding community, or in its academic program and requirements. Many of its administrative officers and some members of its faculty had, for years, been aware of the need for revisions and reforms and had spent countless hours in discussing the necessary changes and in bringing some of them into being. But if Columbia was not perfect, if it had defects and required reforms, it was like every other human institution since the world began. And it is simply untrue to say that this University was so hopelessly corrupt that it needed to be destroyed or revolutionized. Any university, and especially one as large and complex as Columbia, is difficult to change rapidly, and this is due far more to the resistance to novelty and to the capacity for long-continued discussion which are natural to most academics than to callousness or insensitivity to problems. (In 1908, the noted English classicist, F. M. Cornford, in his delightful book *Microcosmographia Academica,* warned young academic politicians about the inherent conservatism of scholarly communities; so little has the situation changed that the book is still well worth reading sixty years later in its sixth edition.)

In conclusion, a few words should be said about the likely political consequences of the attitudes and activities of "revolutionary" student activists. It is obvious that nothing approaching the classic revolutionary situation exists in the United States today. The working-class, especially the organized working-class, is deeply committed to the *status quo* and has achieved substantial gains during the last thirty-five years; as a consequence, organized labor is a strongly anti-revolutionary force in the society. They and the middle-class (and the line separating them is often difficult to draw) have no desire to blow up the existing social system; indeed, if they confront efforts to bring about a revolution, they are likely to respond in a sharply negative fashion. The most serious trouble-spot in the society is found in the urban slums, and particularly among the inhabitants of the ghetto. Their frustration and misery, however, are much more likely to take the form of riots and violent protests than that of organized revolution to replace the social and political system. The most likely consequences of violent protests by the left, such as the demonstrations led by student "revolutionaries," are, therefore, a resurgence in ultra-right-wing movements and an even more widespread swing towards conservatism in this country. We already see ominous signs of these developments, such as the sharp rise in former Governor Wallace's standing in the national polls between April and August 1968, and the surprising strength of the pro-Reagan forces across the nation before and during the Republican convention of 1968. It should be remembered that even in France, where student radicals received some support and encouragement from the workers and their unions, the major result of their violent demonstrations was the resounding victory won by General De Gaulle. Some of our young revolutionaries may tell us that they welcome a "temporary" strengthening of reaction, since the far right will eliminate or weaken the social-democrats, liberals, and conservatives and thus sharply polarize society into two completely hostile segments, the forces of revolution and those of reaction, and that they will emerge victorious from this confrontation. Our response can only be that right-wing repression would destroy all that we value in American society, and that the ultimate victory of revolution over reaction in this country is just as unlikely as it was in Germany before Hitler, when the Communist Party defended its tactical alliances with the Nazis by the unrealistic argument that Fascism, having eliminated all the enemies of Communism, would prove unable to deal with the objective social problems, and that its collapse would permit the German Communist Party to emerge as the "residual legatee."

## APPENDIX II

# Symbols of the Revolution

## by MARK RUDD

DURING THE COURSE of the Columbia strike a whole set of symbols and slogans inevitably emerged. It is difficult for someone who wasn't there, or more accurately, for someone who's not part of the New Left to understand these symbols and their significance. Red flags, red armbands, "Up against the wall, motherfucker," communes, all became integral parts of the strike, helped to define the strike.

### UP AGAINST THE WALL, MOTHERFUCKER!

Perhaps nothing upset our enemies more than this slogan. To them it seemed to show the extent to which we had broken with their norms, how far we had sunk to brutality, hatred, and obscenity. Great! *The New York Times* put forward three interpretations of the slogan, the only one of which I remember is the one which had to do with putting the administration up against the wall before a firing squad—apparently our fascistic "final solution." The truth is almost as bad: the slogan defined Grayson Kirk, David Truman, the Trustees, many of the faculty, the cops as our enemies. Liberal solutions, "restructuring," partial understandings, compromise are not allowed anymore. The essence of the matter is that we are out for social and political revolution, nothing less. This, of course, puts the administration of Columbia University in somewhat of a bind: if they accede to any of our demands they will be the first representatives of the ruling class to have fallen under to a motley mob of student rebels. Secondly, they will only be whetting our

At the time of the crisis, Mark Rudd was a junior in Columbia College and chairman of the Columbia chapter of Students for a Democratic Society (SDS).

insatiable appetites. Better to beat us down: 1,100 busted, hundreds to be thrown out of school.

"Up against the wall, motherfucker" defines the terms. It puts the administration and the interests they represent on one side, leftist students and the interests of humanity on the other. Those undecided in the middle are forced to choose sides. The great victory of the strike was that so many joined our side and so few supported the administration (the few hundred or so in the "Majority Coalition" were the most isolated and pathetic people on campus). The "organized" left on campus had been small—perhaps 150 were active in SDS, if that—but the number who identified with the left, with opposition to the war and to racism and now, the whole structure of capitalism, grew to immense proportions.

"Up against the wall, motherfucker" has had a long odyssey. It originated in the ghetto, with the cops using it when they stop and search or bust people. Columbia strikers, to their mixed reaction, found the cops really do use it. LeRoi Jones got two years in jail for using it in a poem:

> The magic words are
> Up against the wall, motherfucker,
> This is a stick-up.

(Of course, when quoted in *The New York Times,* the poem contained the word "mother-blank.") An SDS chapter on the lower East side, a group organizing hippies, winos, drop-outs, neighborhood people with a program of revolutionary politics and life-style, adopted the slogan as its name. We picked it up in our chapter, using it for the title of one edition of our newspaper, the edition which appeared on April 22, 1968, the day before the demonstrations began. In that paper appeared an open letter to Grayson Kirk in which I defined our goal as socialism, and Kirk and the ruling class as our enemies. The letter ended with the quote from LeRoi Jones. From there, the slogan became a natural for the strike, ranging in use from graffiti to shouts of the entire Math commune against the police.

We co-opted the word "motherfucker" from the ghetto much as we adopted the struggle of blacks and the other oppressed as our own. When young people start calling those in power, the people whose places we're being trained to fill, "Motherfucker" you know the structure of authority is breaking down. We recognize that our own quest for freedom puts us against "the man" just as black people and Vietnamese fight him. The war comes home.

The obscenity, too, helped define our struggle. Finally, we could say in public what we had been saying among ourselves. We could use our own language, much more expressive than the repressed language of Grayson Kirk. When I told a meeting of the Ad Hoc Faculty Group that the talks we were having with them were bullshit, I expressed myself thoroughly, naturally. The reaction to the style was stronger than the reaction to the content. All forms of authority, traditional "respect" (you show respect, obviously, by not using your own language), had broken down. The norms of repression and domination, maintaining the hierarchical structure of the classroom and the society, were swept aside. The revolution frightened some, broke others, freed many.

### RED FLAG, RED ARM-BAND

The arm-band craze swept the campus just as the hula-hoop fad swept the country a few years ago. First the blue arm-bands of "peace" which very soon took on the opposite meaning when adopted by the Majority Coalition: reaction, the status-quo, the war, The Right. Next came the white arm-bands of the faculty and the regular city plainclothes cops who manned the faculty line with them. Green arm-bands were for amnesty—and were worn by a peculiar breed of strike-supporters known variously as the "Sundial crowd," "the step-sitters," or just "the green arm-bands." They held a vigil at the Sundial and pledged themselves to stand between those in the buildings and the cops if a bust came. At the time of the bust, black arm-bands of mourning appeared, but they did not last past the "shock" Grayson Kirk is so fond of talking about. Then there are the red arm-bands.

People have asked me what the red arm-band signifies, and I can say without any hesitation that it means Revolution. They began in Math and Low, the two most militant communes, as a first articulation of the fact that the strike transcends the limits of simple student-oriented issues and demands. In effect, the strike is a protest against the entire society—its wars, exploitation, racism—and our position in it—young people involved in meaningless studies at an exploitative university being channeled into taking our places in business, government, etc. The red arm-band and red flag identify us with historical struggles for freedom as well as struggles going on right now throughout the world.

Red flags and flags of the National Liberation Front of South Vietnam flew over Mathematics and Fayerweather Halls. What an incredible sight! One might ask, aren't you only doing that for the shock value? Or, aren't you scared of alienating people? There is no shock value except that of waking people up to the fact that there is a revolutionary movement in existence and that we, hundreds of students of an elitist university, are involved in the struggle for liberation. Many liberals still do not understand this struggle, still believe that the real fight is to get a few reforms in the university's structure. As far as alienating people, most people are alienated from the revolutionary Left, originally, precisely because they have been taught that reforms can be accomplished within the system. But identifying the nature of the Left, showing its relevance to people's lives wins support for us, since so many young people are dissatisfied and looking for alternatives, looking for a way to fight the system which is so clearly oppressive.

The more people are exposed to the symbols of revolution, and the more they deal with real individuals involved in a revolutionary movement, and not abstract nouns like "Communists," the less they fear those symbols and those people. The red flags at Columbia helped prepare people for acceptance of us as revolutionaries, since they already knew what we were saying was just.

Our red arm-bands also help to identify us as Columbia strikers, sometimes with good, sometimes harmful results. At demonstrations elsewhere in the city we are treated as something of an elite corps by other demonstrators and cops alike. Thus, we're usually among the first to get busted. A striker wearing a red arm-band was busted in a city park for sitting on the grass while making out with a girl.

### COMMUNES

I was unfortunate in not being able to spend the period of liberation of the buildings in one of the communes. During that time, communities grew up in which people ate, slept, discussed, debated, fought, got busted together. For many, it was the first communal experience of their lives—a far cry from the traditional life-style of Morningside Heights, that of individuals retiring into their rooms or apartments. One brother remarked to me, "The communes are a better high than grass."

I really am not competent to discuss the life of the communes adequately, so I'll stay with their political significance. Historically, the Paris Commune of 1871 has long been a symbol of revolutionary will, dedication, and struggle. If just for the identification with the Paris Commune and the international socialist revolutionary movement, "commune" is a proud name for our liberated buildings. But the communal life, especially the political life, gives the communes a unique political significance.

The communes were the locus of political power. This was one of the first times in our experience that "participatory democracy" had been put into practice. Questions such as negotiations, the demands, whether to resist the cops, the goals of the strike, the goals of the movement were debated fully by nearly everyone in the commune. The original Strike Coördinating Committee had an understanding that no major policy could be changed or initiated unless each of the four liberated buildings agreed. That meant hours, even full days, before decisions could be made. It also meant intense discussion, sometimes lasting as long as twelve hours, in which people participated and grew in their political understanding.

Like the red flags, our use of the word "commune" has accustomed people to a concept alien to the culture. The bailiff in the special part of the criminal court which hears only Columbia cases occasionally admonishes people for talking with, "This is a courtroom, not a commune." He gets the same kind of kick out of saying "commune" as he would get with the word "fuck."

### EXTERNAL SYMBOLS

People outside Columbia generally don't have the foggiest notion of what has happened in the insurrection or what it is about. Even those potentially sympathetic, having had to rely on information from the mass media, have formed opinions not far from those of Grayson Kirk, David Truman, etc. Common interpretations, including Rites of Spring, general unfocused reaction to the war in Vietnam, a plot by national SDS, and manipulation by a nihilist hard-core to destroy academic freedom, as well as other fantasies, have been put forth by the press in an attempt to dilute the strike of its political significance. As I've tried to express, the strike, to the radicals, went far beyond the campus: it was an insurrection against the repressive structure of this society; specifically, against racism and imperialism. Since journalists lack the tools to report events outside the accepted limits of action and thought, and since many newspapers are committed to an ideological position, as is the liberal *New York Times,* the truth of the Columbia rebellion had a hard time coming through.

The press created two predominant symbols of the strike, both of which helped to divert attention from the issues. The first is that of the strike leader as a symbol of the strike, i.e., focusing attention on my actions, words, past history, creating stories about plots, "Maoist-cores," etc., all of which masks the political significance and mass nature of the strike.

My role in the strike, along with other strike leaders, was to try to pull together a political organization out of the huge mass of students put into motion by the events of the initial stage—the occupation of the buildings. Secondarily, it was to serve as spokesman of the strike to press and others. One great failing on my part (of which there were many) was the fact that I allowed this role as spokesman to be converted into that of symbol. To some extent, though, this was inevitable, since the press by nature has to point to one man to exemplify and personify an entire movement. Ideologically, however, the press is not equipped to see that the strike is a mass movement, that we had developed forms of democracy in which each person could and did participate in decision-making, that the strike came out of the failings and problems in our society, not the plottings of a well-organized cabal.

The view of one person as symbol allows the causal responsibility to be shifted onto that person. Thus, the administration very much wanted to make me and the SDS leadership appear as a nihilist "hard-core of 35" (David Truman), somewhat less than a minority. We must be fantastic hypnotists to have tricked hundreds of people into following us. As a matter of fact, the strike leadership emerged on the spot as a result of the needs of the political situation: the SDS Steering Committee did not meet after April 24, and SDS as an organization ceased to function.

In the minds of Grayson Kirk, Drew Pearson, and J. Edgar Hoover, one diabolical madman sat down last October, worked out a plan which would be executed to the week, the following April, and closed the University by manipulating the entire student body into confrontation with the police. It didn't matter to them that the position paper I wrote in October had been rejected; mostly, they want to deny that the demands we are raising are valid.

One further proof that those in power hold to an individual-conspiracy theory is the fact that they chose to come down hard on "the leaders." Eliminate the leaders and you eliminate the movement. (No matter what they say, their actions show that they recognize the existence of a movement. But to David Truman, the radical movement must be a few hard-core leaders.) Thus the extremely heavy riot charges the New York City Police, District Attorney-Columbia Trustee Frank Hogan brought down on me. Thus the attempt to throw strike leaders out of school.

Mass political movements cannot be comprehended by those we are fighting. They think only in terms of power-brokering, behind the scenes. Principled spokesmen, responsible to a base which effectively makes the decisions are a far cry from the facts of decision-making locked away in Kirk's files.More fundamentally, those in power cannot conceive of individuals directly acting in their own interest—against racism, the gym, the war in Vietnam, the arbitrary power of the University. According to Kirk, you oppose the war in Vietnam by word, not by deed. Most fundamental of all, however, we acted against the interests of those we were fighting—seizing their property, fighting their exploitative policies, fighting their power over us, so they could do nothing but capitulate or fight—with every weapon at their disposal.

Lies, slander, threats, the cops, suspensions, the courts, the DA, liberal coöptation (channelling dissent into harmless discussions of "restructuring"), all were used, some effectively, some not. But in spite of the tremendous power and organization on the side of the administration, the radical movement grew.

The other symbol of the strike dwelt on by the press and others was our tactics. To them, minority action in seizing buildings constituted an absolute crime. This became the major issue of the strike, at least to those who obtained their information from the press. As a matter of fact, many of those on campus understood that we had acted only after legitimate means had been exhausted. More important, those in the buildings understood their action as an attempt to fight policies which were criminal in themselves—Columbia's expansion into the community, her support of the war in Vietnam. Who ever measured the violence done the victims of Columbia's policies? How can you weigh that violence against the act of seizing a few buildings? Depriving a few individuals of their "right" to an education (i.e., "I paid my $1,900") is certainly a lesser evil than allowing Columbia to continue its policies.

In a sense, by seizing the buildings we took back our university. Believing the propaganda of the "academic community," we decided that we had had enough of bureaucrats and trustees deciding policies against our interests.

But the documents, why did you take the documents? Because they were the proof of our thesis about a ruling elite in this country. Because they show that decisions such as building a gymnasium on public land are made behind the scenes, with threats, cajolings, manufactured propaganda (one of the liberated memoranda concerned an interview Kirk arranged with A. M. Rosenthal, managing editor of *The New York Times,* for a news story defending the gym). Because they belong in public hands, since they concern everyone. The public should know how Kirk picks the new president of the Asia Foundation from Socony Mobil nominees (it should also know what the Asia Foundation does, what the CIA uses it for). These documents should become the new textbook on the American governmental process, refuting David Truman's claims of counter-vailing interests freely competing for power. Do the interests of black people in Harlem appear in Kirk's correspondence on the gym, or those of the people of Vietnam in his correspondence on the Asia Foundation? In Kirk's files pluralism appears as a lie created to trick us into believing that "the American system" is a democracy.

If Grayson Kirk had had a mistress and we had found his letters to her while we spent time in his office, we certainly wouldn't have released them.

# *Chronology*

### Tuesday, April 23

Noon. SDS Sundial rally
12:40 P.M. March on gymnasium site, Morningside Park
1:35 P.M. Sit-in begins in Hamilton Hall
1:40 P.M. Dean Coleman held hostage in his office
2:50 P.M. Six Demands formulated; students decide not to leave until demands are met

### Wednesday, April 24

5:30 A.M. White students evicted from Hamilton by black students
6:15 A.M. Students break into Low Library and seize Kirk's offices
7:45 A.M. Police enter Kirk's offices but make no arrests
3:00 P.M. College Faculty meets
3:30 P.M. Coleman released
8:00 P.M. Administration makes unsuccessful compromise offer to black students
10:00 PM. Avery Hall occupied

### Thursday, April 25

2:00 A.M. Fayerweather Hall occupied
4:00 P.M. Formation of Ad Hoc Faculty Group; formulation of its first proposals to end demonstrations
7:00–8:00 P.M. Strikers reject Ad Hoc Faculty proposals
8:00 P.M. Harlem activists address rally at Columbia gates, march across campus
9:30 P.M. Counter-demonstrators attempt to invade Fayerweather

### Friday, April 26

1:05 A.M. Vice President Truman announces impending police action to Ad Hoc Faculty
1:05 A.M. Mathematics Hall occupied

2:15 A.M. First negotiating session between faculty and students held in Math Library
3:00 A.M. Police charge crowd at Low Library
3:20 A.M. Truman announces police action canceled; gym construction suspended
1:10 P.M. H. Rap Brown and Stokely Carmichael enter campus
4:00 P.M. Galanter committee submits proposals for tripartite commission on discipline

### Saturday, April 27

1:00 A.M. Mark Rudd delivers "bullshit" speech before Ad Hoc Faculty
10:30 A.M. Petersen-Trustee statement released on campus
11:30 A.M. Faculty cordon around Low Library established to prevent access to demonstrators
6:00 P.M. Rally of anti-war demonstrators held near campus
11:00 P.M. Faculty negotiators report deadlock on major issues

### Sunday, April 28

8:00 A.M. Ad Hoc Faculty announces final resolutions ("bitter pill") to end crisis
10:00 A.M. Joint Faculties meet in Law School
5:15 P.M. Majority Coalition establishes cordon around Low
7:00–8:00 P.M. Demonstrators attempt to pass food through counter-demonstrators' cordon into Low

### Monday, April 29

3:30 P.M. Kirk issues negative response to bitter pill
6:30 P.M. Strikers reject bitter pill
11:30 P.M. Ad Hoc Faculty appeals to Mayor Lindsay, tables amnesty motion

### Tuesday, April 30

2:30–5:30 A.M. New York City police remove students from occupied buildings and clear campus; 712 arrested, 148 injured
Noon. Ad Hoc Faculty meets in McMillin; strike resolution presented and withdrawn
2:00 P.M. Joint Faculties meet in St. Paul's Chapel, establish Executive Committee of the Faculty
8:00 P.M. Students hold strike meeting in Wollman Auditorium

### Wednesday, May 1–Sunday, May 5

Classes suspended in most of University; academic calendar and grading procedures revised to permit completion of semester; Executive Committee establishes fact-finding commission

### Monday, May 6–Thursday, May 16

University reopens but thousands of students participate in boycott of classes; discipline commission proposes that criminal charges against students be dropped, and that most strikers be placed on disciplinary probation; Kirk rejects proposals, then accepts them; moderate Students for a Restructured University splits with Strike Coordinating Committee

### Friday, May 17

Community activists seize Columbia-owned apartment building, Columbia students stage sit-in at tenement in support; police move in within hours and arrest 117 (56 students)

### Tuesday, May 21

Students reoccupy Hamilton Hall in protest against disciplining of four SDS leaders; threatened with suspension, demonstrators refuse to leave; police empty building, clear campus as students erect barricades and fires break out in two campus buildings; 138 arrested, 66 later suspended

### Tuesday, June 4

Columbia holds 214th Commencement Exercises; several hundred graduating students walk out of ceremonies and hold counter-commencement on Low Plaza

### Friday, August 23

Grayson Kirk announces his early retirement as President of Columbia University, and Andrew Cordier is appointed Acting President

# Cast of Charactors

## STUDENTS

Ray Brown, class of '68, member of SAS and Hamilton Hall Steering Committee.
Lewis Cole '67, member of SDS and Strike Steering Committee.
Nick Freudenberg '70, vice-chairman of SDS.
Dave Gilbert '66, member of Strike Coordinating Committee.
Ted Gold '68, former vice-chairman of SDS.
Juan Gonzalez '68, member of Strike Steering Committee.
Morris Grossner '69, member of SDS Steering Committee.
Tom Hayden, graduate of Michigan University, a founder of SDS, leader of Mathematics Hall strikers.
John Jacobs (JJ) '69, member of SDS.
Ted Kaptchuk '68, former chairman of SDS.
Tony Papert '67, former member of Progressive Labor Party and leader of Low Library strikers.
Robby Roth '70, member of SDS and negotiator for Low Library strikers.
Mark Rudd '69, chairman of SDS.
Bill Sales, graduate student, member of Hamilton Hall Steering Committee.
Jon Shils '68, member of Strike Steering Committee.
Paul Vilardi '68, leader of Majority Coalition.
Cicero Wilson '70, chairman of SAS and member of Hamilton Hall Steering Committee.

## ADMINISTRATION

Henry Coleman, acting dean of Columbia College.
Herbert Deane, professor of government, former acting dean of Graduate Faculties, now vice provost for academic affairs.
George Fraenkel, dean of Graduate Faculties.
Grayson Kirk, President of the University.
William Petersen, chairman of the Board of Trustees.
Alexander Platt, associate dean of Columbia College.
David Truman, vice president and provost of the University.

## FACULTY

Robert Belknap, AHFG,[1] professor of Russian.
Daniel Bell, AHFG, ECF,[2] professor of sociology, author of *The End of Ideology* and *The Reforming of General Education*.
Eric Bentley, Brander Mathews Professor of Dramatic Literature, translator of Brecht and author of *The Theatre of Commitment*.
Sam Coleman, associate in philosophy.
Alexander Dallin, AHFG, ECF, Adlai E. Stevenson Professor of International Relations, author of *The Soviet Union at the United Nations*.
Robert Fogelson, AHFG, assistant professor of history, advisor to the President's Commission on Civil Disorders.
Morton Fried, professor of anthropology, author of *Political Anthropology: An Evolutionary View*.
Eugene Galanter, head of Galanter committee, professor of psychology, taught course in *Individual Motives and Their Socio-Political Amalgamation*.
Marvin Harris, AHFG, professor of anthropology, author of *The Nature of Cultural Things*.
C. Lowell Harriss, professor of economics, author of *Money and Banking*.
Richard Hofstadter, De Witt Clinton Professor of American History, author of *Anti-Intellectualism in American Life, The Paranoid Style in American Politics*.
Carl Hovde, member of Galanter committee, associate professor of English, appointed Dean of Columbia College, July, 1968.
Peter Kenen, AHFG, professor of economics, author of *International Economics*.
Seymour Melman, AHFG, professor of industrial engineering, author of *The Depleted Society*.
Walter Metzger, AHFG, ECF, professor of history, teaches colloquium on American Civilization, authority on academic freedom and university structures.
Orest Ranum, associate professor of history, author of *Richelieu and the Councillors of Louis XIII*.
David Rothman, AHFG, faculty negotiator, associate professor of history, author of *Politics and Power*.
Warner Schilling, professor of government, author of *Strategy, Politics and Defense Budgets*.

[1] AHFG: member of Ad Hoc Faculty Group.
[2] ECF: member of the Executive Committee of the Faculty.

Allan Silver, AHFG, faculty negotiator, assistant professor of sociology.
Michael Sovern, co-chairman of Executive Committee, professor of law, author of *Legal Restraints on Racial Discrimination in Employment*.
Fritz Stern, Seth Low Professor of History, author of *The Politics of Cultural Despair*.
Lionel Trilling, member of Galanter committee, ECF, Edward Woodberry Professor of Literature and Criticism, author of *Beyond Culture* and *The Liberal Imagination*.
Immanuel Wallerstein, AHFG, negotiator with students in Hamilton Hall, associate professor of sociology, author of *Africa: Politics of Unity*.
Alan Westin, chairman of AHFG, faculty negotiator, co-chairman of Executive Committee, professor of public law and government, author of *Privacy and Freedom*.
Robert Zevin, AHFG, lecturer in economics.

## COMMUNITY LEADERS AND CITY OFFICIALS

William Booth, New York City commissioner of human rights.
Kenneth Clark, professor of psychology, City College of New York.
Sid Davidoff, member of Mayor's Urban Task Force.
Sanford Garelik, chief inspector, New York Police Department.
Barry Gottehrer, head of Mayor's Urban Task Force.
Theodore Kheel, labor mediator.
Jay Kriegel, member of Mayor's Urban Task Force.
Basil Paterson, state senator from Harlem.
Percy Sutton, Manhattan borough president.
Eldridge Waithe, assistant chief inspector, New York Police Department.

# Index

Ad Hoc Faculty Group, 92 ff., 96–7, 99–102, 104–6, 112–13, 134–5, 144, 146–8, 153–5, 159, 161, 165–6, 168, 171–2, 178–80, 204–12; negotiations with strikers, 110–13, 139, 152–3; steering committee of, 135, 142, 155–9, 205–6, 211
administration, *see* Kirk, Grayson; Truman, David B.; Fraenkel, George; etc.
amnesty, 52, 78–80, 82, 90, 97, 135, 140–1, 143, 152–3, 162–3, 167, 173, 174–5, 179, 180, 251
Avery Hall, 85–6, 125, 129, 229; April 30 police action at, 190–1

Belknap, Robert, 100, 152, 153
Bell, Daniel, 69, 74, 155; proposal before College faculty, 76–9
"Bitter Pill," 157–8, 159, 161–2, 168 ff., 174–5
Booth, William, 71, 110
Brown, H. Rap, 19–20, 133–4
Brown, Ray, 51, 55, 81, 254, 271–2

Colahan, Thomas, 41, 45–6, 70
Coleman, Henry, 40, 49–51, 54–5, 56–7, 63, 73, 75–6, 77, 79, 81, 98–9, 107, 108, 258–9
Columbia College faculty, 229; April 24 meeting, 76–80
Commencement, 278–81
confrontation politics, 32–3
conspiracy, 36n.
counter-demonstrators, 89, 99–103, 163, 165, 186, 188–9; *see also* Majority Coalition; Students for a Free Campus
Cox Commission, *see* fact-finding commission

Deane, Herbert, 69–70, 283, 285–90
discipline, 21–22, 25, 33–4, 41, 52, 53, 72, 77, 78, 83, 87, 92, 135–6, 156, 171, 172, 245–52, 259, 277; ultimate authority, 79, 132–3, 143–4, 154, 170–1, 176, 247–50; *see also* Joint Committee on Disciplinary Affairs; tripartite commission

Executive Committee of the Faculty, 213–14, 217–18, 230–4, 235, 250, 283

fact-finding commission (Cox Commission), 207, 235–6, 252n.
faculty, *see* Ad Hoc Faculty Group; Columbia College faculty; Executive Committee of the Faculty; Independent Faculty Group; Joint Faculties; Low Library, faculty cordon
Fayerweather Hall, 88, 94–5, 99–101, 123–5, 129, 162–3, 184–5; April 30 police action at, 191–2; fire in, 268–9
Fraenkel, George, 74, 87–8, 102, 146, 248–9

Galanter, Eugene, 59, 69, 88, 132, 228–9
Garelik, Sanford, 110, 197, 243–5, 267
Gilbert, Dave, 66, 70, 97, 220
Gold, Ted, 37, 46, 51, 94, 152, 263
Gonzalez, Juan, 104–5, 111, 138, 260, 266
Goodell, Warner, 23–4, 85
Gottehrer, Barry, 71, 73, 109, 179, 198, 262
gymnasium, 77, 78–9, 82, 87, 90, 92, 115–16, 144–6, 153–4, 156–7, 159, 163, 170–1, 257–8; April 23 demonstration at site, 44–7;

gymnasium (*continued*)
    demonstrations against, 20, 53, 82; history, 18–20, 82

Hamilton Hall, black students in, 87, 126–8, 150, 169, 182–3, 186–7, 201; occupation of April 23, 49 ff.; occupation of May 21, 255 ff.; steering committee, 71, 74–5, 134, 145–6, 153–4, 172, 187, 235–6
Harlem militants, 58, 73, 82, 92, 97–9, 150, 183–4
Hayden, Tom, 29, 111, 112, 129, 151
Hofstadter, Richard, 212–13, 279–80
Hovde, Carl, 89, 132

IDA Six, 34, 153, 251
Independent Faculty Group, 233–4, 282
indoor demonstrations, ban on, 21, 52
Institute for Defense Analyses (IDA), 53, 78, 82, 163; history, 15–18; March 27 demonstration against, 17, 21, 23–4, 25, 32, 33, 52, 257

Jacobs, John ("JJ"), 62, 106, 107, 118, 166
Joint Committee on Disciplinary Affairs, 245–52, 277, 283; *see also* discipline; tripartite commission
Joint Faculties, 146–7, 158, 159–61, 212–17

Kaplow, Jeffry, 94–5, 106–7, 166, 208–9
Kaptchuk, Ted, 31, 35, 46–7, 280
Kenen, Peter, 140, 149–50, 159–60, 200
Kheel, Theodore, 172–3
Kirk, Grayson, 8, 24–5, 67, 72, 82, 87, 89, 90, 108, 170–1, 173, 197, 198–9, 200, 215, 217, 234, 247–50, 259, 271, 276, 277; take-over of offices, 64, 110, 115, 118, 122, 132–3, 148–9

Low Library, April 30 police action at, 188–90, 192–3; faculty cordon at, 135, 146, 165–6, 168–9, 174; Majority Coalition cordon at, 163–5, 168–9, 173–4, 177–8; occupation of Kirk's office, 64 ff., 86, 118 ff., 200; security entrance, 44, 64, 114–16, 188–90

Majority Coalition, 96–7, 136–7, 163–5, 168–9, 173–4, 177–8, 182, 256, 257; *see also* Vilardi, Paul
Mathematics Hall, 107, 110–13, 125–6, 182, 201–2; April 30 police action at, 193
McMillin Theatre, 40–3, 205
Melman, Seymour, 100, 109
Morgenbesser, Sidney, 93, 100, 108, 115, 192
Morningside Heights community, 13–14, 39, 121–2, 242–3; apartment house occupied, 241–5

Papert, Tony, 66, 68, 86, 106, 108, 221, 262
Patterson, Basil, 71, 72, 75, 82
Petersen, William, 142 ff.
Platt, Alexander, 40, 42, 82–3, 110, 112, 113, 189, 251–2, 253–5, 257–8, 272–3, 276n.
Police, New York City, 66–8, 73–4, 85, 104, 108, 114–16, 135, 217, 218–19; April 30 action, 181, 187–99, 201–3, 244–5; May 22 action, 262, 265–76; *see also* Tactical Patrol Force

Ranum, Orest, 43, 57, 68, 268
Rothman, David, 79–80, 93, 110, 113, 139, 261
Rudd, Mark, 17, 25–7, 28, 31–2, 44, 47, 48–51, 53–4, 61, 62–3, 64–5, 80–1, 87–8, 91, 104–6, 108, 110–13, 137–41, 151–2, 185–6, 193, 215, 220–2, 228–9, 240–1, 245, 251, 255, 256–7, 258, 259, 261, 262–4, 267, 278, 291–7

Sales, Bill, 48, 51, 52, 55
Silver, Allan, 106, 110, 111, 152, 156
Six Demands, 52–3, 95, 97n., 221; *see also* amnesty; discipline; gymnasium; Institute for Defense Analyses
South Field, April 30 police action, 195–6, 197–8; May 22 police action, 274–6
Sovern, Michael, 209, 213–14, 215–16, 218, 231, 250
Strike Central, 128–9
Strike Coordinating Committee, 51–2, 129, 137–8, 150–1, 161, 168, 174–5,

Strike Coordinating Committee (*continued*)
204, 217, 220–2, 224, 225–7, 232–3, 234, 236, 237–42, 253, 282
Strike Steering Committee, *see* Strike Coordinating Committee
Student Life Report, 11–12, 24–5
students, moderate, 204, 221–2; referendum on issues, 163; *see also* counter-demonstrators; Majority Coalition; Students' Afro-American Society; Students for a Democratic Society; Students for a Restructured University
Students' Afro-American Society (SAS), 20–1, 82; relations with SDS, 38, 60 ff.
Students for a Democratic Society (SDS), 80–1, 84–5, 203; April 22 meeting, 34–6; history, 9–11, 31; ideology, 29–33, 35, 105, 117–18, 150–1, 240, 260; "praxis axis," 30–1, 80; relations with SAS, 38, 60 ff.; *see also* confrontation politics
Students for a Free Campus, 40–1
Students for a Restructured University (SRU), 241, 279, 283
Sutton, Percy, 71, 82, 83, 85

Tactical Patrol Force (TPF), 48n., 84, 182, 184, 187–99 *passim*, 244–5, 265–76
Trilling, Lionel, 69–70, 88–9, 132, 179, 231
tripartite commission, 77–8, 88–9, 131–3, 136, 156, 159, 163, 170; *see also* discipline; Joint Committee on Disciplinary Affairs
Truman, David B., 28, 40, 42–3, 56, 59, 65–7, 82, 90–1, 107–8, 115, 148–9, 159, 167, 169–70, 197, 198, 200, 214, 215, 228–9, 236–7, 249, 282
Trustees, Board of, 8, 115, 142–5, 179, 231–2, 234–5, 249–50; *see also* Petersen, William

Vilardi, Paul, 101–2, 165, 174, 271

Waithe, Eldridge, 71, 187
Wallerstein, Immanuel, 74–5, 127, 133–4, 140, 145–6, 153–4, 155, 166, 175–6
Westin, Alan, 89–90, 91–2, 93–4, 100, 107, 109, 110, 111–13, 138–41, 152, 153–4, 158, 161–2, 168, 205–12, 214, 218, 231–2
Wilson, Cicero, 38–40, 47, 55, 74–5, 183–4, 241

JERRY L. AVORN is Supplements Editor of the *Columbia Daily Spectator;* ANDREW CRANE is Sports Editor; ROBERT FRIEDMAN is Editor-in-Chief; and OREN ROOT, JR. is Executive Editor. All four are seniors in Columbia College and all have been associated with the *Spectator* since they were freshmen. MARK JAFFE, PAUL STARR, MICHAEL STERN and ROBERT STULBERG are members of the News Board of the *Spectator* and are juniors in Columbia College.

ST. JOSEPH'S COLLEGE LIBRARY

3 1960 0022916 $

Do Not Remove ___10/09___ Date

LD
1256
.A9

36822

Avorn, Jerry L., et al

Up against the ivy wall; a history
of the Columbia crisis

BRENTWOOD COLLEGE LIBRARY
BRENTWOOD, L. I. NEW YORK